A USEFUL DREAM

AFRICAN PHOTOGRAPHY 1960 2010

TABLE OF CONTENTS

Yes, Africa does have aspirations. Yes, the African people do have ambitions, dreams, a vision for their continent. That is why the title chosen for this series of exhibitions and events is so apposite. *Visionary Africa* stands in stark contrast to the Afro-pessimism about what some call the 'hopeless continent'. This exciting array of exhibitions is also in stark contrast to the reductive clichés about a continent where 'the people are poor but full of joie de vivre'. As if the whole of Africa could be reduced to a binary reality of misery and cheerfulness, between which and around which nothing else can exist.

To begin with, it makes as little sense to speak about 'Africa' as it does to speak about 'Europe' or 'Asia'. Africa is a continent with a thousand languages. Africa is a breathtakingly diverse continent. There is the Africa of the Maghreb, of the desert, of the savannah, of the lush green forests, of the mountains, of the lakes, of the coasts and of the cities bursting at the seams, *les villes tentaculaires* to borrow a phrase from the Belgian poet Emile Verhaeren. The architect David Adjaye and the Brussels architecture office SUM have done an exceptionally fine job of highlighting this diversity.

The works of art brought together in this exhibition hold up a mirror up to this African diversity. They are also a testimony to another multiplicity because they pick out various epochs. They are a combination of tradition and modernity, traditional themes with contemporary techniques, themes from the outside world involving traditional African working methods. Working together, curators Anne-Marie Bouttiaux and Koyo Kouoh rightly urge us to look at these works and judge them with an open mind, without trying to squeeze them into the criteria of the international art world, without asking whether they are art or 'only' decorative crafts, without expressing doubts about their 'authenticity'. Who is the outsider to tell African artists what is authentically African?

Africa has to trace its own path, in all areas. Many countries are still searching for this direction, for many countries are still young. This exhibition is a celebration of the 50th anniversary of the independence of 17 African countries. This independence was exuberantly celebrated, in the midst of an euphoric spirit of joy, of optimism and high hopes. Many of these hopes were dashed. The talented Senegalese writer Aminata Sow Fall described this movingly in her beautiful short story 'Independence: tomorrow it will be too late!', featured in the collection *African Renaissance*s, which is being published to coincide with this exhibition.

Independence, she writes, is more than symbols of sovereign power. Independence means 'to build the country, to generate and redistribute wealth, to educate and care'. Independence also means not being kept by others. She quotes a Wolof proverb from her country: 'He who feeds you mortgages your dignity'.

As the Prime Minister of a country endeavouring to keep Africa high up on the European and international agenda, I can only endorse these words. The cooperation Belgium is seeking in Africa is one between partners, not between donor and beneficiary. Belgium believes in the future of Africa. That is why I am delighted that these events at the Centre for Fine Arts are turning a spotlight on Africa during Belgium's European Union Presidency. And I extend my sincere congratulations to all those whose vision, courage and talent is behind the success of this welcome and many splendored initiative.

Yves Leterme, Prime Minister

A Useful Dream is a splendid exhibition of African photography from the 1960s to today. This exhibition, part of the prestigious project *Visionary Africa*, is taking place in a year during which our country has the responsibility to reflect on its relations with Africa.

2010 marks the 50th anniversary of the independence of the Democratic Republic of the Congo. The colonial era ended a half century ago. It had started with the creation of the Congo Free State by King Leopold II in 1885. In 1908, the Congo Free State became the Belgian Congo colony, which it remained until 1960, the year the Republic of Congo was founded. As such, this anniversary is a special event for both D. R. Congo and Belgium.

Like other former colonial states, Belgium has a colonial past made of contradictions: conquest versus charity, subjection versus elevation, pride versus shame, nostalgia versus self-criticism. All these paradoxes appear in the media and publications, which means that the colonial past is still under debate and that the discussion should continue. In that context, projects like *Visionary Africa* can help us contemplate history in a serene and committed way, and have therefore a positive effect on the relations between our countries.

For Belgian-Congolese relations did not come to an end with the independence of Congo. Our shared history has created strong ties. Our relationship goes far beyond an economic and humanitarian partnership. In a certain way, we are for ever a family. This explains why many Belgians have an emotional tie to Congo.

2010 will be a year of celebrations in 16 more African nations, including Nigeria, Mali, Senegal, and Burkina Faso. These partner countries of the Belgian Development Cooperation also celebrate 50 years of independence. I would therefore say that *Visionary Africa* quite rightly highlights the whole African continent.

The European dimension is also present in the project *Visionary Africa*. In the second half of the year, Belgium will take over the presidency of the European Union. Several important meetings between Africa and the European Union will be held under our presidency, including the third EU-Africa summit, on 29 November in Tripoli.

Africa will also shine on a global stage in 2010 as it will be hosting—for the first time ever—the World Cup, the biggest sport event of the year. The tournament, which starts on 11 June, will bring multitudes of fans together and create a feeling of solidarity and brotherhood beyond frontiers.

In all respects, 2010 will be a major year for Africa. As regards Belgium, this year will be a time to review the past, give attention to the present and reflect upon our future relations with Africa in general and the Congo in particular.

For all the reasons above, the Belgian federal Government has decided to support *Visionary Africa*.

Steven Vanackere, Minister of Foreign Affairs

The mission of the Centre for Fine Arts has always been to bear witness to the kaleidoscopic and, increasingly, interconnected society we live in. As a result, we try, in our programme, to represent the different cultures of the world. In 2010, seventeen African states celebrate fifty years of independent rule, and the African continent in general celebrates the beginning of a wave of independence that would eventually sweep the entire continent.

It is in order to celebrate this important anniversary that the Centre for Fine Arts has launched a complete and multi-faceted season dedicated to unfolding Africa's creative genius in all its forms: the visual arts, music, cinema, literature, and photography.

The exhibition *A useful dream*, part of this broader pro-gramme, highlights the many and varied role that photography played in the years leading up to independence—with covers from *Drum* Magazine and with the black-and-white images in which Gosani captures the first intimations of freedom—and throughout the past fifty years.

All creative forms and media play an important role in the development of a society, any society. *A useful dream* suggests that photography, in Africa, was a seminal tool. In the West, photography has by and large become a commodity, a means to sell goods, influence opinion, and generally promote as little reflection as possible—outside the art gallery, of course. The trajectory in Africa has been quite different, and photography, there, has always been a serious matter directly implicated in the aspirations, grievances, hopes, and disappointments of the pop-ulace. From the studio portrait of the early sixties to the abstract landscapes and photo-montages of the twenty-first century, the human being is the essential cipher in the visual language of African photographers. An important example taken from the exhibition and printed in this volume are the images produced in the seventies in South Africa, at the height of the apartheid regime, and whose makers were assimilated to freedom fighters; another are the portraits of young men and women aspiring to become a integral part of the world captured by Malick Sidibé.

With *A useful dream*, curator Simon Njami, perhaps the foremost authority on African photography, puts together a story where hope walks hand in hand with despair, where pride is never far from disillusion, where beauty is earned not at the expense of the ugly, but in spite of it. Ultimately, though, it is a story in which we bear witness to the evolution of a conti-nent that for much too long was an object, and that suddenly, as suddenly as the click of shutter, becomes an active subject through the gaze of its photgraphers.

Photographs were, in Africa as everywhere else, an invita-tion to a dream; in Africa, though, this dream was useful.

Étienne Davignon
Chairman of the Board of Directors
Centre for Fine Arts, Brussels

Paul Dujardin
General Director
Centre for Fine Arts

A useful dream: *photography as a metaphor of freedom and self-esteem*
Simon Njami

To mom and dad

I have borrowed the title for this exhibition from my friend, the Guinean writer Tierno Monenembo. For the desperate poetry I perceive in it. For the metaphorical power it contains. For its oxymoronic style. How can a dream become useful? How can something as immaterial and ethereal as a dream be brought back down to the decidedly earthly dimension of usefulness? Indeed, André Breton, the great guru of Surrealism, accused traditional African art of being functional, utilitarian, of grounding belief in a desire for earthly immanence, to sum up a long story. This almost desperate desire for efficiency is precisely what I would like to dwell on here for a moment. A dream is a driving force. In this sense, it is synonymous with visions, inspiration and desire… It is the origin of great projects, great ambitions.

On gaining independence, each African nation was driven by a dream that would transform the continent into a wonderful space to live in, one where freedom, equality, fraternity, peace, justice and prosperity—happiness, in a word—would be within everyone's reach. An inalienable right. Space here should be understood both as a physical and as a mental concept. It covers a field of investigation that goes beyond pure geography to touch the edges of psychology and psychoanalysis. If we are even to think of applying it to the field of the African continent—and more specifically the contemporary artistic practices arising there—we must deconstruct its different implications through an historical approach. This history, which covers approximately fifty years, is very immediate, and thus adds to the notion of space its indispensable corollary: time.

The borders established during the colonial era defined an artificial African space, for its contours were determined exogenously and with an eye to political coordinates that by and large ignored the populations concerned. Although the continent displayed a tectonic unity in terms of geography, in the interests of the 'occupying' forces the partitioning arrived at the Berlin Conference helped to cut Africa up, or 'Balkanise' it, as Léopold Sédar Senghor put it. Even though the tools they have used have so far proved ill adapted, Africans have been trying to recreate this lost entity since before the wave of independences. For they intuited that a space with no known centrality cannot exist, as Homi Bhaba stresses: 'If, in our travelling theory, we are alive to the *metaphoricity* of the peoples of imagined communities—migrant or metropolitan—then we shall find that the space of the modern nation-people is never simply horizontal. Their metaphoric movement requires a kind of 'doubleness' in writing; a temporality of representation that moves between cultural formations and social processes without a centred causal logic'.[1]

The notion of 'metaphoricity' refers to a *de facto* virtuality. And contemporary Africa is indeed different, due to the impalpable immateriality of the imagined 'community'—an intellectual construction, if you will, that politicians have rather unsuccessfully been trying to turn into a concrete and tangible reality for the past fifty or so years. Africa in the wake of independence was the result of an exogenous negotiation among the colonial powers, which means that the continent paradoxically found itself faced with a multitude of exogenous centres, all of which corresponded to a colonial cartography. The centres were outside the continent, they were what was called the 'home' countries. This external appropriation of African centrality doubtless played a part in structuring a chaos that would become the main *modus operandi* for all. The decisions made in the ruling countries had no real materiality, for the people concerned by these decisions were not entitled to discern their logic, much less to discuss it.

Hence the confusion that appeared, despite all the attendant hope, when it came to defining what Africa could be following the independences of many countries in the 1960s. The terms of the debate have greatly evolved and numerous attempts have been made to answer that question, but this difficulty is still today the stumbling block in every discussion focused on the continent. Politically speaking, the strength of the dream for renewal that drove the first continental leaders turned this African space into a virtual space. At the end of the day, the only function of an organisation such as the Organisation of African Unity, today the Africa Union, was to materialise a reality that had no substance. The different policies implemented all failed to give rise what Fanon called the 'new man', for the only thing that was new about this man was this recently gained freedom: 'Decolonisation never goes unnoticed, for it focuses on and fundamentally alters being, and transforms

---

1 Homi K. Bhaba, *The location of culture* (London: Routledge, 1994) 141.

the spectator crushed to a nonessential state into a privi-
leged actor, captured in a virtually grandiose fashion by the
spotlight History. It infuses a new rhythm, specific to a new
generation of men, with a new language and a new humanity. Decolonisation is truly the creation of new men. But
such creation cannot be attributed to a supernatural power:
the colonised "thing" becomes man through the very process of liberation'.[2] Has the 'colonised thing' really become a
man by proposing and inventing a new way of grasping the
world? We can, despite the very real work of reappropria-
tion, have our reservations about how successful politicians
have been on this score. There can be no doubt, however,
that Africa's artists and intellectual have given us the most
convincing translations of these aspirations. We will see
later which strategies were used to reach a truly *post-colo-
nial* state, i.e., one liberated from the weight of the past.

Independence came as a liberation. In some countries, it was won with a fight, in others it was the result of
a process of negotiation. In both cases, it spawned a sense
of hope throughout Africa that would then be shattered
by harsh economic, political and historical realities. 'The
Fathers of Independence', as the first leaders of liberated
African countries are habitually known, had a vision for
their countries. They were hungry for emancipation and
experimentation. They were eager to build countries, to accompany peoples who had at long last been given back their
pride. This period of theoretical proliferation gave rise to
the notion of Pan-Africanism, itself a prelude to the creation
of the Organisation of African Unity. It would be wrong
to conceive an event commemorating this period without
taking these political and historical facts into account.
Incidentally, this is why art will always be the most appro-
priate field for perceiving the complex and subtle evolutions
of any society, African societies in particular. And of all the
visual media, no doubt the most immediately palpable form
is photography. As soon as it reached the African continent
in the late 19th century, this medium—which gained its
autonomy and flourished in the field of artistic creation—
represented the best tool for the process of emancipation
and for that of writing an endogenous history. It gave life,
though sometimes unwittingly, to the 'new man' that Fanon
hoped for by leading Africa into the production of endogenous images. Images where the subject would no longer
be a passive being beleaguered by the desires and fantasies
of an outside gaze, but an actor in his own biography.

In our modern societies, the role of images is overdeter-
mined by codes whose main objective has become to ma-
nipulate the people they are targeted at. We are so swamped
in increasingly globalised clichés, so persistently prey to
the more or less subtle exploitation of which we are the
object, that we have unlearned how to see. We've forgotten
how to read an image, not in terms of whatever it is that
someone is trying to sell, but in terms of what it expresses,
which is not always manifest. For what are images, if not
the prime location of an ontological attempt to define the
visible? This was obvious to the Ancients, who, contrary to
current practice, did not separate the image from its sub-
versive force, or from its capacity to lead us through the
looking-glass of reason. Hence the mistrust towards images
harboured by those whose role it was to be the enlightened
guides of a tenebrous world. The Ancients, iconoclasts one
and all, worked on the assumption that it was impossible
to represent the visible world, of which God was the only
master. Hence the injunctions found in the three monotheist religions: 'I am the Lord thy God, which have brought
thee out of the land of Egypt, out of the house of bondage.
Thou shalt have no other gods before me. Thou shalt not
make unto thee any graven image, or any likeness of any
thing that is in heaven above, or that is in the earth beneath,
or that is in the water under the earth'.[3] By creating a single
aesthetic aimed to assuaging his political and moral ambitions, the coloniser was temporarily able to replace the
implacable custodians of divine law.

This prohibition, wrongly attributed solely to Islamic
peoples, poses the terms of an age-old dilemma. According
to Baudrillard, any attempt at representation must be assimilated to a simulacrum—if not, more radically, to blas-
pheme. Taking religious icons as an example, the author of
Simulacra and simulation shows how every representation
is inevitably a mask thrown over the reality of the absence
of God. As soon as they appeared, i.e., as soon as human
beings appeared, images were prone to be mistrusted. The
need to represent, characteristic of the human being and
found already in cave paintings, differentiates itself from
faithful materiality in order to seek out an essential duality.
When prehistoric men covered the walls of their caves with
paintings, the divinity to which they *might* have been referring was a pure abstraction. This abstraction was material-
ized in Ancient times by a multitude of gods, gods so numerous and so close to human nature they did not partake

---

2 Frantz Fanon, *The wretched of the earth*, trans. Richard Philcox
(New York: Grove Press, 2004 [1963]) 2.

3 Exodus 20:2-4.

in the mystery that Judaism, Christianity and Islam would instate. The image, i.e., the representation, became divorced from the idea of God through the institution of Mystery, which Moses codified in a series of fundamental laws.

In its essence, art, which stands at the heart of this debate, signifies the separation from God, or the celebration of God's death. Art is blasphemous. What are we representing when we go about the Promethean task of stealing the sacred fire? Representation can only be interpretation and this, in the eyes of iconoclasts, is where its danger lies. The artist, the sculptor, the painter and, today, the photographer and the video artist take the place of divine power by claiming to see what cannot, by definition, does not show itself. In the violent battle that is still raging between Iconoclasts and Iconolaters, what is at stake is the very meaning of religion and its application in monotheist societies. Iconoclasts, scrupulous guardians of the temple, follow the divine commandment to the letter. But there was, in their rage to destroy images, something more than the scrupulous application of a Divine Law. As the guardians of a temple built on immanent and unverifiable principles, they knew that the only thing that could enable God to outlast his revelation and popularisation was the Mystery. Baudrillard even claims that this rage can only be explained by the fact that, beyond the simulacra that pious images and icons represent, there is nothing. The philosopher analyses the divinity and asserts: 'But what becomes of the divinity when it reveals itself in icons, when it is multiplied in simulacra? Does it remain the supreme power that is simply incarnated in images as a visible theology? Or does it volatilise itself in the simulacra that, alone, deploy their power and pomp of fascination—the visible machinery of icons substituted for the pure and intelligible Idea of God?'[4] Iconoclasts were afraid that images would end up replacing what they were supposed merely to represent. Images therefore jeopardise much more than the Platonic idea of God: they are the other, empty side of an all-too-perfect picture. Thus iconoclasts, wrongly seen as the enemies of images, actually only adopted their attitude because they feared these images, feared their irreverence and strength. Perhaps in doing so, they endowed them with a power they do not hold.

Iconolaters, however, with their licentious attitude to images, are perhaps the ones who have confined images to their primary function by sending them back to trivial materiality: 'Mental images of things are more easily associated with the images referred to things which we clearly and distinctly understand, than with others'.[5] In this case, God cannot content himself with being his sole representation, for he does not correspond to any image we know. What this means, in other words, is that the appropriation of an image is above all recognition. Hence projection and subjectivity. It is as though the meaning of the image preceded its existence. Consequently, our interpretation of representation is essentially cultural, in the sense that the way in which we give meaning to an image we are shown depends on our background—where we grew up, our understanding of symbols, etc. These inform how we read the underlying message. An image can thus be unintelligible because we do not have the codes that would allow us to penetrate and reveal it. This is why God cannot be reproduced. He is, by essence, immaterial.

The prohibitions linked to images are directly derived from clearly established social, political or religious codes. Nudity, for example, is lived differently in different societies, and an image that seems banal here will come up against rigorous laws elsewhere. There can be no sacred images, because sacred is by definition the opposite of visible. Just as we decipher the meaning of images through the codes we have at our disposal, each possible reading of an image becomes an empirical construction, an artifice fed by our subjectivity. Sartre says just that when he asserts that the image 'is a certain way in which the object appears to consciousness, or, if one prefers, a certain way in which consciousness presents to itself an object'.[6] According to this existentialist vision of the world, we need to project ourselves. There would be no object without consciousness, i.e., no image that is not vested with a particular meaning. The mistake that has sometimes been made is that of thinking that an image can be gratuitous, stolen, or *real*. That it has no concept. Being unable to translate our intention or emotion into words does not rob visual writing of its intrinsic content.

Visual writing, a priori like all writing, is a language. Which means it aims to communicate to others what you do not necessarily master yourself—this language which, if memory serves, Henri Delacroix described as one of the instruments that transforms the chaotic world of sensations into a world of objects and representations. If this definition applies to all works of art, then photography and video, as media through which representation takes a human form, are perfect vectors for translating that which cannot be said/shown. There is inevitably an inherent degree of loss in this translation exercise, for there is no such thing as a per-

4   Jean Baudrillard, *Simulacra and simulations*, trans. Sheila Faria Glaser (Ann Arbor, MI: The University of Michigan Press, 1994 [1981]) 4.
5   Benedict de Spinoza, *Ethics*, translation by R.H.M. Elwes (London: 1883).
6   Jean-Paul Sartre, *The imaginary: a phenomenological psychology of the imagination*, trans. Jonathan Webber (London: Routledge, 2004 [1940]) 7.

fect language—a language that would be entirely capable of transcribing this world of constantly shifting sensations whose essence can never be grasped.

One of the recurring misunderstandings in the gaze we cast on the other, notably the gaze the West has cast and still casts on 'others', is the illusion of a universal language underwritten by shared fantasies or, at least, by an essential truth. The scientific illusion of deciphering and equating the world is part of the same determination that leads to objectifying that which cannot be objectified. How to bring a gust of wind or a storm into a language that can be understood identically in all four corners of the globe? This is the universalist illusion. The place of being in pre-industrial societies, for example, lies at the heart of this misunderstanding, one that still opposes the West to the rest of the world. But again, just as was the case with God, we must not confuse being with its appearance, as Jean Loup Pivin reminds us: 'The icon not only expresses being; it also prevents it from becoming anything other than its portrayal. If photography were a mirror of reality, it could merge being and its photographed counterpart, as being is indeed realistic, although the counterpart is abstract and does not content itself with being a mere portrayal. It is part of a much greater reality. Can this be why people being photographed are so willing to be shown in costume, or even disguise…?'[7]

The profound philosophy that still governs the peoples of Africa, both north and south of the Sahara, is essentially based on being, that is to say, on the embodied essence rather than the abstraction of an equated world. The very Christian separation between being and nature is the touchstone of this missed opportunity. The word, i.e., one of the first forms of language, constitutes the revelation of being while it simultaneously puts it at a distance. The face that I observe in the mirror is already no longer me. It is something else that I can contemplate at leisure—I can grasp features which will elude me at other, ordinary moments, when I only appear as an image of myself. Merleau-Ponty calls this the 'power of looking', which, if we pay attention to it, can be similar to a mystic experience: 'My body simultaneously sees and is seen. That which looks at all things can also look at itself and recognise, in what it sees, the "other side" of its power of looking'.[8] This experience of *dédoublement*, or duality (we shall see how Sartre envisages it later), is the core concept in the work of the photographers brought together here—regardless of whether they

are conscious of it while producing their work, or whether their pictures is the fruit of an *immediate consciousness* or, which is the same, an 'instinctive consciousness'.

The experience of being a stranger to oneself is shared by all peoples who have known the yoke of colonisation. But while, when colonised, they experienced this duality solely as a loss, an absence of part of themselves, following Independence they acquired the ability to see. Applying this new talent in full consciousness is no easy task. You have to start by unlearning to look at yourself as an unchanging image defined by the other's gaze. You then have to take over your own gaze and give it meaning, which is tantamount to giving yourself meaning. The 'shock of being seen' Sartre refers to in *Black Orpheus*, when he evokes the sudden power gained by the ex-colonised to cast an objective gaze on their colonisers, must be understood in a double sense. In this text announcing the immanence of decolonisation and the emancipation of peoples who had been the victims, or at least the objects, of the other's gaze, Sartre underscores the act of seeing—i.e., the capacity to judge or, at least, to form your own opinion—as a founding element of freedom. But while he stresses the humility with which the West should henceforth consider itself, he forgets to mention that this shock also affects the (newly) seeing subject. Having emerged from a long night of blindness, it is as though he was gradually opening up to the world and to the magic of discovering himself as he had never imagined.

In the current century, the production of images is probably the last realm in which our freedom and individuality can be fully expressed. Up until the late 20th century, the West had a monopoly on seeing, i.e., a monopoly on the power to describe, and thus define, the world according to a hegemonic point of view. The anthropometric photographs of natives in the Southern Sahara, just as orientalist photography in the northern part, was part and parcel of the conscious effort to reduce every different, every *other*, mode of being to a set of comfortable clichés; in the instance, the other, the exotic, etc. All those old books by travel writers and geographers are as result chockfull with typical portrait galleries and timeless scenes. Leni Riefenstahl's Nuba are but one example of this. Mastering your own image means bringing into the world voices and colours that elude globalisation and uniformisation, it means refusing to be just the fruit of the other's gaze. It means assuling, in a kind of silent contradiction, your own vision

7   Jean Loup Pivin, 'The icon and the totem', in *An anthology of African photography: the twentieth century*, eds. N'Goné Fall and Jean Loup Pivin (New York: D. A. P., 2002). Reprinted in this volume; for passage, see p. 16.
8   Maurice Merleau-Ponty, 'Eye and mind', trans. Carleton Dallery, in *The primacy of perception*, ed. James M. Edie (Evanston, IL: Northwestern UP, 1964) 162.

of yourself, following your cultural codes and aesthetics. It means taking back your own measure of time, which, according to Merleau-Ponty, 'stays the same because the past is a former future and a recent present, the present an impending past and a recent future, the future a present and even a past to come; because, that is, each dimension of time is treated or aimed at as something other than itself, and because finally at the core of time there is a gaze…'.[9]

The keyword here is *gaze*. Let's imagine for a moment that the human being can be assimilated to time and that the different phases of this multiple present to which Merleau-Ponty refers are none other than the essence of mankind. Thus, in a kind of eternal return of the same, as Nietzsche's famous concept goes, we try in vain to define an object—man—that never corresponds to the moment at which we envisage it. For as soon as we have frozen this object, we are already in the past, in history. How then to define the future, if not through an extrapolation of the moment lived and a projection whose only merit will be the strength of its subjectivity, the strength of the light shed by this gaze? The strength and weakness of any gaze is its fragmentariness—its existence as the lone element in a puzzle whose general contour will always elude us, as Théodule Ribot reminds us: 'With the image, the intermediate stage between percept and concept, the reduction of the object represented to a few fundamental features is still more marked'.[10] Once you become aware of the impossibility of representing reality, you gain access to the creator's freedom. This distance is necessary in photography more than elsewhere, for it alone, through the subjectivity of its poetry, allows us to attain a truth that suffers no contradiction precisely because it will never claim to be universal.

The importance of images in propaganda serves to remind us of the subliminal function that is vested in every image. The reversed mirror that the colonised peoples started to present to the world from the 1950s onwards showed the beginnings of the internalisation and deconstruction of the images that went before. This symbolic emancipation traded in politics, as well as in the ideological choices that translated a fierce desire to turn the colonial page and challenge the prevailing models that had been invested with the status of absolute truths. This translated into a policy of non-alignment nevertheless accompanied by a flirtation with Moscow, which, at the time, was seen more as an alternative to the Western model than a viable philosophical choice. But in the race for history launched by Independence, in the urgency to invent nations, the formerly colonised peoples perhaps missed the chance they were given to confront what Ernst Bloch calls the essential question, viz.: the question of *We* in itself.

This is question Deleuze tackles in other terms in the *The logic of sense*. The complex problematic of *We* refers to two notions (the duality of the being again), without which it is hard to determine oneself in one's essence: the group and the individual. The group, the *We* to which Bloch refers, is a set of interdependent groups that form what Deleuze calls the 'contact surface', i.e., the realm of appearance. The family group, the ethnic group, the religious group, the national group, the continental group, etc. represent so many sets within which the individual must find his or her place. Identity, for this is what it is all about, becomes the synthesis of these various sets in a unique and singular actualization. If to be is to think oneself, to paraphrase Descartes, it should be added that our thinking determines the way in which we appear to the world. Alongside the exogenous image of ourselves that threatens to define us and lock us into archetypes, is the endogenous image asking to be released and to express Delacroix's 'chaotic world of sensations'. If language has a fate, it is this. Yet how to translate this world into the reality of an image? How to turn chaos into an organised and balanced whole? This is the challenge facing Africa's contemporary artists. The question of this *We*— their central concern, incidentally—is a mystery that seems destined to be endless. Tangled up in the twofold trap of the local and the global, African artists today have to invent a hybrid being that can respond to the grievances of the two groups, the local and the global, simultaneously. For contemporaneity is necessarily universal.

Photography and video allow this ontological discussion because, perhaps more so than any other, they are both media of embodiment. Images cannot exist without some form of embodiment. The imaged body is a place of narration. It is the intimate body, but it is also the social body, the body of the other. In the figuration that photography and video allow, displaying oneself is a way of tangibly expressing an emotion that is no longer abstract at all. The slightest landscape becomes a kind of self-portrait and *takes shape*, becomes *embodied*. The duality we evoked earlier becomes an instrument that we can play with over and over again. The body, therefore, stops belonging to its owner and becomes the metaphor

9   Maurice Merleau-Ponty, *Phenomenology of perception*, trans. Colin Smith (New York: The Humanities Press, 1962) 490.
10   Théodule Ribot, *The evolution of general ideas*, trans. Frances Alice Welby (Chicago: Open Court, 1899 [repr. 2009]) 5.

of a *We* that the 'seer' has to grasp. It becomes matter. The paradox, of course, is that its embodiment turns it into an idea, as Henri-Pierre Jeudy reminds us: 'Images of the body do not relate to the body as an isolated entity; rather, they occur simultaneously as images of the world. Language only allows for the organisation of arbitrary classifications, a fact which gives interpretation a sense that is always close to that of illusion. To a certain extent, the collision of body images teaches us that there is no real body language. The manner in which this is spoken already implies a negation of the image by objectifying the sense it is given'.[11]

There is no need here to go back over received images and race typologies, because the body we are referring to is multiple. If we want to envisage the reality of an *oriental body*, for example, it is up to us to give it a substance that dissociates it from the clichés that surround it. The oriental body is only oriental because it is said to be such. What telegraphs the message is not the body itself, but the way in which the artist shows it. The body becomes metaphor. The body, like a landscape—and this is no coincidence—becomes metaphor: a cryptic canvas onto which the artist transposes his vision of our humanity. As an instrument of mediation through which the artist speaks to the other—the one who looks and who cannot refrain from qualifying—the body is the first concrete element by which we are perceived. It is the seat of a permanent conflict, because the body is the site where the contradictory question of perception is played out. On the one hand, there is the image that we transmit to others; on the other, there is the image they perceive of us. An image that is part of appearance. Mastering this dual image amounts to putting your soul into it immediately, in order to avoid any misunderstandings, or, better said, in order to catch the *missed perceptions* that underlie the initial gaze. Here we are in the realm of representation, i.e., of *being-in-the-world*. The realm, that is, in which we project ourselves to others as we want to be seen, and negotiate the conditions of our humanity while avoiding the tragic trap that condemned Narcissus.

The meaning of the body must escape its primary nature and blur the messages of its appearance. The reference, or rather the referent, is often the stranger, the other. We do not describe ourselves for people close to us but for those who are far away, those who perceive an image of us that does not necessarily match our sensibility. My body could therefore be the *atopos* Barthes talks about, and which

he suggests corresponds to a singular truth that cannot be confused with the truth of others. This truth would then appear as such to those who do not know me. Challenging this frozen image and thinking about your place in the world supposes an ascetic reflection that starts with yourself. It involves plunging back into the very depths of your being to evaluate the different ways of presenting yourself. It is a relatively schizophrenic exercise, for it supposes a Janus-like stance that looks both inward and outward at the same time. Sartre is referring to this duality in the following passage, in which, for 'Black', we should understand 'non-White' or 'colonised': 'The herald of the black soul has gone through white schools, in accordance with a brazen law which forbids the oppressed man to possess any arms except those he himself has stolen from the oppressor: it is through having had some contact with white culture that his blackness has passed from the immediacy of existence to the meditative state. But at the same time, he has more or less ceased to live his negritude. In choosing to see what he is, he has become split, he no longer coincides with himself. And on the other hand, it is because he was already exiled from himself that he discovered this need to reveal himself.'[12]

No longer coinciding with oneself no doubt represents the awakening of political awareness. It means, first of all, that we are capable of taking the indispensable step away from ourselves, which is necessary if revelation is to follow. Considering our body and our environment as foreign objects makes it easier for us to manage to recreate them in the totality of their signifieds. This duality supposes mastering the parameters by which the world is governed. The act of creating is no longer, indeed, it never was, the gratuitous, light-hearted act that some have wanted to portray it as, but an undertaking that exceeds the simple individual and turns the artist into a living illustration of a singularity. To create is to reveal the ultimate duality—that of art itself: 'Aesthetics suffers from a wrenching duality. On the one hand, it designates the theory of sensibility as the form of possible experience; on the other hand, it designates the theory of art as the reflection of real experience. For these two meanings to be tied together, the conditions of experience in general must become conditions of real experience; in this case, the work of art would really appear as experimentation'.[13]

It is this experimentation, duality and quest for meaning among African photographers that this exhibition, and this book, intends to illustrate.   *SN*

---

11   **Henri-Pierre Jeudy, *Le Corps comme objet d'art* (Paris: Armand Collin/Masson, 1998).**

12   **Jean-Paul Sartre, *'Black Orpheus'*, trans. John MacCombie, in *'What is literature?' and other essays* (Cambridge, Mass: Harvard UP, 1988) 298.**
13   **Gilles Deleuze, *The logic of sense*, trans. Mark Lester (New York: Columbia UP, 1990) 260.**

The icon and the totem
*Jean Loup Pivin**

Why, when writing and photography come together, does one feel that the exercise is a waste of time, that it will be in vain? There are many texts written on photography that manage to be at once enriching and relevant while avoiding any claim to being definitive. And yet, theoretical considerations on photography are distinguished by their lack of impact on the taking of pictures itself, and on the myriad interpretations of those pictures by billions of eyes around the world.

At the time when photography was exploding onto the scene, modern European painting was being born out of theory and thought: for more than a century and a half, not a single new art form or new art movement has come into existence without being preceded by a theoretical declaration drawn up, not by thinkers, but by the artists themselves. Kandinsky, Duchamp and Breton are the archetypal examples.

In the field of photography, no major theory of aesthetics, no matter how vast, has ever had the slightest impact on the concept or production of photographs. Handbooks emphasise techniques, making recommendations, for example, about how to frame a shot. But, as the subject is highly technical, the discussion it generates is inevitably academic. Today's cameras, with their automatic diaphragm settings and autofocus, still attach great importance to the centre of the viewfinder, so that the focus is determined by technical needs. The history of photography has mainly been influenced by technical advances, so that new practices and new aesthetics are tied to the increasing potential afforded by the camera and by the development of new techniques. Theoretical writings on aesthetic issues involved in depicting reality in photographs are virtually non-existent, and the few texts there are have had no impact on the taking of pictures.

Photography is a medium that uses machines. The use of these machines is functional or commercial; it is not artistic. From the very outset, a vast number of photographs were taken outside the scope of art and art-related issues, so that photography was able to set up and develop in total autonomy from the 'art world'.

In time, photography came to have its own critics, its own history, and its own critical vocabulary, one that is far removed from art criticism and history. Less than twenty years ago, we often heard art historians and critics confessing to knowing nothing about photography, which is why they refused to exhibit photographs in museums or galleries. This isolation from the artistic mainstream, which confined photography for many long years to the ranks of inferior art forms, left it free to explore reality without suffering from any complexes, allowing it to become a form of expression so common and widely practiced that it can now claim to be a truly popular art form, one free from all the trappings of 'high art'.

Photography is now on an equal footing with painting or sculpture as an art form in its own right; it has no outside references, no influence other than its own. A photograph can only be compared to another type of photograph. What the photograph evokes or tells us is autonomous.

Interpretations must always be made with caution and will inevitably remain an exercise external to the object. If text must be written to accompany a photograph, the only forms of writing which are equal to the task are poetry and metaphor—writing in images. All we can do, really, is to sort out a series of photographs, a series that we can collect, combine or discard in different orders as we attempt to incorporate or fathom the different worlds of forms created by photography: the setting, the pose, the expression of the subject photographed (particularly for portraits); the light, the movement, the framing; the inspiration, the expression, the environment. The written text will review and describe contextual references: the date and place, the biography of the photographer and of the subject (whether human or inanimate). It will be impossible to stop the written text from conveying a moral message, a statement, even while we remain aware of its relativity.

Sometimes writing and photography are closely interrelated, as is the case with books and posters (think of the posters made for advertising, informational or political purposes). The famous slogan of the French weekly magazine *Paris Match*—'the weight of words, the impact of photos'—acknowledges the inevitable manipulation of photographs by words. The words offer an instant interpretation of the visuals, stirring both the individual and the collective subconscious in order to endow the photograph with one specific, easily decipherable meaning. It is the slogan that uses the picture. Written commentary, and the caption or *legend* (a quaint choice of terminology for the few words that accompany a photograph, and a term which highlights the ambiguity of written commentary) guide and steer the eye across the image.

* in **An anthology of African photography: the twentieth century**, eds. N'Goné Fall and Jean Loup Pivin (New York: D. A. P., 2002). The original translation was substantially revised for this edition.

The paper totem

It is possible that photography in Africa could be less a realistic representation of reality than an example of iconic vision. By renouncing documentary value or personal, private value, the photographic image itself may become, not a depiction of reality, but a social and spiritual counterpart of the subject photographed. Hence the photographer view of him/herself as a mediator, as an interpreter of social values and an intercessor, one who goes beyond the role of the clever technician to become the producer of icons. This may be an explanation for the reluctance certain communities feel at the prospect of being photographed, not wishing to have their souls stolen away. African photographers are not exempt from this suspicion: the Congolese-Angolan photographer, Antoine Freitas, described this in notes made during a visit to a village in Kasai country in 1939.

We are not trying to quantify the level of subjectivity in a picture, as that would involve acknowledging the obvious fact that each viewer interprets things as his or her heart and mind see fit. What we are talking about, instead, are the values carried by a photograph. These are never what the photograph is; instead, they are what it signifies, at the point where the photograph carries its own inner meaning (independent of any intended by the photographer) not simply on an individual, but on a universal, scale, thus enhancing the intrinsic value of a visual image in the perception of reality, without recourse to writing and words. Yet this does not imply that universal values are conveyed by photographic images, because it is clear that the cultural essence of each civilization will develop its own, sometimes contradictory and conflict, meanings and significances. 'This fork is not a fork'. It is a fork only for the person who knows what a fork is and who wants it to be a fork: we can see this again and again, especially in surrealist and conceptual paintings.

The icon not only expresses being; it also prevents it from becoming anything other than its portrayal. If photography were a mirror of reality, it could merge being and its photographed counterpart, as being is indeed realistic, although the counterpart is abstract and does not content itself with being a mere portrayal. It is part of a much greater reality. Can this be why people being photographed are so willing to be shown in costume, or even disguise right up to the 1980s? 'I am my portrayal'; 'my portrait is myself'. In the same way, a totemic portrayal, the emblem of the person, embodies broader values and is far more than just a realistic depiction of the subject. The resemblance between the photograph and the subject, or the totemic portrayal and the subject, is not intended to be absolute, even if it actually is. Instead, it is the attitude, the gestures and the costume which proclaim the inner identity of the subject. The use of traditional costumes and ritual poses assumed by the man or woman being photographed illustrates this clearly. And the use of modern costume or disguise is not intended to have a different purpose: on the contrary, it is the revival of the traditional social values of the ancestors displayed in new attire.

Such a photograph parallels the poster of a singer or football player on the bedroom wall of any young person anywhere in the world: both express values and confer an identity, even 'protection', on the person associated with them. The sports star and the singer are not gods, but totems in which gods are embodied.

This is similar to young people's tendency to adopt nicknames borrowed from current stars—rap stars especially—for their music groups, or even fashion designers. Young people in the US and in Zaire identify, for example, with Yves Saint Laurent or Versace. The image of the other person becomes a fragment of oneself. One's own image, similarly and by the same token, is also a fragment of oneself: here we have the icon and the totem. The above phenomenon is also a means of anchoring one's individuality in a communal value shared by as many people as possible.

We are far removed from what had originally seemed to be a self-evident truth: we are now at a point where photography is not a neutral object observed as if it were a fixed reality at a given point in history, but has a different value, no doubt deep down inside each and every one of us at the most fundamental level. Photography is not the proof that something has existed (a meeting, birth, political event, accident or war). It stands, rather, as testimony of what such reality depicts. Once again, photography has become an icon.

Communal values or the relevance of a parenthesis in the flow of text

In Africa, the extended family of fathers and mothers, plus aunts and various spouses, underscores the broad concept of community operative in the continent: it can include the even wider dimension of the cultural family, name, caste and civilization. And this is indeed the key issue when a photograph is taken: it is taken in relation to the imagined or real social context of the subject; the photograph defines the role the subject's actual or intended role in that context.

Something crucial has disappeared in Europe, along with the loss of the concept of the social individual, viz.: the notion of the individual who does not exist outside society. In the past, it was not parents who procreated, but society which produced children. This is how things were all over the world, including in Europe, until the 18th century. But this concept completely disappeared in the West in the latter part of the 20th century, and it is fading—though it has not disappeared entirely—in the rest of the world, including in Africa. The European family, reduced to the procreating couple, is no longer the first link in society, but merely a barrier behind which the still unborn child withdraws. The victory that was won for the respect and freedom of the individual has been transformed into rampant individualism. Relationship with others has been reduced to a sharing of commodities on the international market, and these commodities have in turn become moral values: as the shoe manufacturer, Nike, says, 'Just do it!' Consumer goods have become the promised land of individual fulfillment that in images manufactured for the territory they can occupy in the subconscious of each individual. Once again, these are images which portray, not reality, but a value carried by reality.

Societies in a state of weightlessness regarding the communal values by which each individual lives no longer bind individuals on the basis of common rules, other than rules of material values. They can no longer break down the loneliness they have produced. And yet this does not mean that we must return to a state where the individual is negated and confined to a social mould that offers nothing more than communal contentment: the price paid for individual liberty over the past century has been too great for us to find ourselves at such a dead end.

The nuclear family as the sole bond in society has led to such narrowness in Europe that the only prospect is to extend outwards again in a new movement of sociability. The communal destiny will have be to redesigned so that we can once again share common values and act together, not only in a local context but also at the level of our small planet, Earth. This is probably the angle we need for understanding the contemporary upheavals in modern cities around the world, each of which has become the world (as the song says, 'We are the world!'); and this includes the cities of Africa today.

The 'moral' contained in this view is not an essential prerequisite for understanding the statement which a photograph attempts to convey, or its scope as an icon expressing communal values, as shown so clearly by photography in Africa. It does, however, cast light on the issue involved. It also casts light on the objective view of photography in Africa and probably on an entire area of photography generally. An icon is not merely for individual use, a source of reassurance, but is intended primarily for use by others; in fact, it is intended for the society which produced that individual. Could a photograph from independent Africa of the 1950s to the 1970s (or of some date in the future) be seen as anything other than an expression of communal values overlaid with the external manifestations of modern style? During this period, photography was a special form of expression, as was music. Both provided abundant proof to the individual, to his or her family and to the colonizing power, that attitudes were ready for the modern age. This meant honouring everything in the way of autonomy, liberation and respect for the individual, but always in the context of shared community values. Clearly this interpretation is not applicable to Africa only. It can be seen in a more structured and conscious way in all propaganda photography in which people are represented as groups rather than as individuals.

The photographer

In such a context, in which the African subject can be transformed into a actor playing his or her own role and staking his or her claim on society, the photographer is not the brilliant artist living as a recluse, but the mediator, the stage director, the iconographer. He is not making art. He is, rather, on the sidelines of the artistic, the manufacturer of a paper icon, the producer of a two-dimensional material rendition duplicating another being. His expertise lies in the attention he pays to what the actor wants to convey of his own image, and in his help with the staging of the scene. This aspect of staging is more obvious in regions with 'animistic' traditions. Such careful composition of the scene and deliberate attention to the posture of the subject can be seen in the ritual postures of speech and prayer seen from Côte d'Ivoire to the Congo, but these features are less obvious in Muslim countries, although they are just as strong. One finds evidence of this if one examines photographs of a number of men crouched praying on their mats, in the same studio where, ten minutes earlier, a couple had been embracing and where, ten minutes later, a young girl will appear in a new dress or two boys will announce their friendship to the world. In Ghana, Kenya and Ethiopia the relationship is even stronger because icons, which in the past were painted and placed on coffins, were quickly replaced by photographs. These photographs were often touched up using colour and the delicate airbrushing of features. They literally played the role of icons, not because the photographic depiction was more realistic, but because it provided a better likeness of the deceased person and his or her values: it was a twin. There had been a meeting between the photograph and the person photographed.

The autonomy of African photography

The best way to illustrate what was different about the way photographs were taken in Africa is the persistent gulf, whether conscious or unconscious, one sees between the aesthetics of European teaching and apprenticeship and the aesthetics found in African practice. An important aspect of African photography in its early days was that, despite the colonial photographic model, it developed an autonomous form quite unrelated to colonial subjects and styles. The first African photographers, mostly apprenticed to European photographers (who had settled in the country or were there as expatriate civil servants), had their own parallel, and privately run, businesses. They took photographs which displayed not the slightest stylistic connection to those of their tutors. The distinguishing feature was the practice, almost standard among African photographers, of capturing their fellow countrymen on film, attired in their finest clothes, in carefully arranged poses, with expressions suggesting that they were 'conversing' with the photographer and the camera lens. In these photographs, Africans were showing themselves to themselves. By contrast, shots taken by European photographers, even those who had been based locally for many years, have a tangible quality of awkwardness and distance; it feels as if they have been taken 'from the outside'. European photographers also favoured a particular choice of dress for their sitters, at least in the early years, preferring costumes that created an impression of strangeness or wildness. Such anthropomor-

phic, ethnological, touristic, or exotic photographs served to endorse one single viewpoint: that which was designed to show that the other person was indeed other, different, unknown. Otherwise, why photograph the person? Such an argument obviously served to bolster the legitimacy of the foreign presence as a civilizing influence over these noble or ignoble savages. Photographs taken by Africans were clearly regarded the result of a neutral technique, not of an artistic approach. Within the European tradition, the apprentice painter in an art school—or even the ordinary observer of the Western paintings in circulation—learnt not only the technique, but also what it conveyed regarding assumptions about portraying reality. The same applied to the person teaching or the source of the reference pictures, as the paintings and drawings were mainly bought by Europeans. The autonomy of African photographers was therefore absolute from the outset; they operated within a free zone because they were not targeting the external white market.

Towards a theory of anonymity

Can photography be seen as the return to a communal form of visual expression in a world where the tendency is for spectators to be passive? Does this mean we can see it as part of the traditional practice of making images that our common ancestors passed down to us? More specifically, can we link it to prehistoric rock paintings, where it seems that the most accomplished hands worked side by side with the most inept, and in which all are totally anonymous? Could we dare see a practice such as rock painting, which was built around a ritual as a spiritual exercise achieved through a communal artistic act, as being similar—even in flippant argument—to the practice of photography? This may very well be the case, if we allow for an intuitive inclusion of three objective components: communal practice, artistic experience and anonymous initiatives. However, one distinction must be made: photography aims to exorcise reality, while prehistoric rock art aimed to transcend it.

Even if drawing a link between photography and rock paintings in prehistoric times is simply a leap of intuition, it may help to provide an understanding of the meaning of things unspoken, of form, in the arts in general, and in photography in particular. Such practices are not to be seen as spiritual in the limited religious sense.

Any art form is a carrier of spirituality. Without attempting to develop an argument about art and the nature of producing different forms, it is essential at least to contemplate the anonymous aspect of photographic work for which Africa offers a live illustration on a grand scale.

Art and the hero

Over the last thirty years, photography has become a more common means of expression for artists producing works recognised as art by museums and such. And yet, the camera is still seen as that funny machine with the button we press without knowing why. Its sole purpose seems to be the fascination of seeing one's own image seen through the eyes of another. It is nevertheless difficult to understand why photography, being 'multiple' by nature (i.e., infinitely reproducible), has been forced to remain within the confines of the single, original object: a photograph is made unique by the viewer's perceptions and the accidents of history, where this may never have been the intention of the photographer. While attempts have been made, if only over recent years, to bring photography onto the art market, with numbered prints, vintage photographs and the application of famous signatures with a view to financial speculation, it is still clear that photography is an art of a multiple nature that can be reproduced *ad infinitum* without any concern for the restrictions governing a market based on one-off objects.

The value of the multiple object that can be shared by everyone coincides with the basic communal value. In this way, photography has built a community around the world, in a series of radically different contexts, depending on the geographical areas and civilizations concerned.

From the outset, the photographer is working with multiples that infinitely reproduce what can be shared as an image. His or her subject is reality and the reproduction of the subject is reality: the photographer is only a medium brandishing a gadget, really no more than a simple technician in a communal enterprise. For the public, the art of the photographer is always secondary to the reality effect produced. The subject is the superstar, not the photographer, unlike the painter, who creates seemingly out of nothing. Yet the photographer is equally an artist, with the mind of an artist, which is expressed in his or her photographic vision. The process may not be arduous—a mere fraction of a second to take the picture, instead of hours wielding a brush, pencil or chisel—yet it is quite autonomous in the choices made and the intuitive qualities behind the work.

And yet, this craft is within the reach of millions of fingers and eyes which, every second, press the shutter release or see a picture.

And this is no doubt the point where the shift occurs between practicing one of the 'fine arts' and the art of photography. On the one hand, the revered artist-turned-iconoclast sets up cliques and gradually moves away from the general public to orient his or her message solely towards a cultivated audience of specialists, speculators, paying patrons-of-the-arts and critics (museum curators get added to the list later). On the other hand, photography has invaded the shared, and public, visual imagination. The subject is no longer god or the hero, but me and my relatives, the countryside where we were on holiday or, in the case of pictures taken by others, the countryside we dream of visiting, special moments in the community, new superstars we all identify with, advertising and reporting.   JLP

Chapters heading illustrations

Before dawn
DRUM Magazine, DRUM Cover 03: First DRUM Cover, 1951
© BAHA, courtesy Bailey Seippel Gallery

A useful dream
Mohamed Dib, from the series *Tlemcen ou les lieux de l'écriture*, 1946
© Dokolo, Revue Noire

Lost illusions
Mohamed Mo Amin, MBALE, UGANDA. MBALE, UGANDA. A crowd
of twenty-thousand Ugandans, women and children included, witnessed
the execution, in 1973, of two alleged conspirators from Bugsihu: Tom
Masaba, a former captain in the Ugandan Army, and Sebastino Namirundu. Masaba, who was accused of being a terrorist, was reported to have
said: 'Let those, like me, who are killing innocent people in the country,
come out and report to the authorities'. 02, 1973
© Mohamed Amin, Camerapix, A24 Media

Crossroads
***Idumota, Lagos Island, Lagos* from the series *Lagos. All Roads*, 2001**

No name in the street
Dorris Haron Kasco, *Nue dans la rue, Abidjan*, ca 1990-1992
© Dokolo, Revue Noire

Another country
***Cape Town*, 2009**
© Essop Brothers, courtesy Goodman gallery

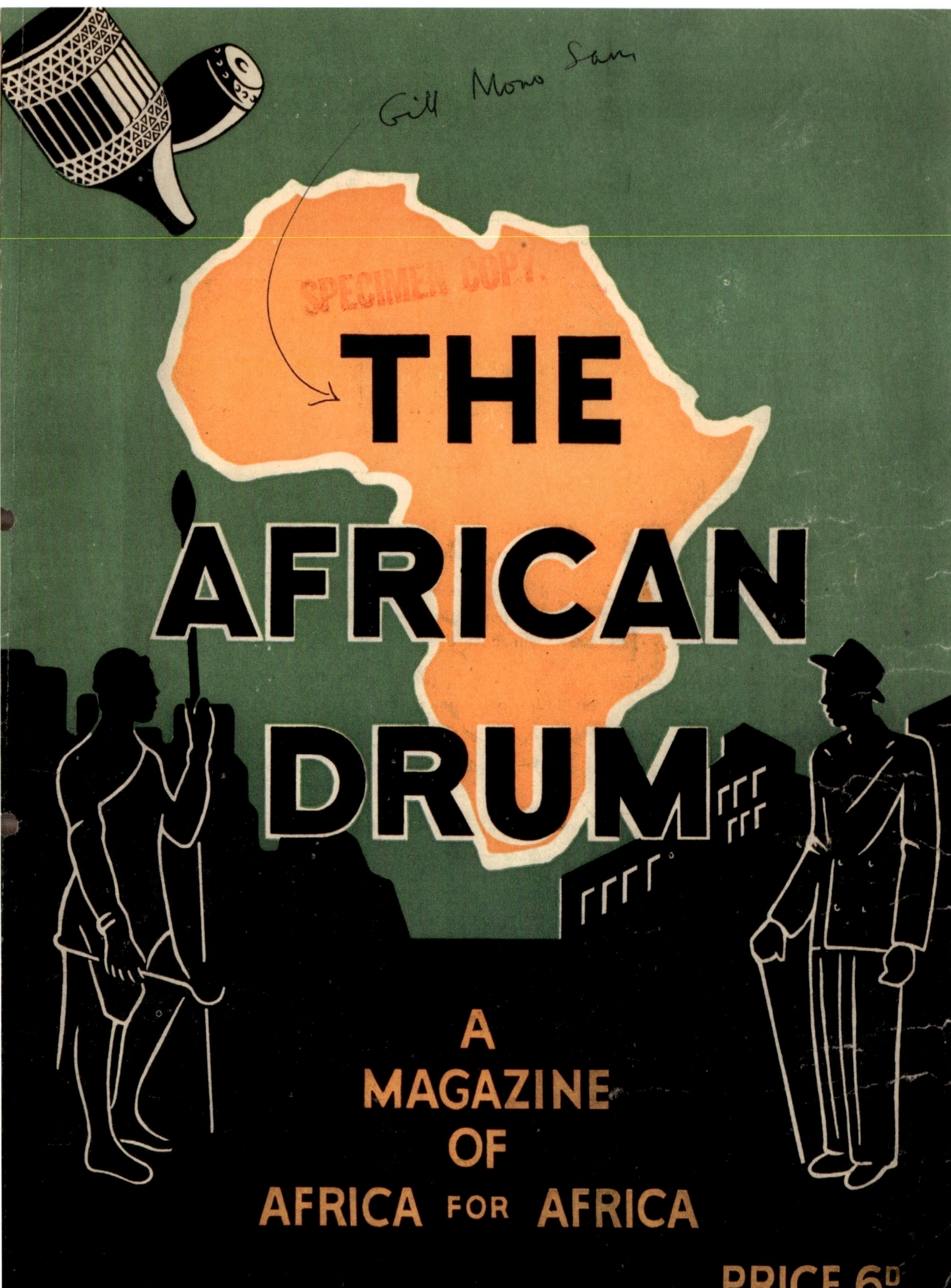

Gill Mono Sans
SPECIMEN COPY.
THE
AFRICAN
DRUM
A
MAGAZINE
OF
AFRICA FOR AFRICA
PRICE 6D
REGISTERED AT THE G.P.O. AS A NEWSPAPER

Before
dawn

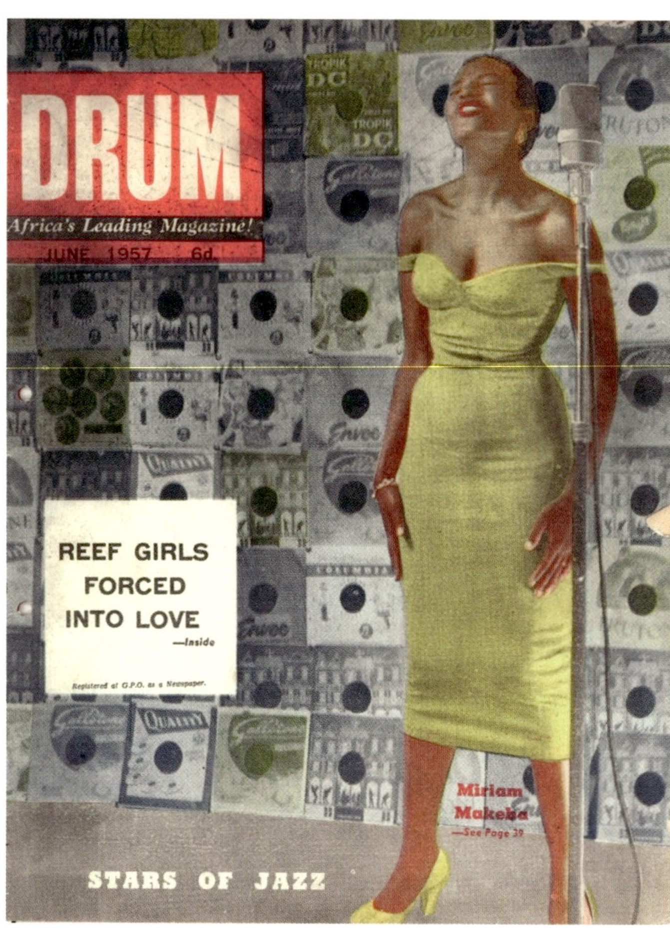

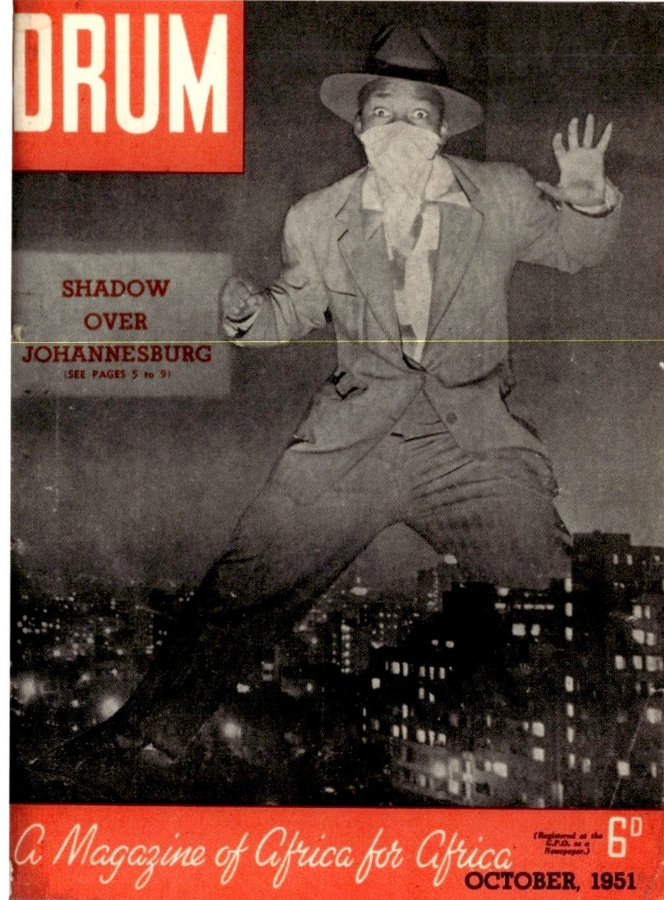

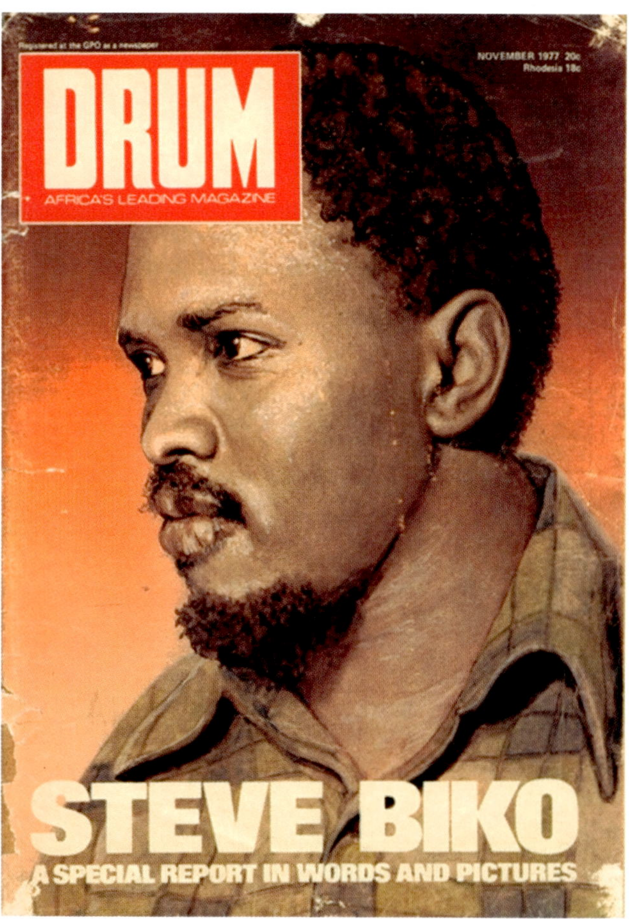

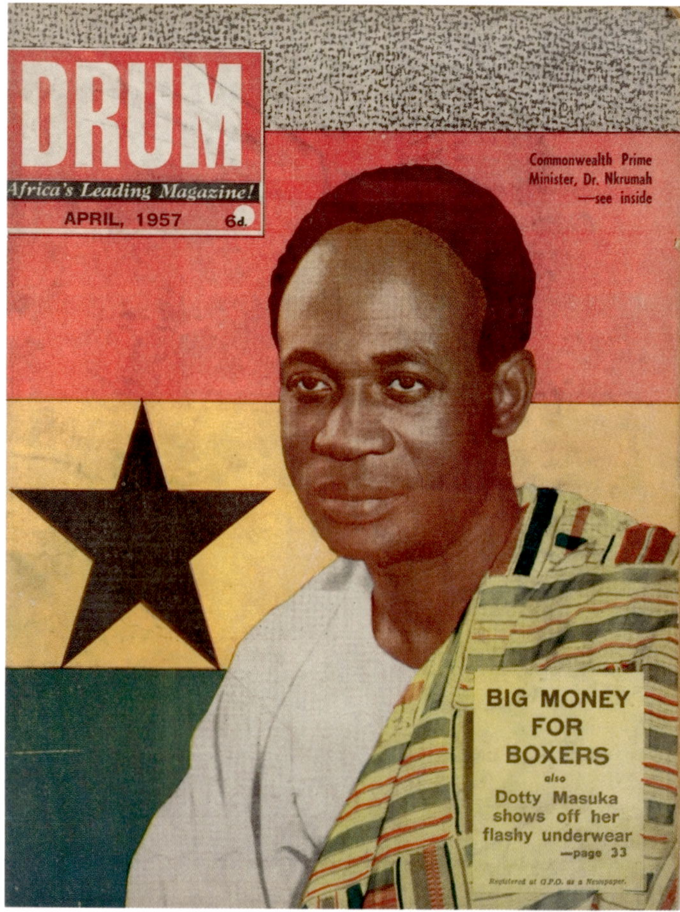

DRUM Cover 06: *Miriam Makeba*, 1957
DRUM Cover 11: *Steve Biko*, 1970

DRUM Cover 10: *Shadow over Johannesburg*, 1951
DRUM Cover 04: *Kwame Nkruma, Commonwealth Prime Minister*, 1957

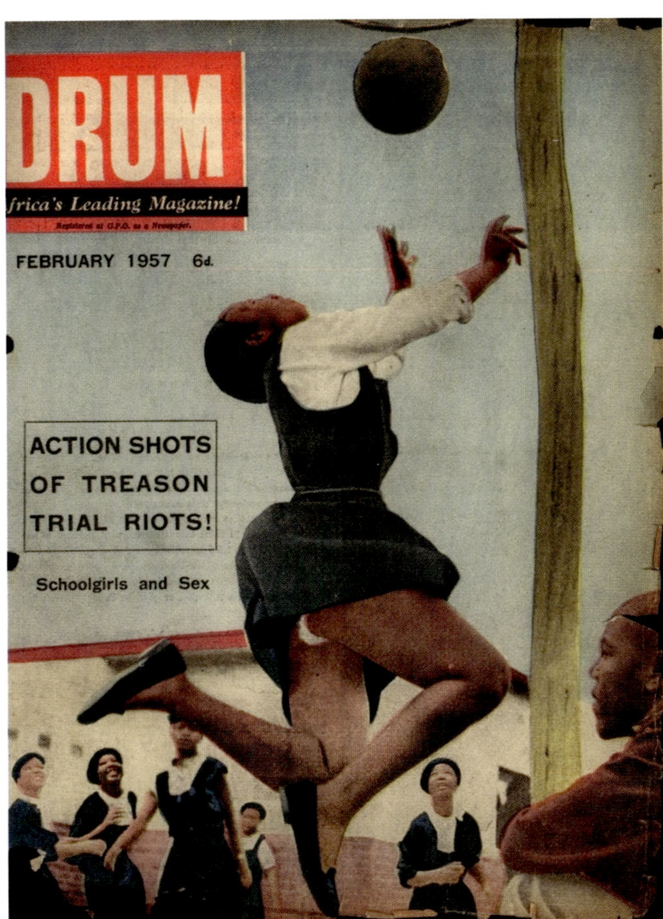

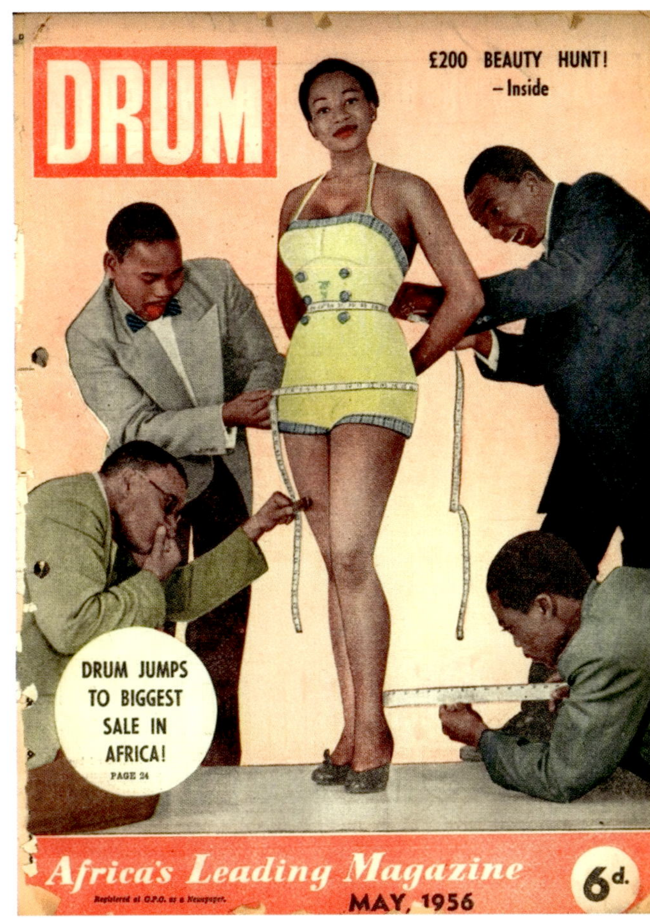

DRUM Magazine
Johannesburg (South Africa), 1951

Drum, edited and directed by the white liberal Jim Bailey, was the first magazine in South Africa to be staffed (in part) by blacks, and to be written for a black audience. It became the most widely read magazine of its time. The publication reflected a vibrant era, the 1950s, which saw both the emergence of an urban black identity and the violent and repressive backlash that followed on its heels. The magazine exerted a subtle but important political pressure on the establishment with its denunciation of living conditions in ghettos. It covered the torturing of prisoners, the proliferation of hangings, and the massacre in Sharpeville in 1960, when the police, in the words of Denis Hirson, 'with the electricity of blind panic flashing in their blood, fired 705 rounds of bullets in less than a minute against the crowd, without previously issuing any warning'. Sixty-seven demonstrators were killed that day. *Drum* provided a conduit for the growing recognition of black South African culture, and was in print during what is considered to be the golden age of black journalism.

DRUM Cover 02: *Treason Trial, Schoolgirls and Sex*, 1957

DRUM Cover 05: *Drum Staff*, 1956

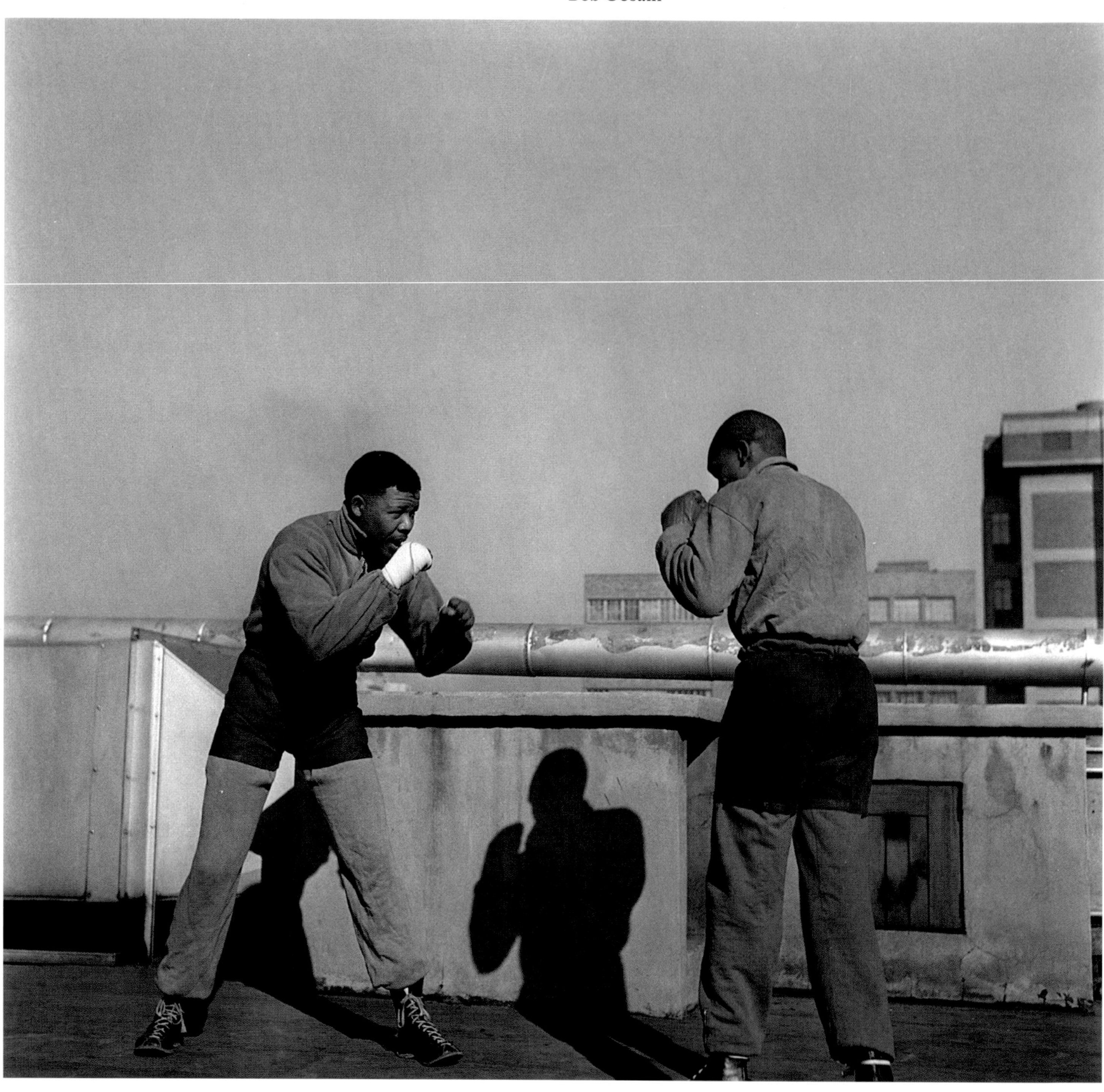

Treason Trial, End of round One, Mandela boxing on the roof top of
a newspaper building in Johannesburg, 1957

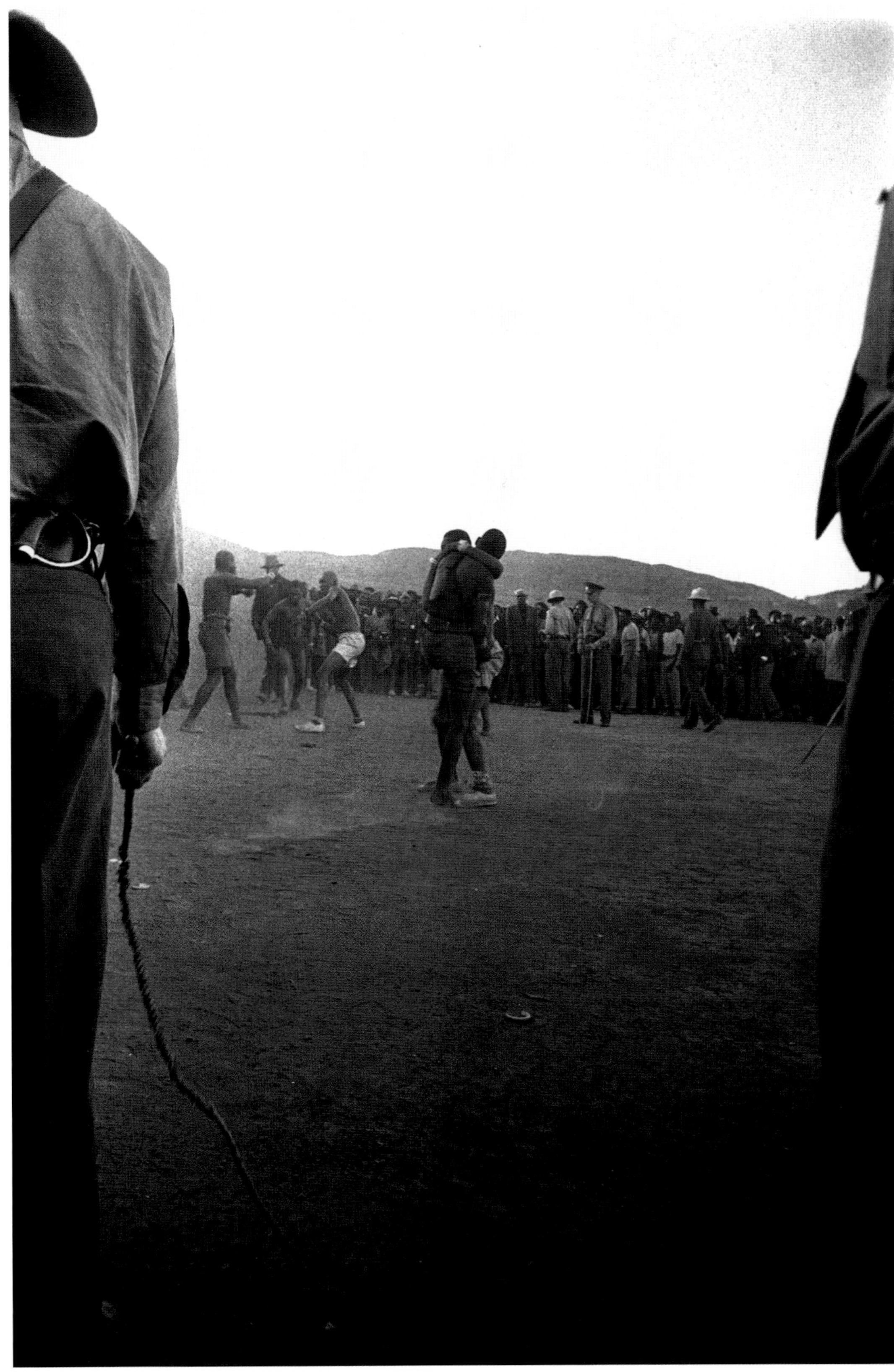

Drum Secret Camera at the Pretoria Bare-fist Fights

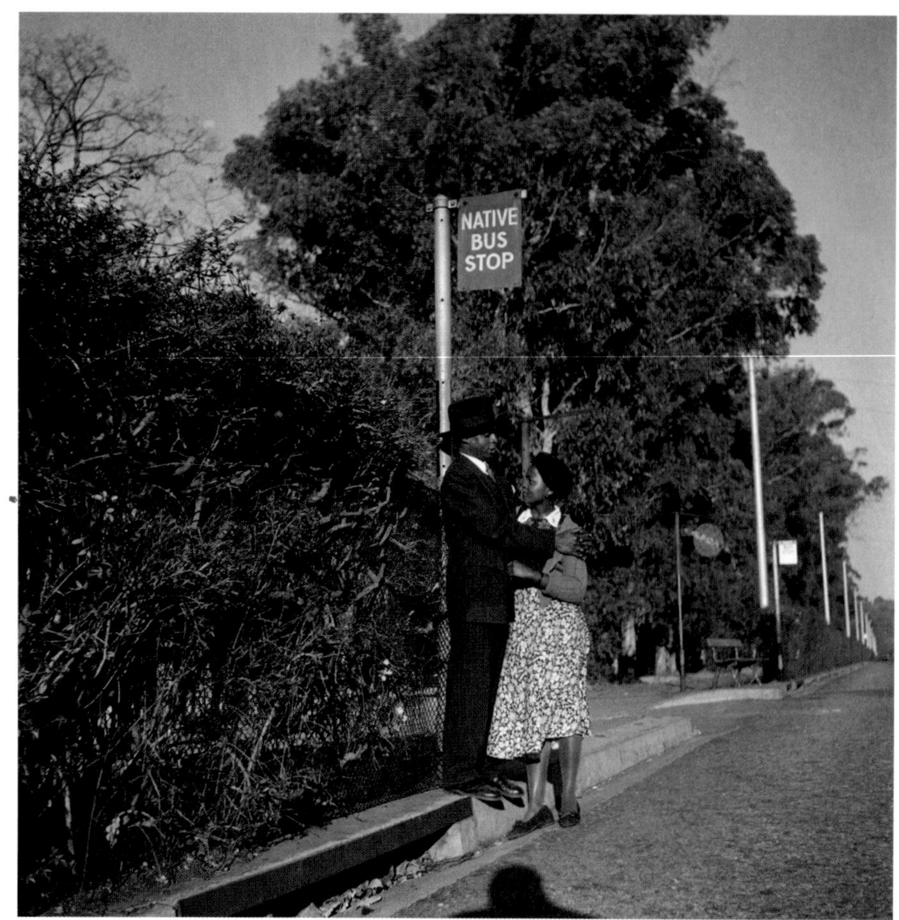

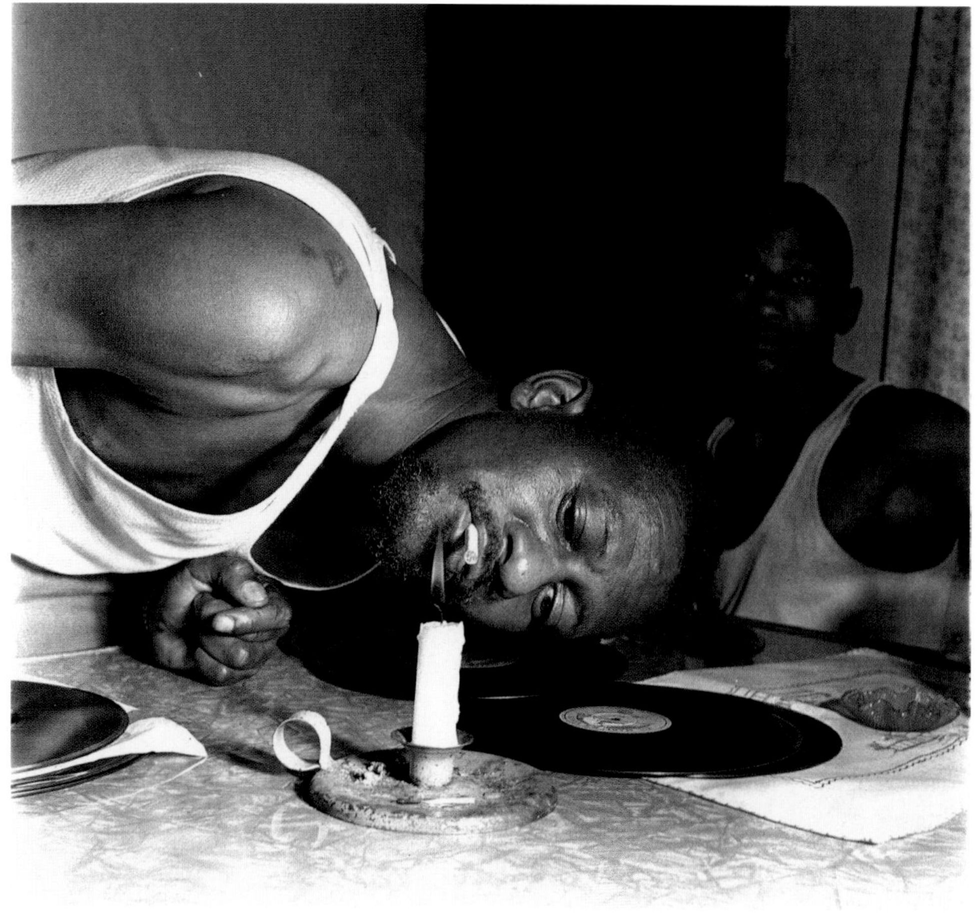

Love Story, 1954

King Force

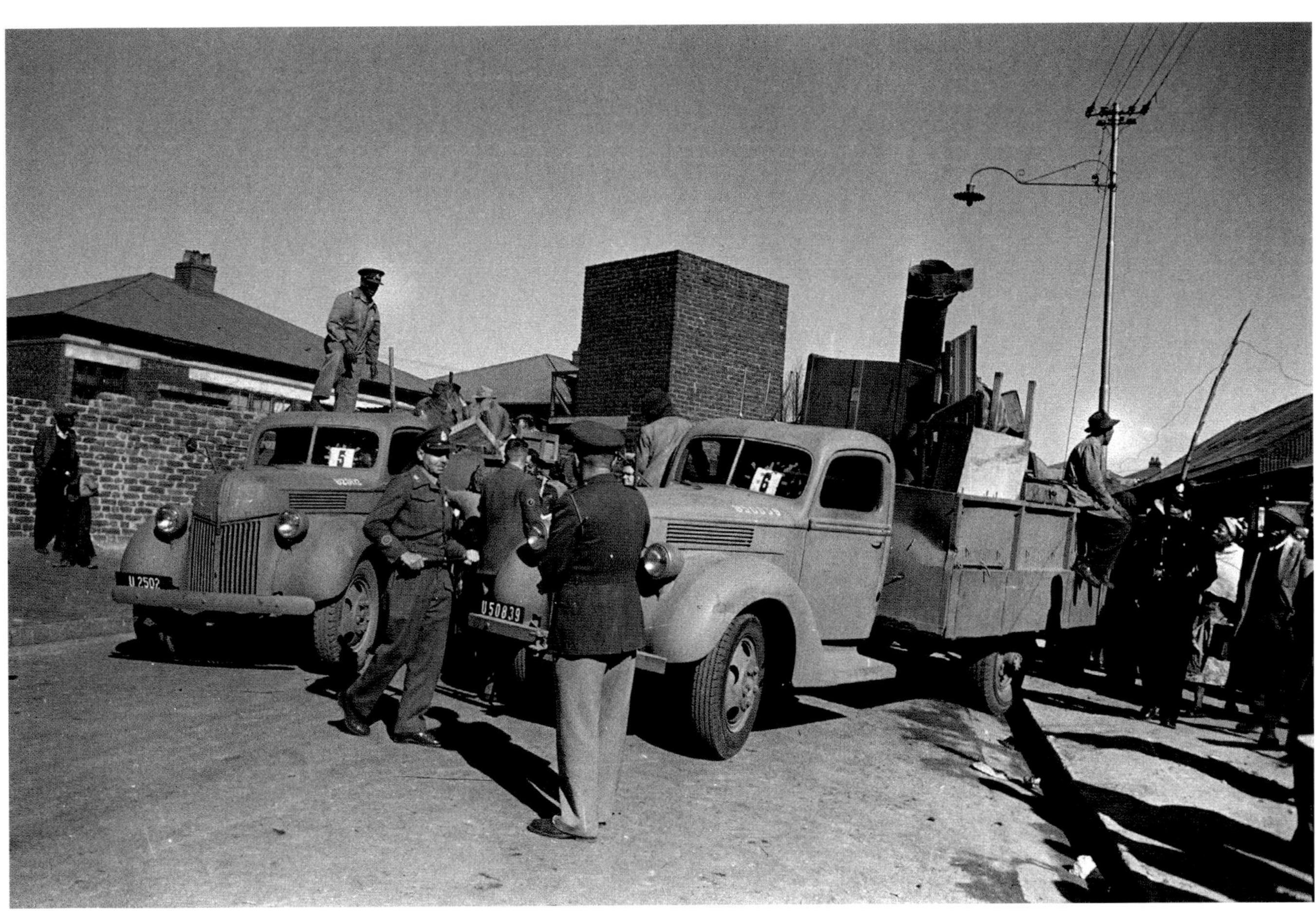

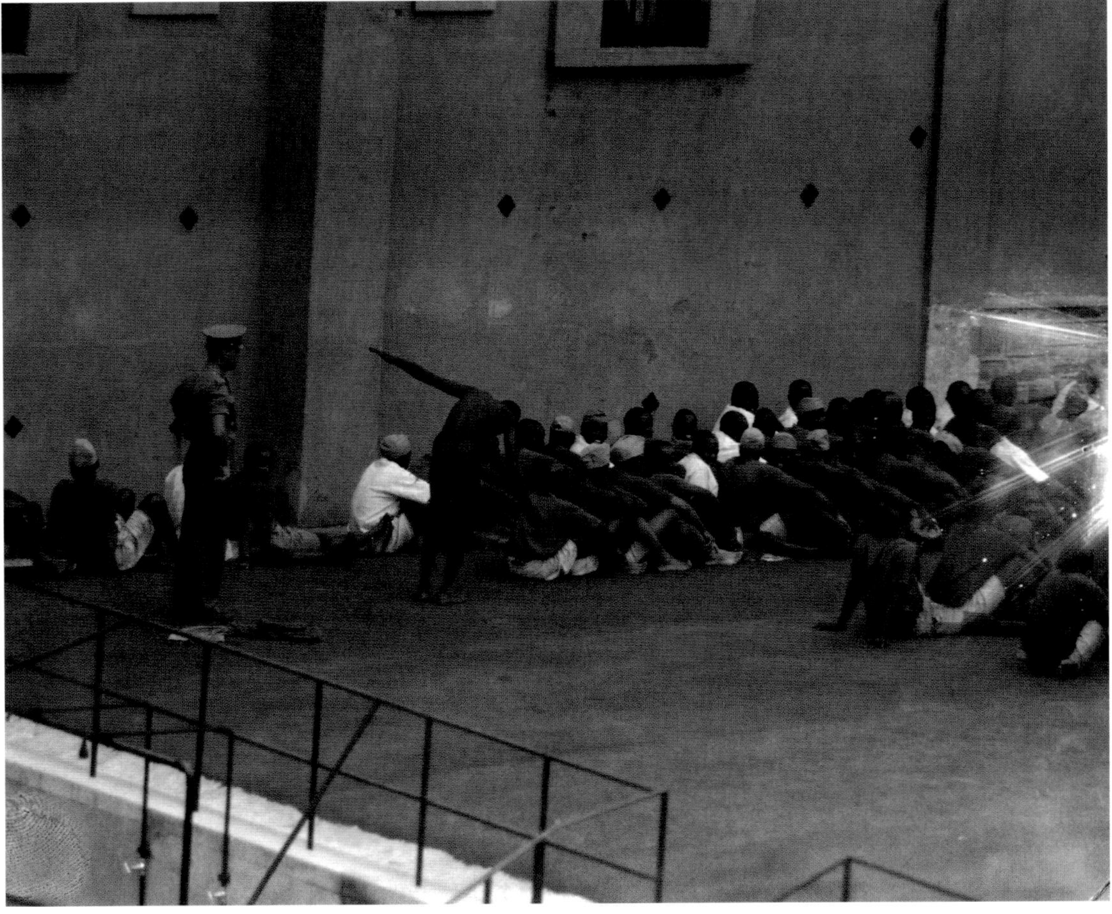

Removal, Sophiatown, 1955

Mr. Drum goes to jail, 03, 1954

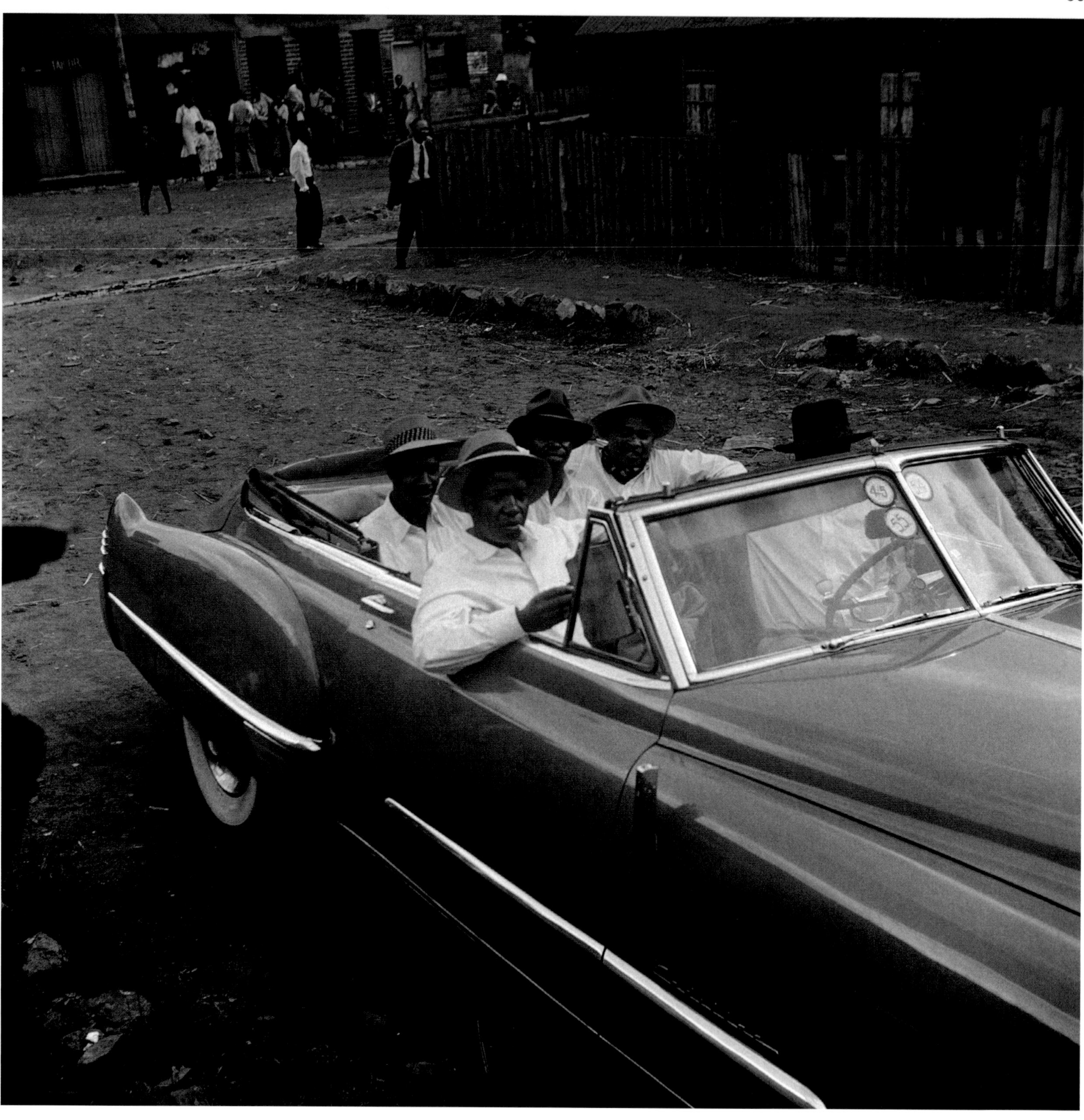

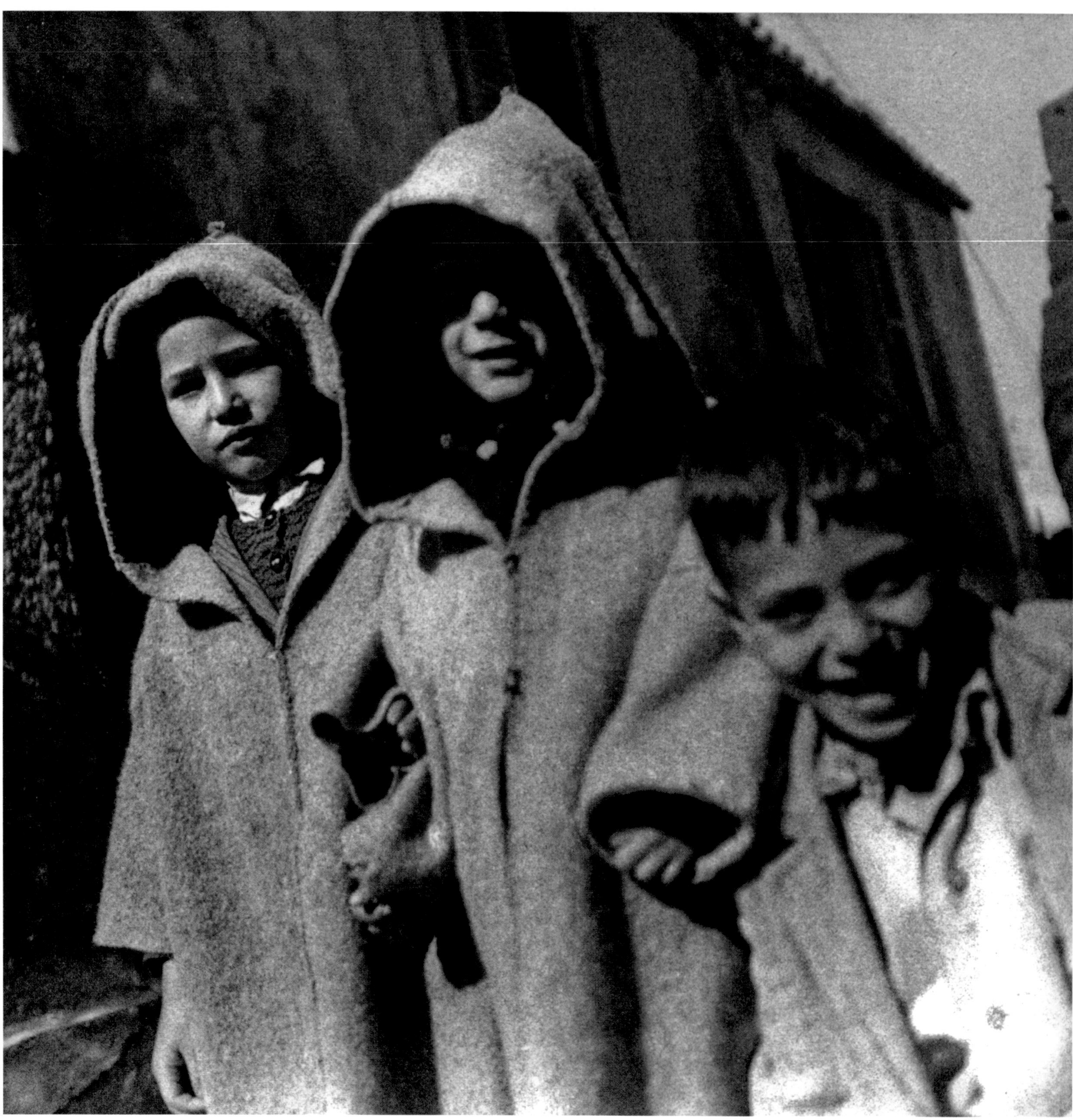

A useful dream *
1960 1969

The dates which organise this book are a way to tell a story that, like any story, is ultimately a fiction.   *SN*

* Tierno Monenembo

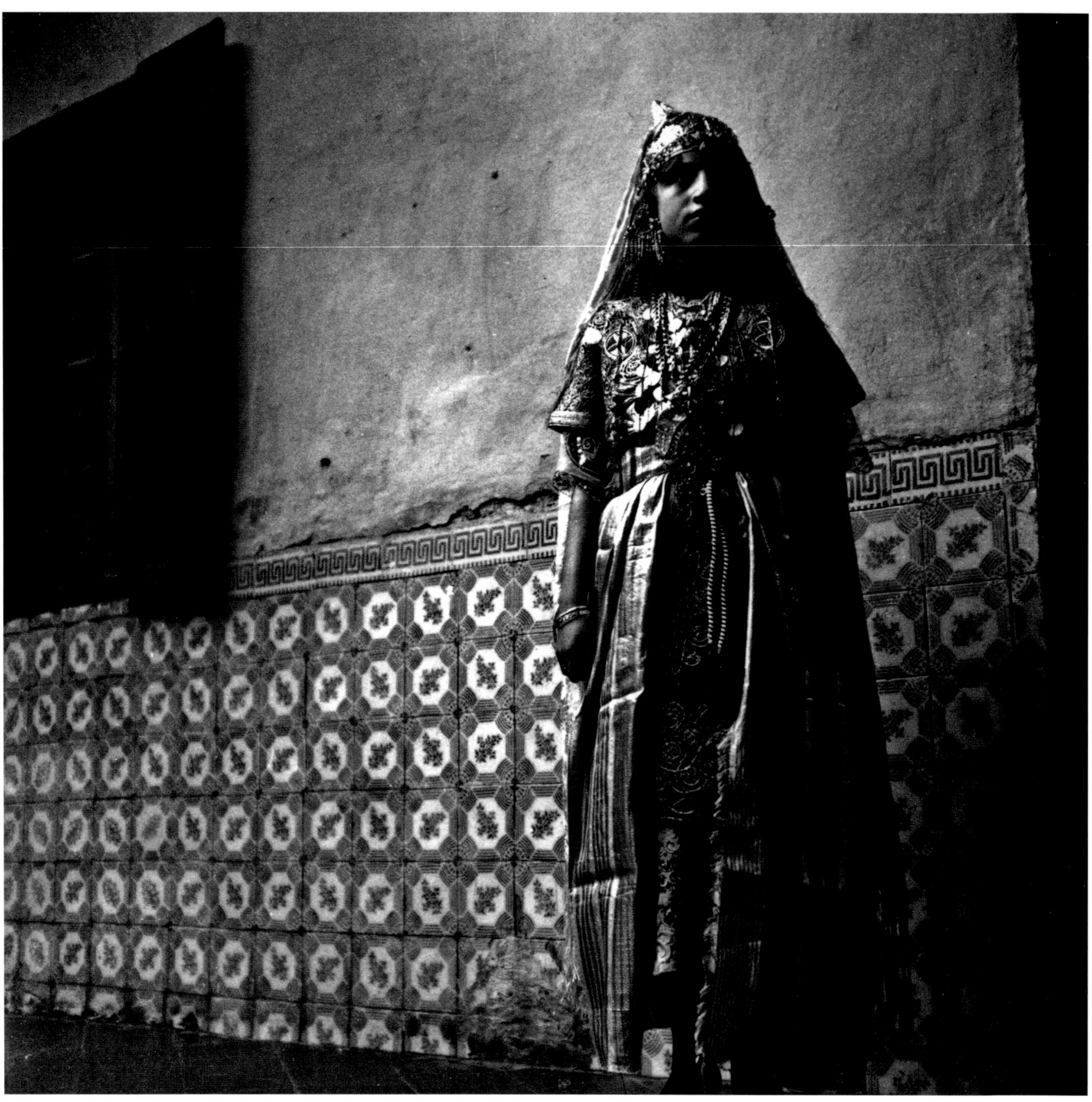

from the series *Tlemcen ou les lieux de l'écriture*, 1946

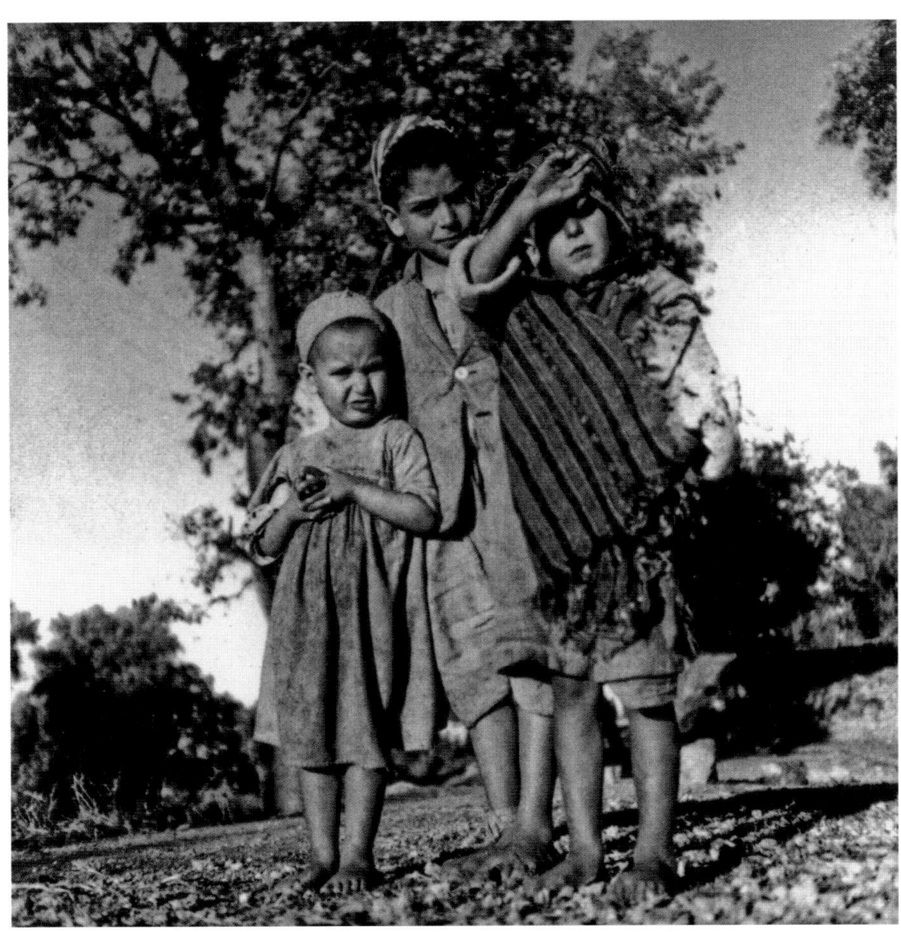

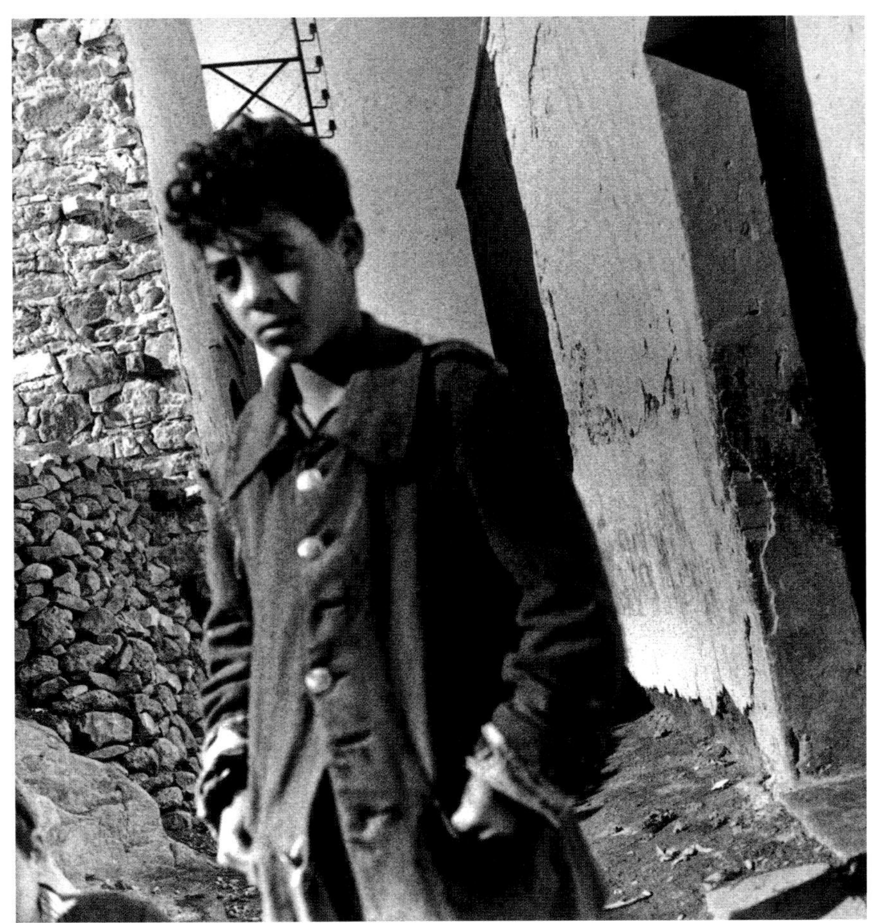

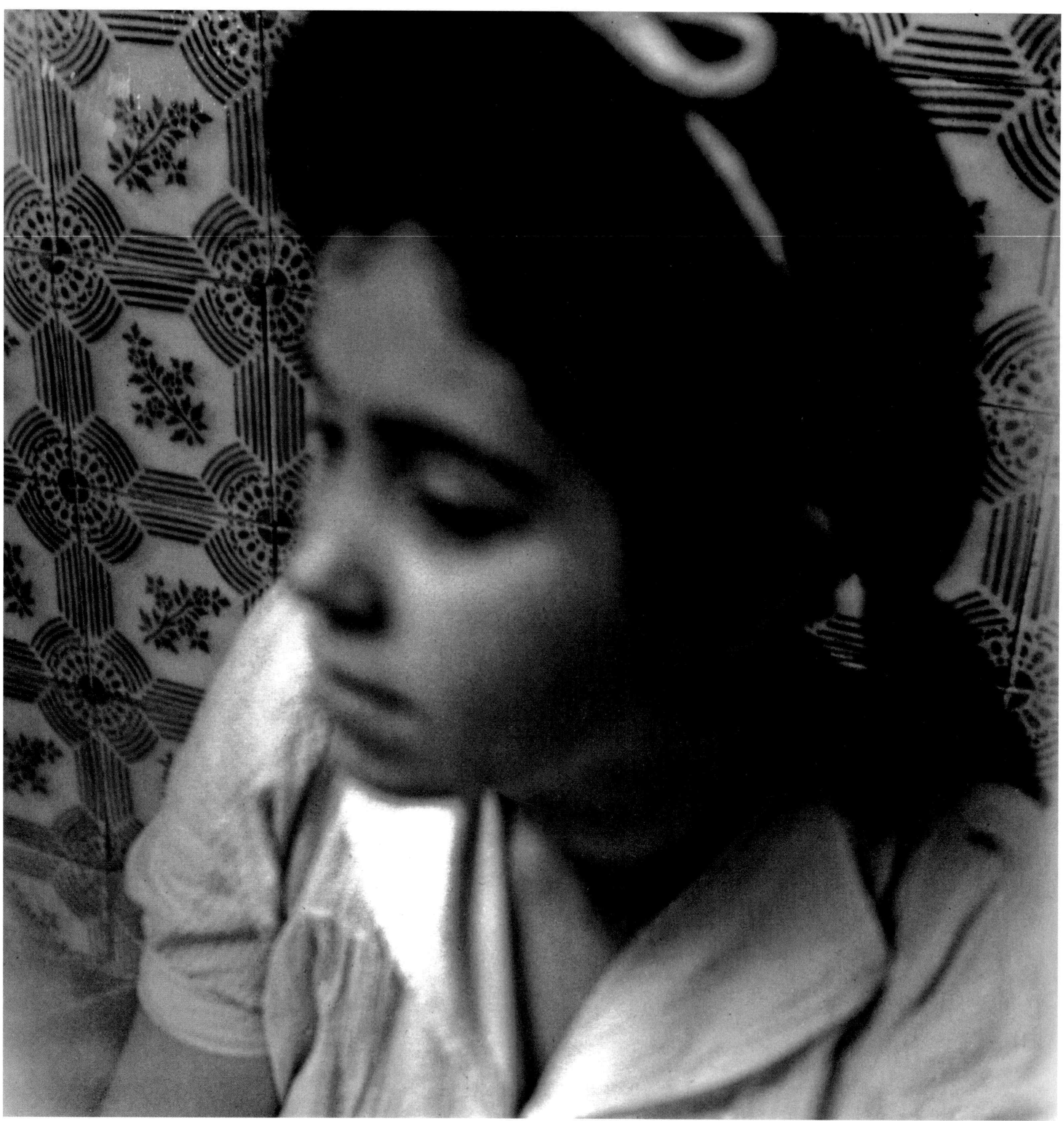

from the series *Tlemcen ou les lieux de l'écriture*, 1946

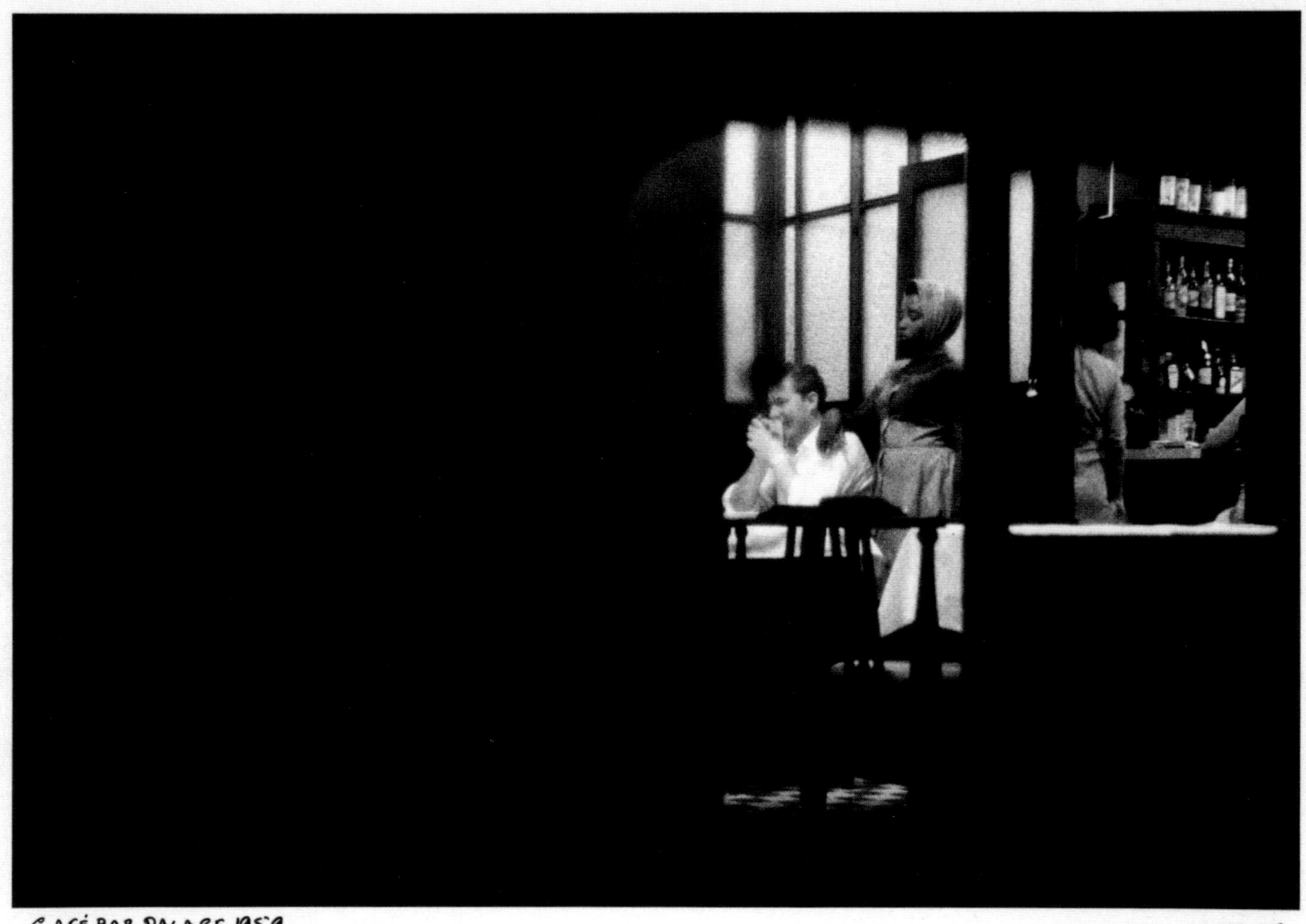

Café Bar Palace, 1959

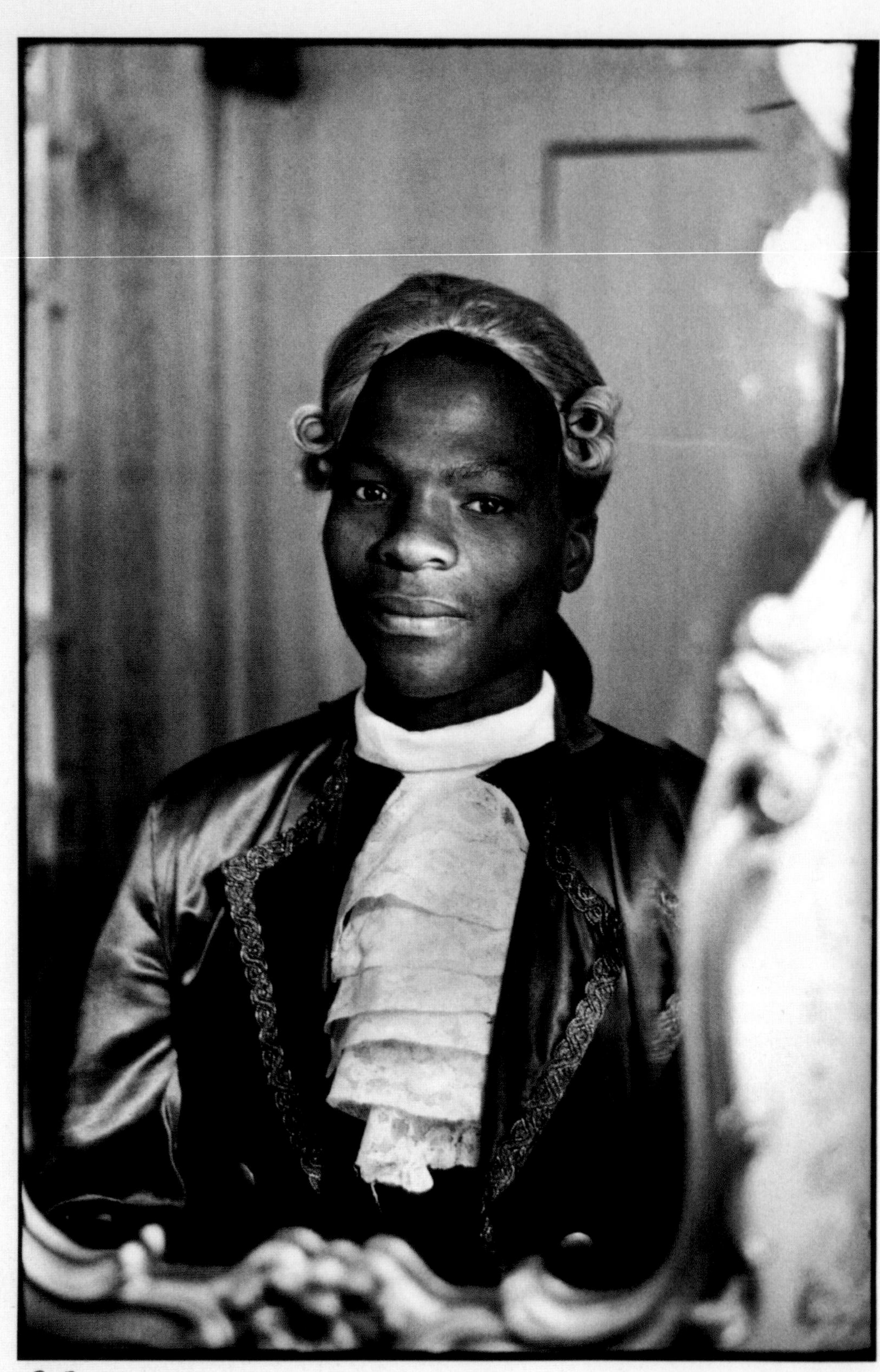

Doorkeeper at the Moulin Rouge, 1970

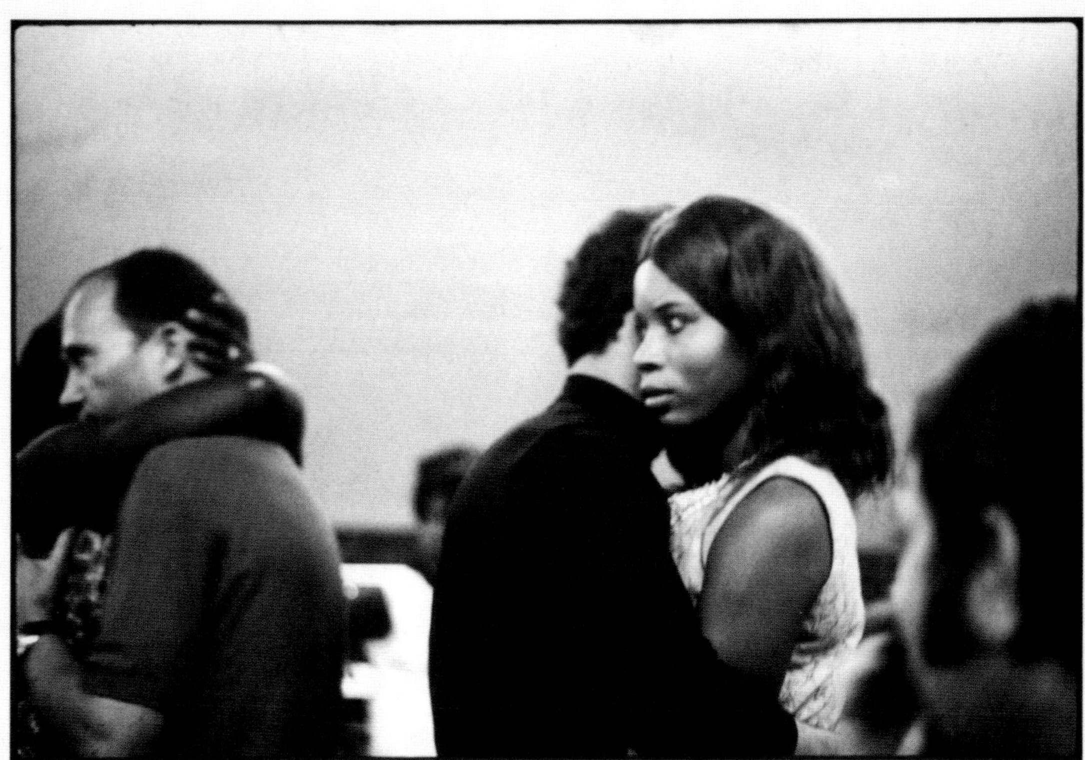

In the Embrace of the Night, 1970

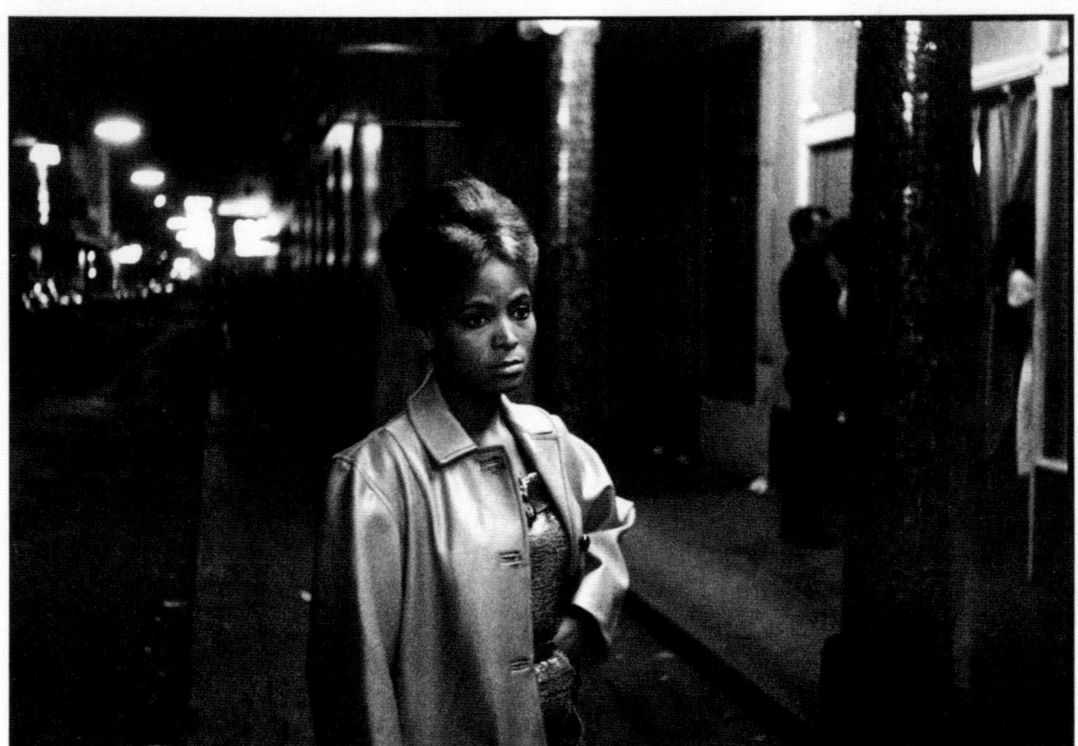

Sad eyed Model, 1962

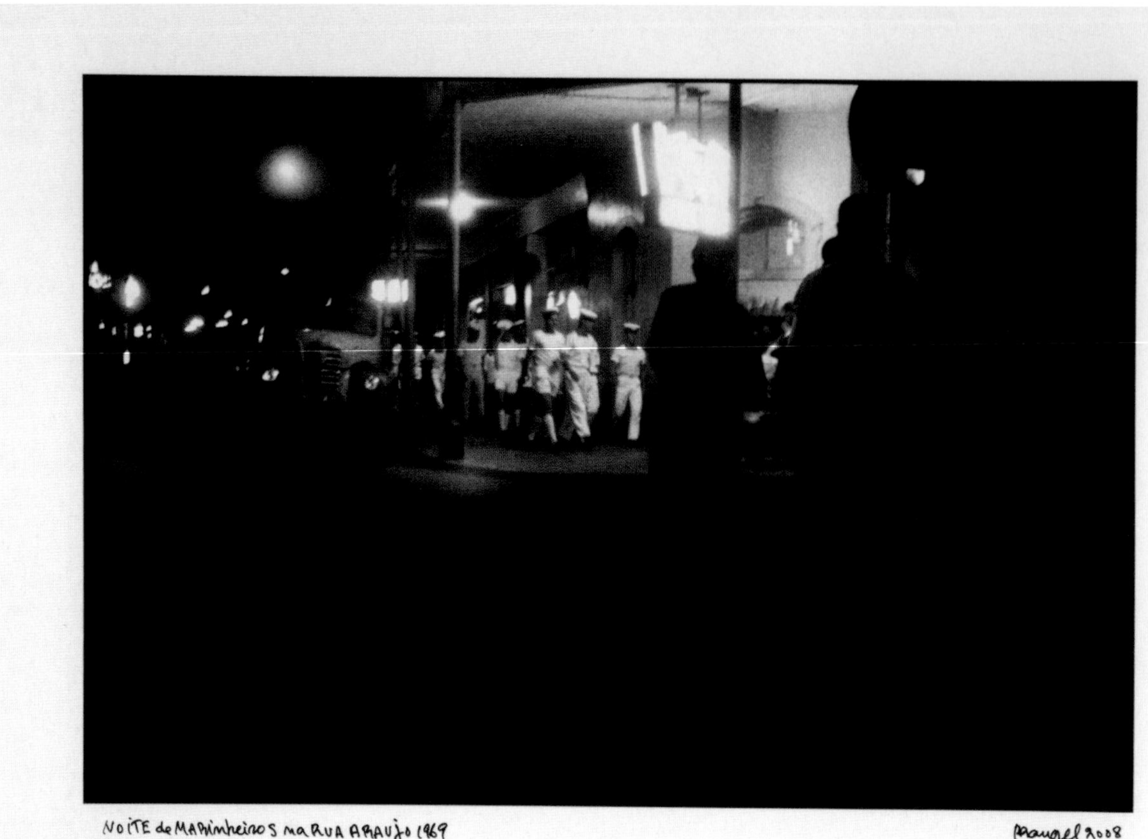

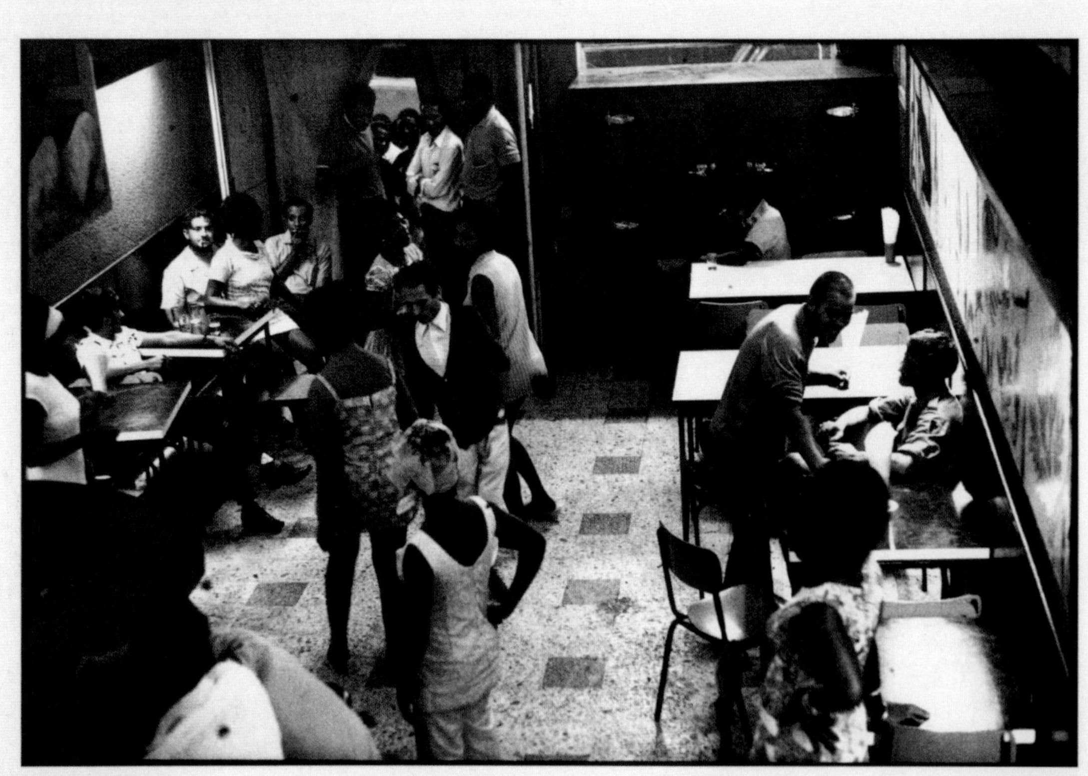

Sailor's Night in the Rua Araujo, 1969   *The Texas Bar*, 1971

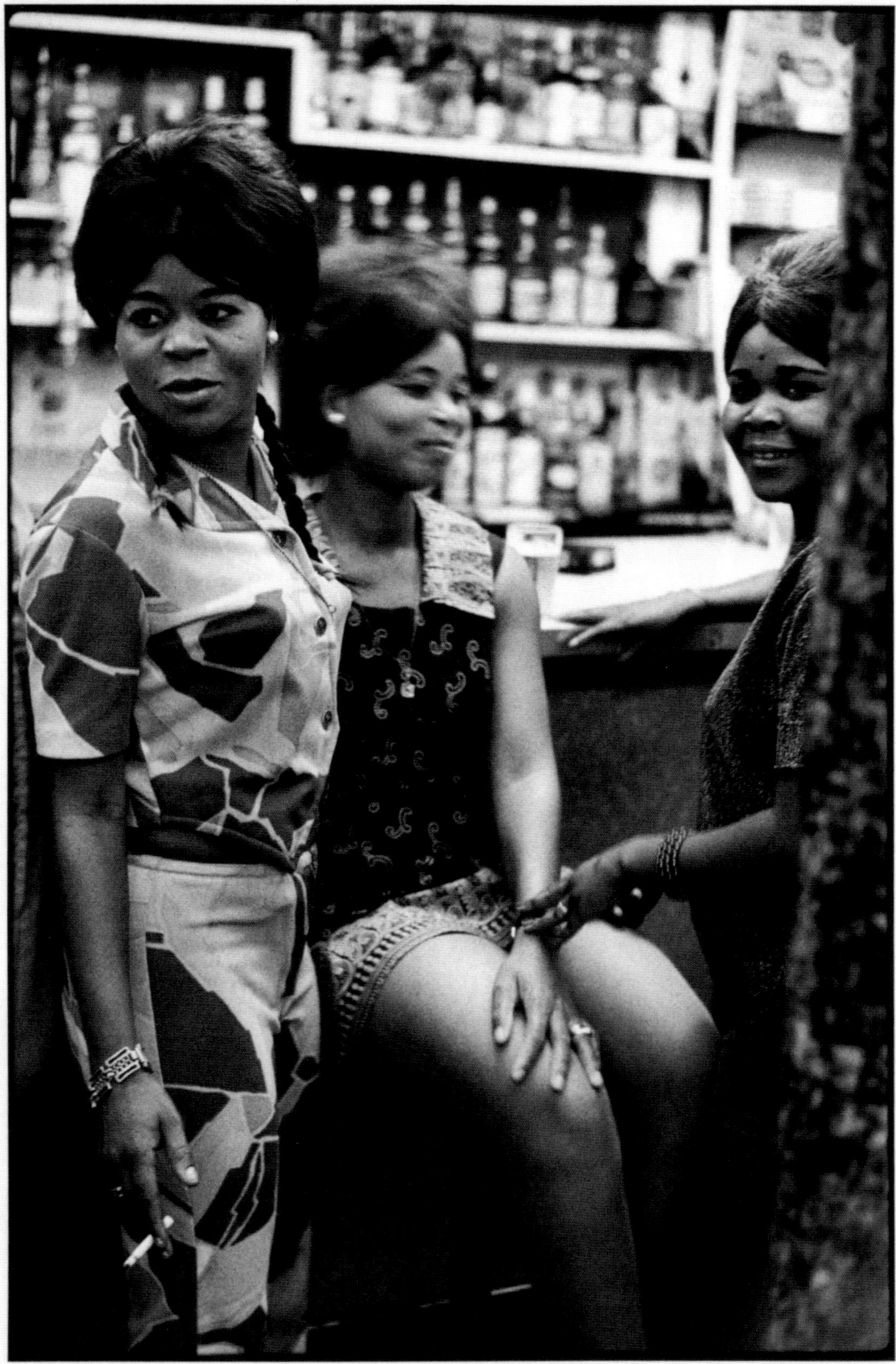

The three Marias, 1970

 Cornélius Yao Augustt Azaglo

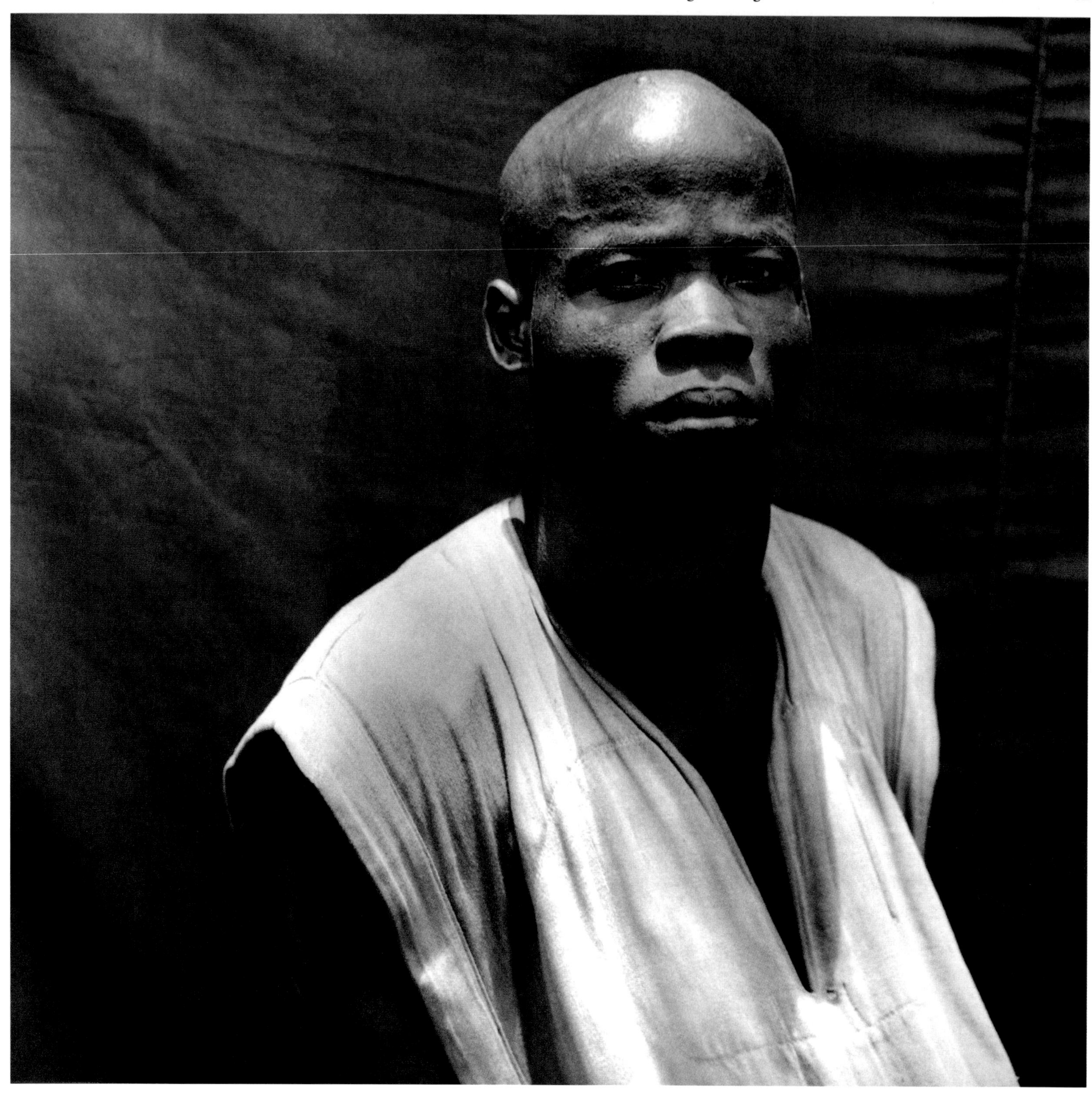

from the series *Sur place*

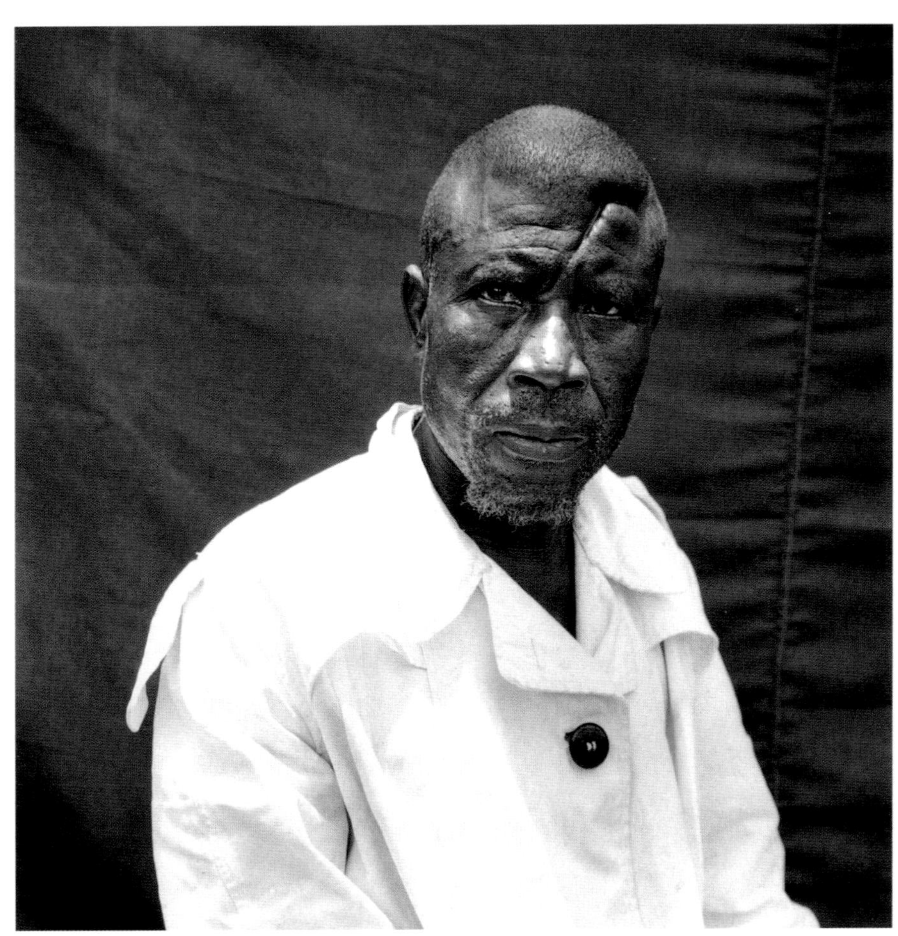

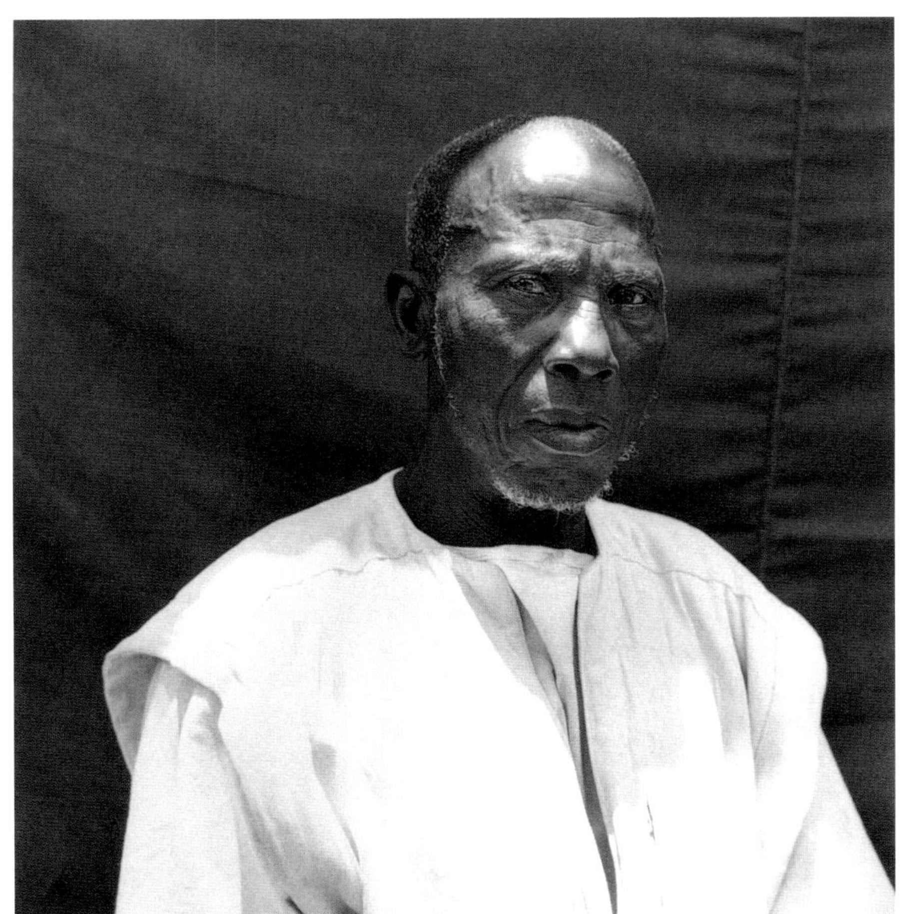

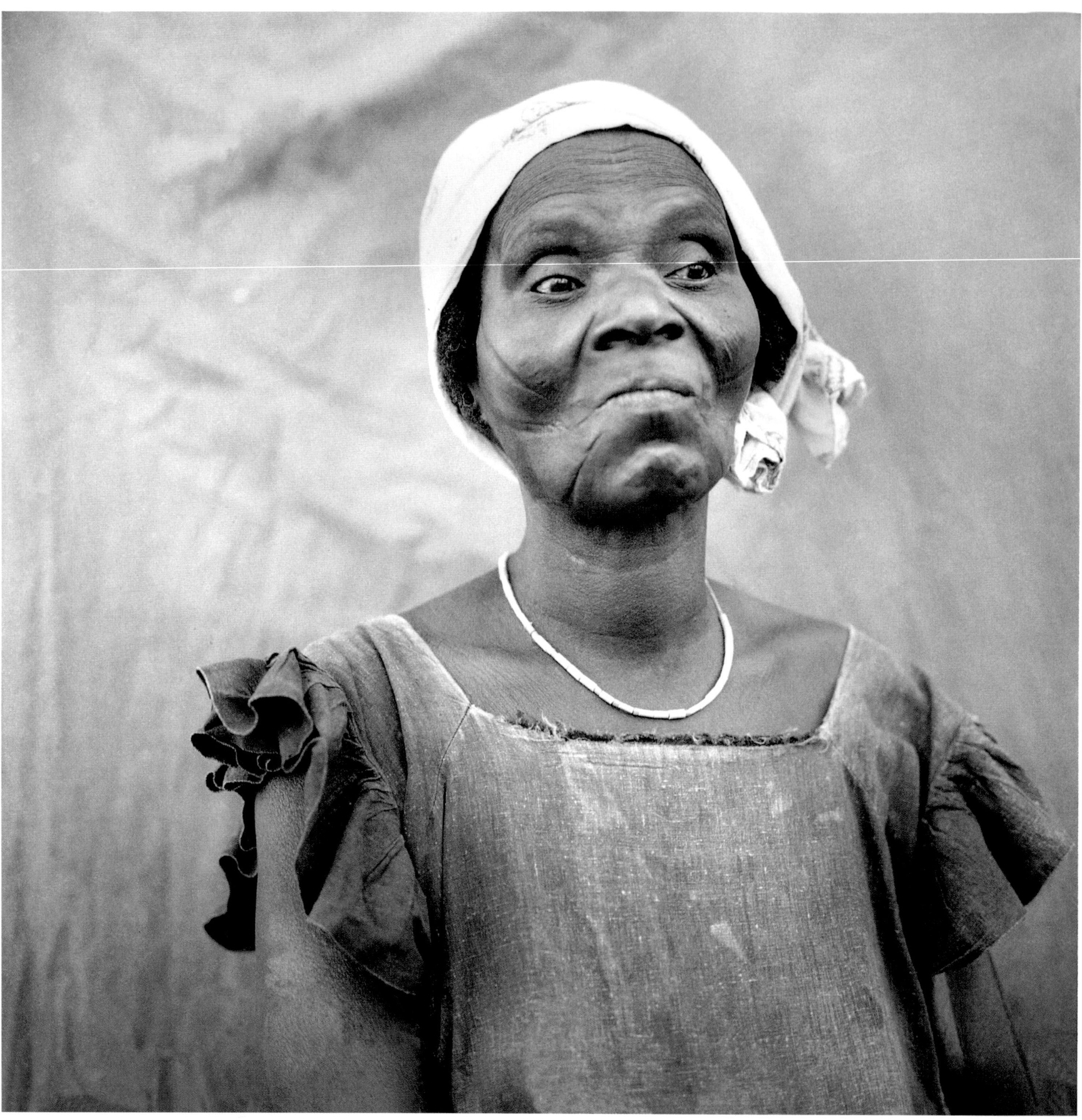

from the series *Sur place*

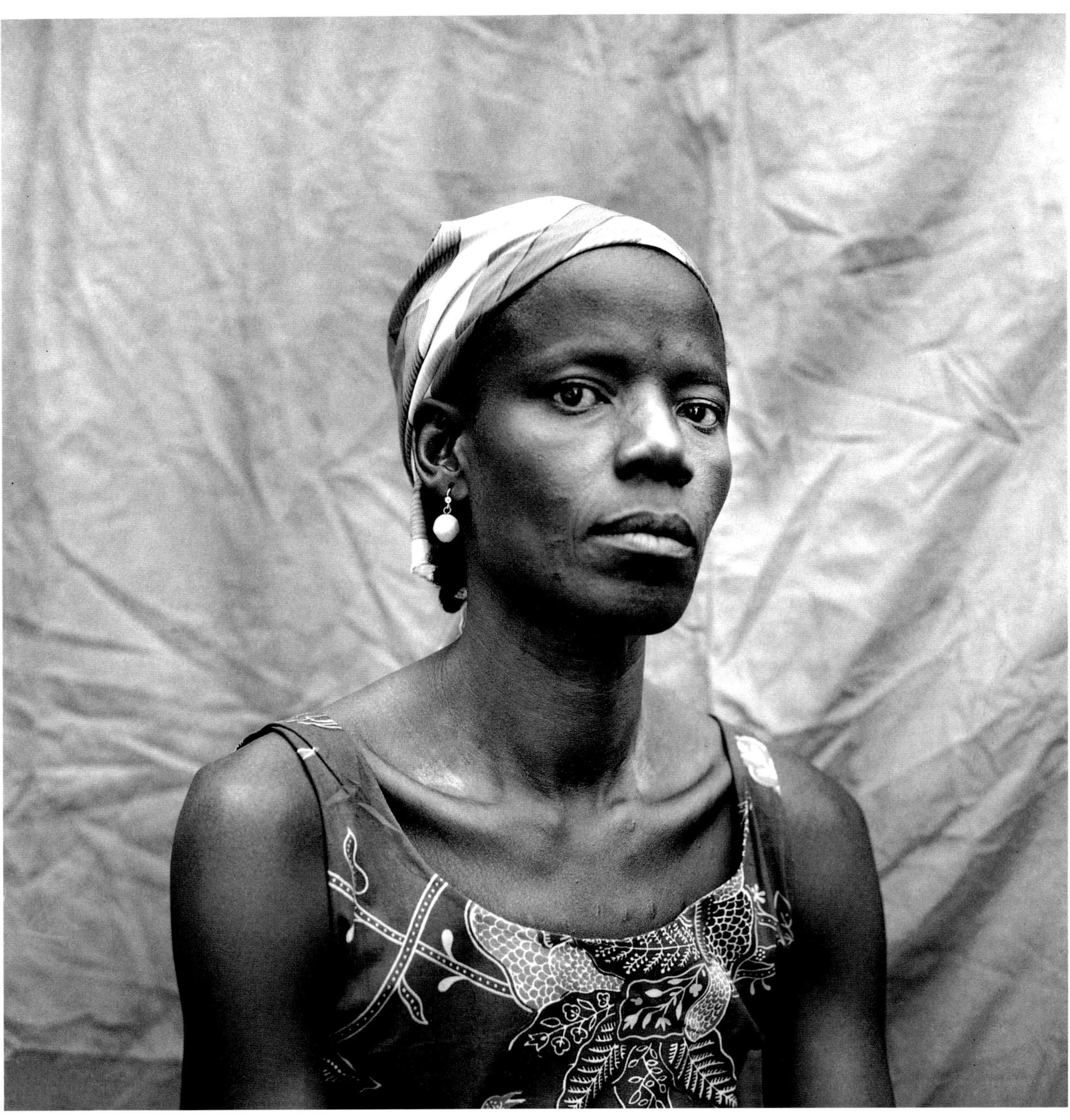

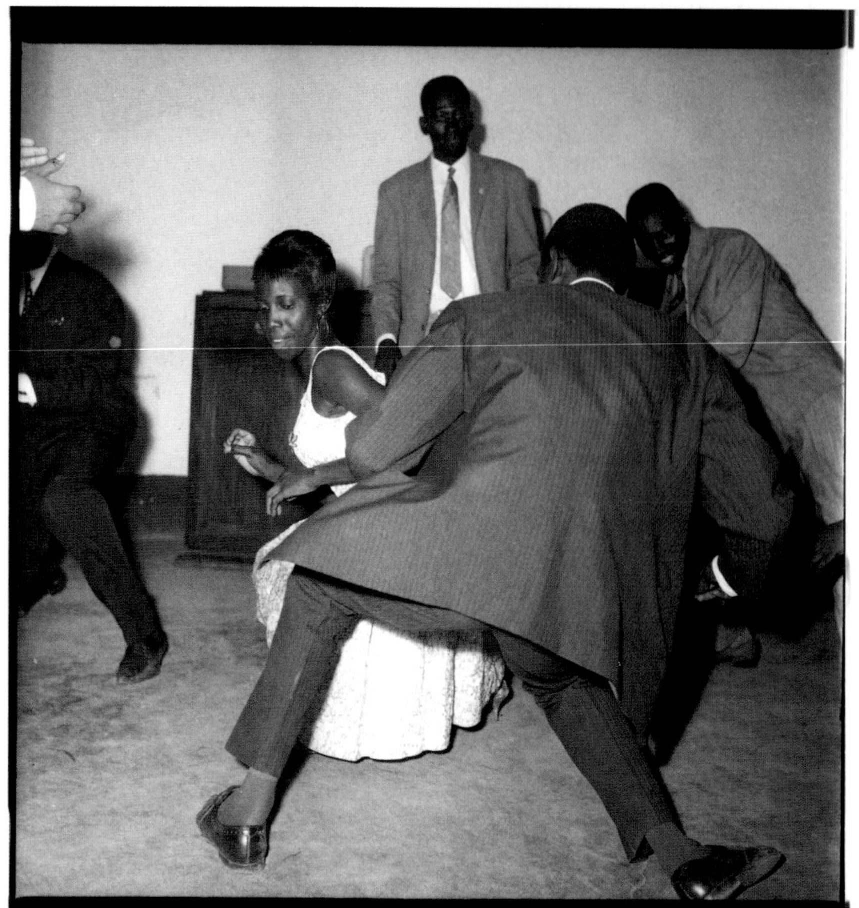

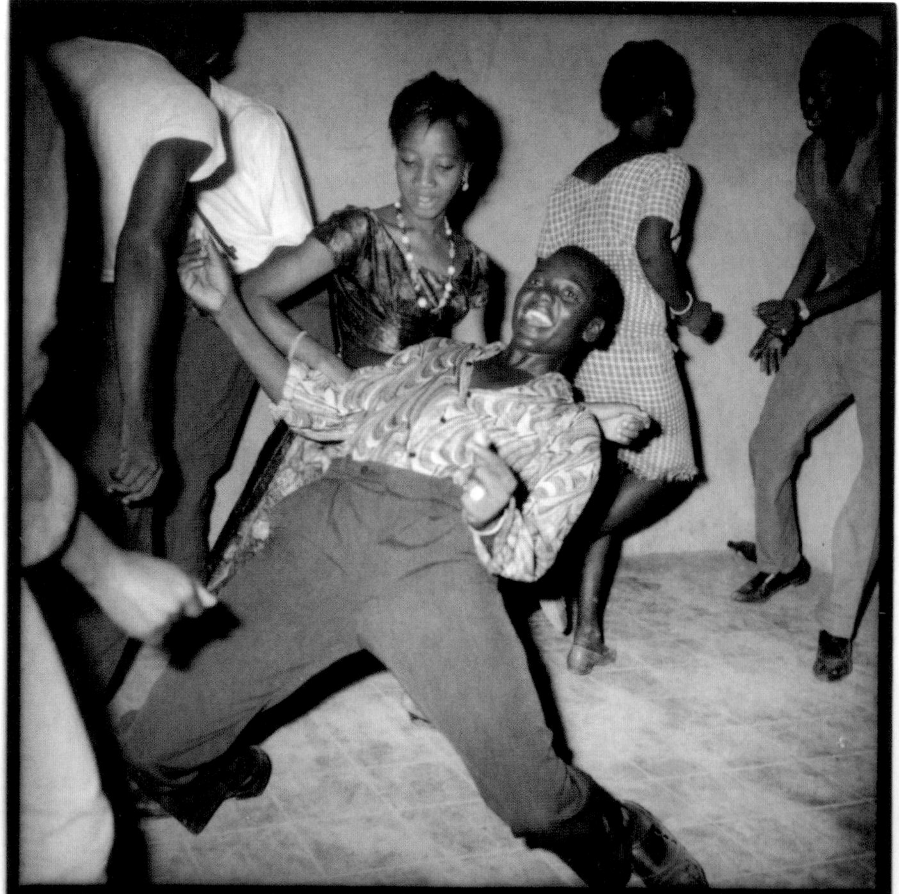

Dansez le Twist, 1965   *Soirée de mariage de Drissa Balo*, 1967

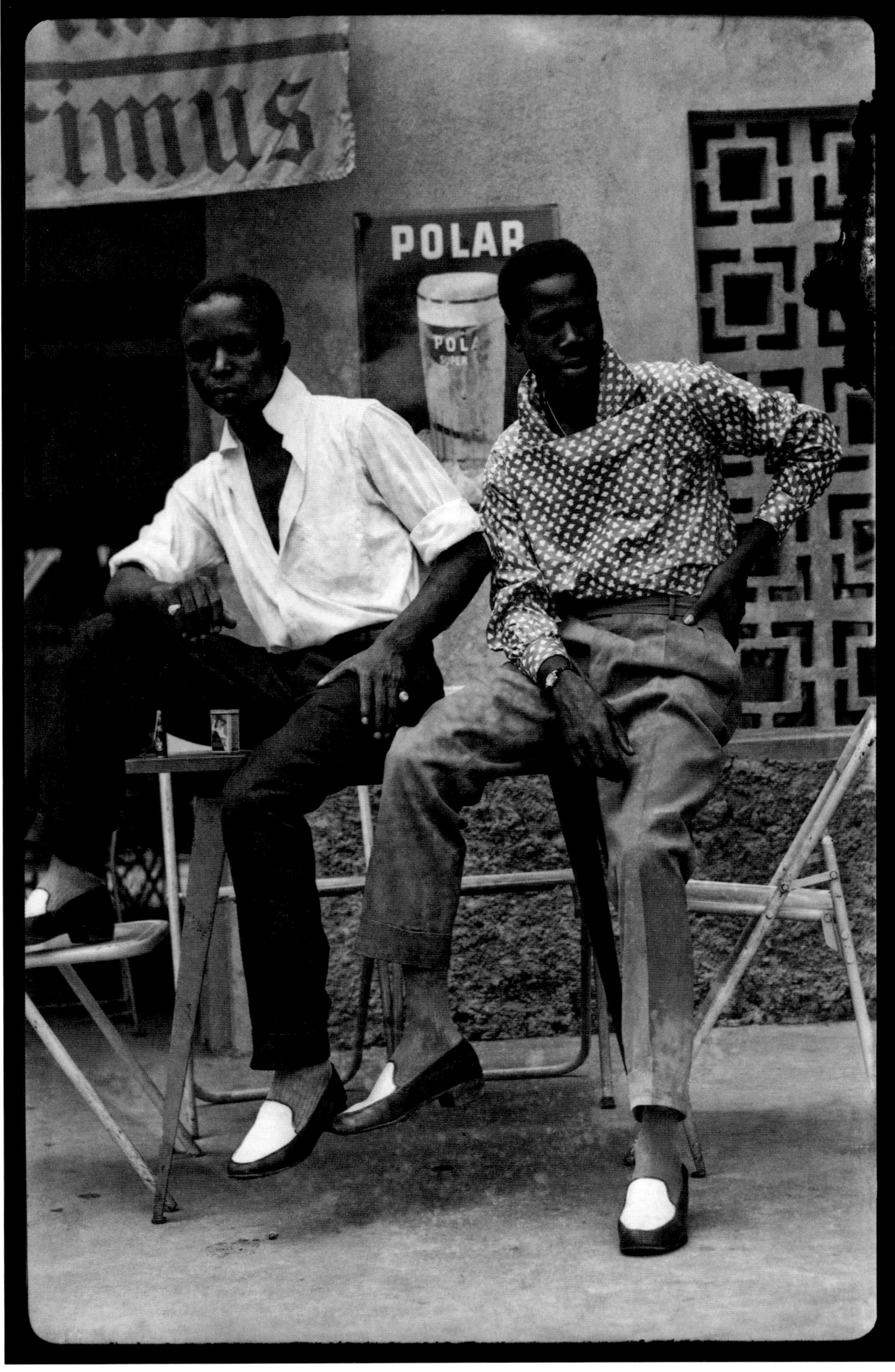

Deux garçons au café, ca 1965

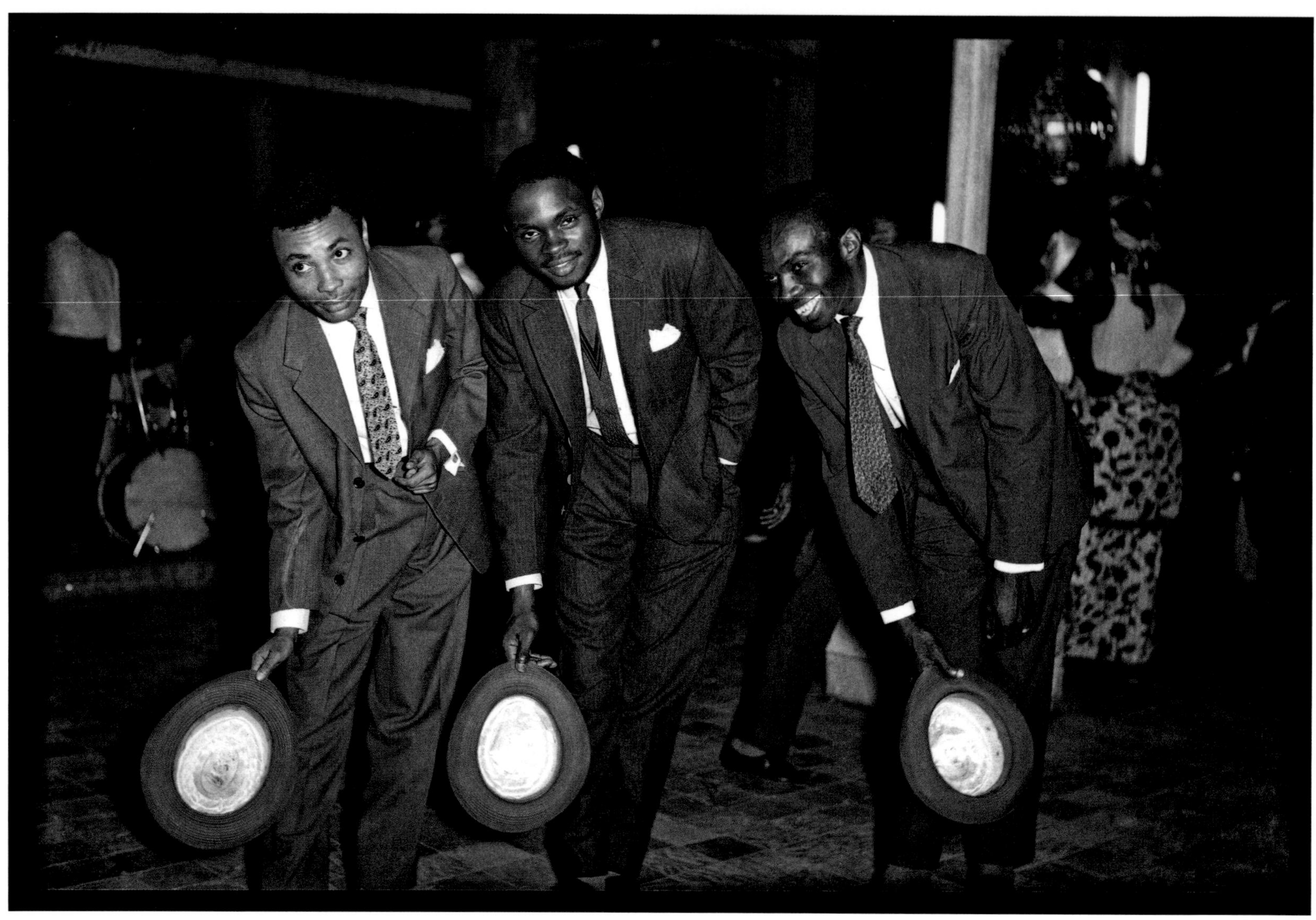

Salutation de Franco après le concert, ca 1965

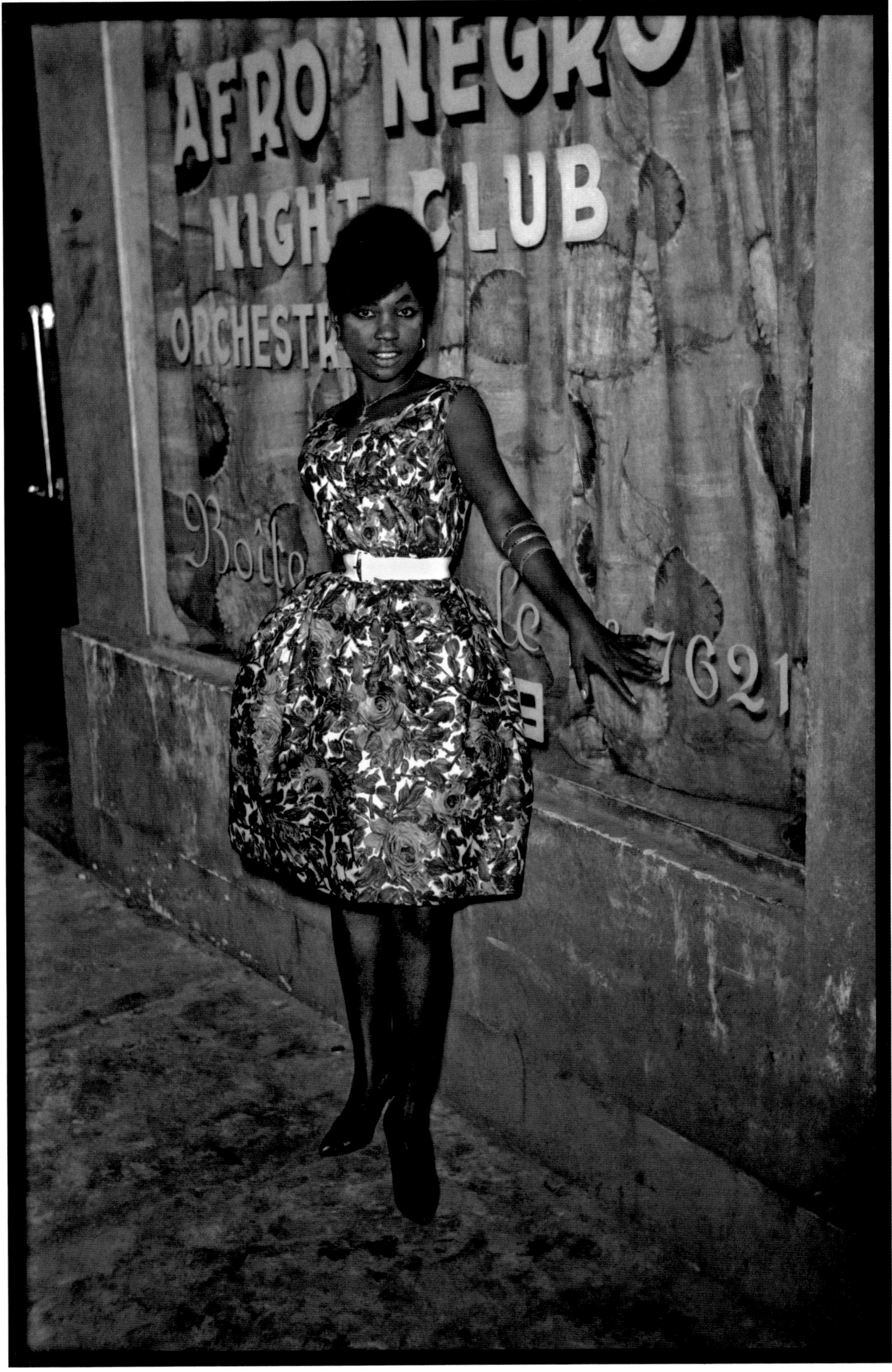

Belle devant l'Afro-negro club, ca 1965

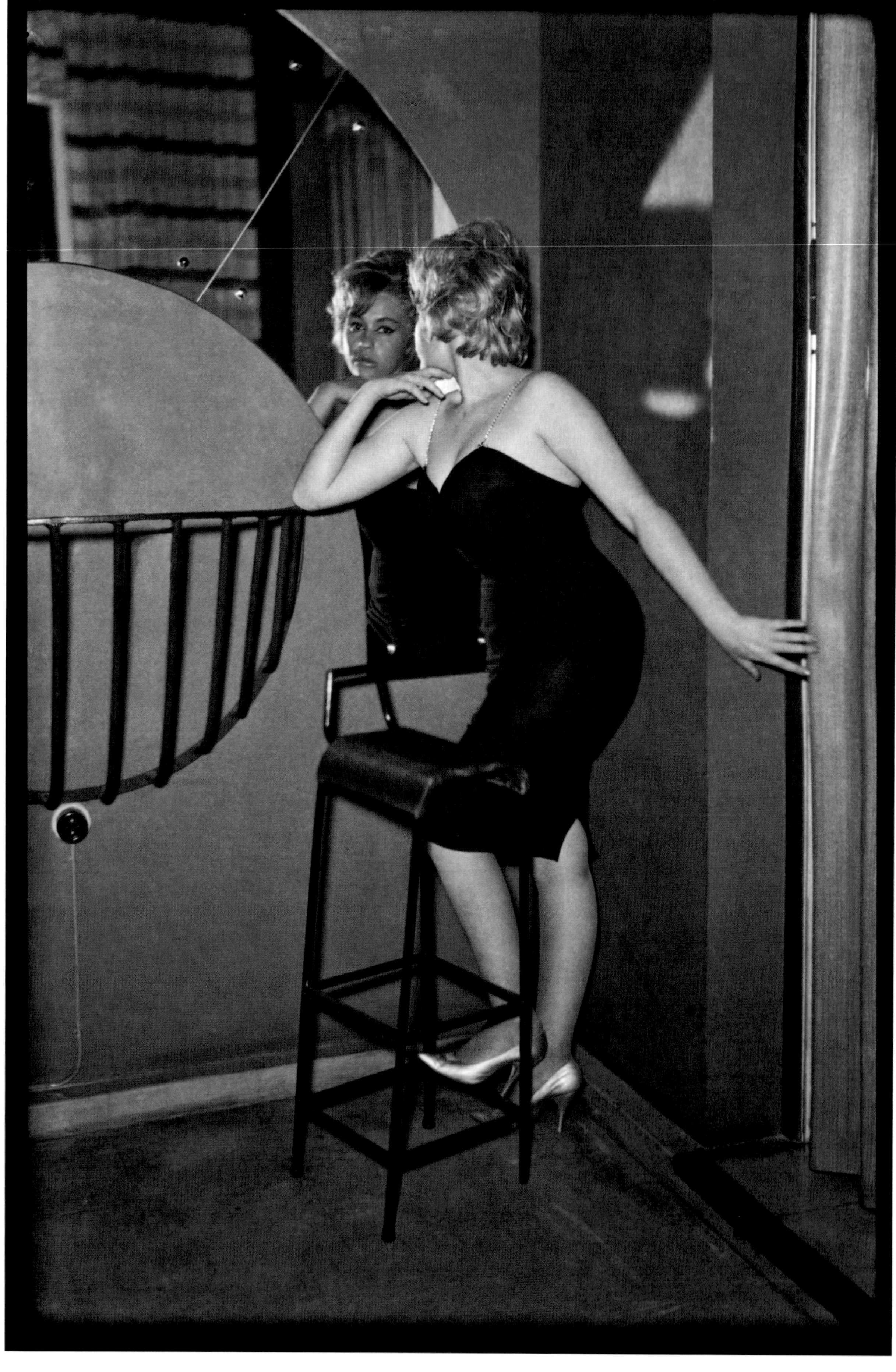

Femme seule devant un night-club, ca 1965

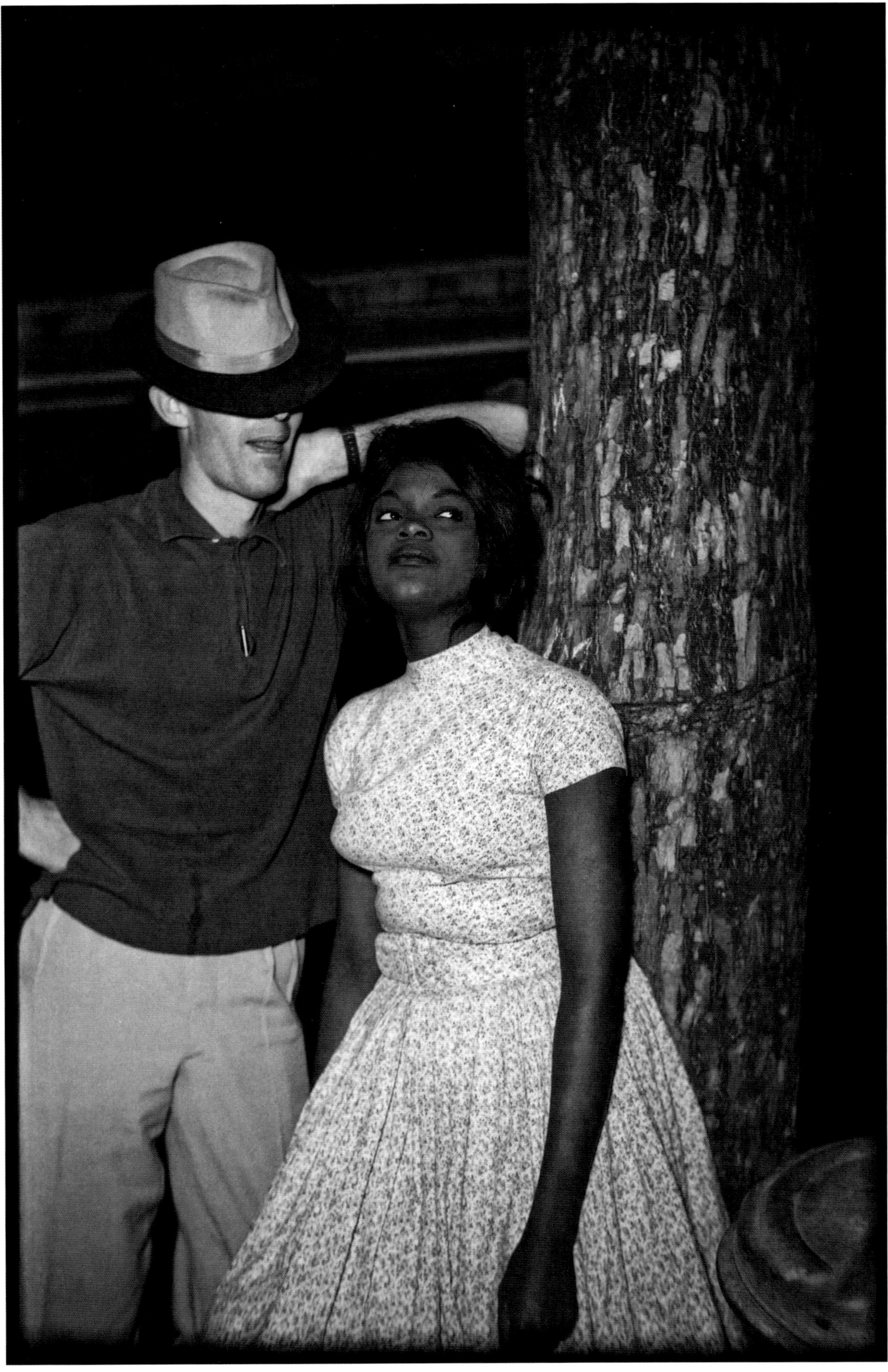

Couple adossé à un arbre, ca 1965

Jean Depara

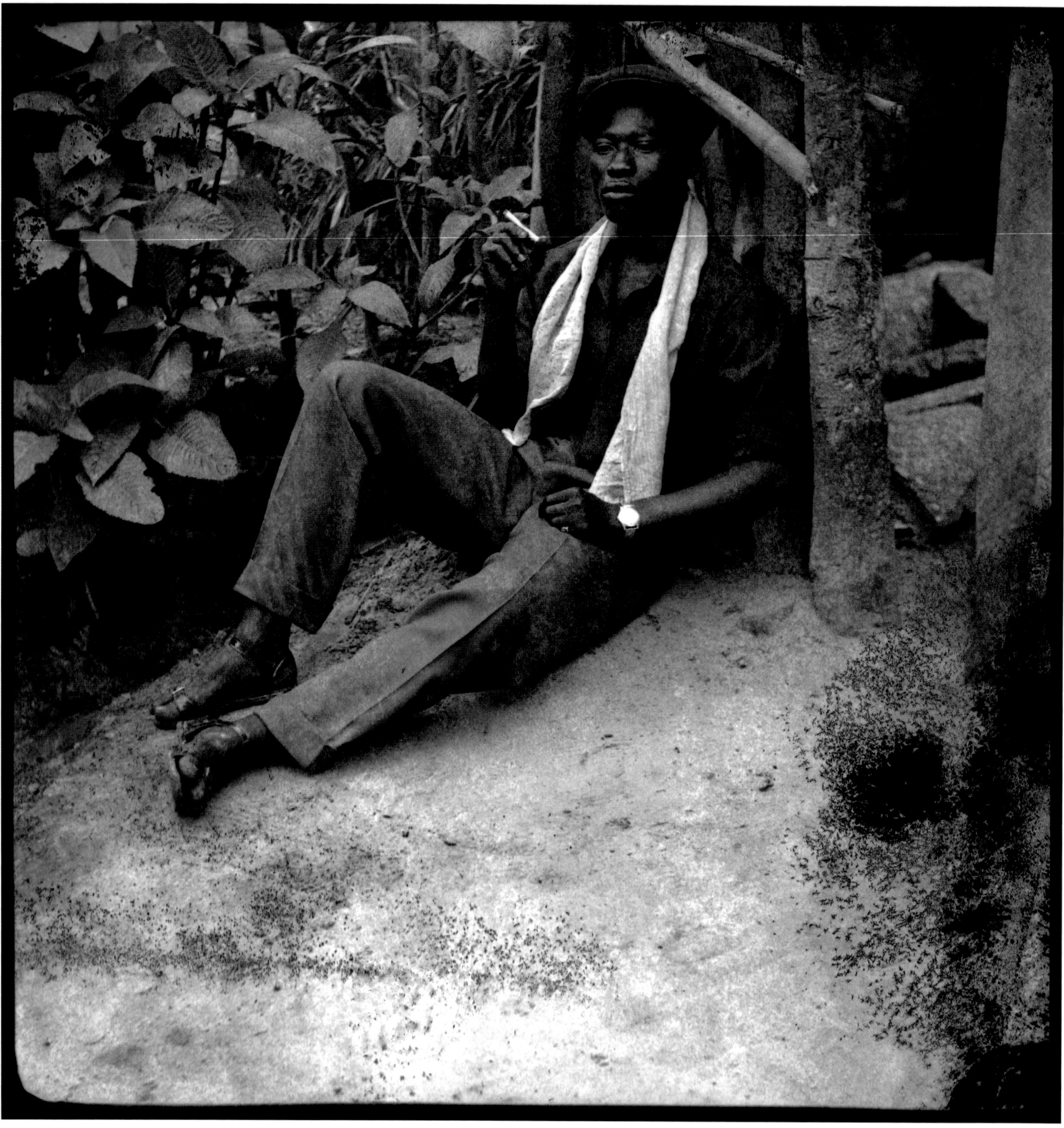

Franco, ca 1965

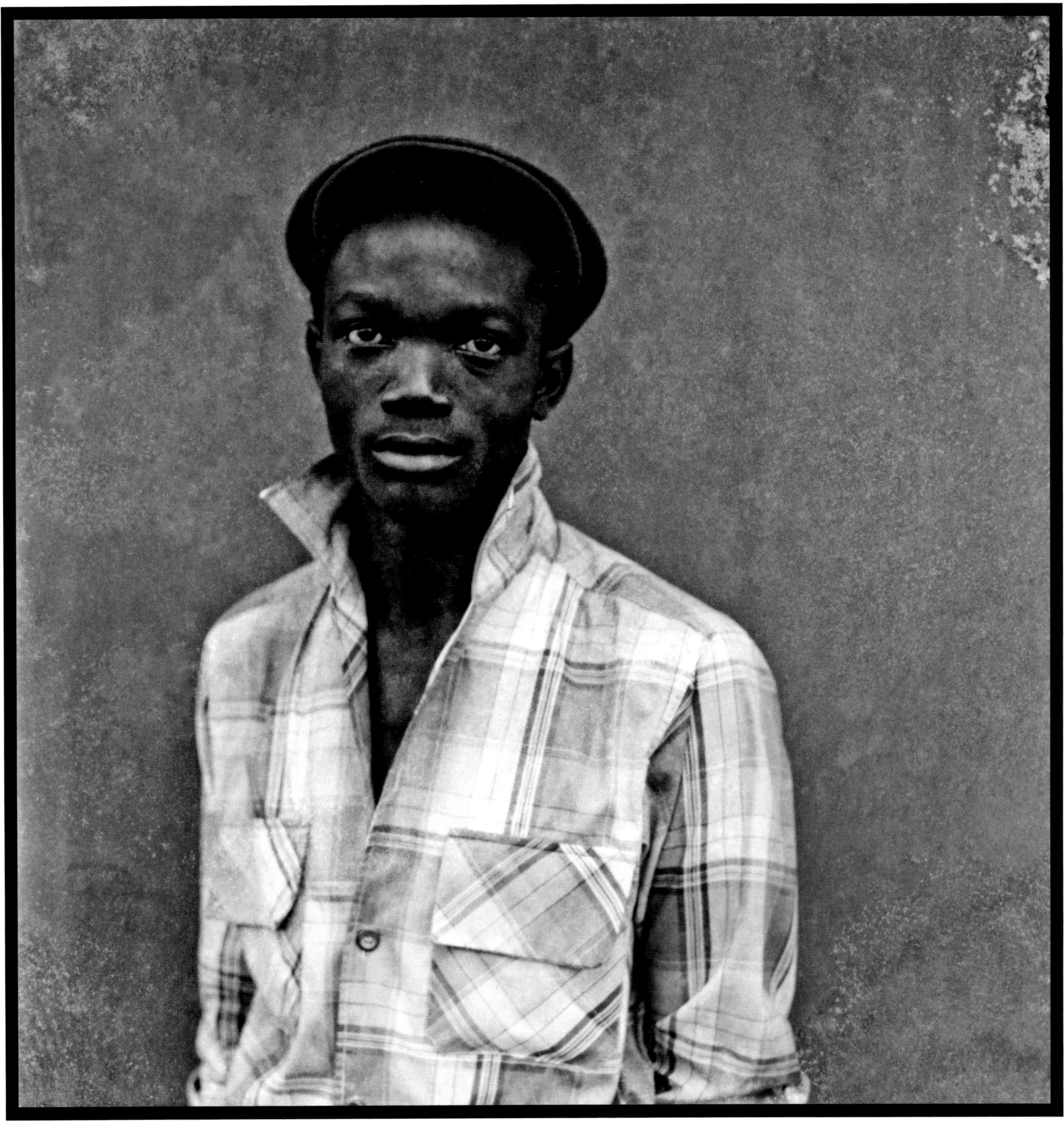

Franco à la casquette, ca 1965

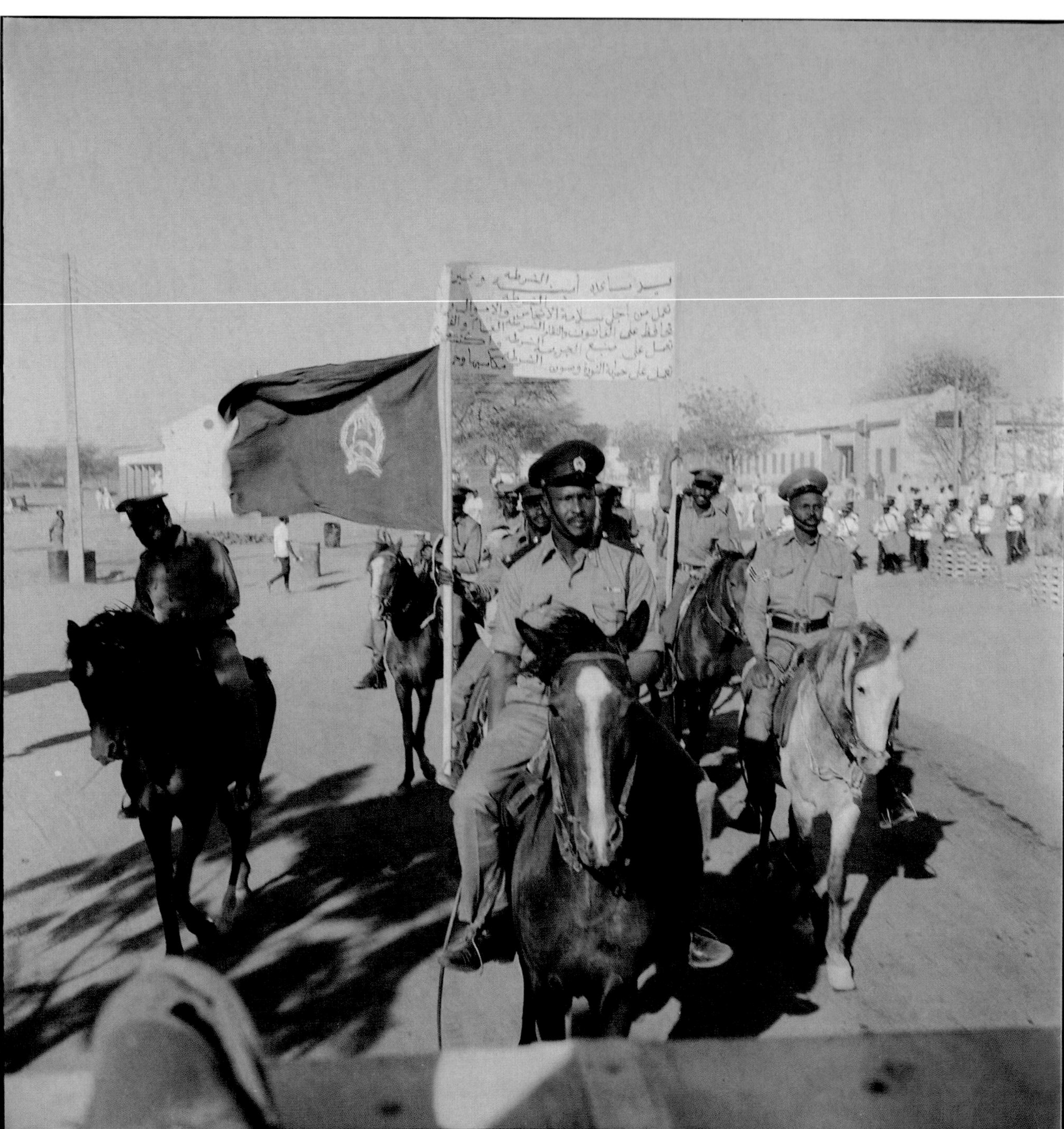

Parade Police montée

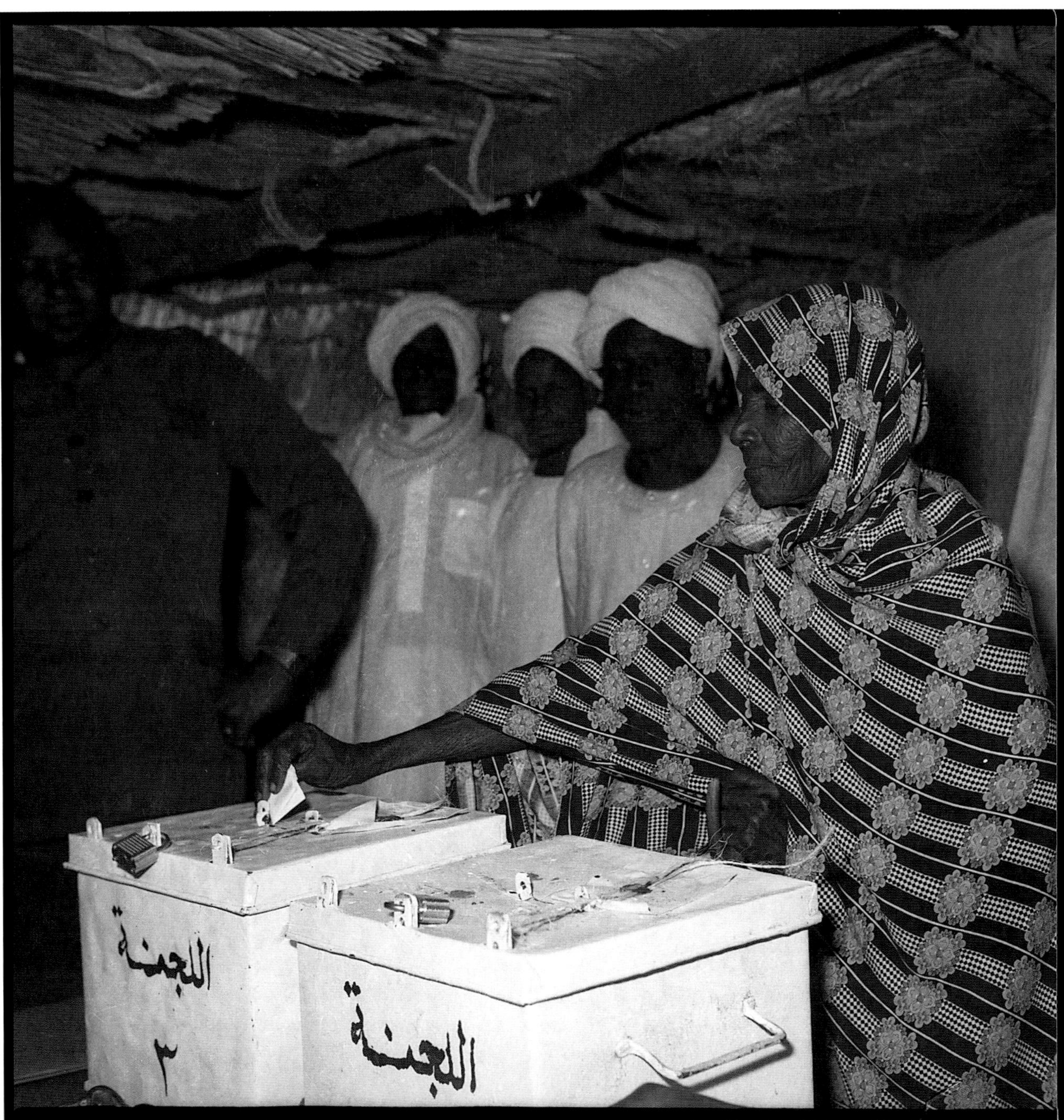

Vote Feminin Elections de 1965

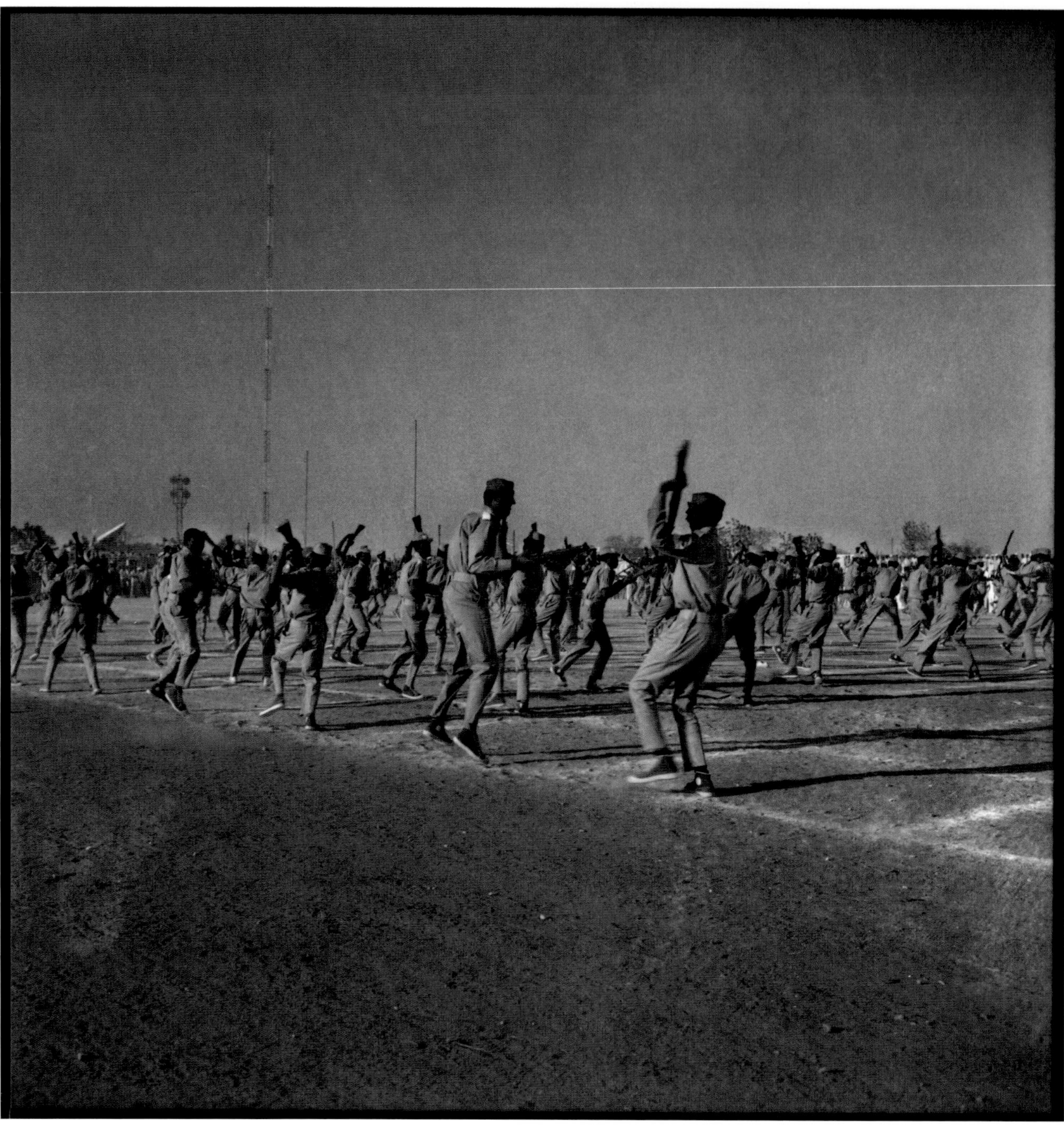

Parade combat

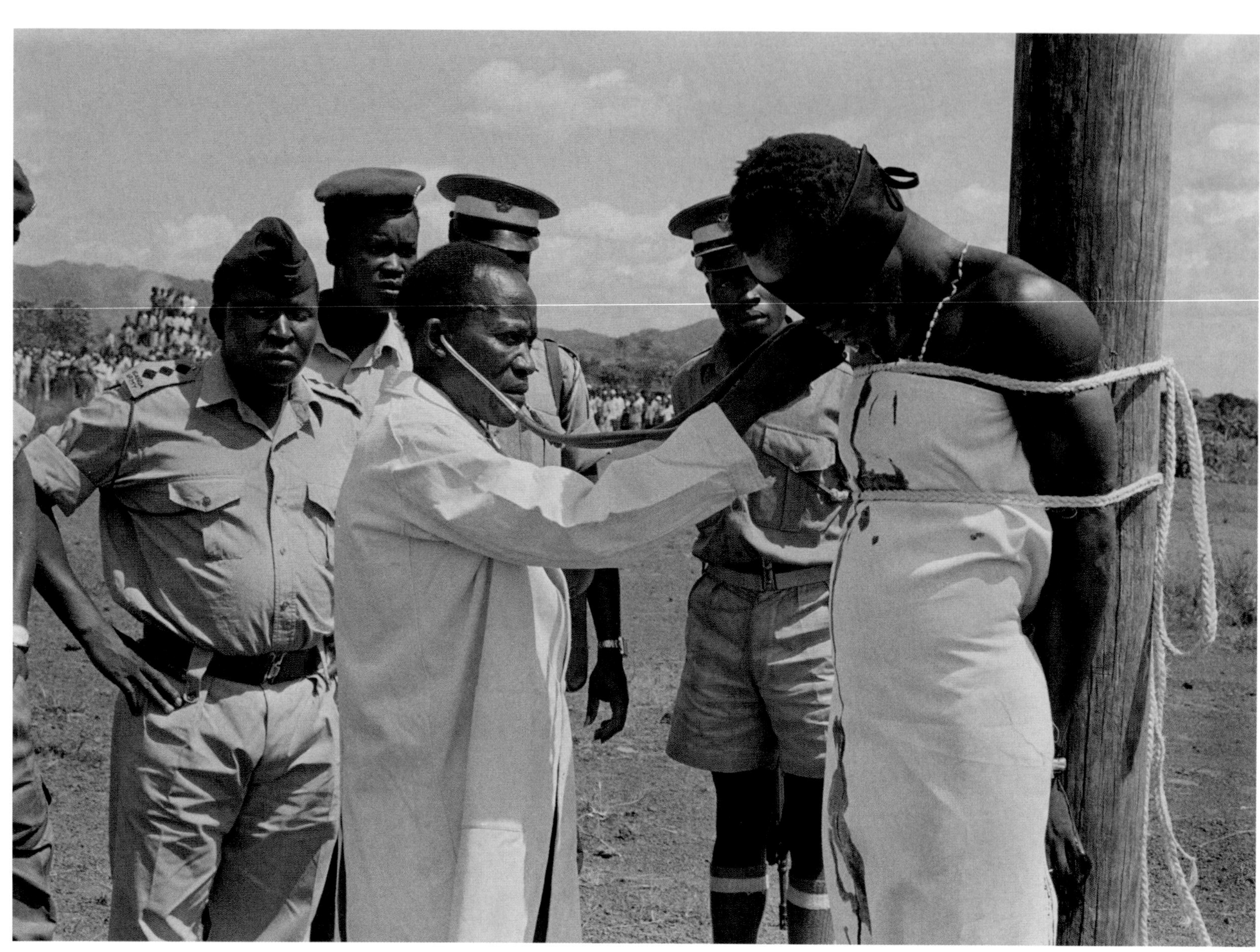

Lost illusions* 1970 1979

* Honoré de Balzac

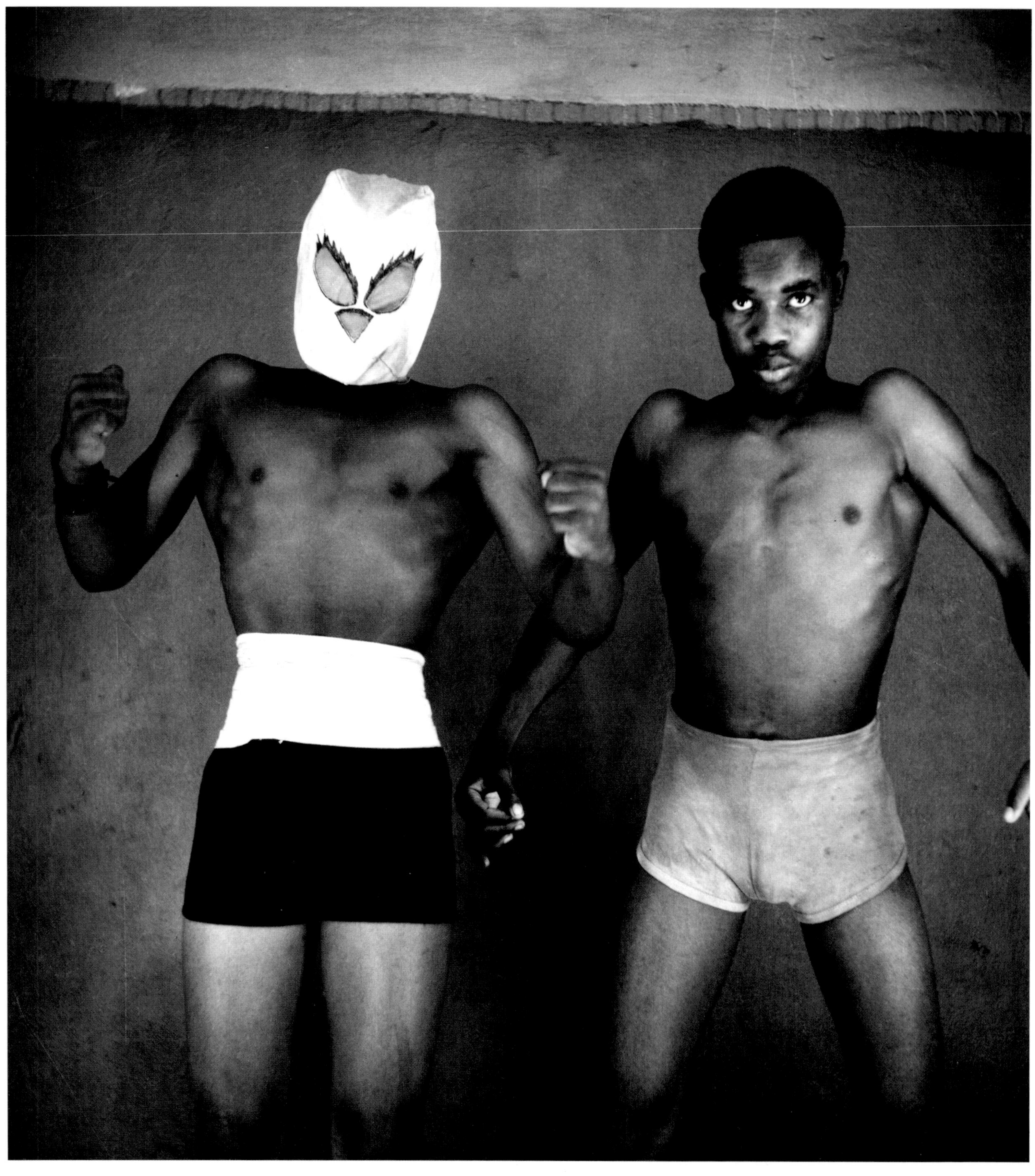

from the series *Kinshasa*, 1975

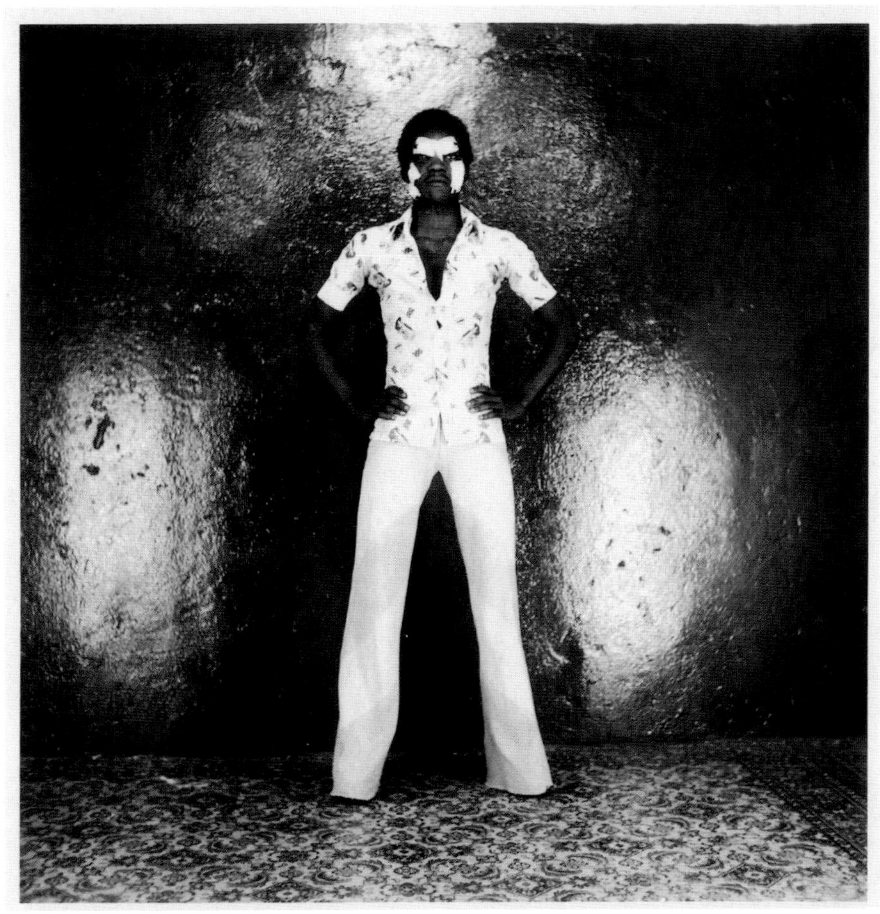

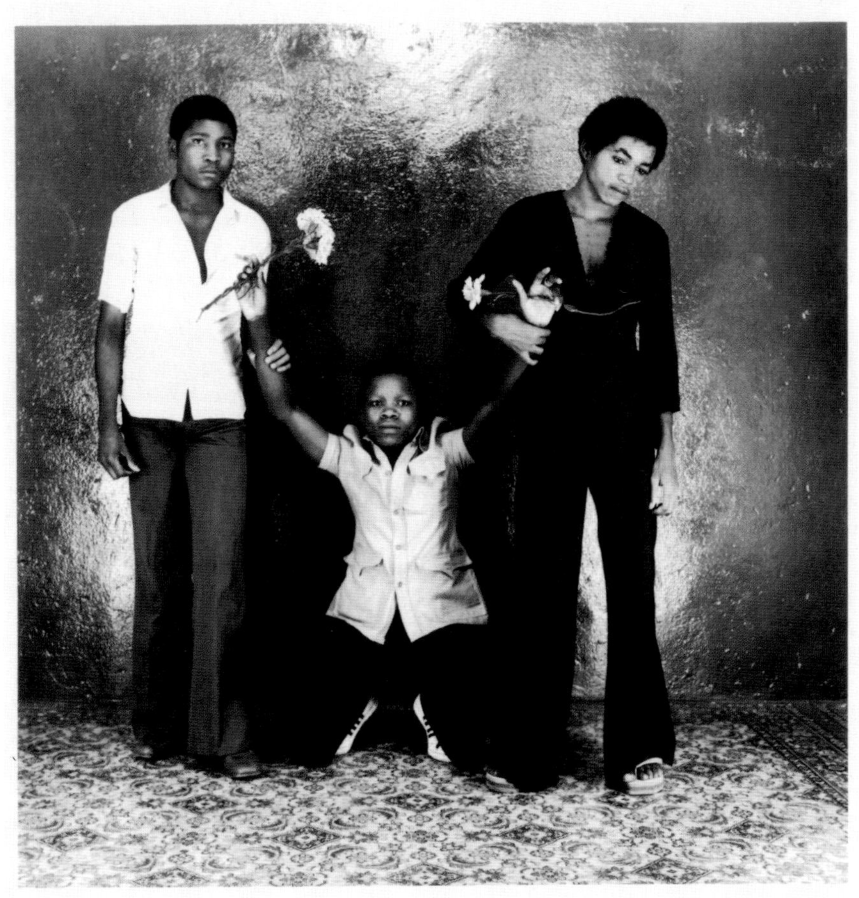

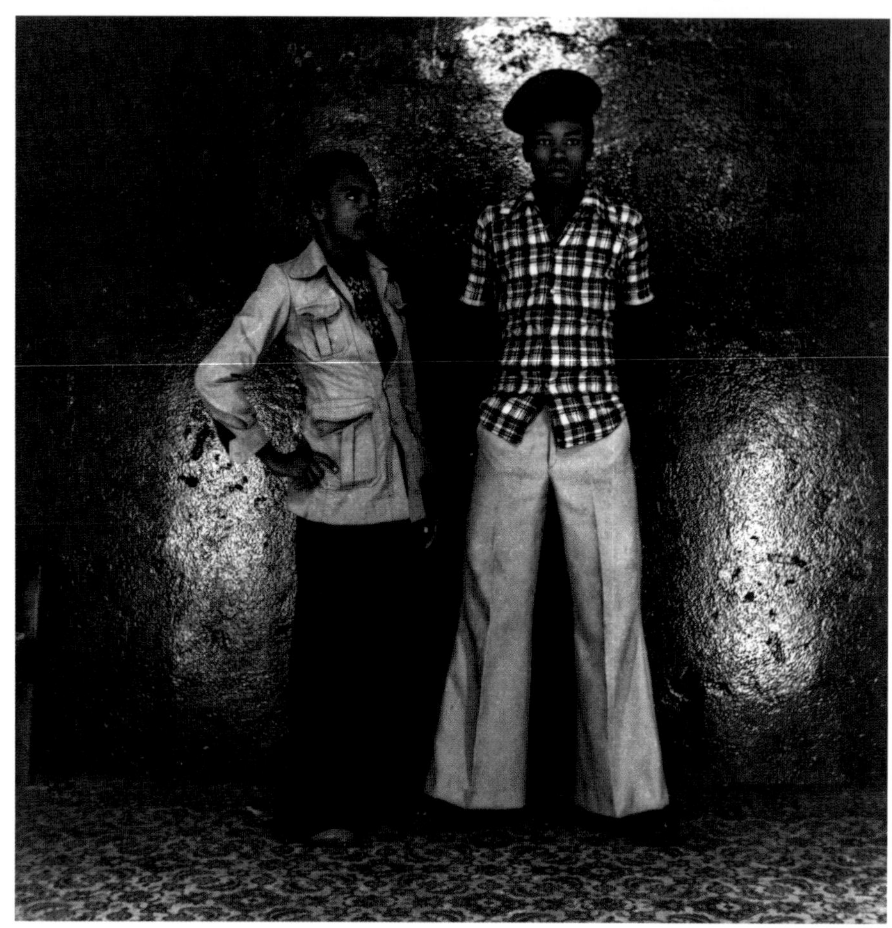

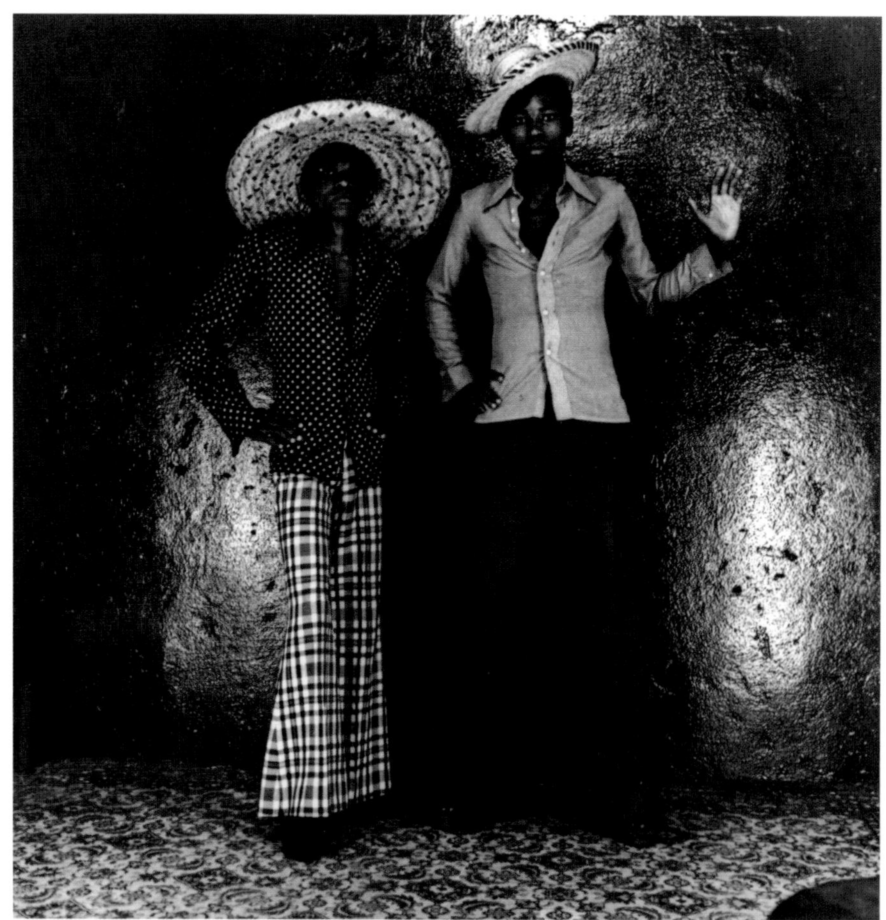

from the series *Kinshasa*, 1975

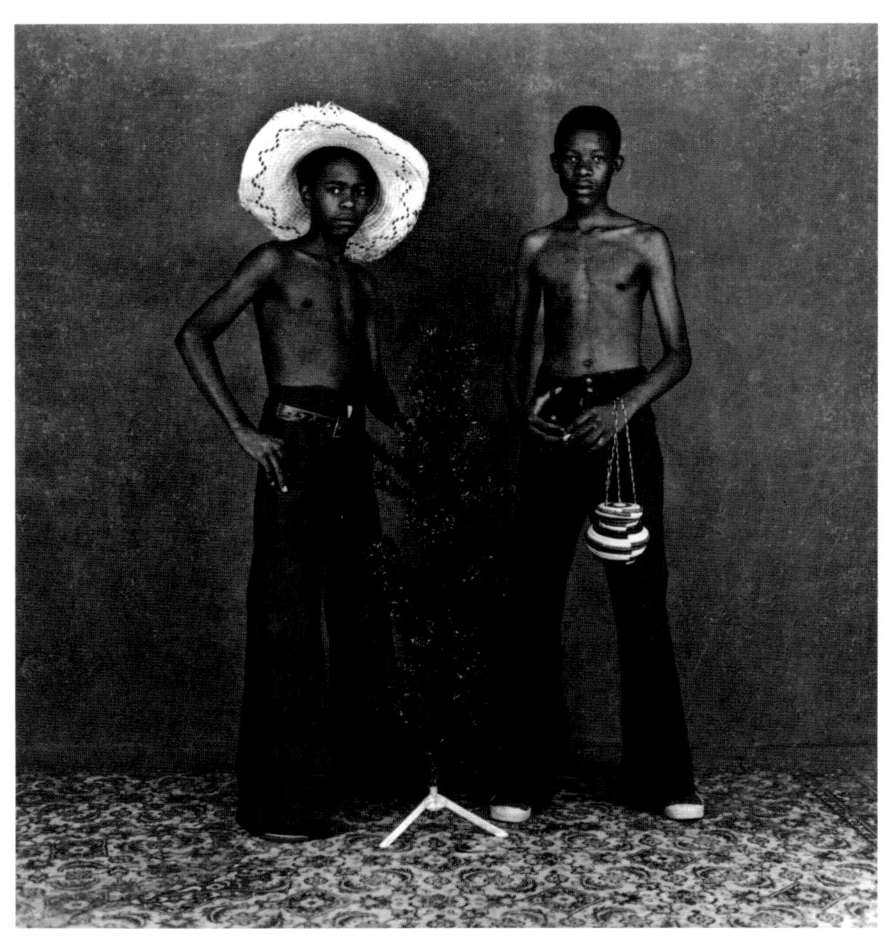

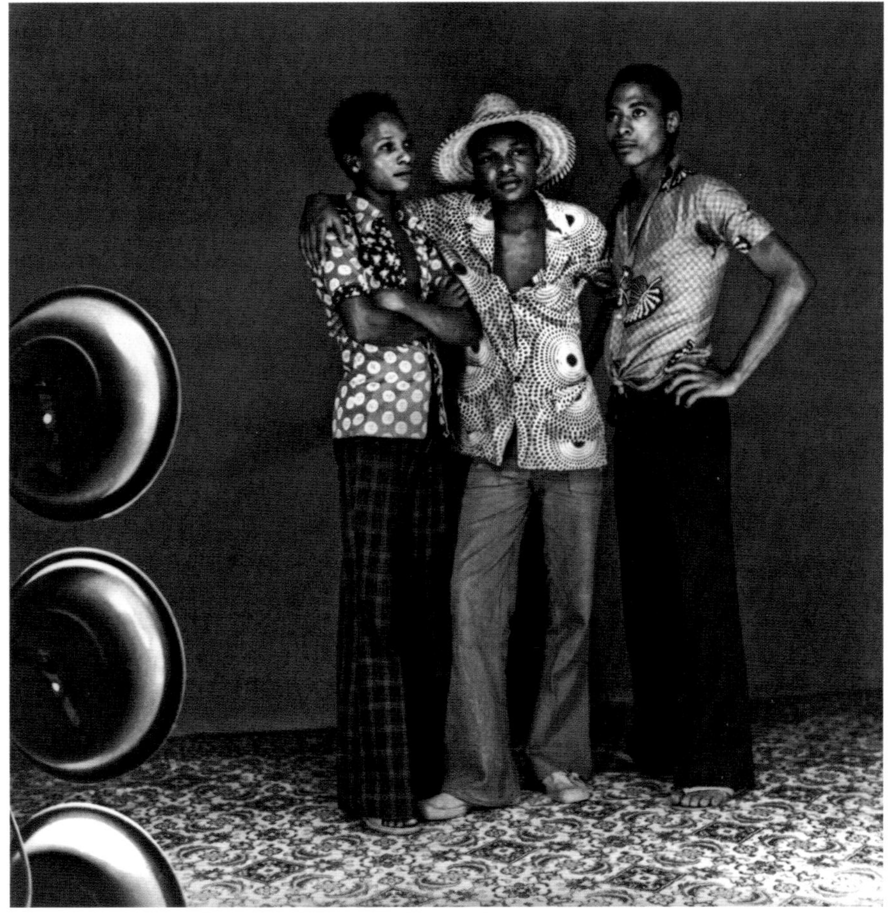

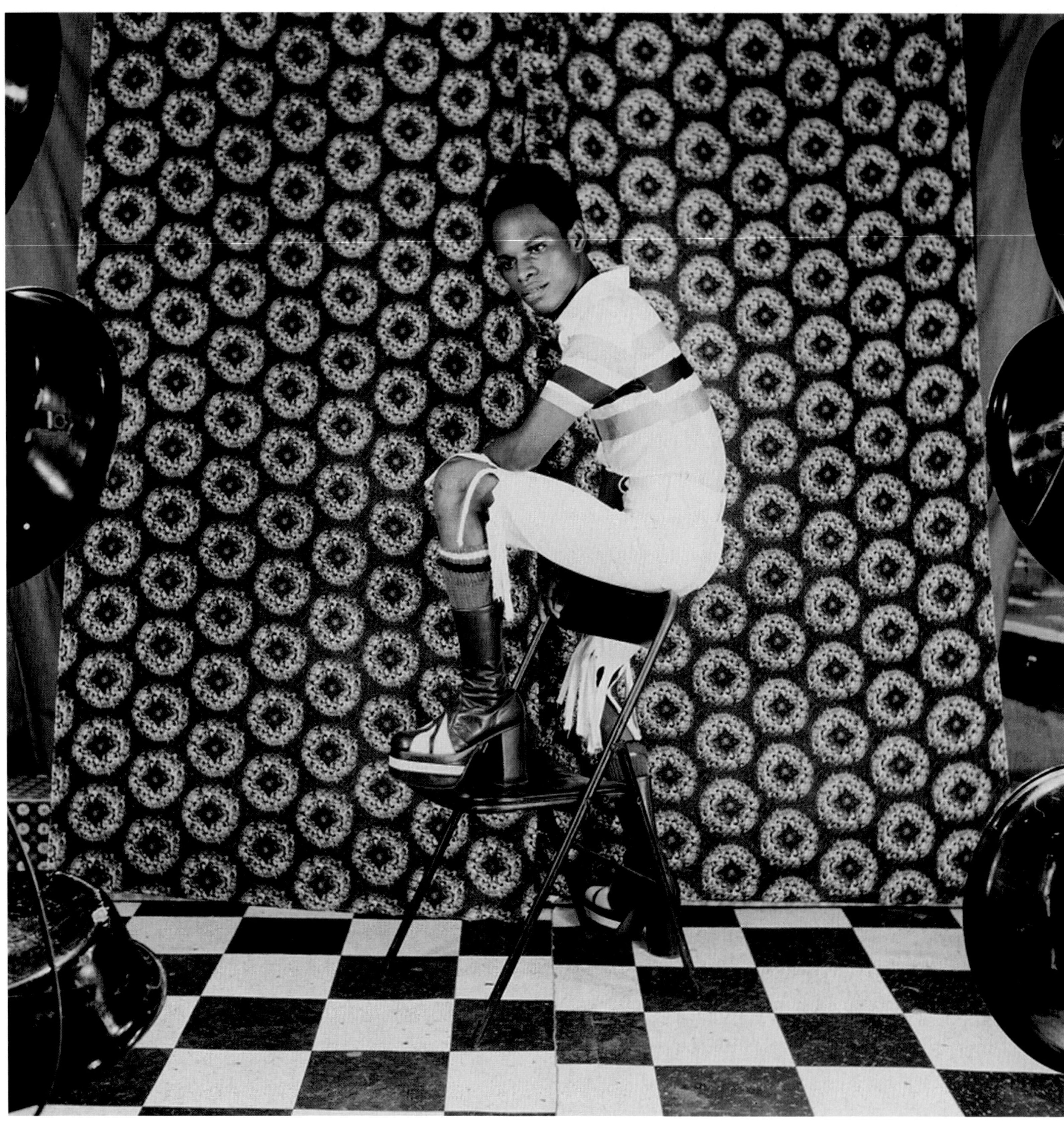

Untitled 13 from the series *Self-portraits of the Seventies*, 1960-1970

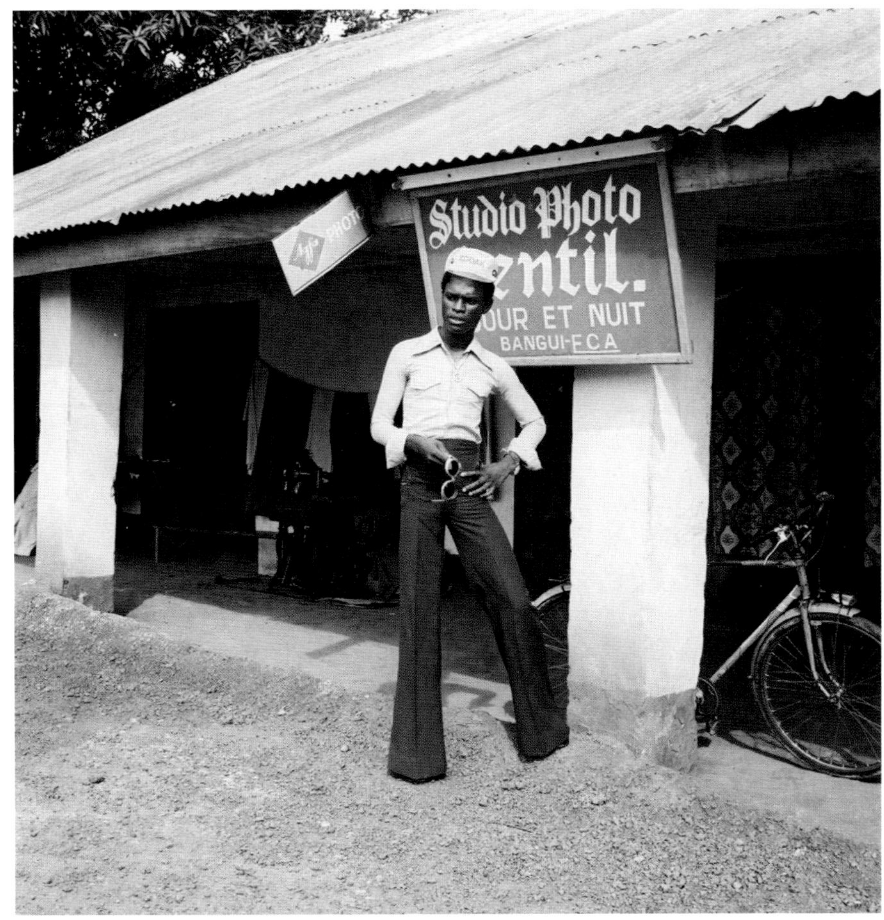

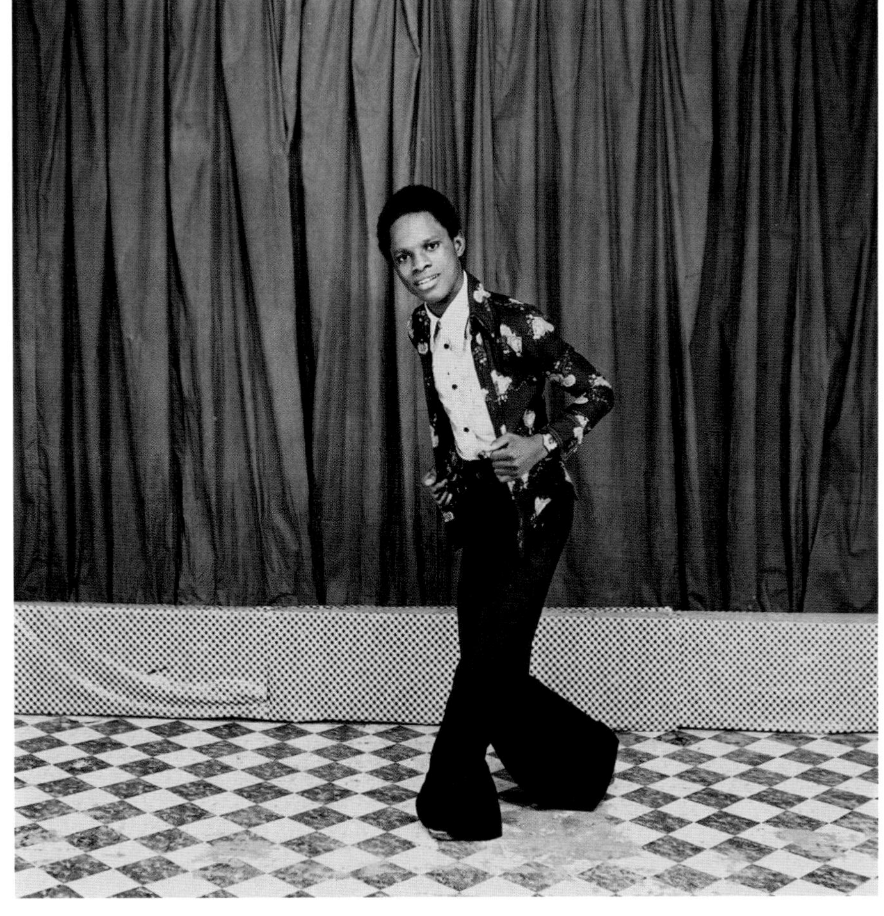

Untitled 16 from the series *Self-portraits of the Seventies*, 1960-1970   *Untitled 10* from the series *Self-portraits of the Seventies*, 1960-1970

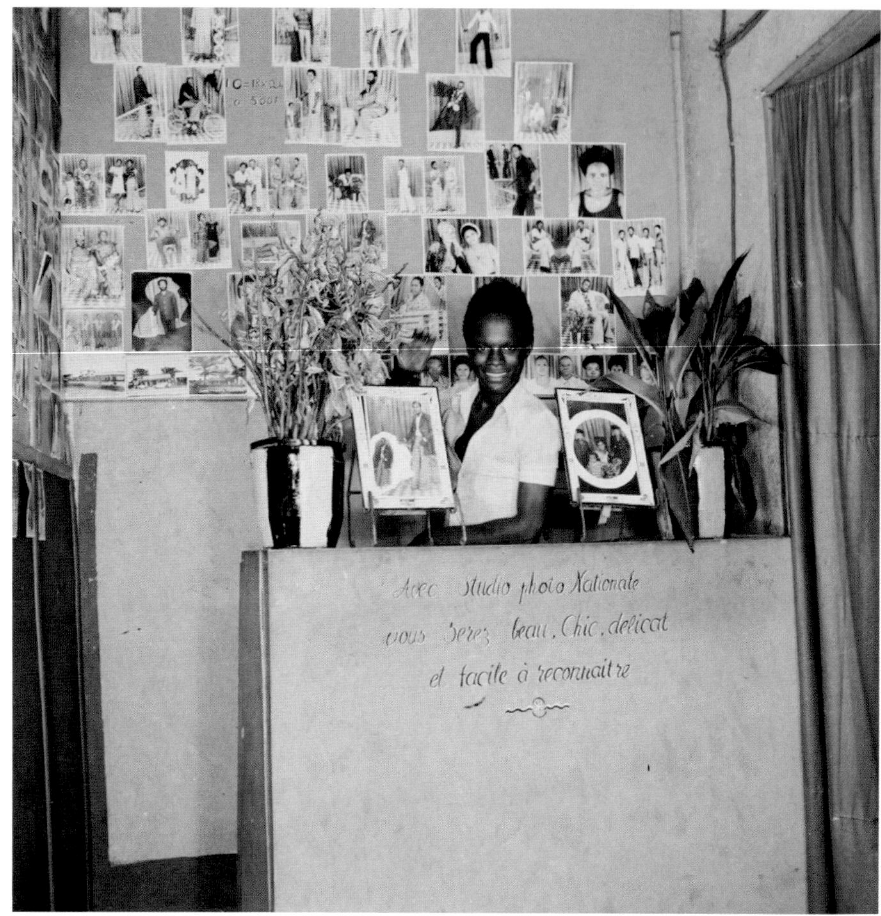

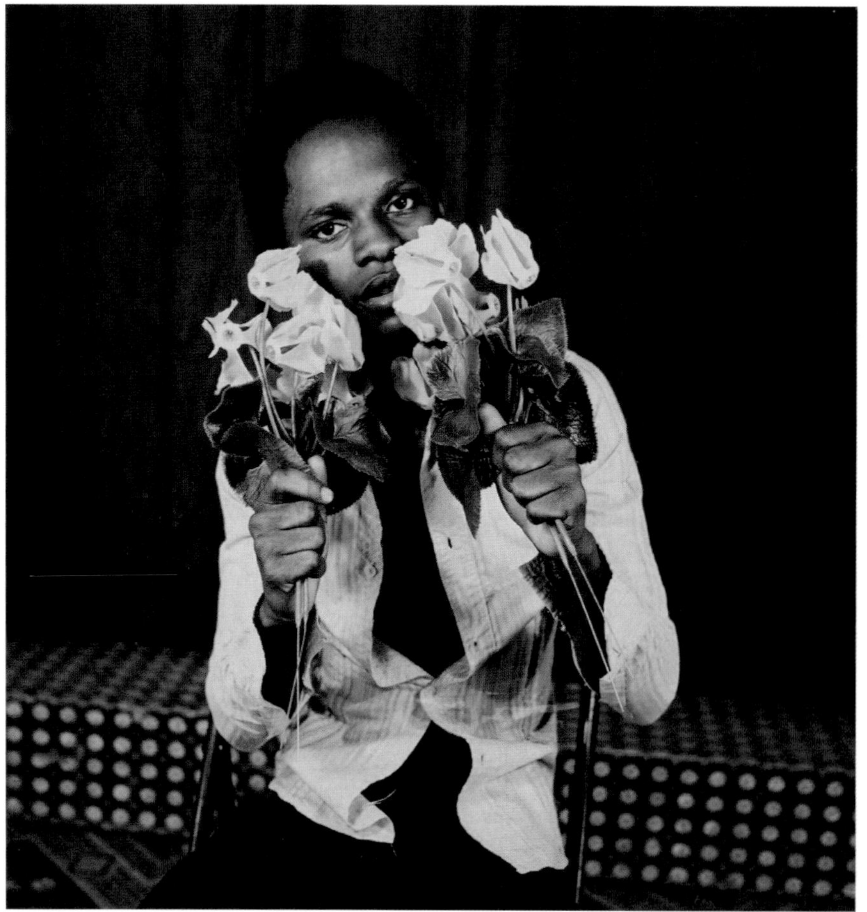

Untitled 15 from the series *Self-portraits of the Seventies*, 1960-1970   **Untitled 16** from the series *Self-portraits of the Seventies*, 1960-1970

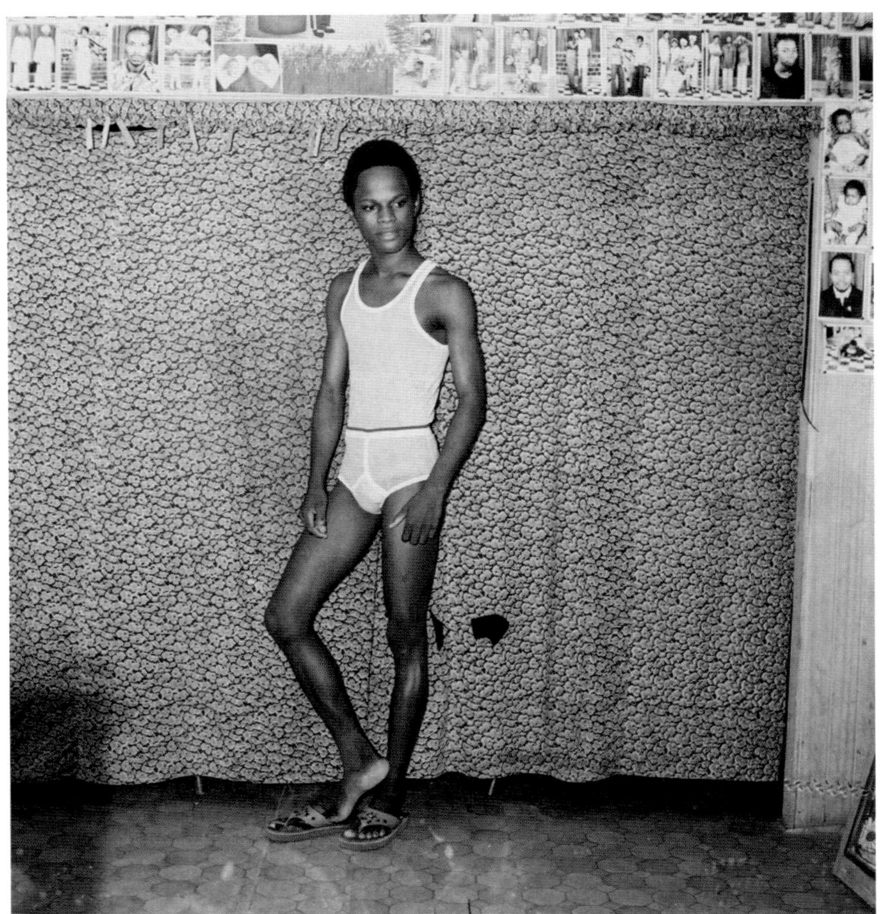

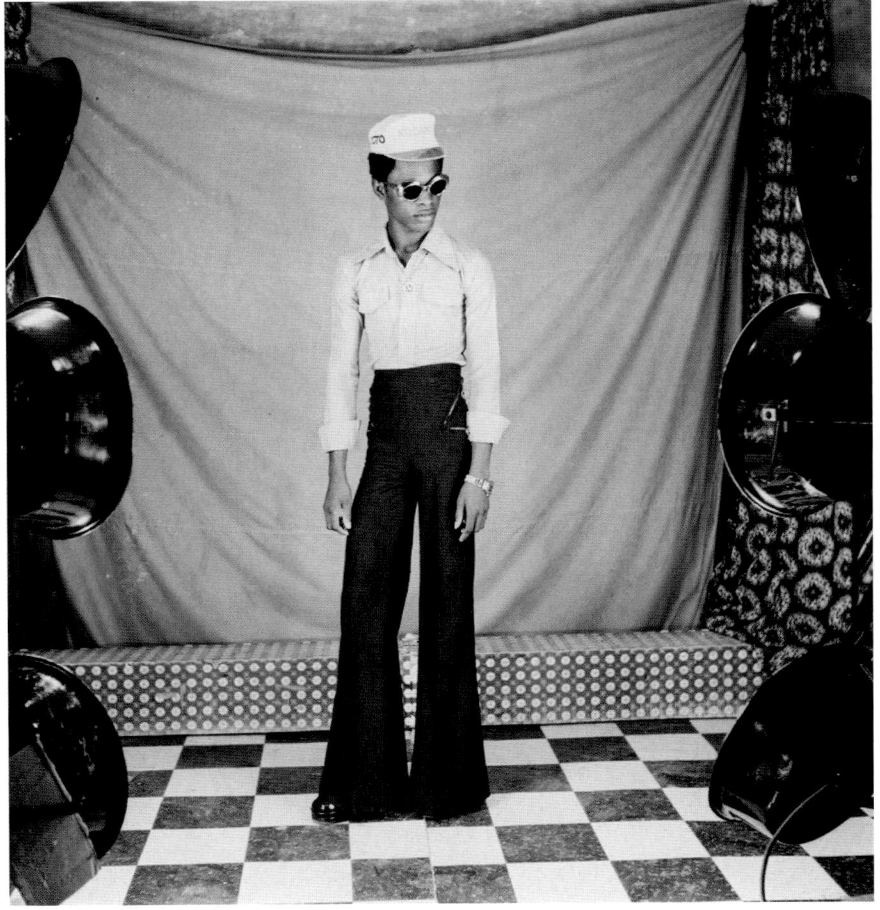

Untitled 25 from the series *Self-portraits of the Seventies*, 1960-1970   *Untitled 05* from the series *Self-portraits of the Seventies*, 1960-1970

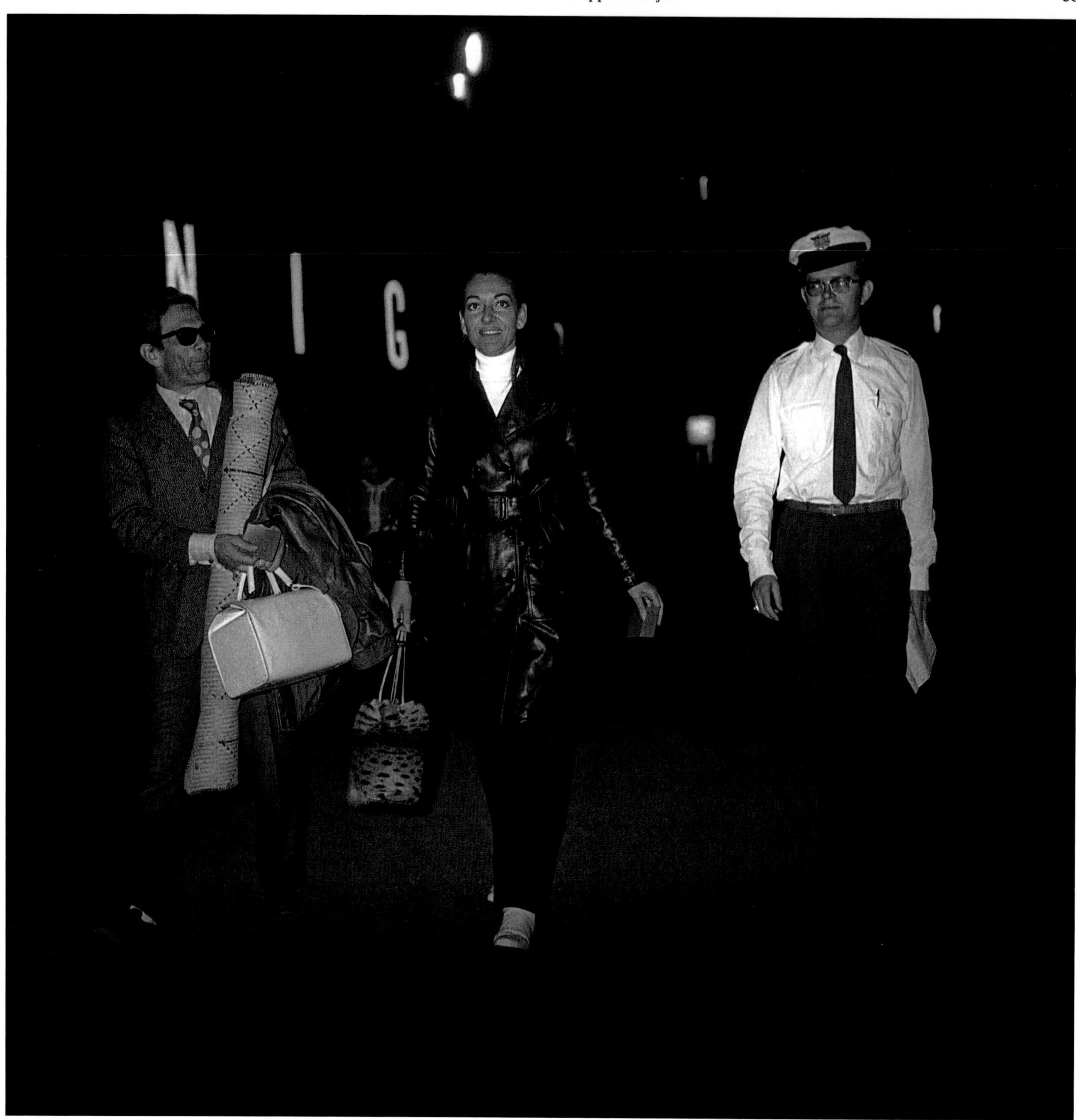

Pier Paolo Pasolini & Maria Callas

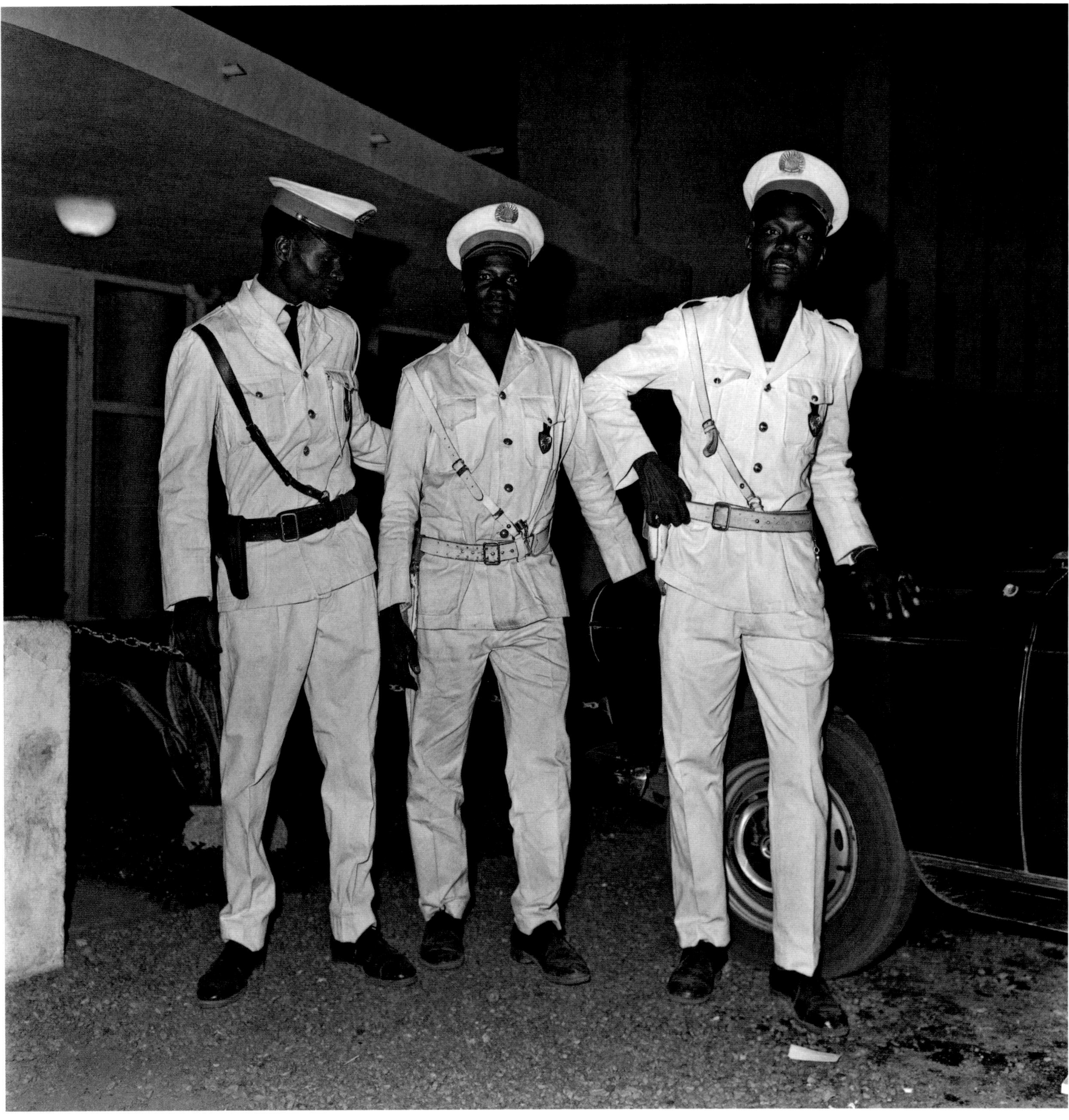

Trois policiers, ca 1965

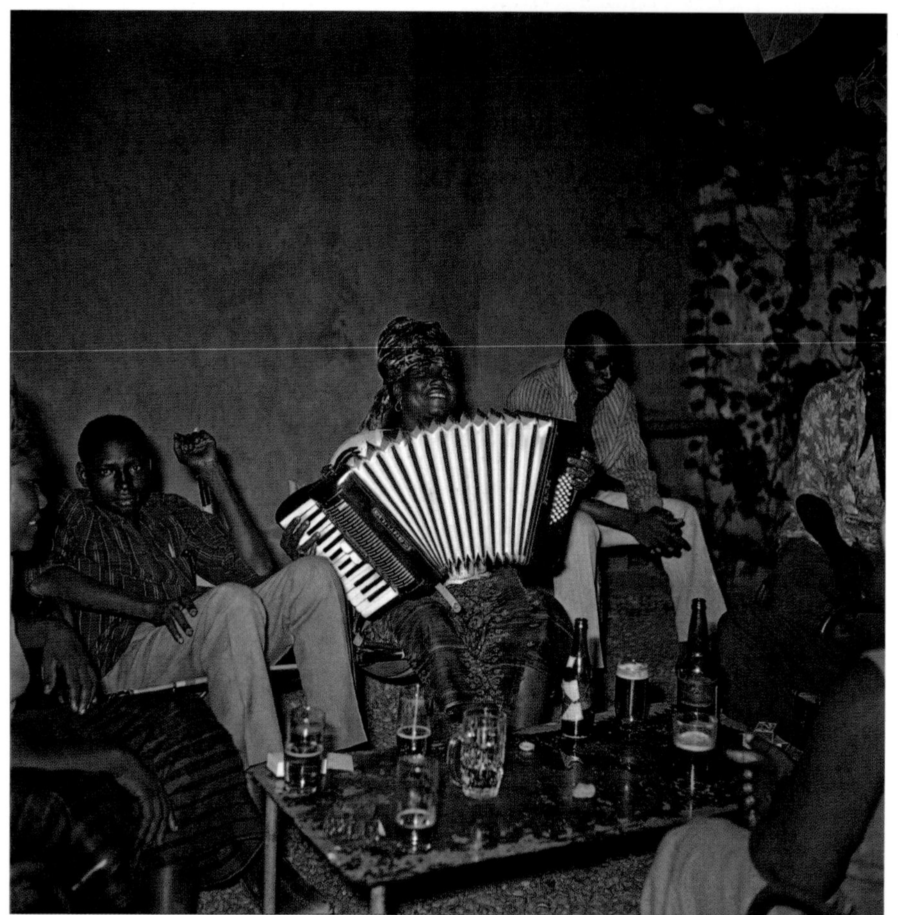

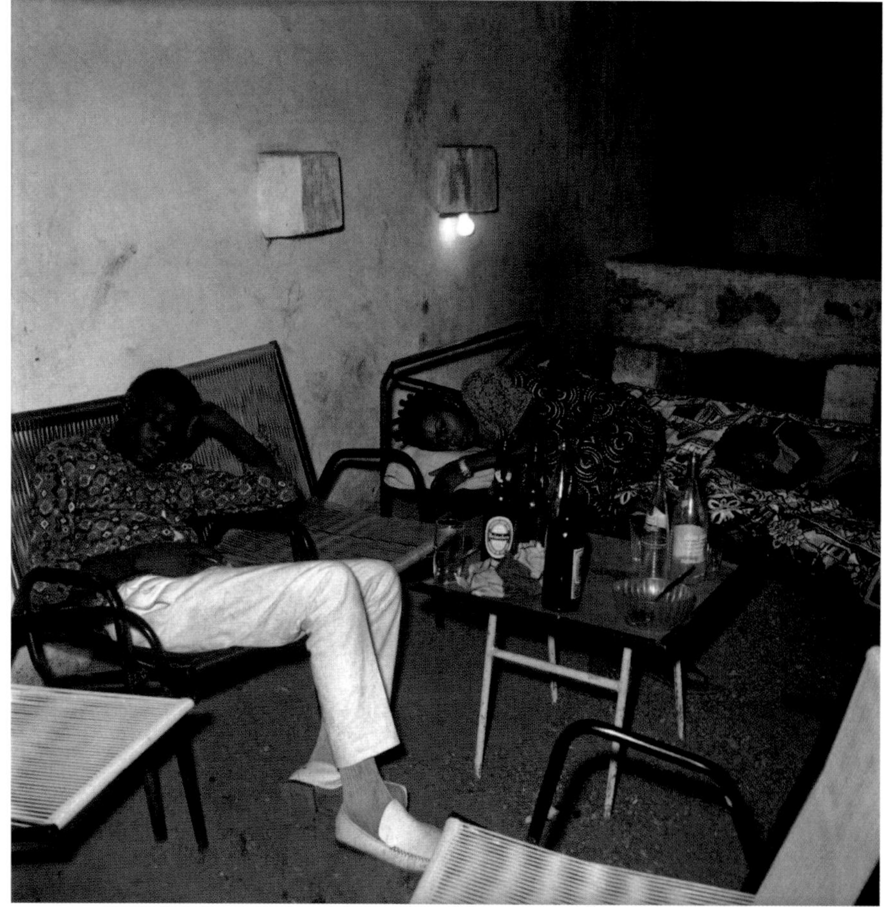

L'accordéoniste, ca 1965

Farniente, ca 1965

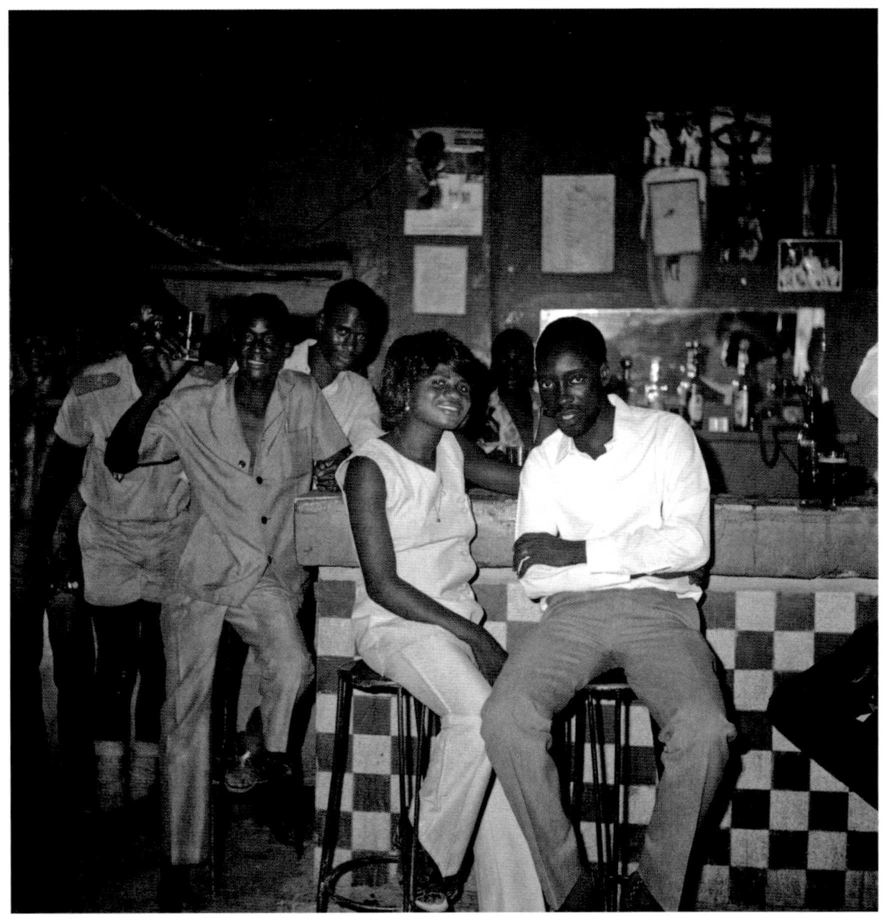

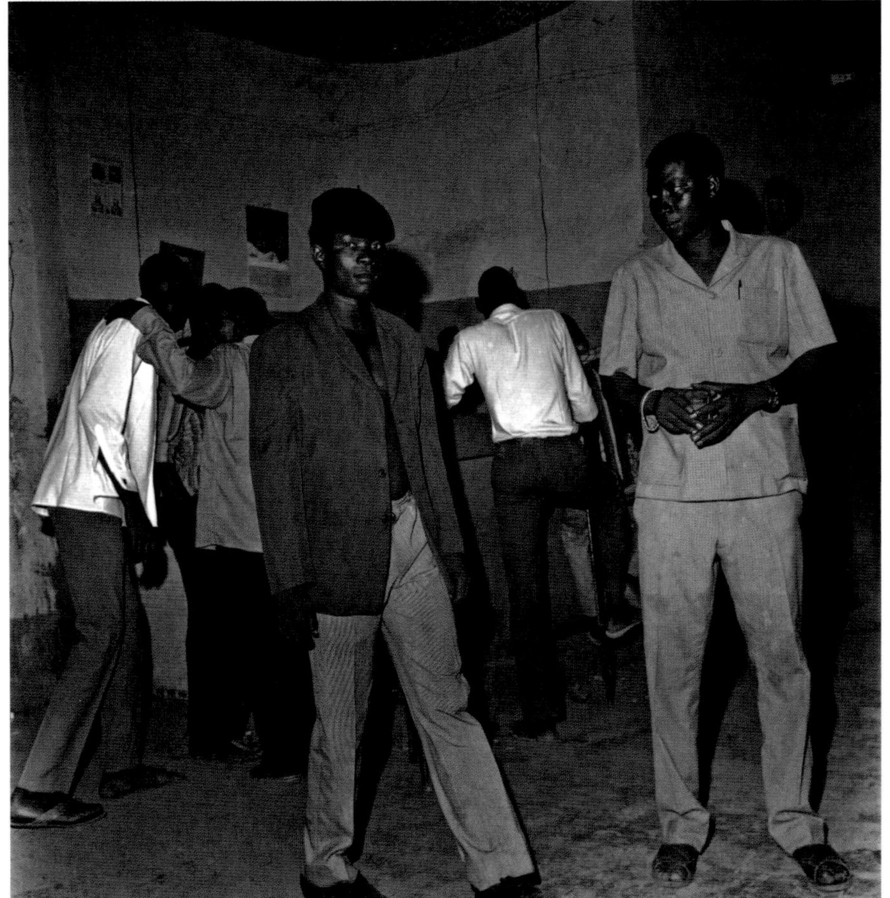

Les amoureux au bar, ca 1965

Garçons au dancing, ca 1965

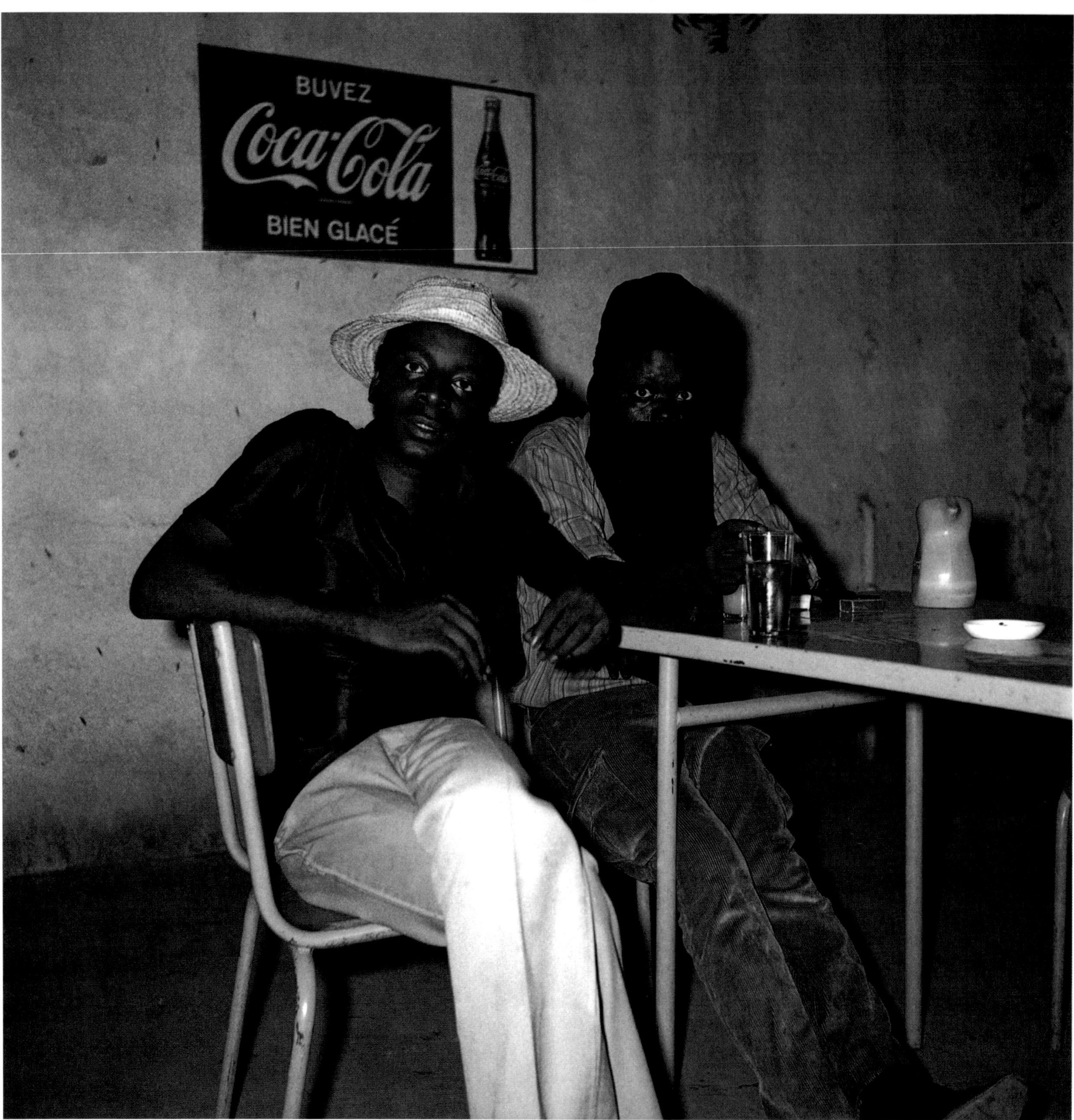

L'attente au dancing, ca 1965

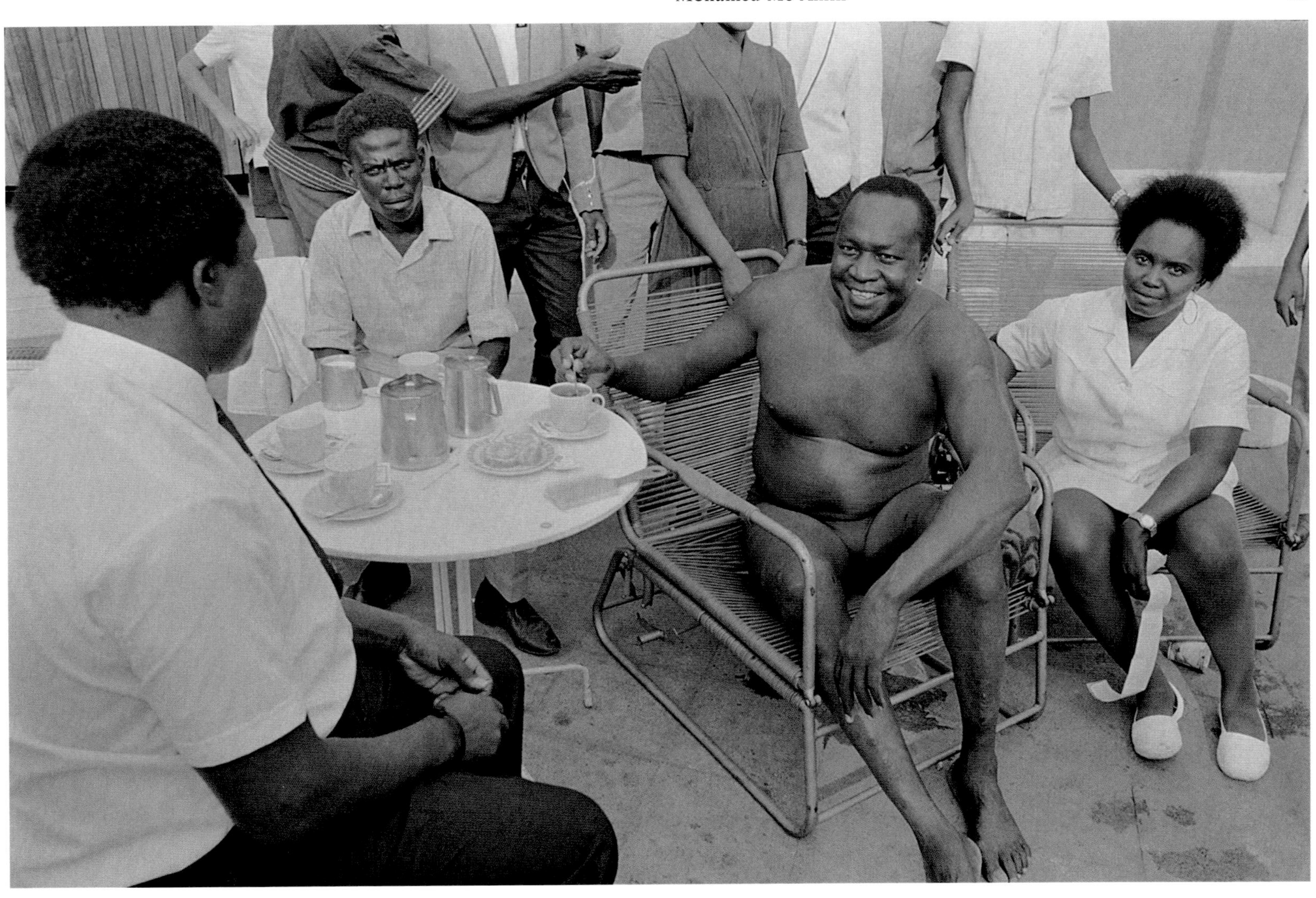

Idi Amin at home.

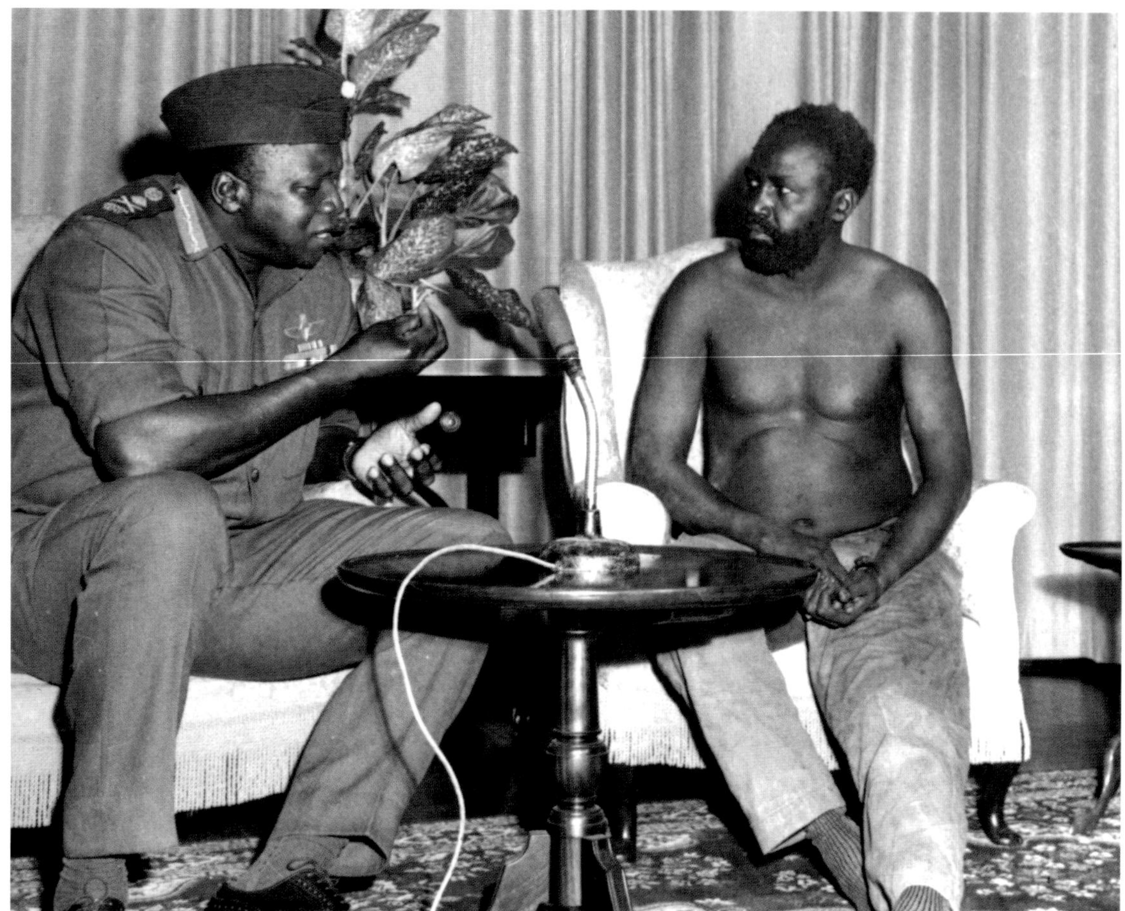

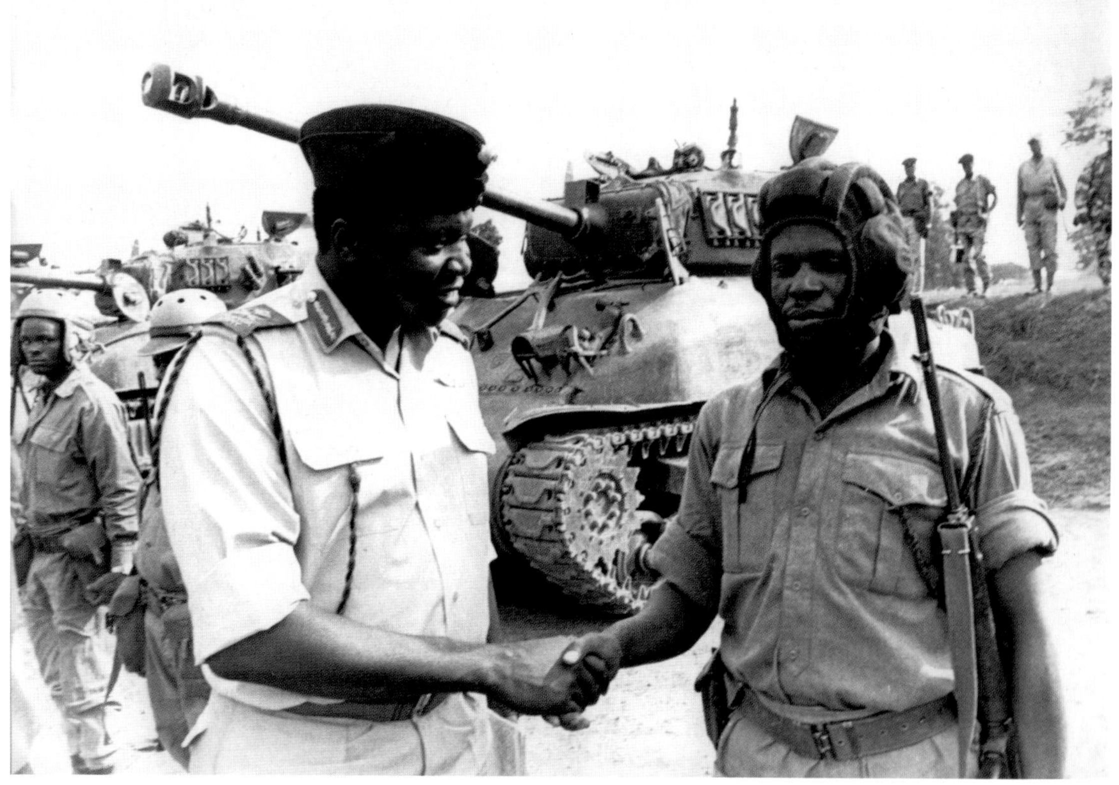

Idi Amin Dada declares himself President of Uganda, on February 2, 1971, one week after taking power as a result of the coup he led against Ugandan President Milton Obote, in January 25, 1971. Under Amin's eight-year reign of terror, from 1971 to 1979, it is estimated that five-hundred thousand people were murdered in Uganda.

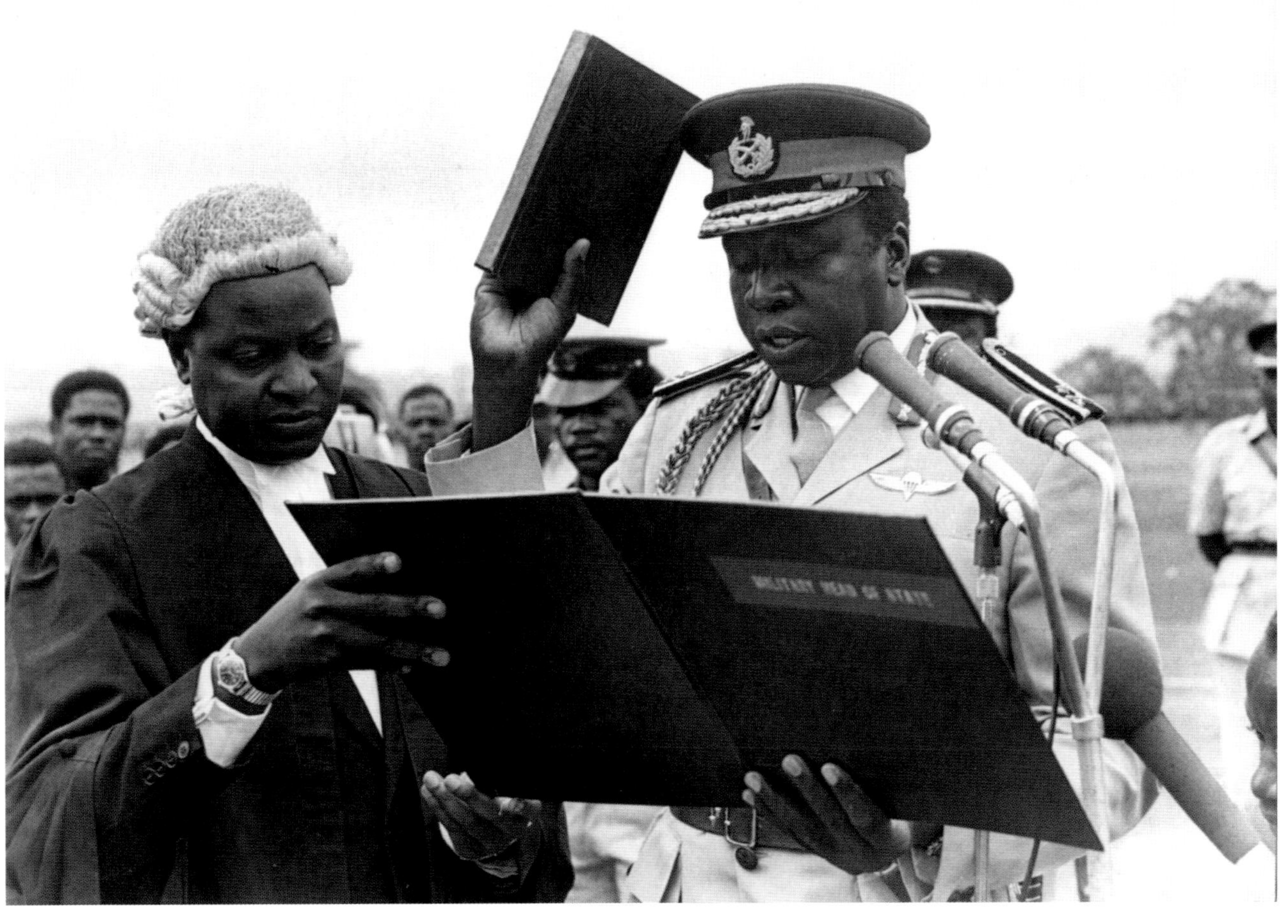

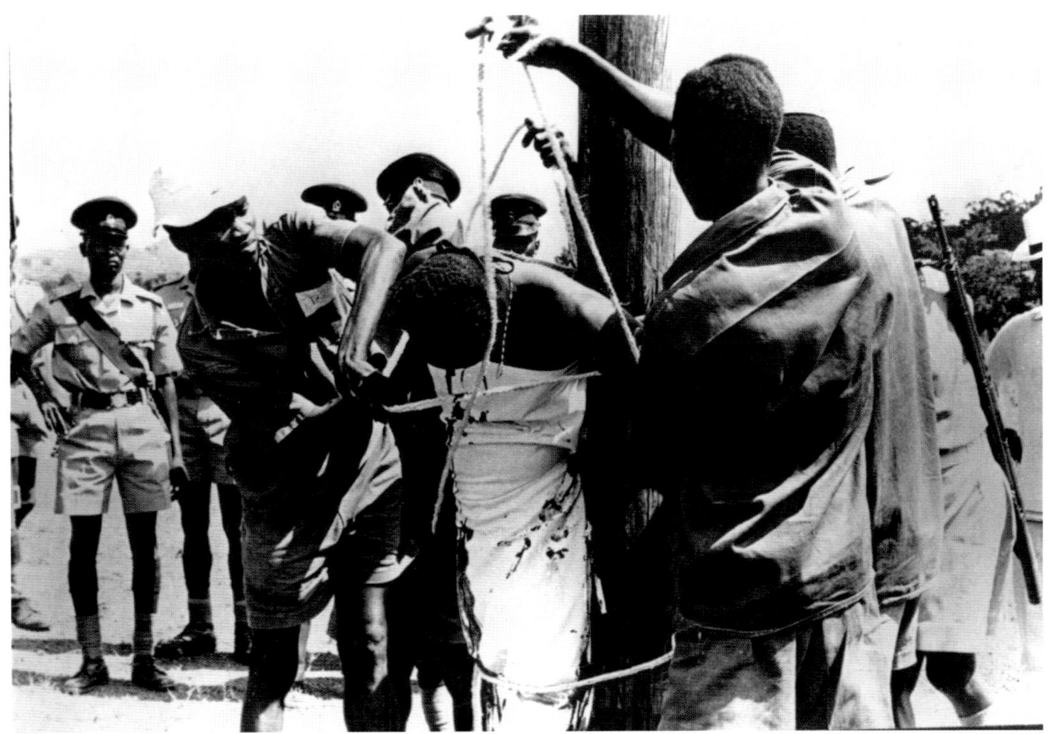

MBALE, UGANDA. *A crowd of twenty-thousand Ugandans, women and children included, witnessed the execution, in 1973, of two alleged conspirators from Bugsihu: Tom Masaba, a former captain in the Ugandan Army, and Sebastino Namirundu. Masaba and Namirundu were interrogated, stripped naked, fitted with short white tunics, and tied to their execution posts. Masaba, who was accused of being a terrorist, was reported to have said: 'Let those, like me, who are killing innocent people in the country, come out and report to the authorities'. 02, 1973*

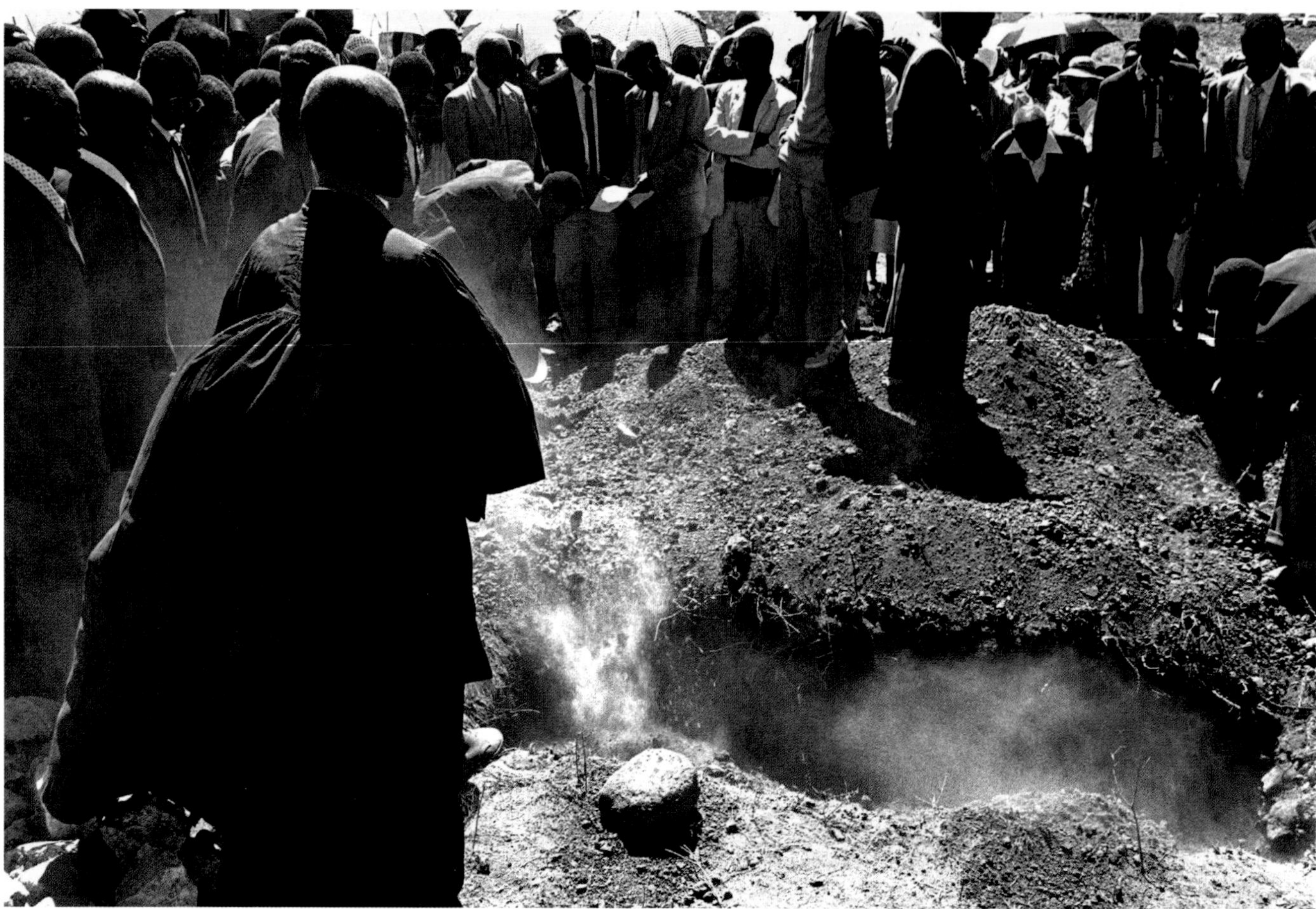

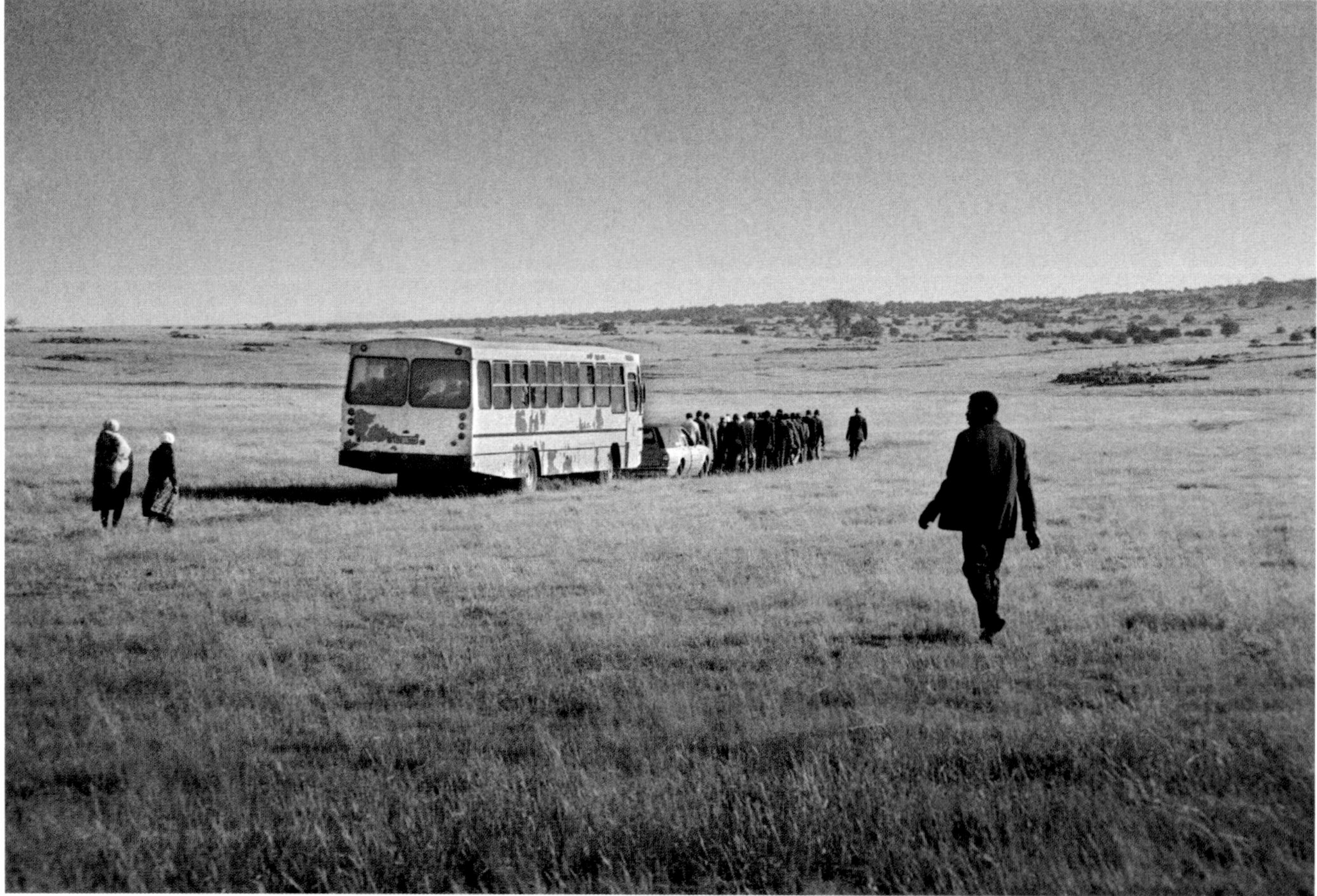

Miriam Maines interment, Vaalrand, ca 1986   *Chief More Funeral, Gamogopa-bus*, ca 1986

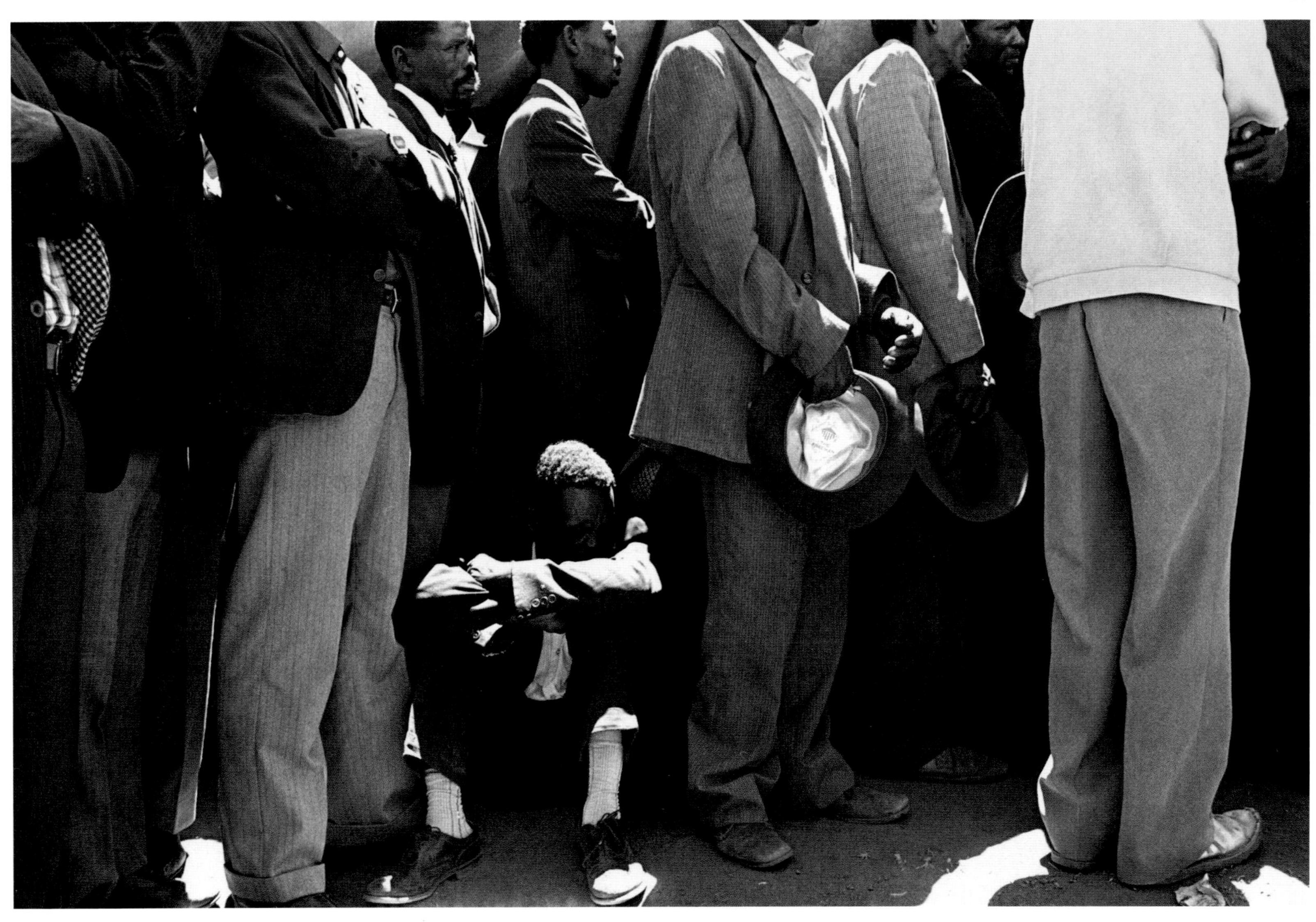

Miriam Maines Funeral, ca 1986

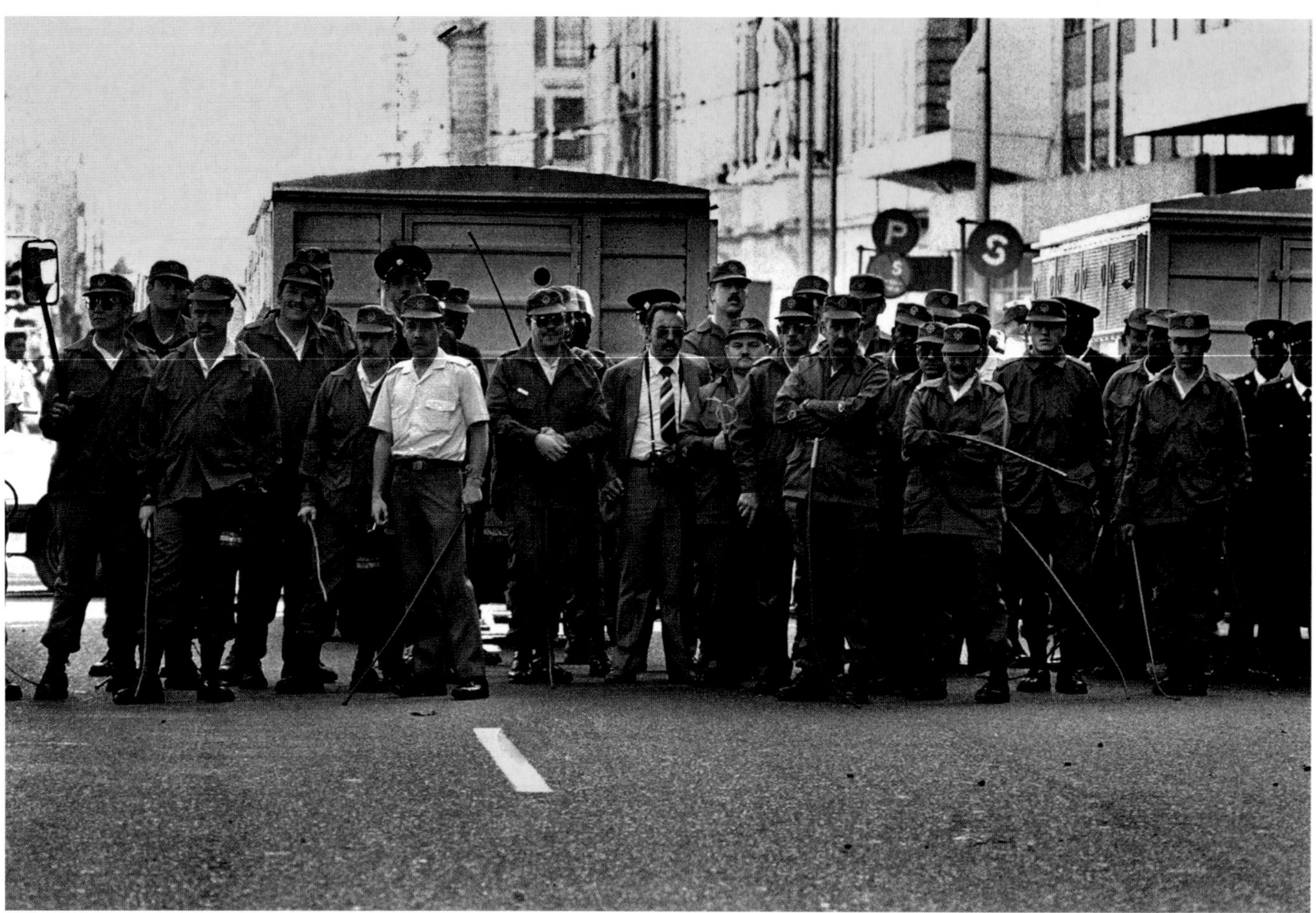

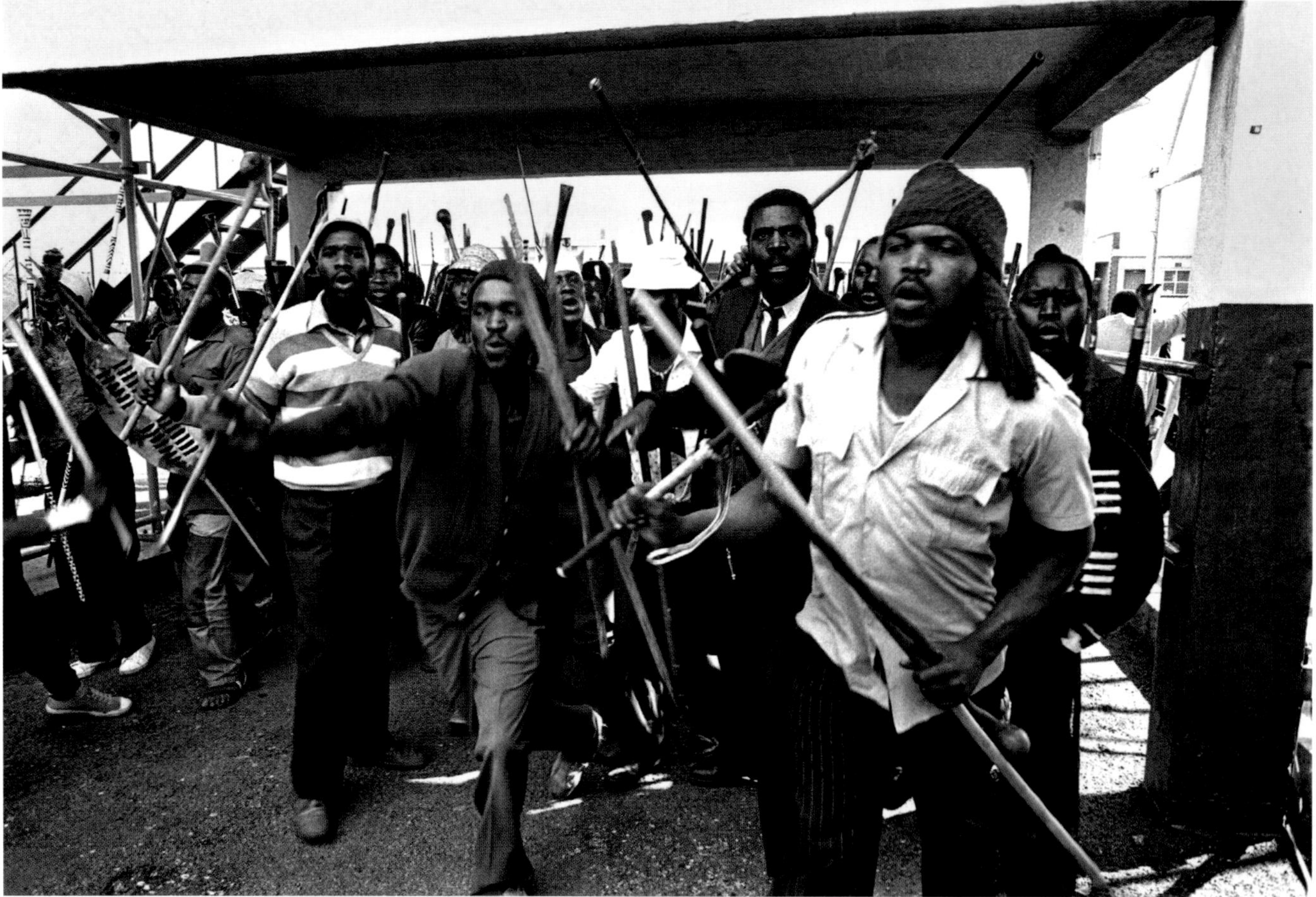

Police with Sjamboks, Plein Street, ca 1986   *Inkatha Rally, Jabulani Amphitheater*, ca 1986

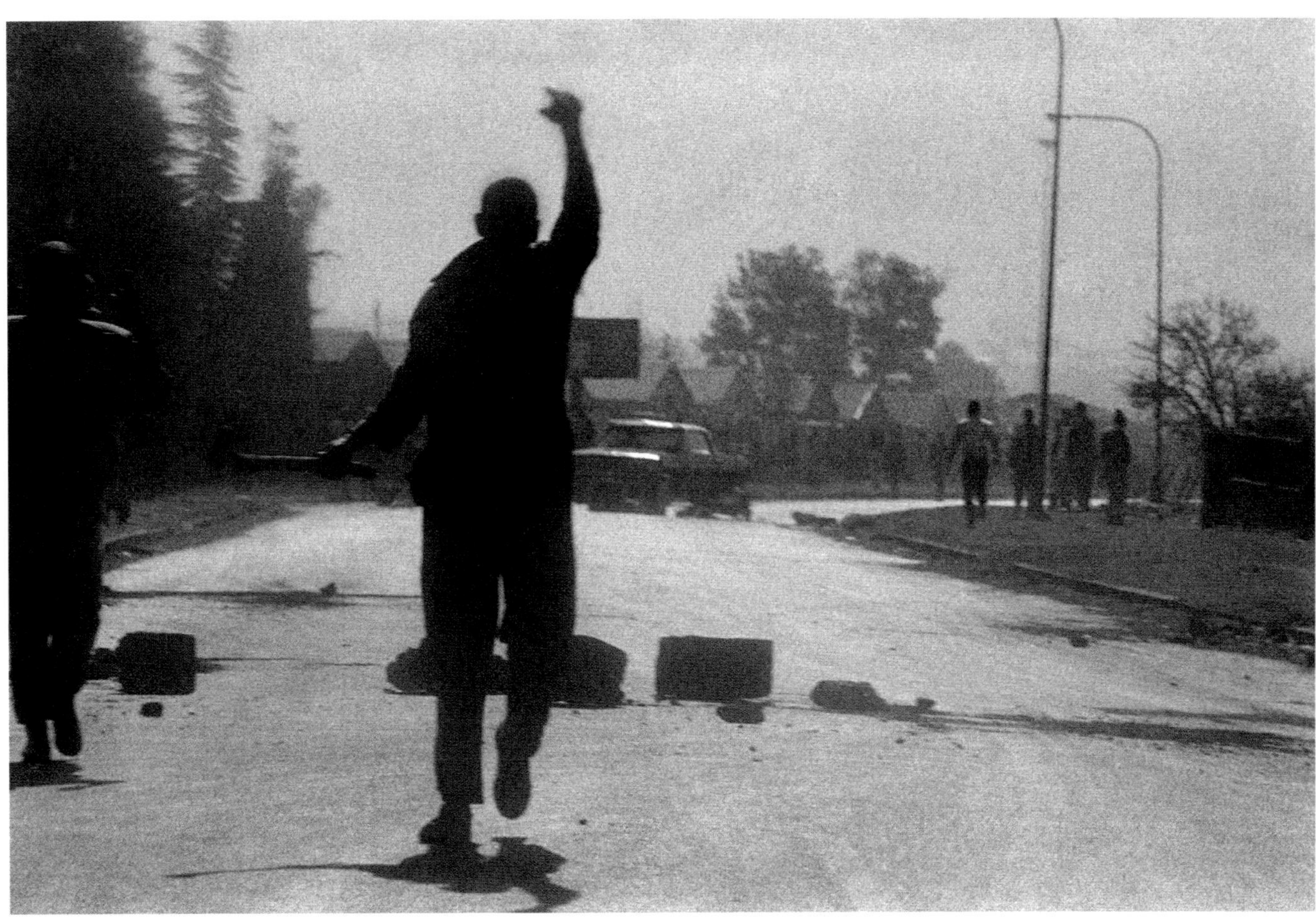

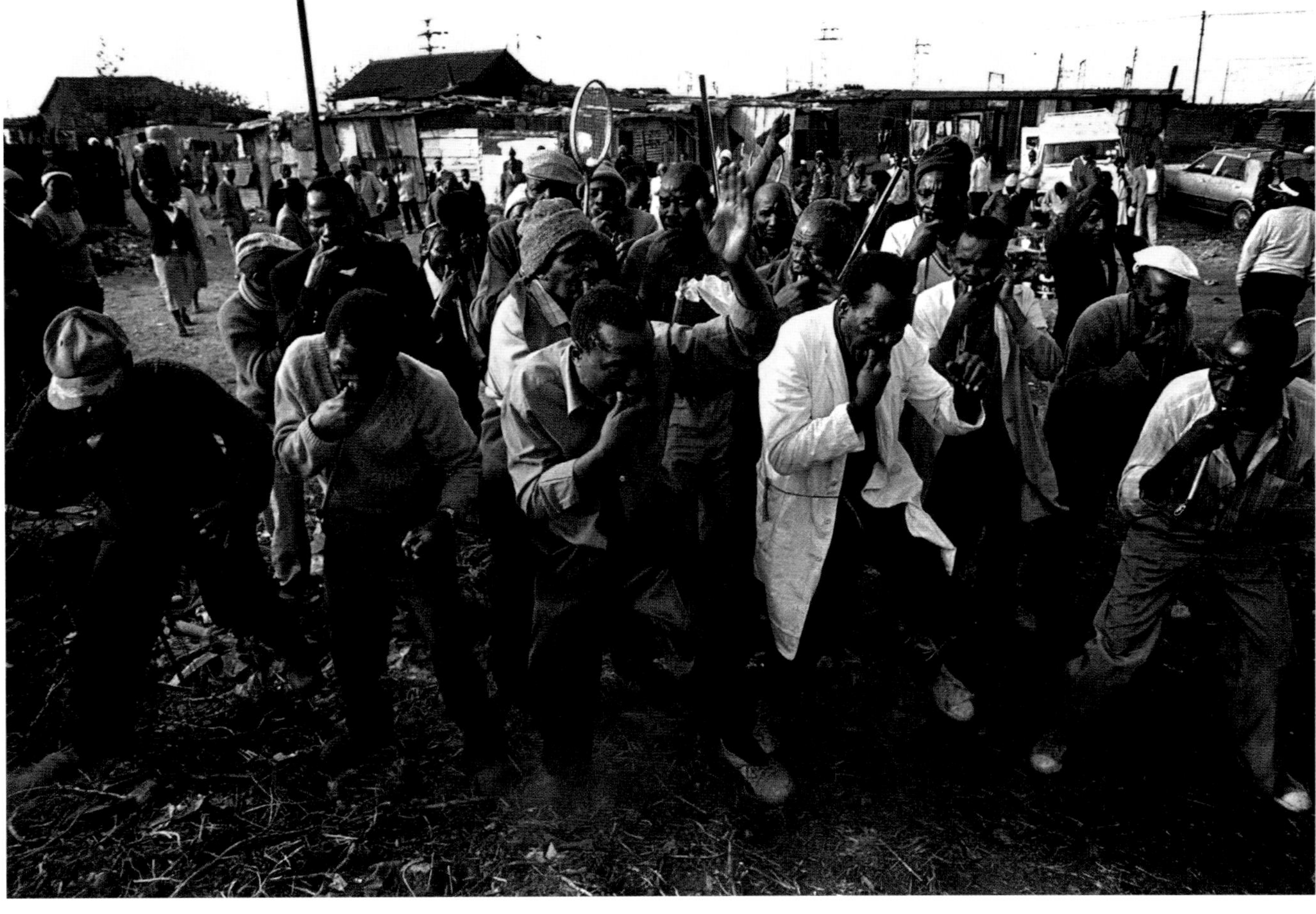

Street Blockade Merafe, ca 1986   *Pedi Dancers, Dukathole,* ca 1986

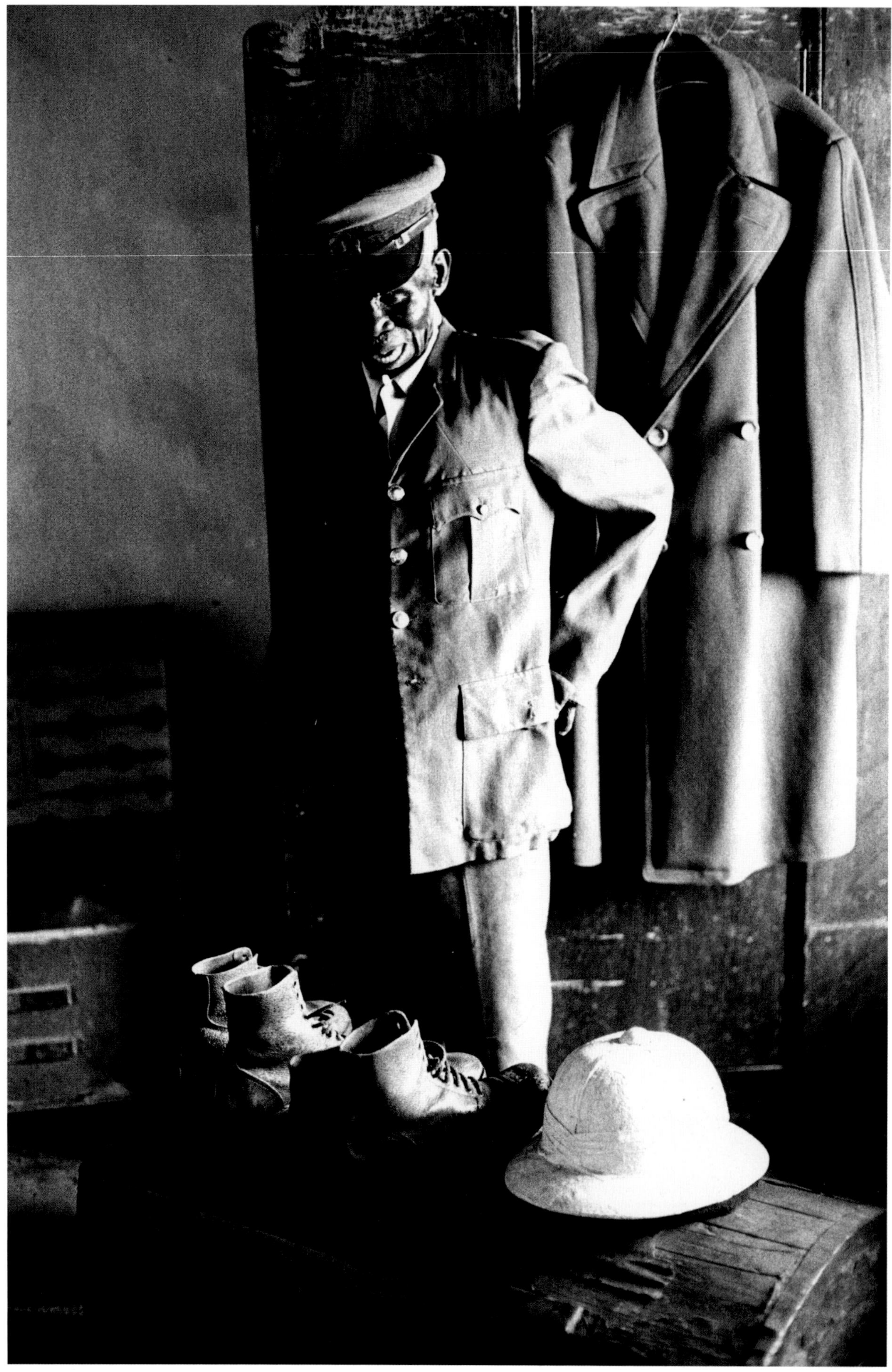

Raflaga Matau Bapong, ca 1986

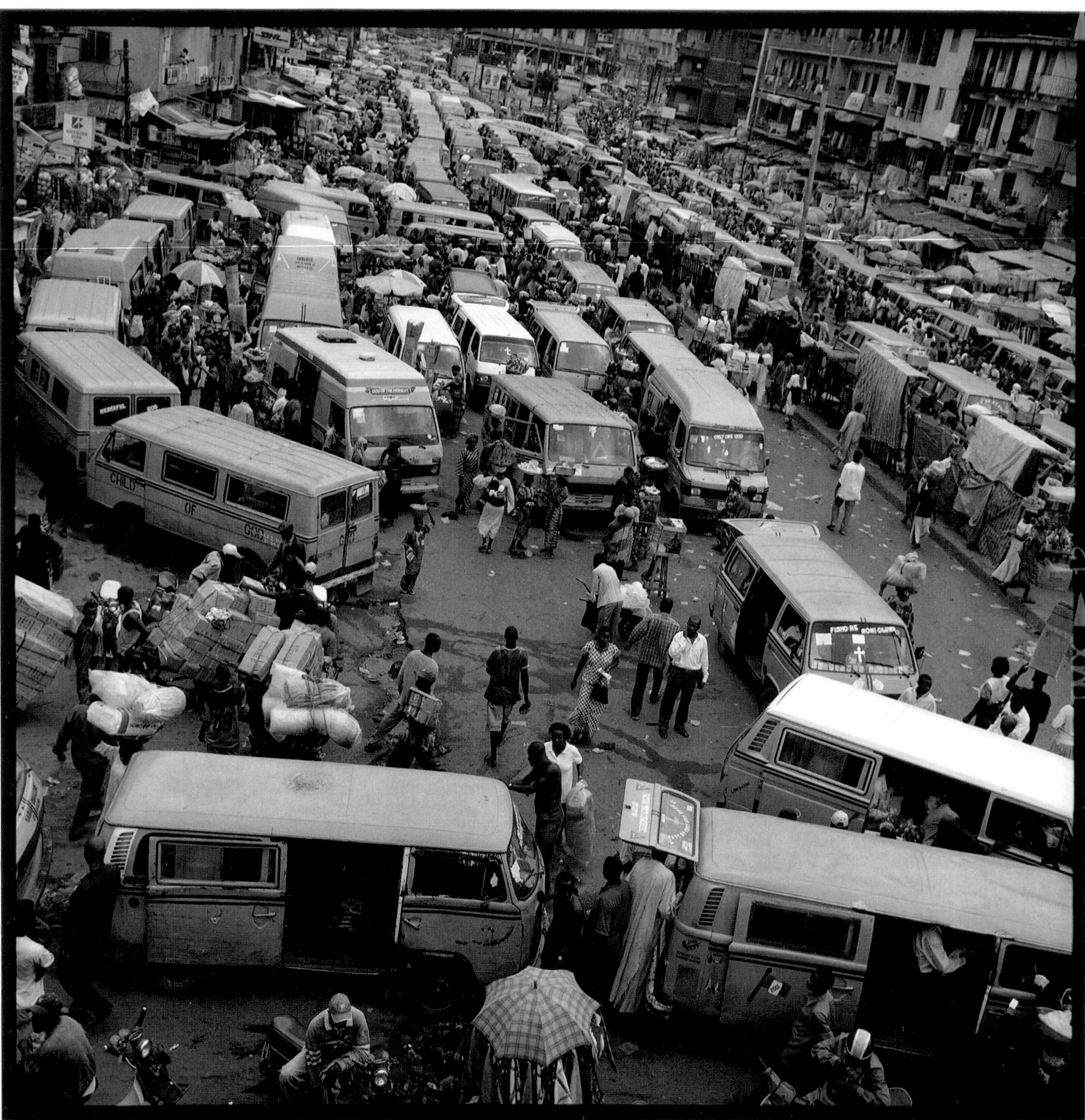

Crossroads[*]
1980 1989

* Tracy Chapman

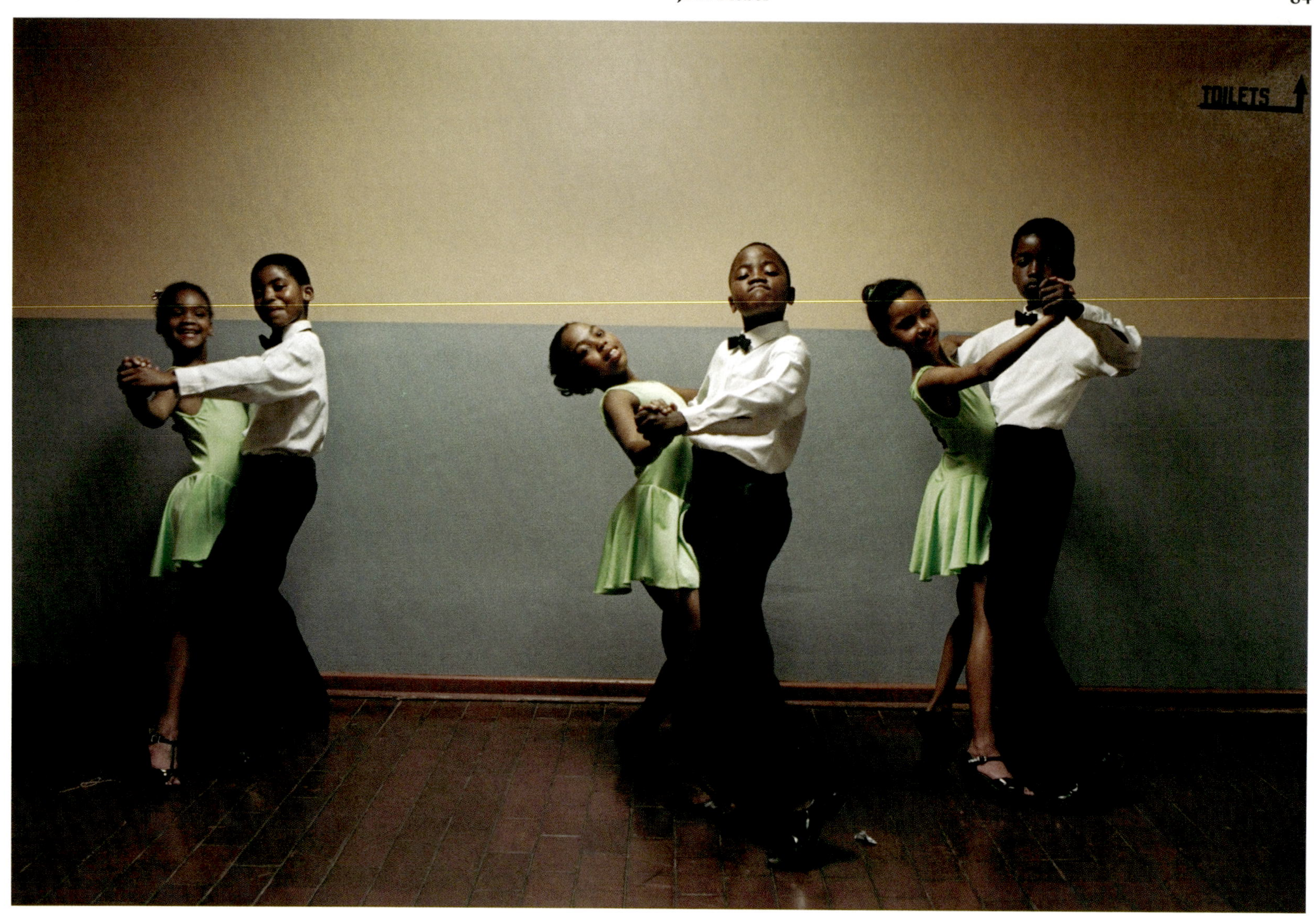

*One, two, three and… The Ennerdale Academy of Dance, south of
Johannesburg, 1997*

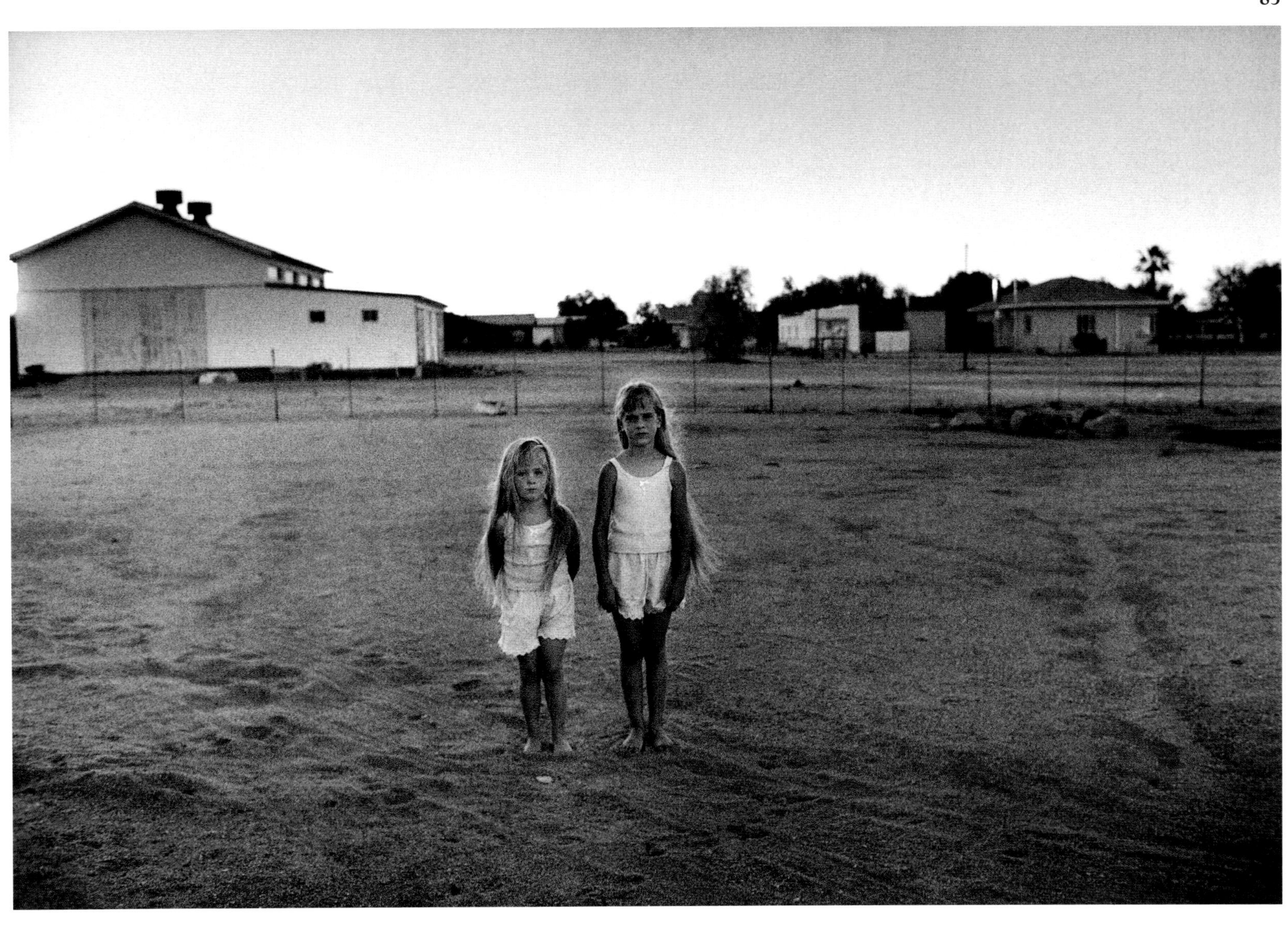

Namaqualand daisies, Pofadder, Northern Cape, ca 1998-1999

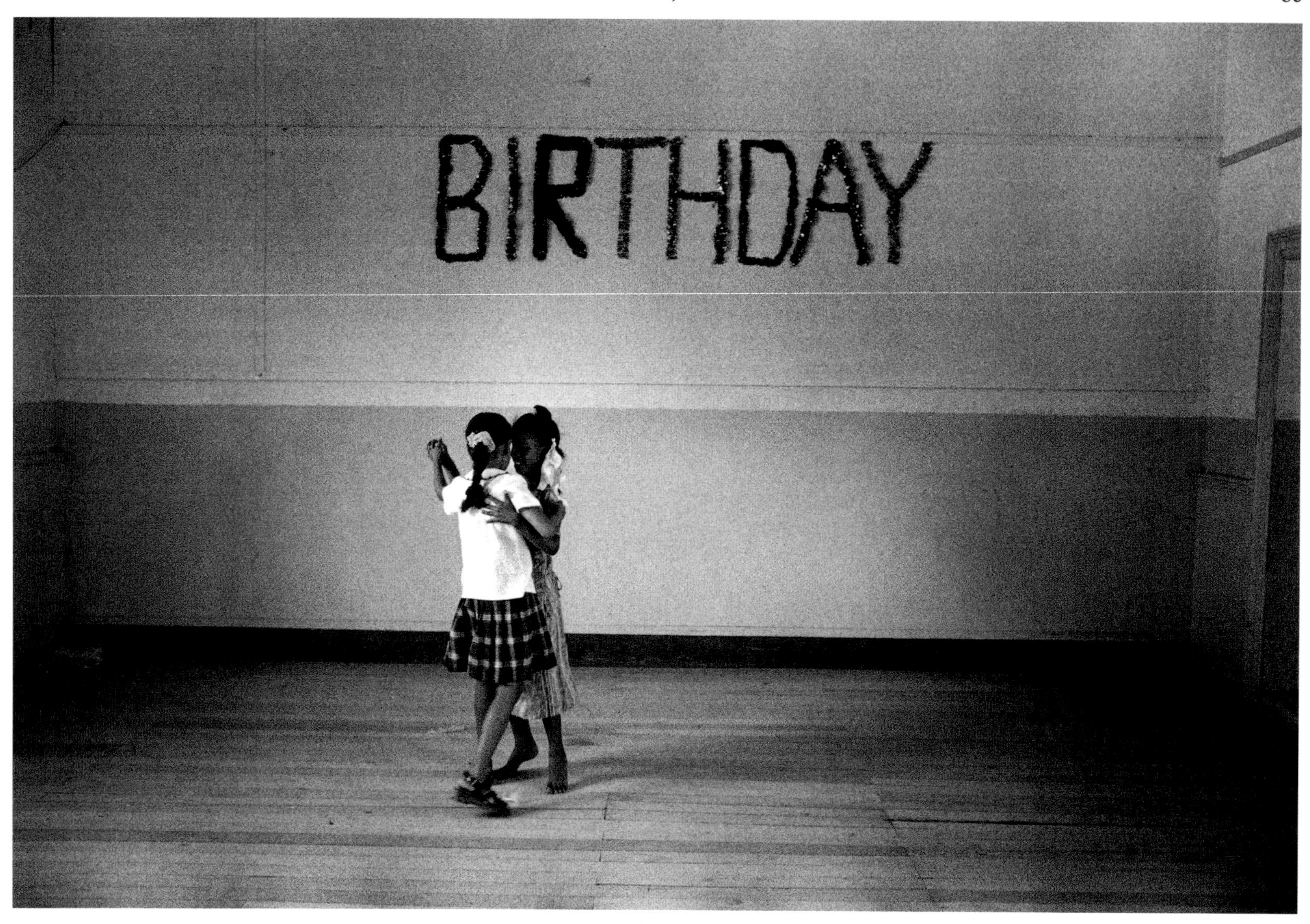

Sunday School, Nababeep, Northern Cape, ca 1998-1999
Nababeep is a copper mining town in the Northern Cape. More and more
of the local men were looking elsewhere for work, as copper was running
low and it looked as if the mine would close down in three years time. The
family unit was crumbling because of work migration.

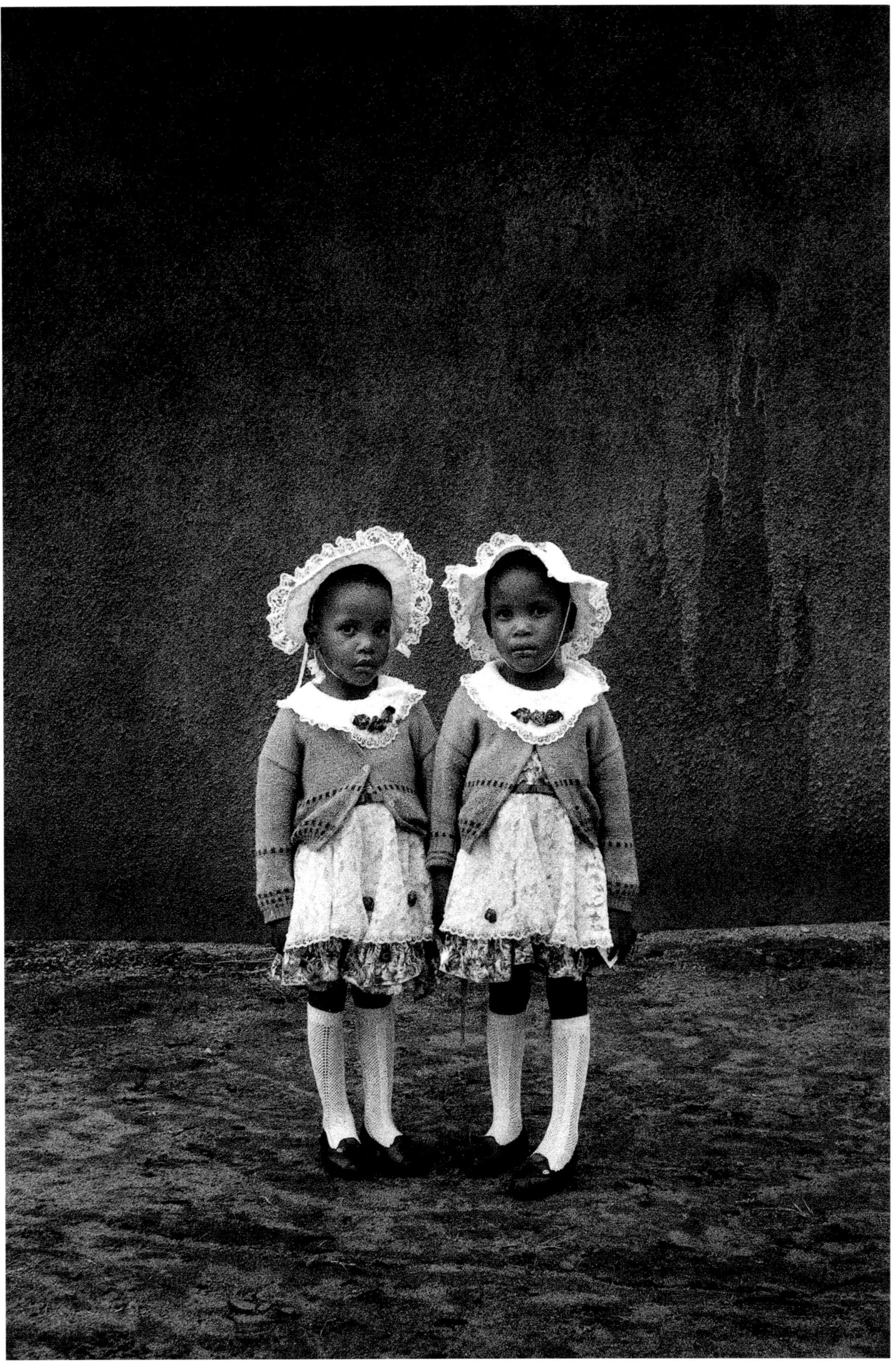

The Silence of the Ranto Twins

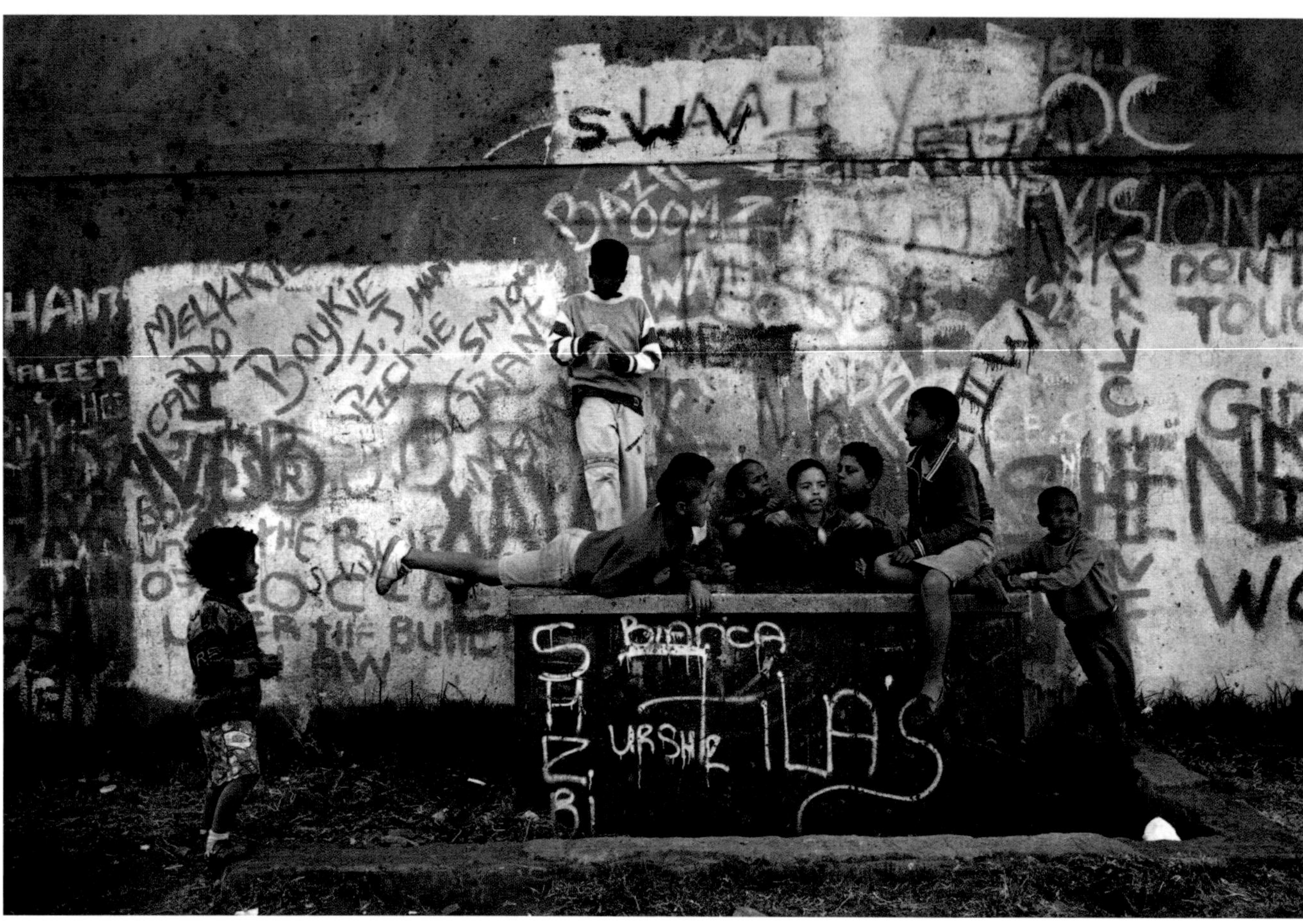

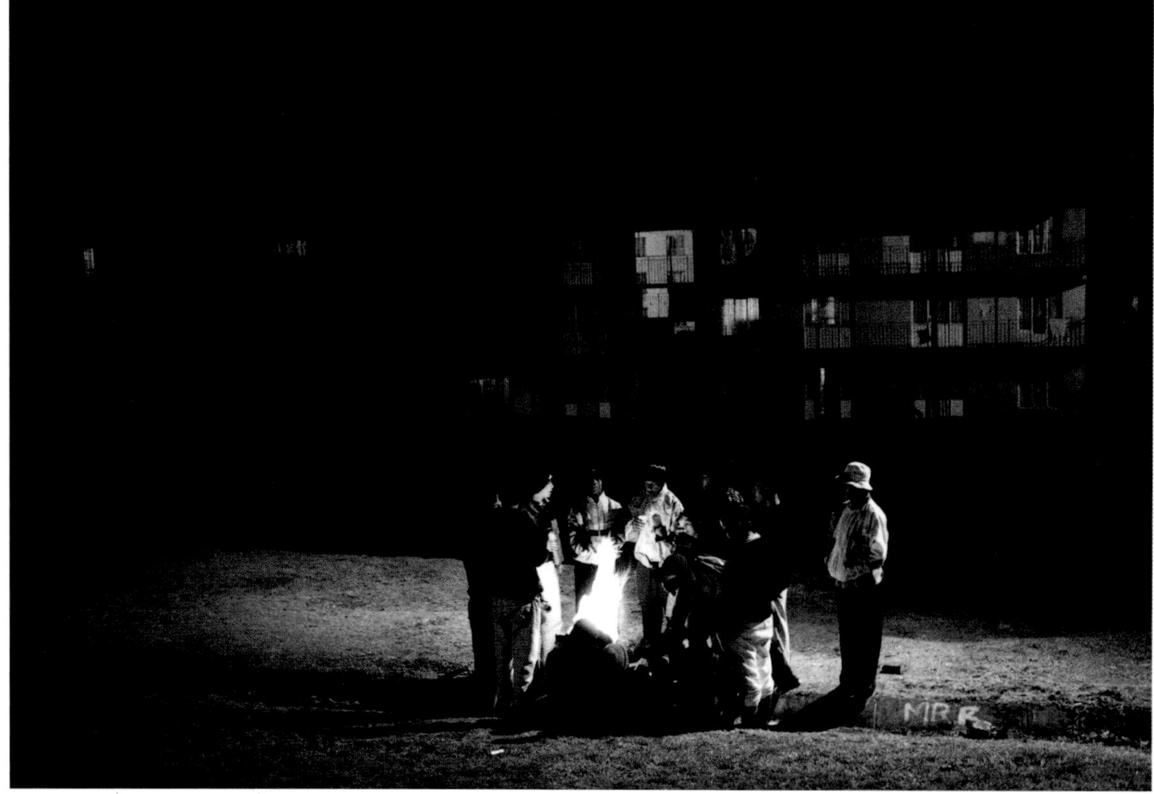

Come hang out with us, ca 1996
Overcrowding and broken family life contributes to children moving onto the streets at an early age in Westbury. Brotherhoods or gangs develop as a means of survival on the streets. They are an extension of family.

Come hang out with us: *Jonathan D Boyz*, ca 1996
At night the Jonathan D Boyz hang out around a fire, making plans or telling stories. Most of the community in Westbury remains within the safety of their hoes. Revenge attacks in the form of drive-by-shootings take place during these hours.

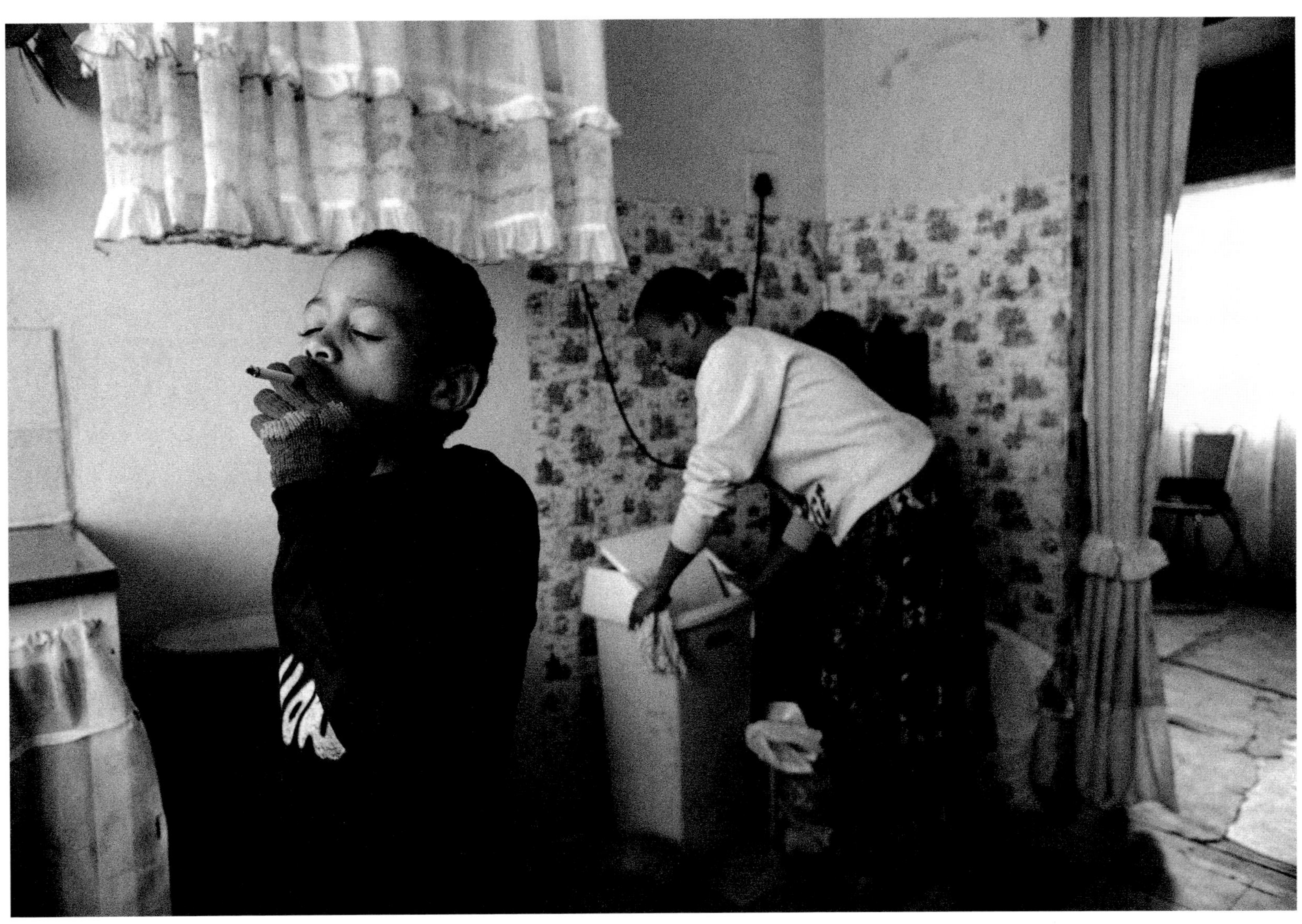

Bradley and Lynette, ca 1996

Lynette is a single mother with three young boys, a live-in lover and a dog. She lives in a council block, in a flat which consists of one room, a kitchen and bathroom. She and her children have often had to move, even sleeping in a school classroom for a period when her husband abandoned the family. Her day is spent doing household chores. Danny, her lover, is a retired gangster who spent time in jail for murder and is now a storeman at a private hospital.

Wardlen, her eldest son (11), was expelled from school and hangs out on the streets with the Jonathan D Boyz. When Bradley, her youngest son (7), gets angry he responds with a knife; behaviour learnt on the streets is brought back home. The only way Lynette seems to know how to discipline her children is by threatening or striking them with a leather belt. Her son Wardlen once stabbed her. Many women are left alone to care for and discipline their children, as their husbands are either in jail, on the run from the law or have been killed through gang violence. Lynette has pleaded with the Welfare Department to take her kids away from Westbury, as she believes it is not a suitable place for children to grow up. However, life goes on…

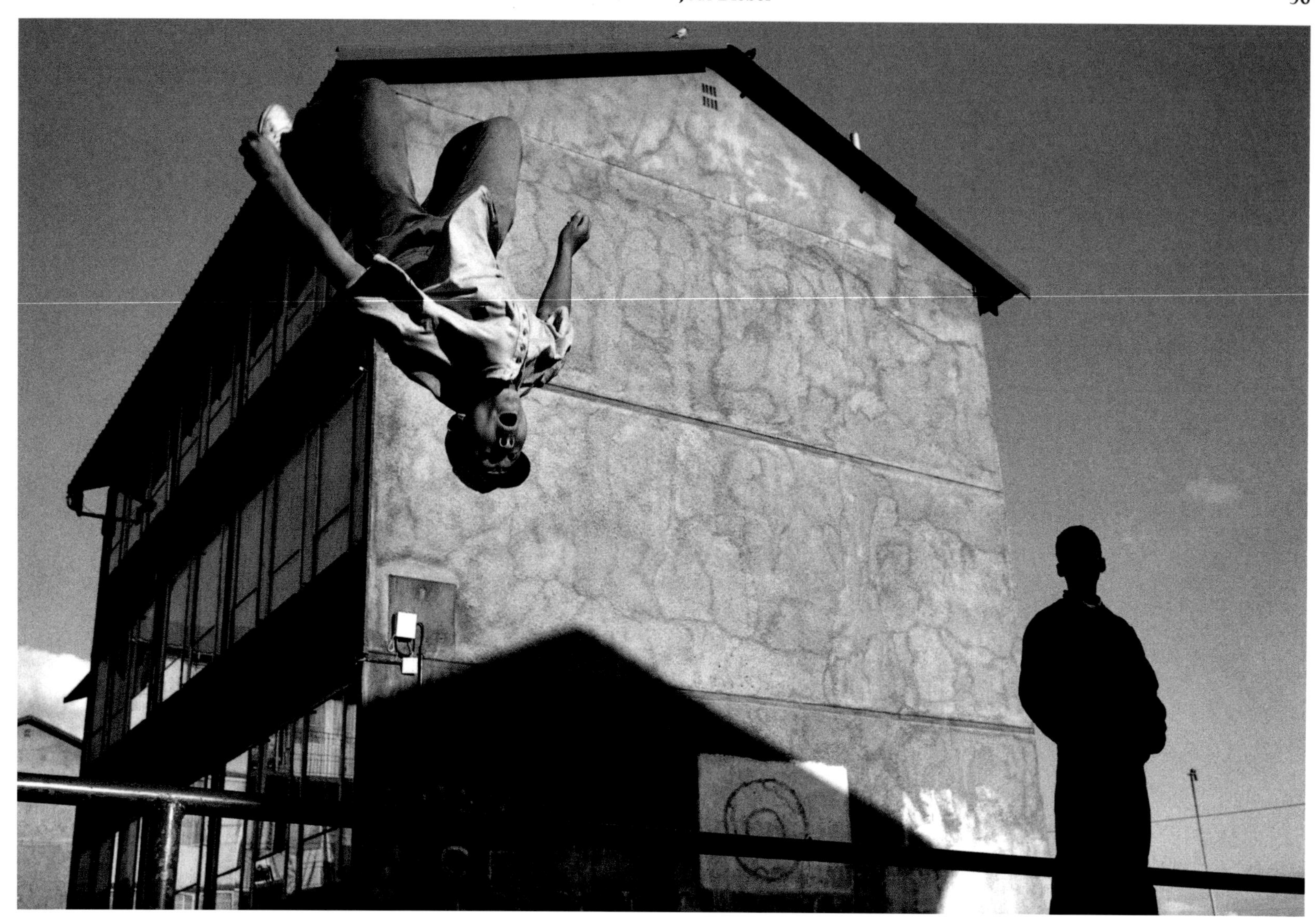

Come hang out with us, ca 1996
Everyone has a nickname in Westbury. Q.T was known as a brilliant
gymnast. I was introduced to many people—'Rapist', 'Rap Artist', 'God-
father', 'Car Thief', 'Drug addict'. Sometimes a lucky few with talent
are recognised and get the opportunity to develop their skills outside the
confines of their environment.

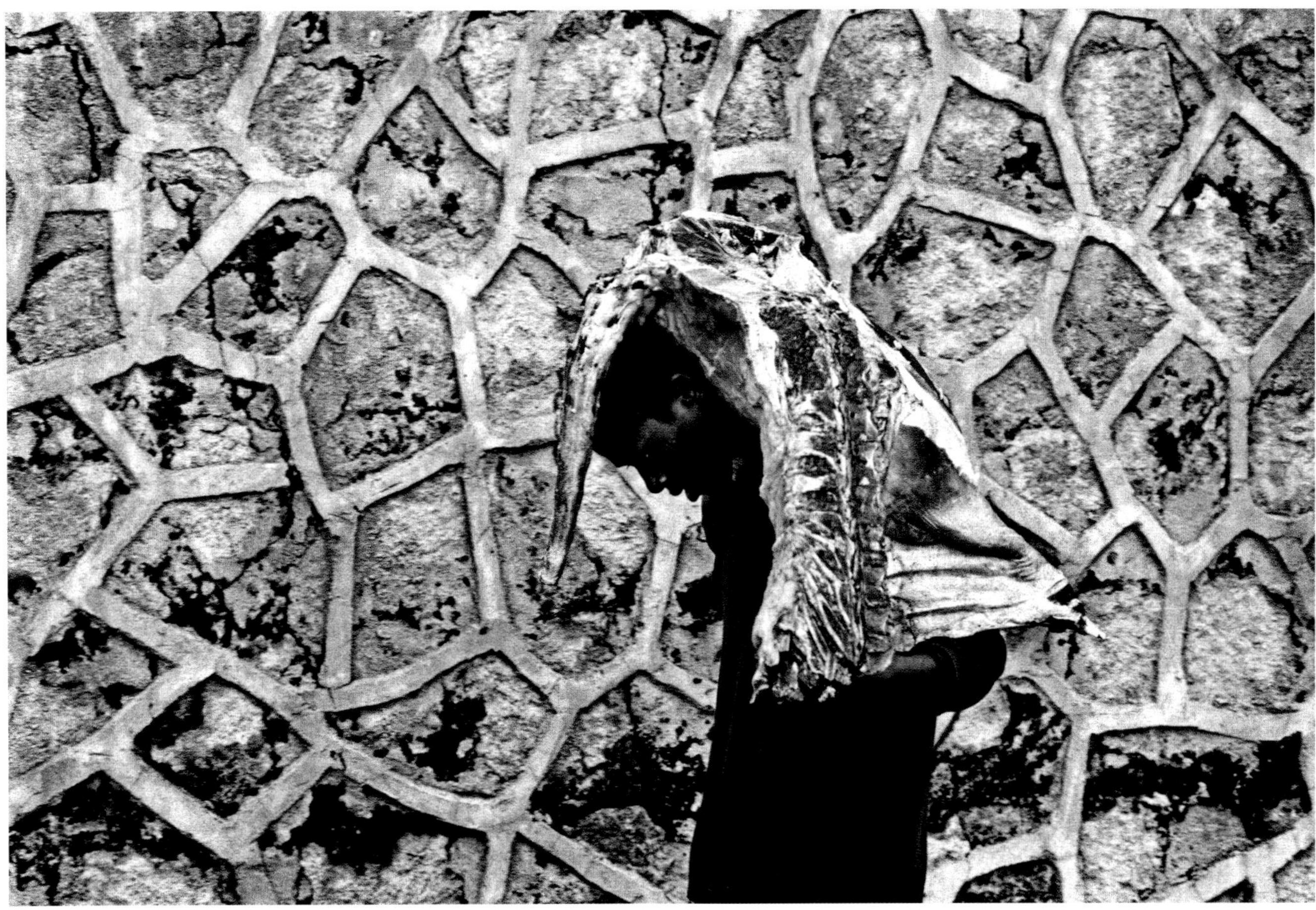

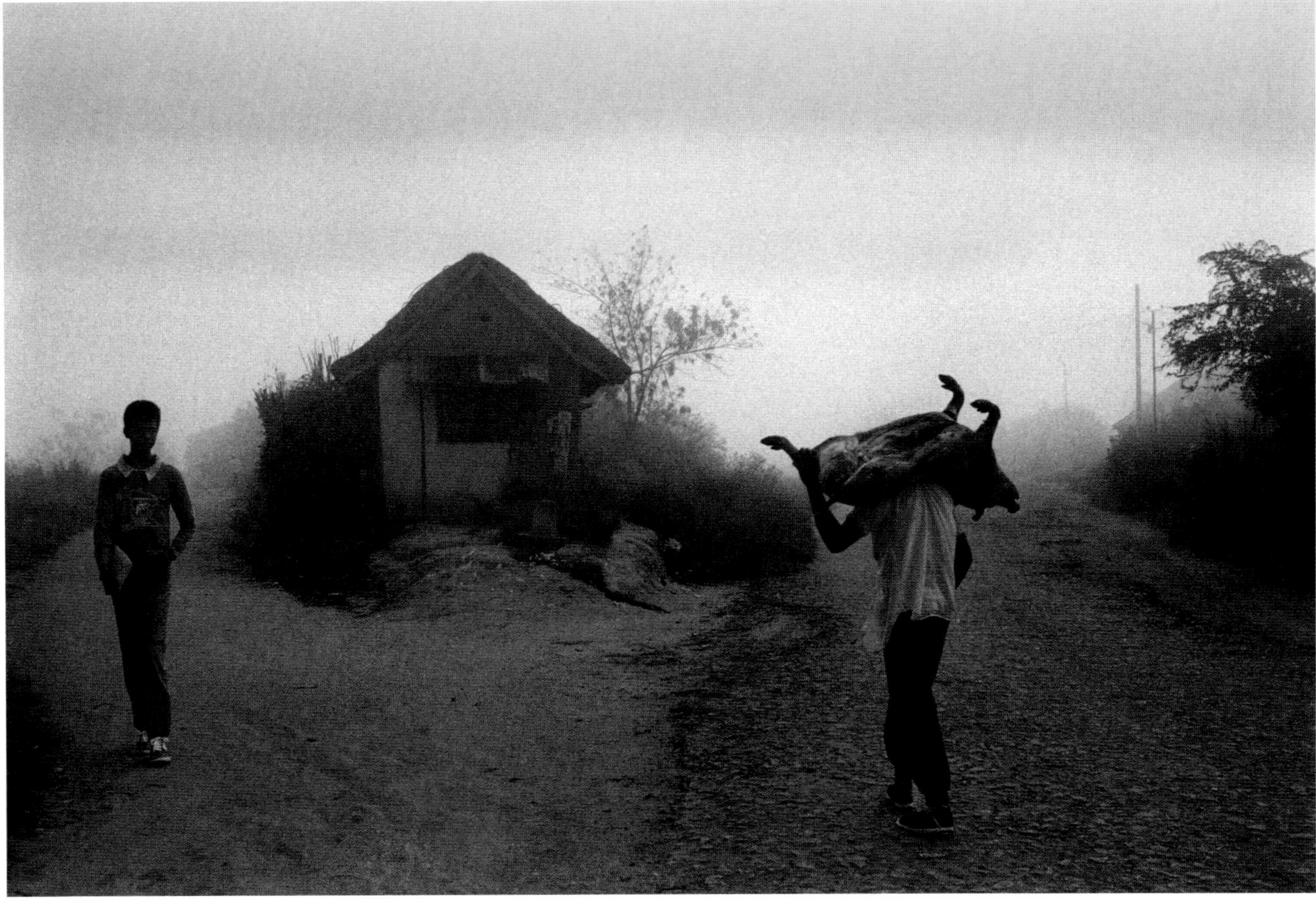

from the series *Fianarantsoa*, 1990

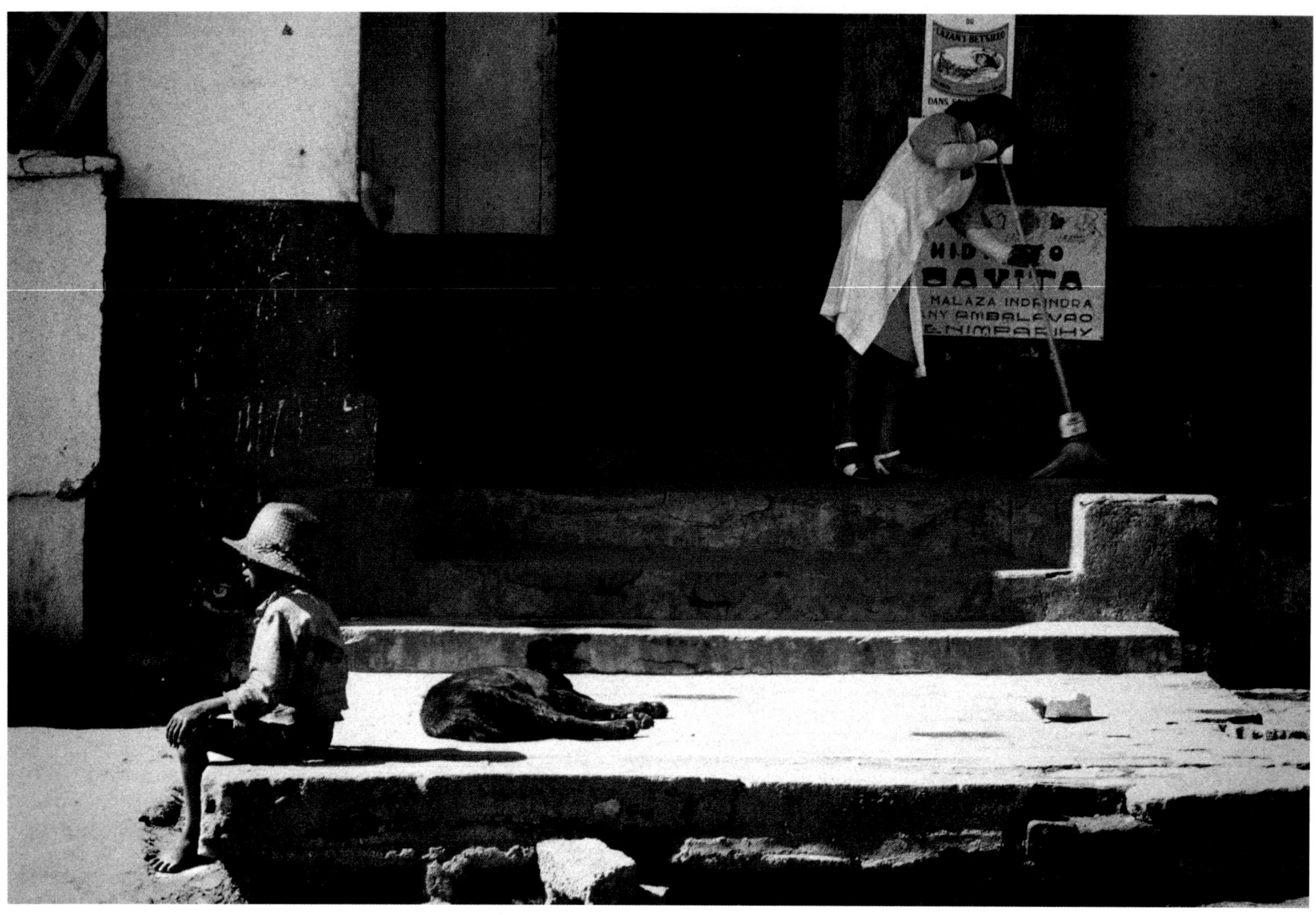

from the series *Fianarantsoa*, 1990

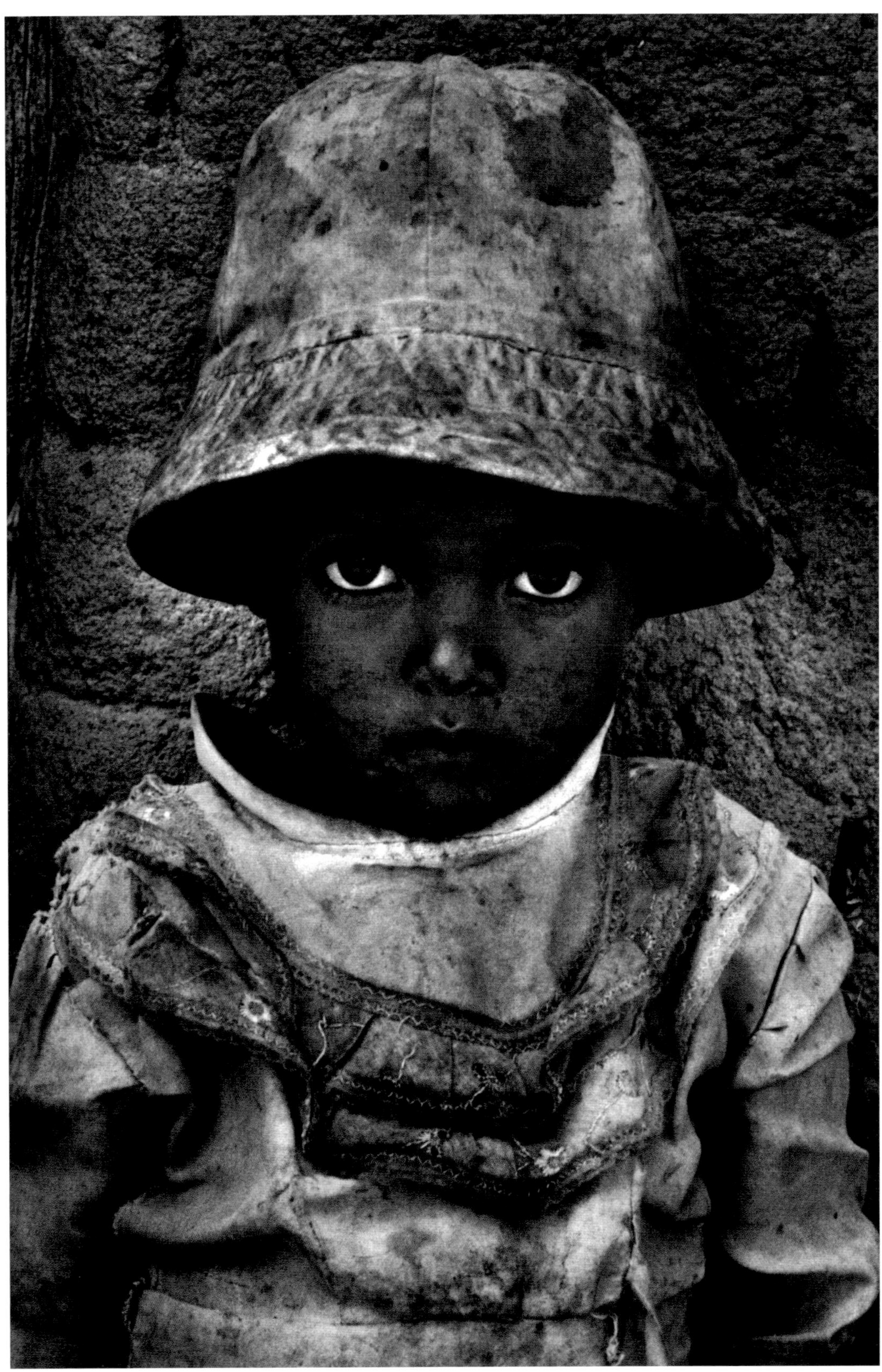

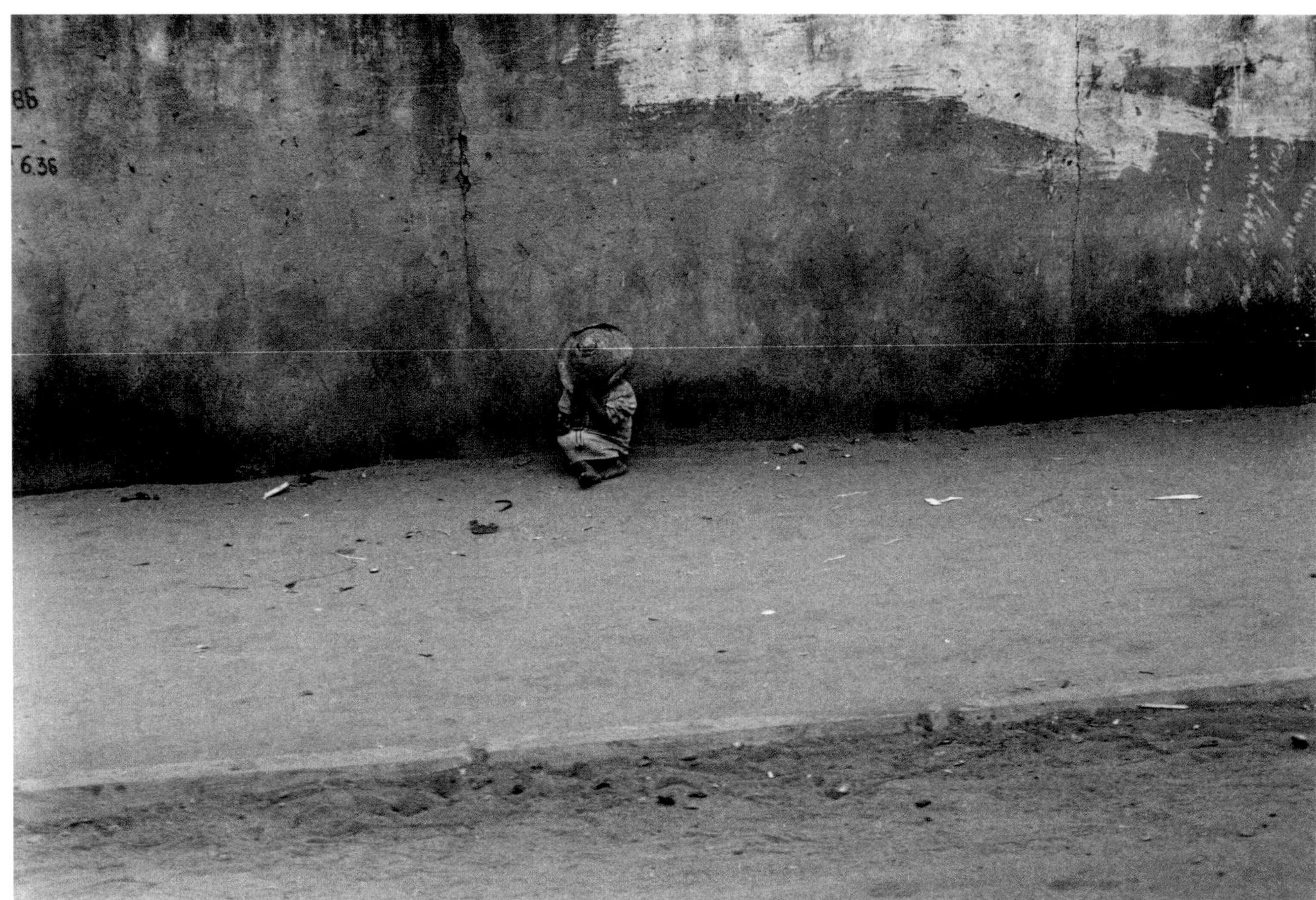

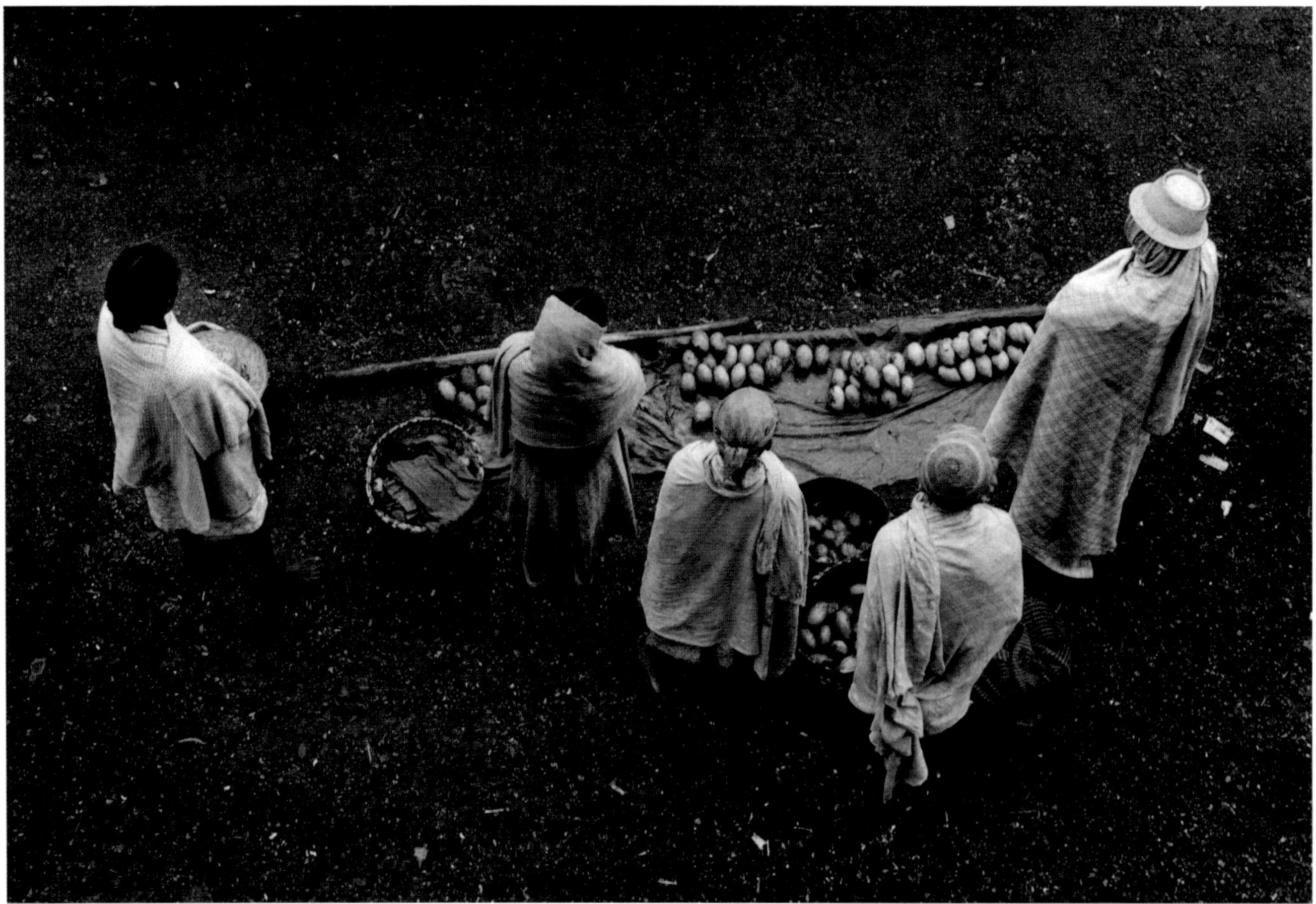

from the series *Fianarantsoa*, 1990

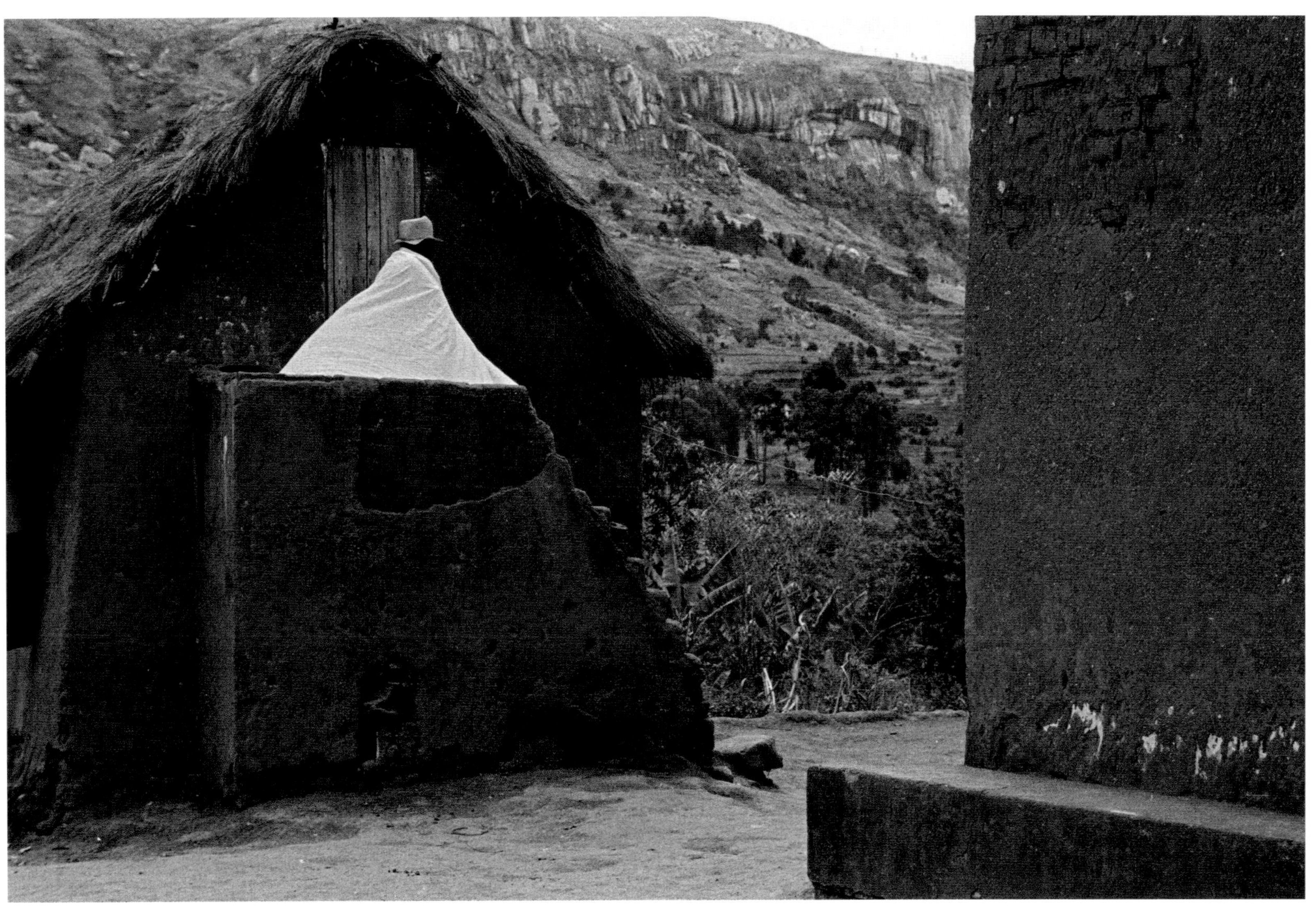

Stanley from the series *Alexandrie revisitée*, 1997

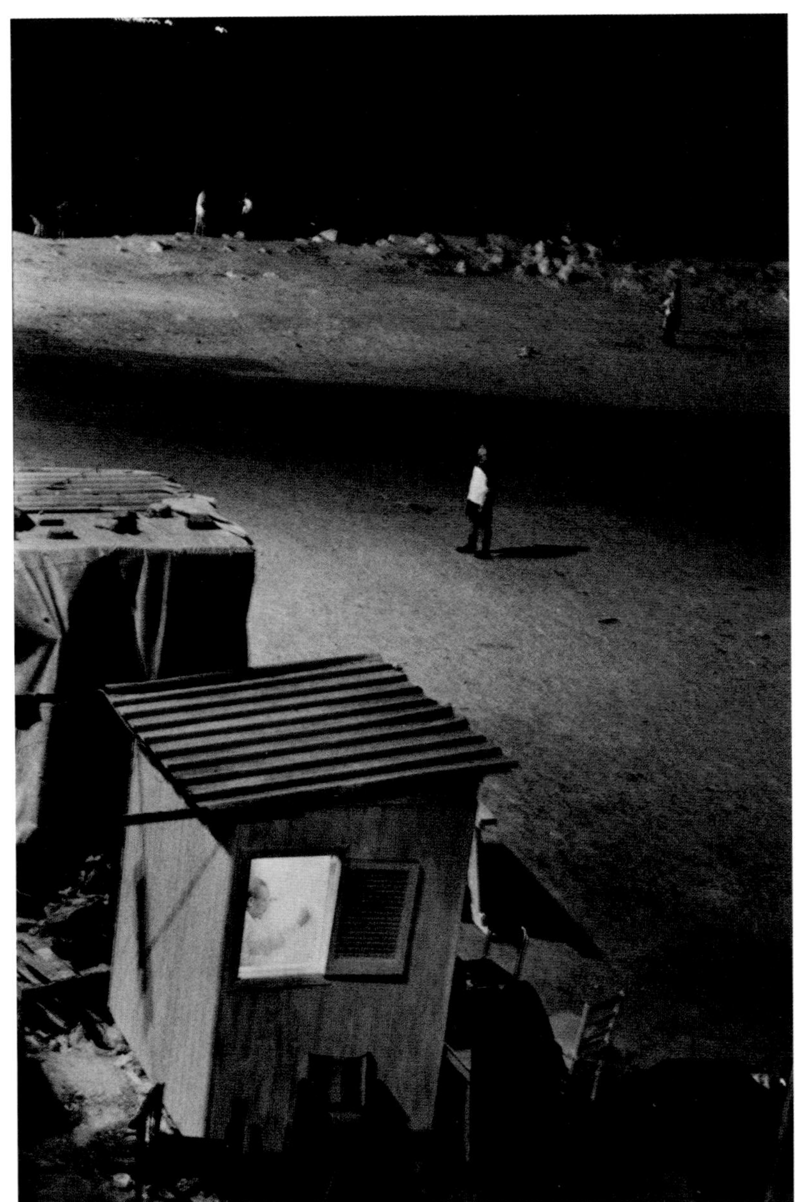

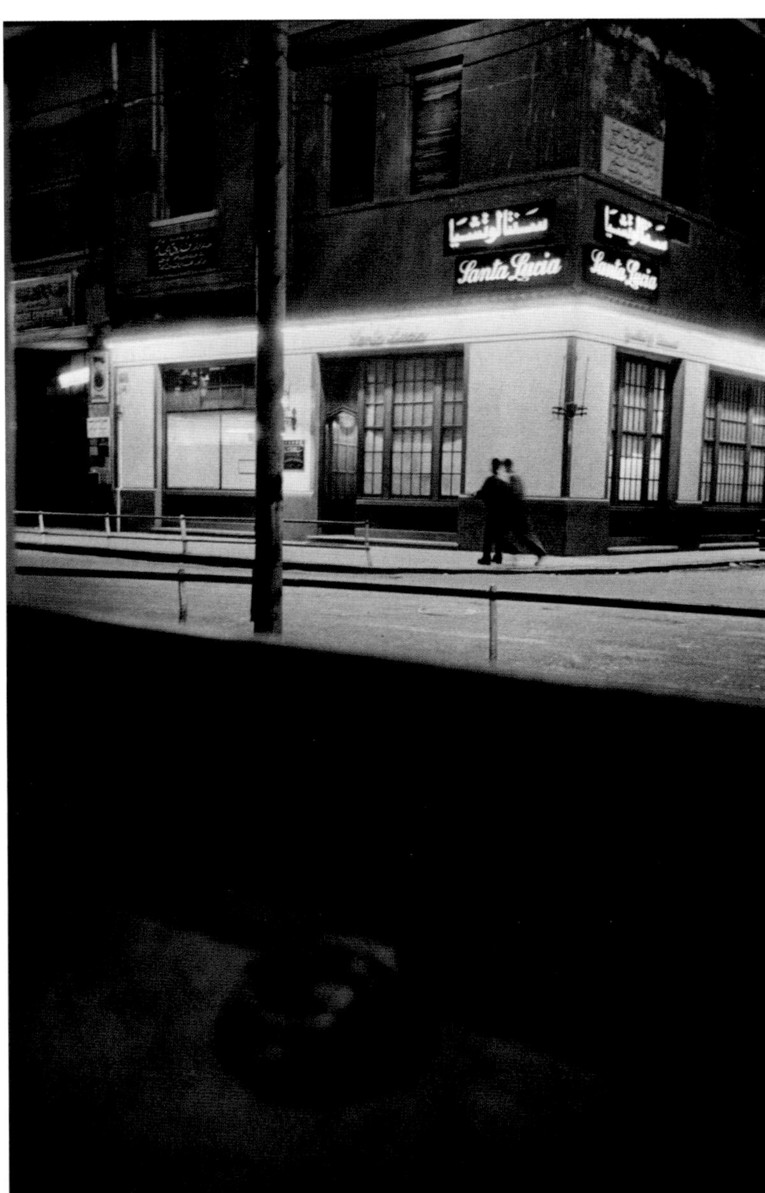

Chantier du port de Stanley from the series *Alexandrie revisitée*, 2001   *Santa Lucia, Ramly* from the series *Alexandrie revisitée*, 1997

Nabil Boutros

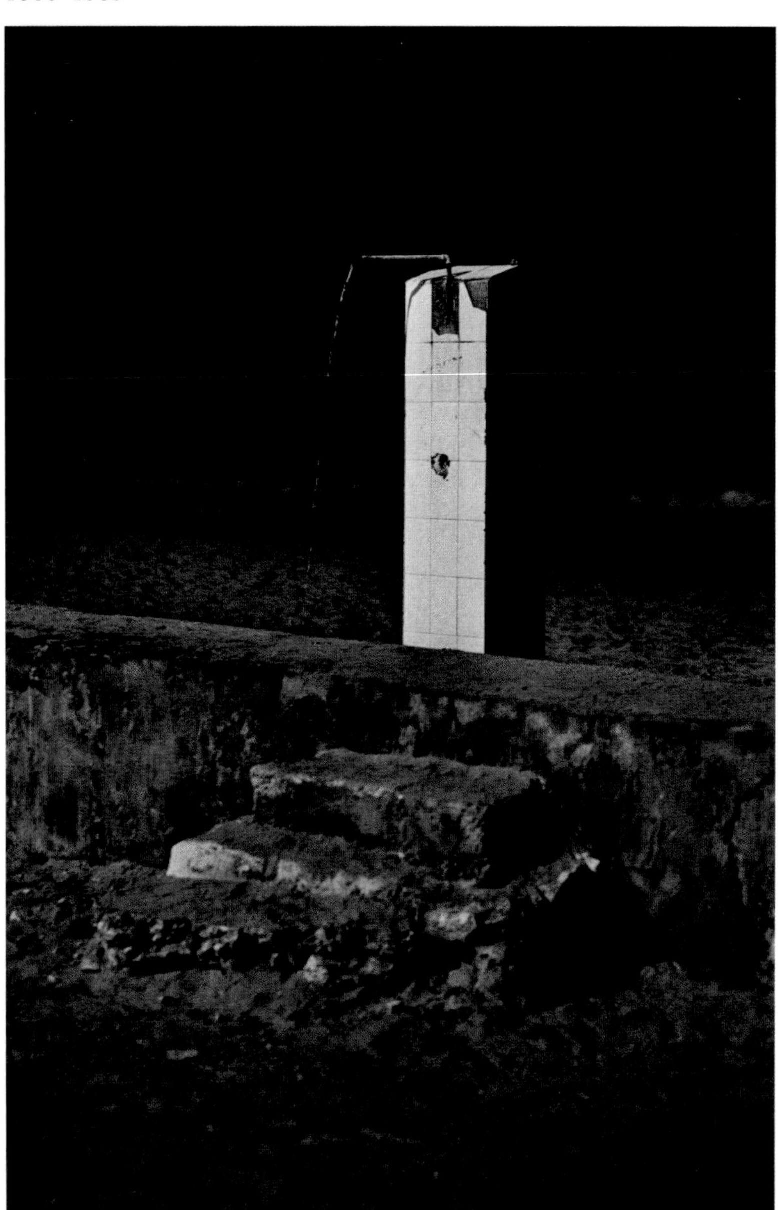

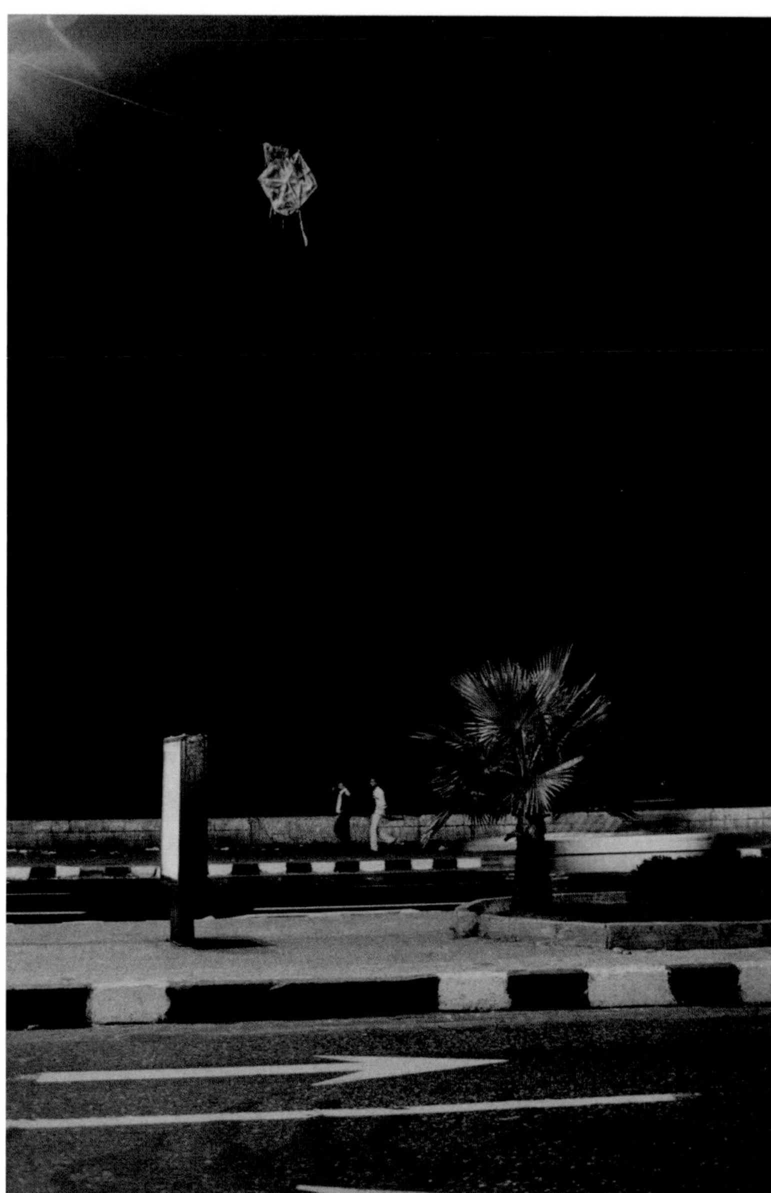

Miami from the series *Alexandrie revisitée*, 1997

Corniche à Ramaly from the series *Alexandrie revisitée*, 2001

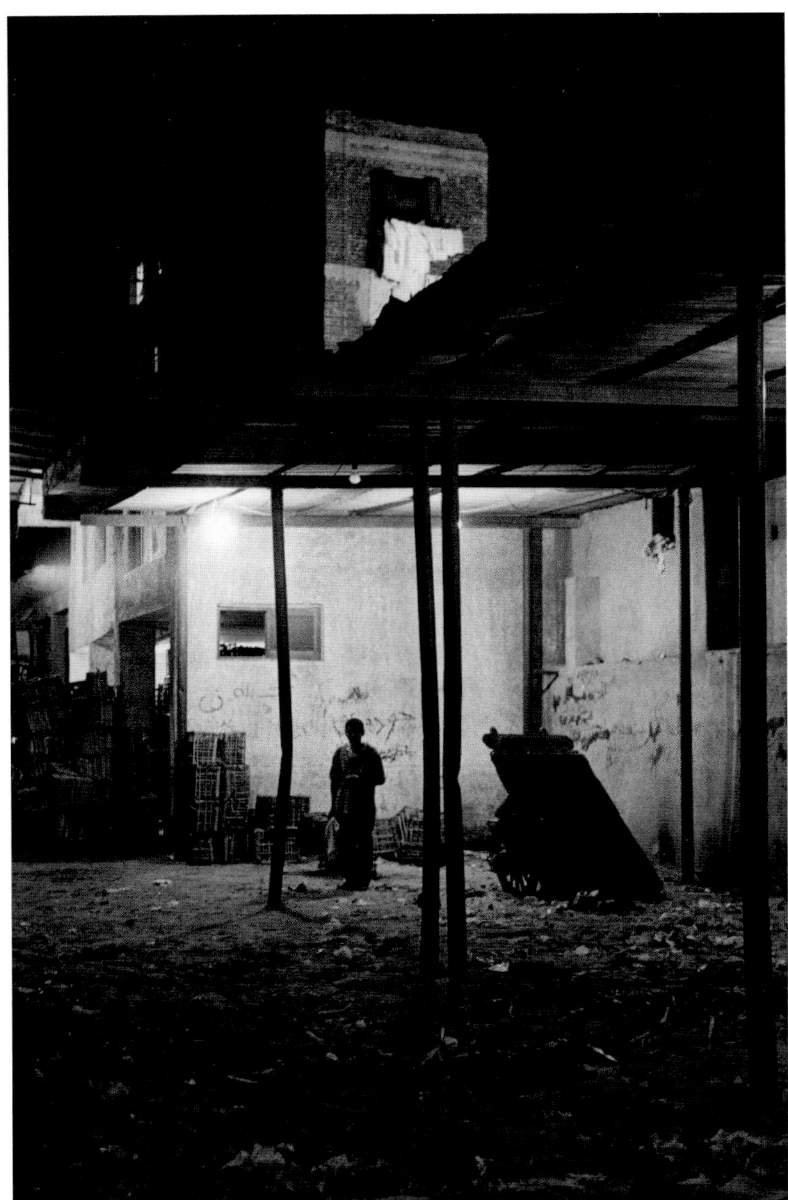

Marché aux légumes, Mahmoudeyah from the series *Alexandrie revisitée*, 2001

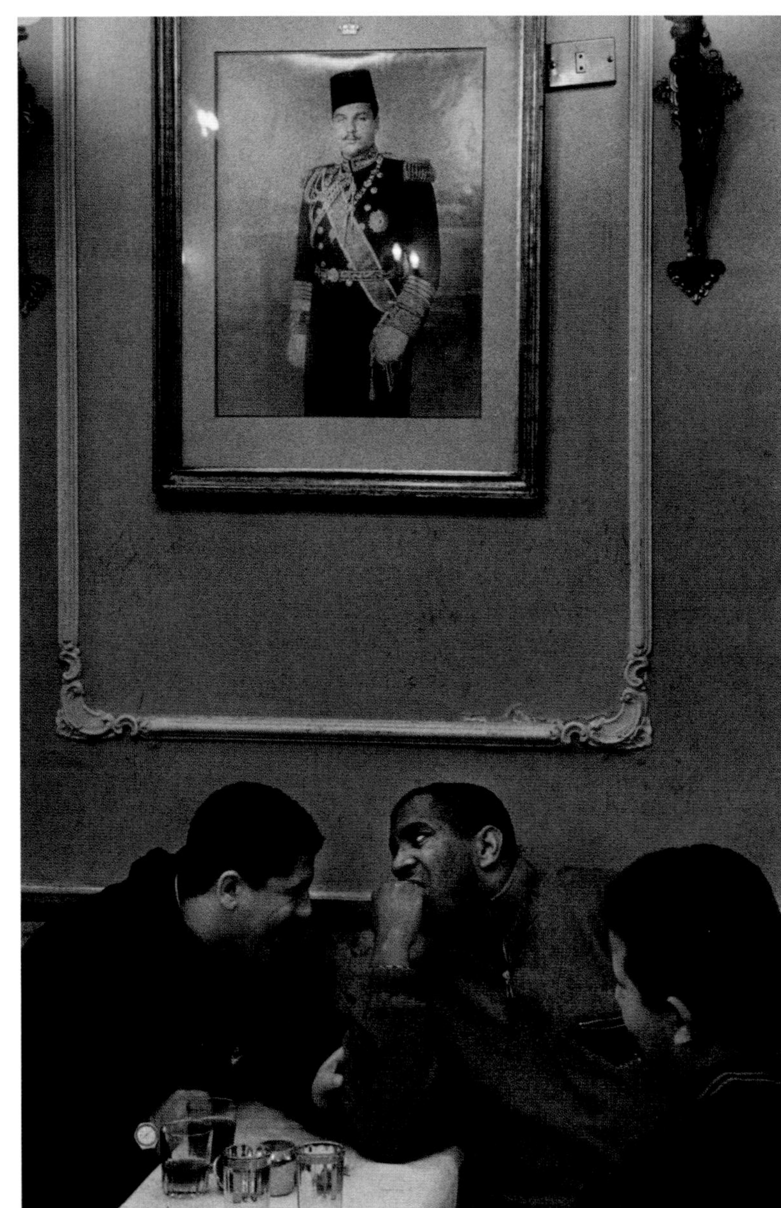

Café Farouk, Anfouchy from the series *Alexandrie revisitée*, 2001

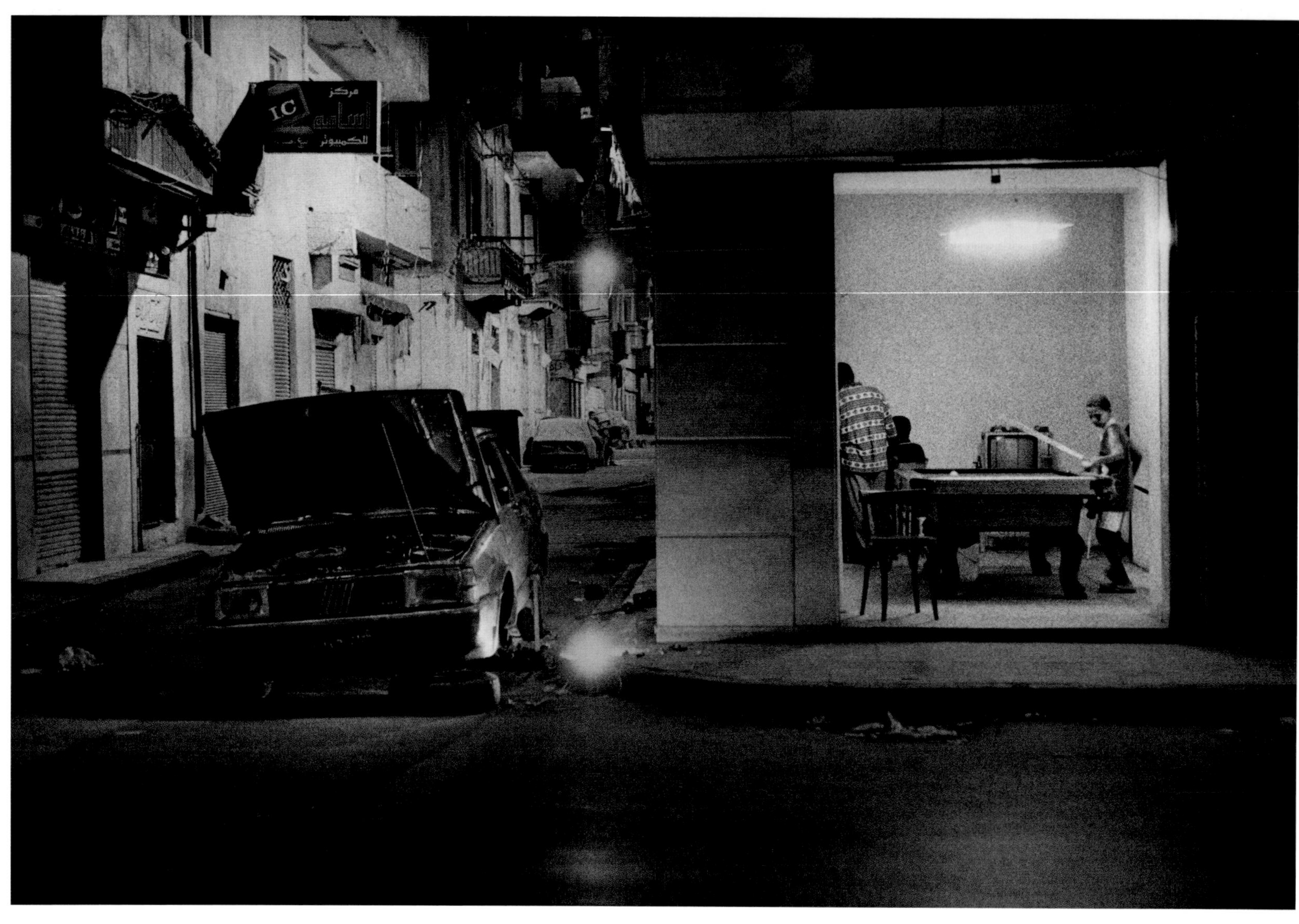

Attarine from the series *Alexandrie revisitée*, 2001

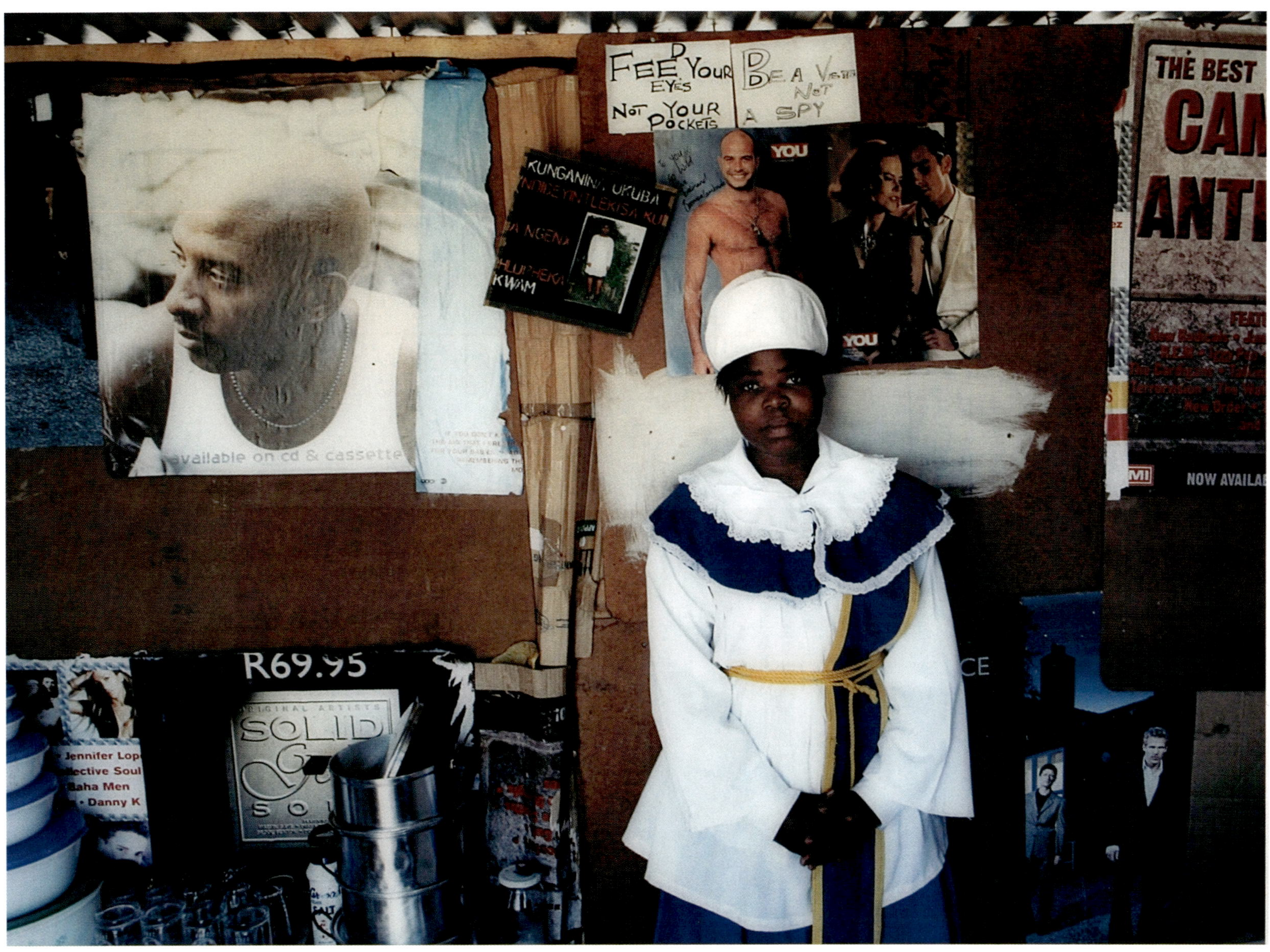

Untitled from *interior* series, 2006

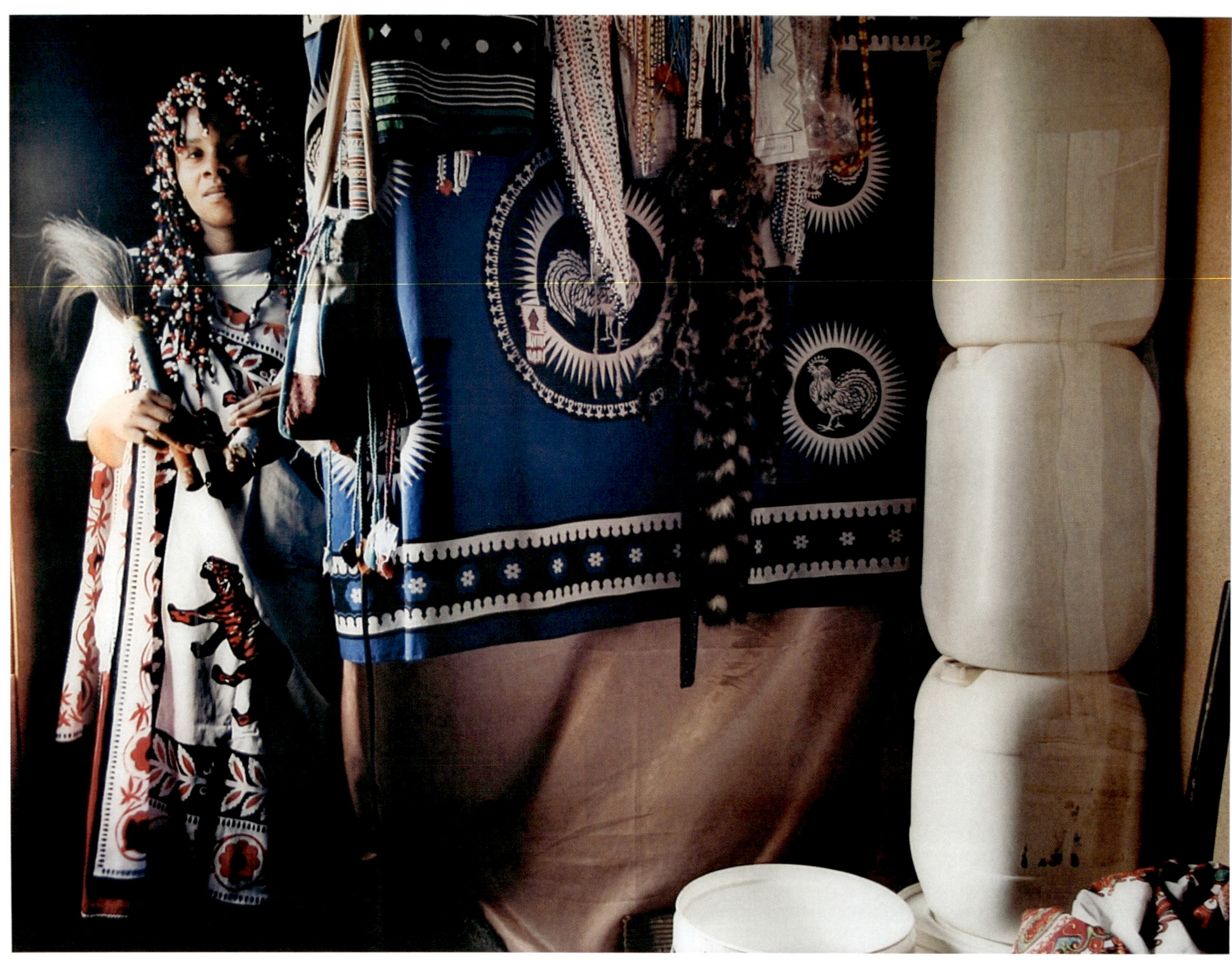

Untitled from *interior* series, 2006

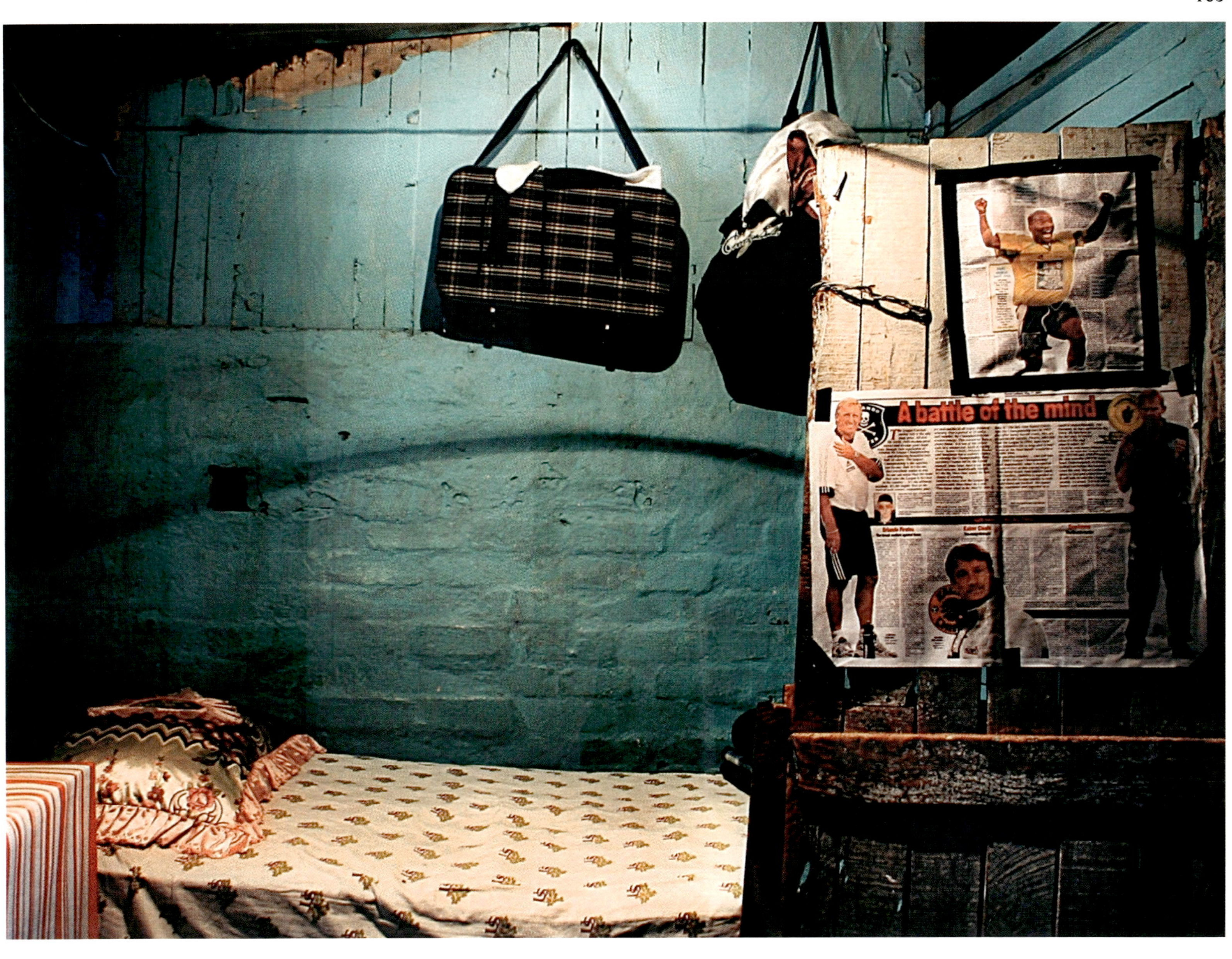
A battle of the mind

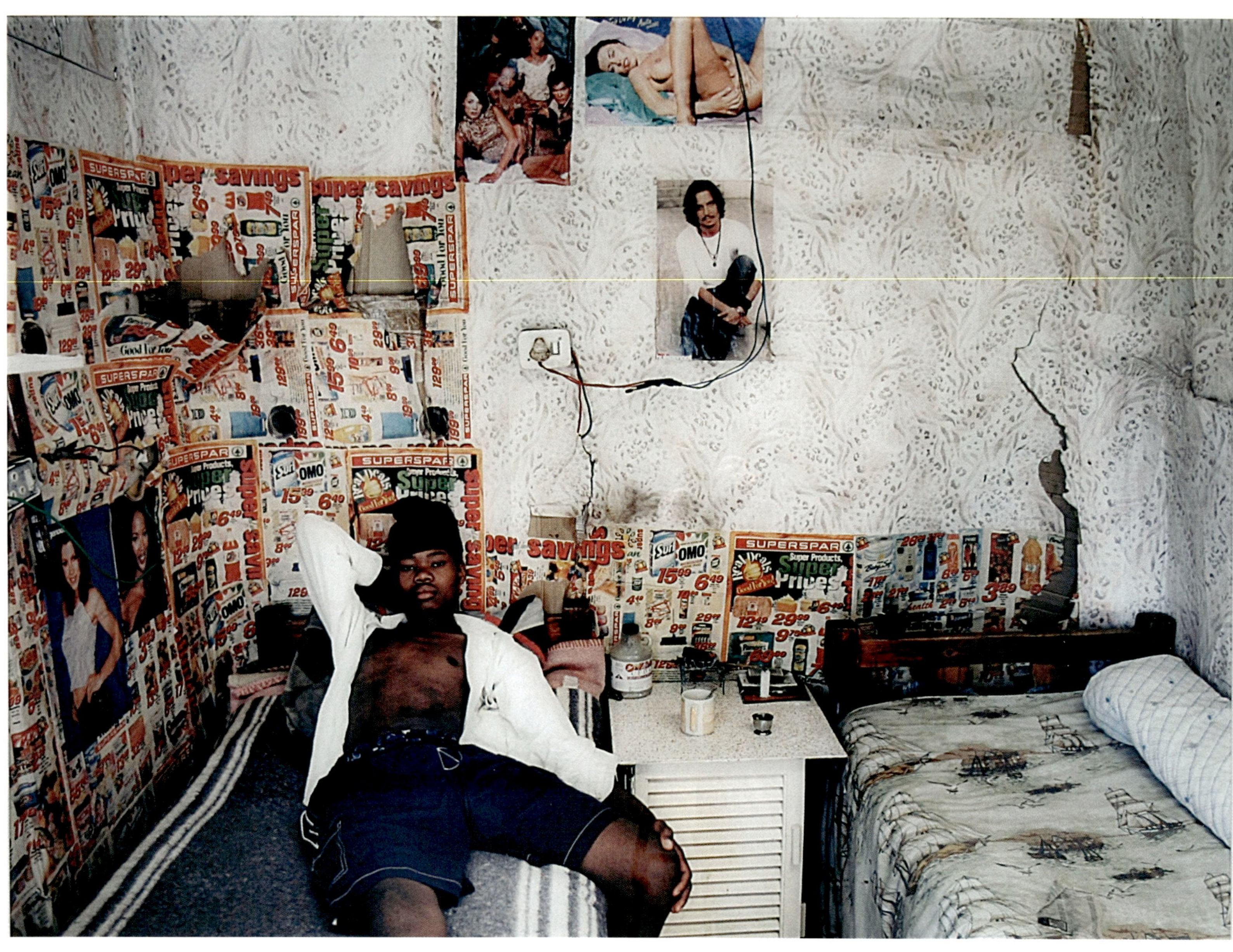

Untitled from *interior* series, 2006

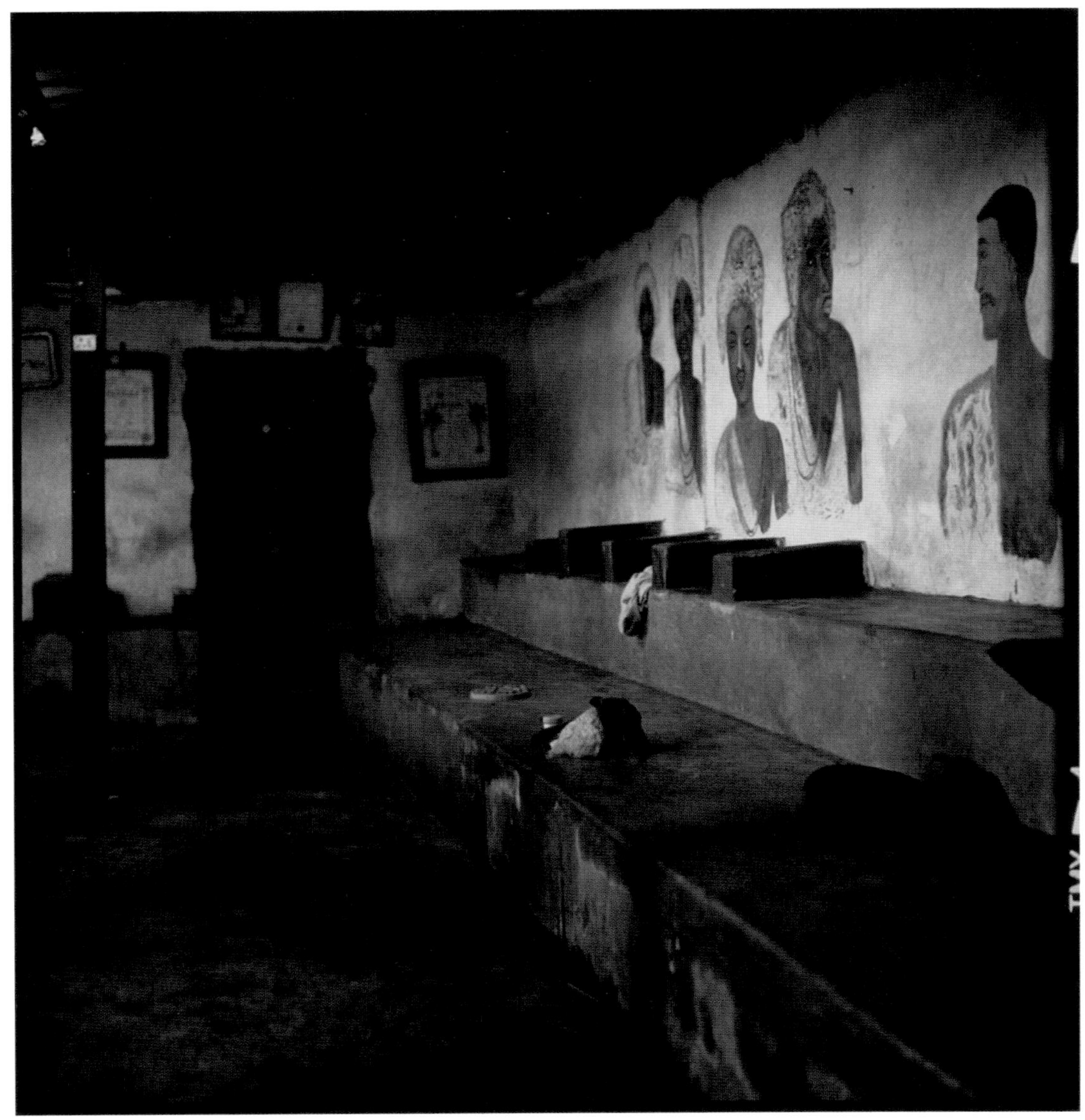

Ijeh, Lagos Island, Lagos from the series *Lagos. All Roads*, 1999

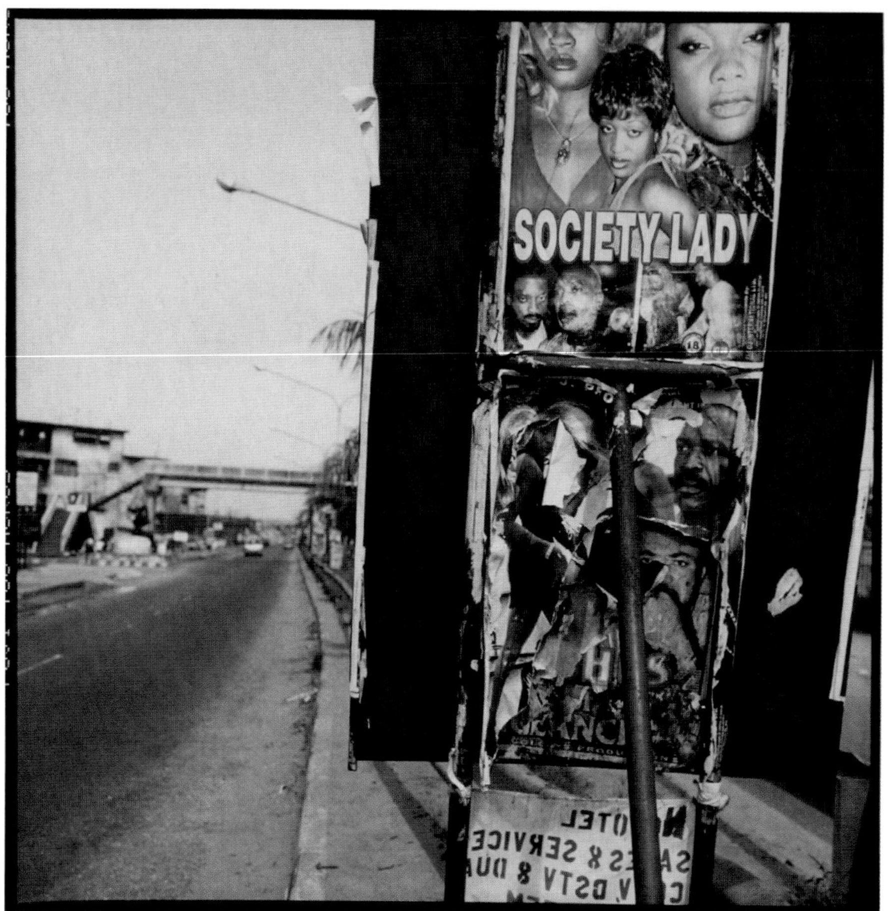

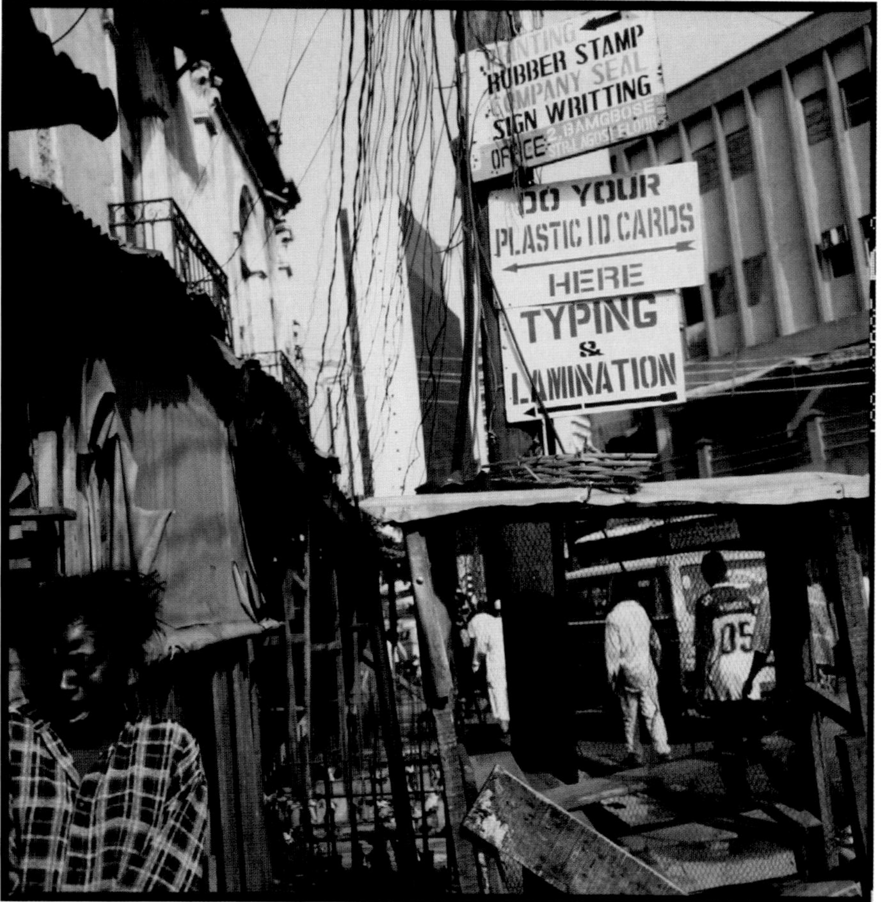

Surulere, Lagos from the series *Lagos. All Roads*, 2003   *Popo Aguda, Lagos Island, Lagos* from the series *Lagos. All Roads*, 2001

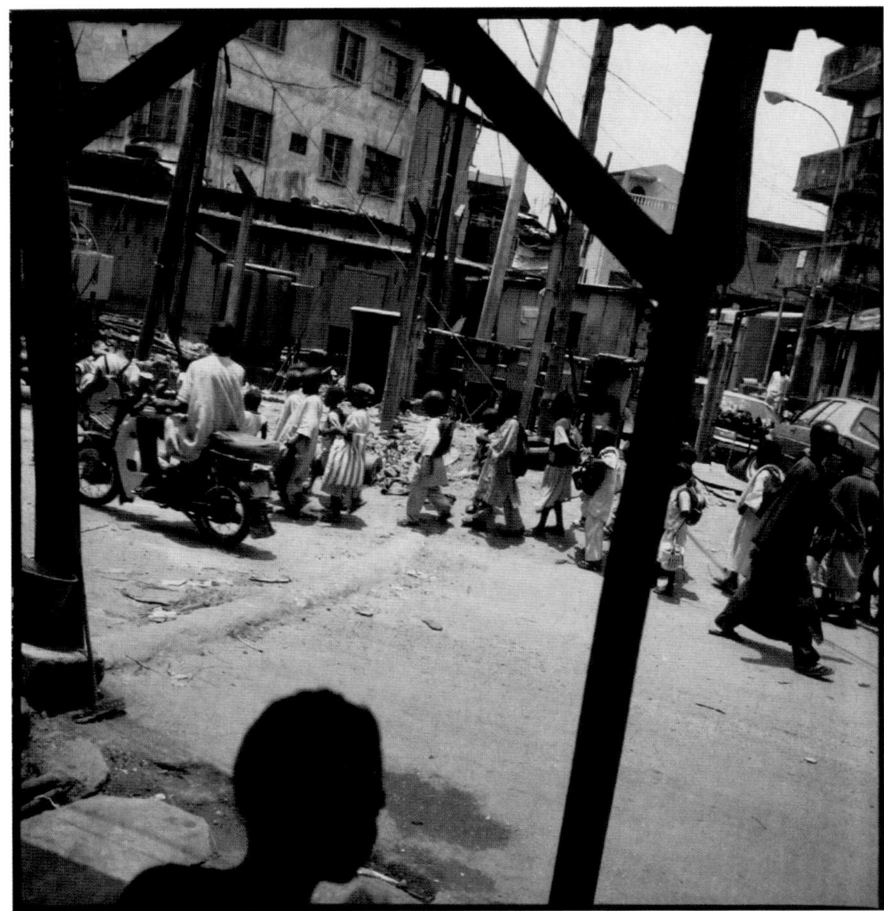

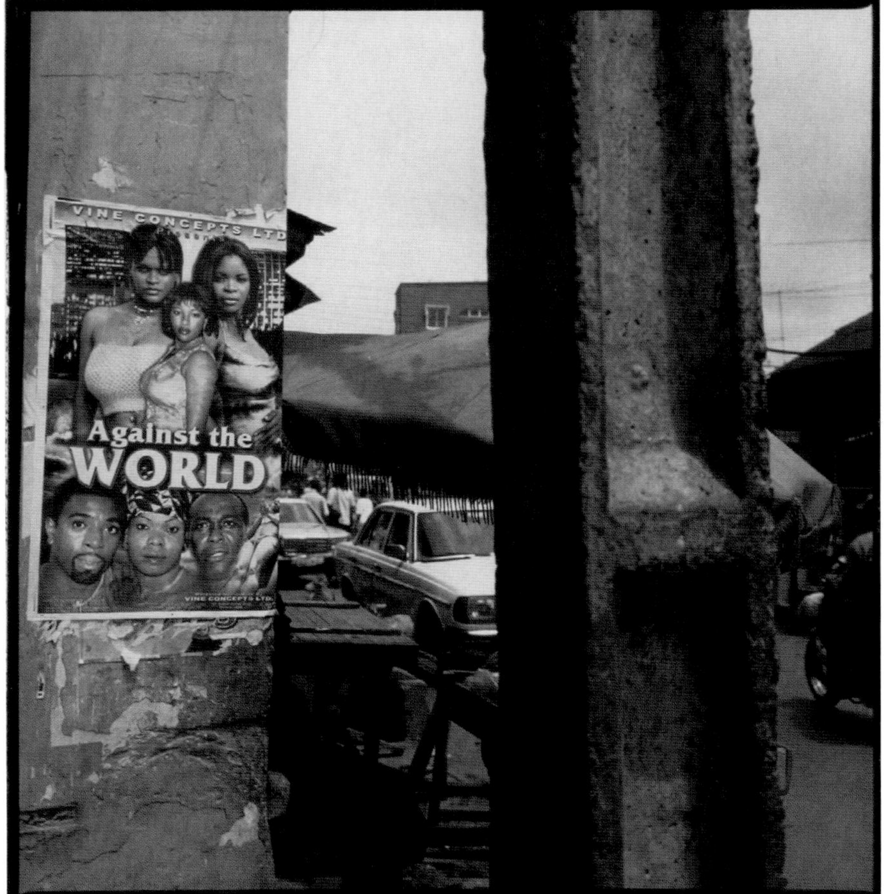

School Children, Lagos from the series *Lagos. All Roads*, 2001   *Popo Aguda, Lagos Island, Lagos* from the series *Lagos. All Roads*, 2001

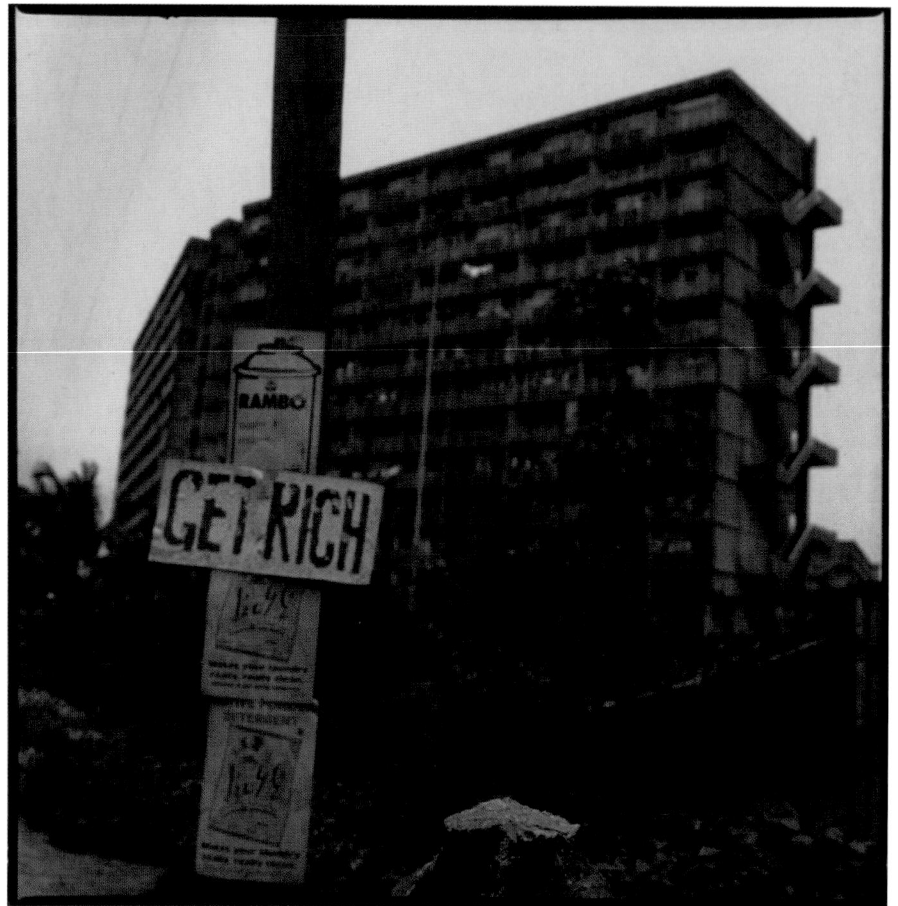

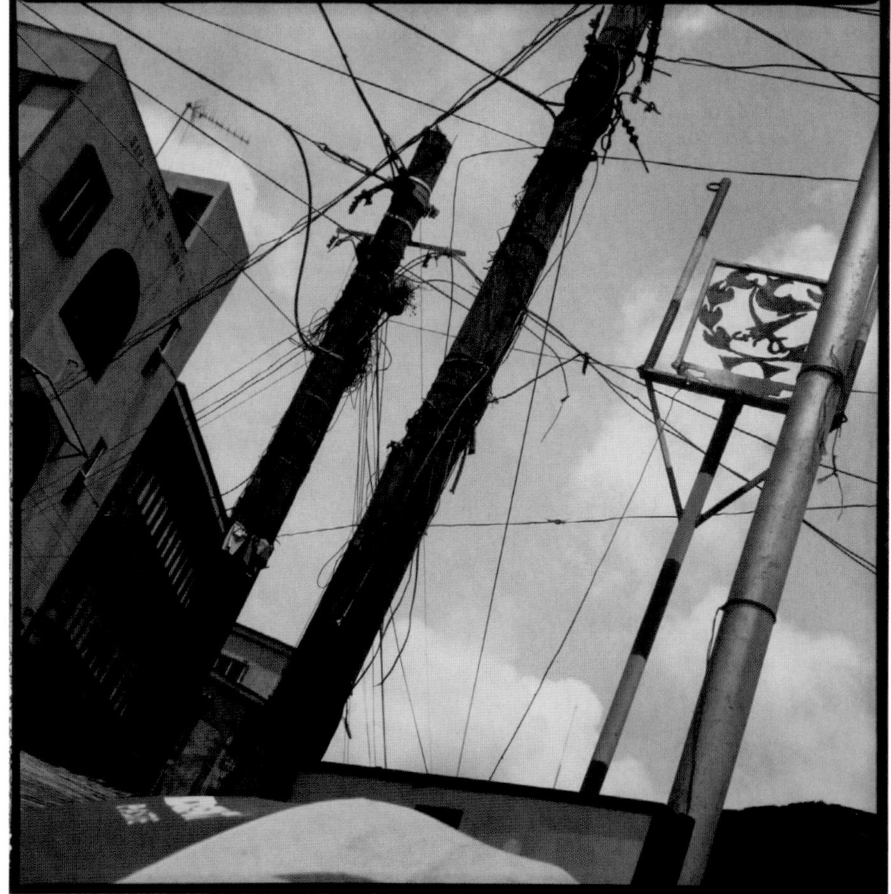

Victoria Island, Lagos from the series *Lagos. All Roads*, 2001   *Balogun, Lagos Island, Lagos* from the series *Lagos. All Roads*, 2001

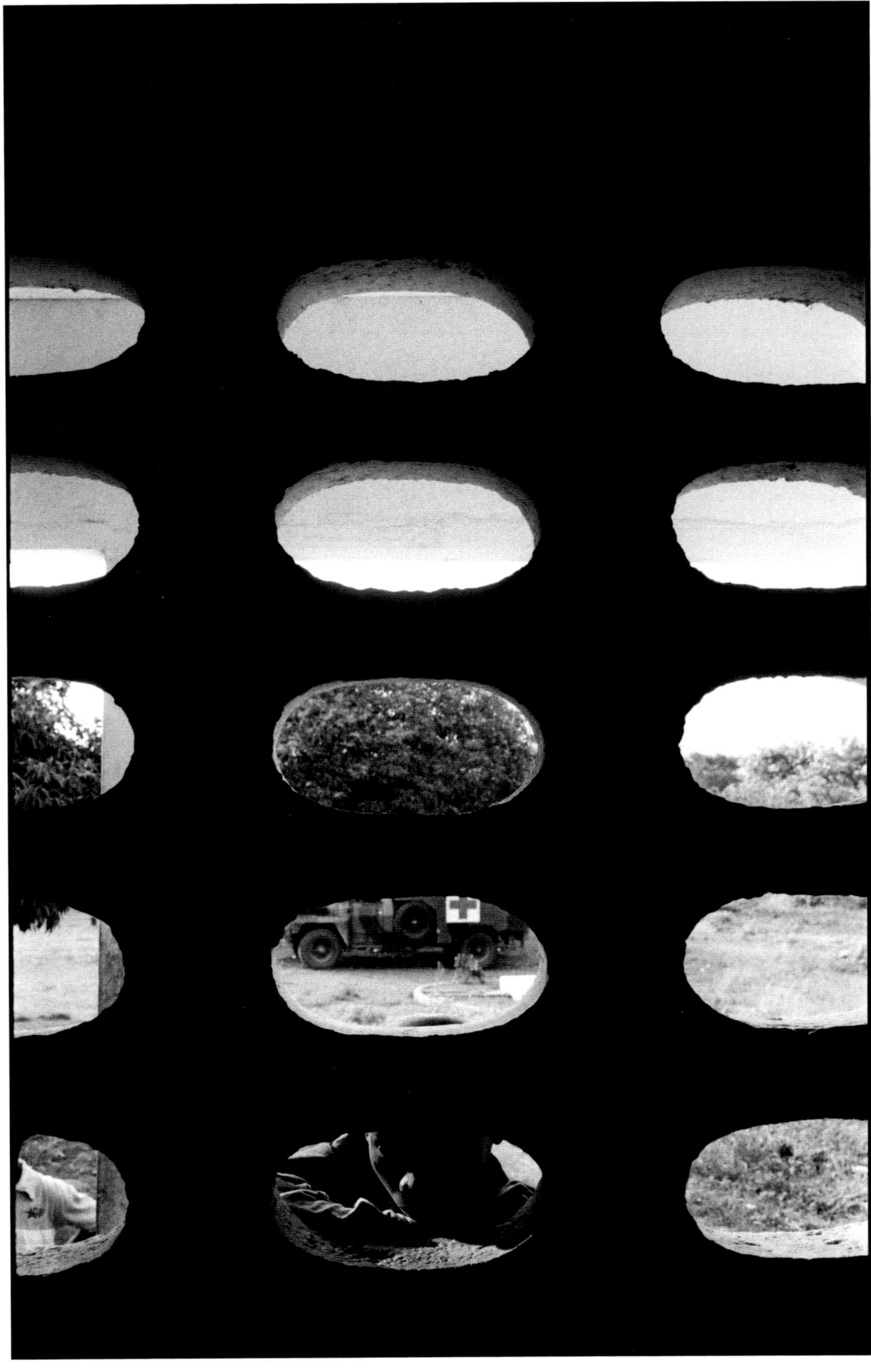

Côte d'Ivoire, zone ex-rebelle from the series *Embedded*, 2008

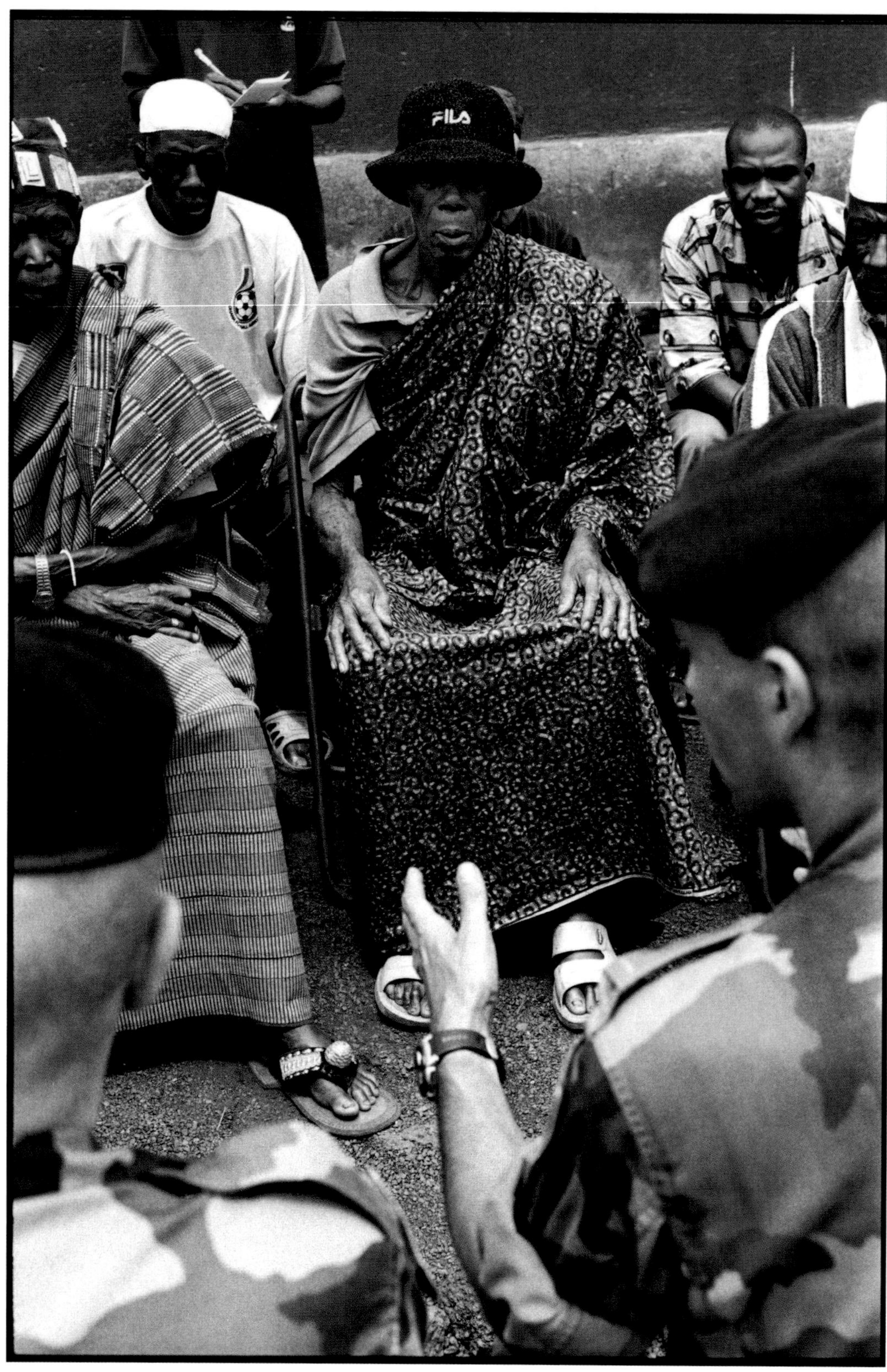

Côte d'Ivoire, zone ex-rebelle from the series *Embedded*, 2008

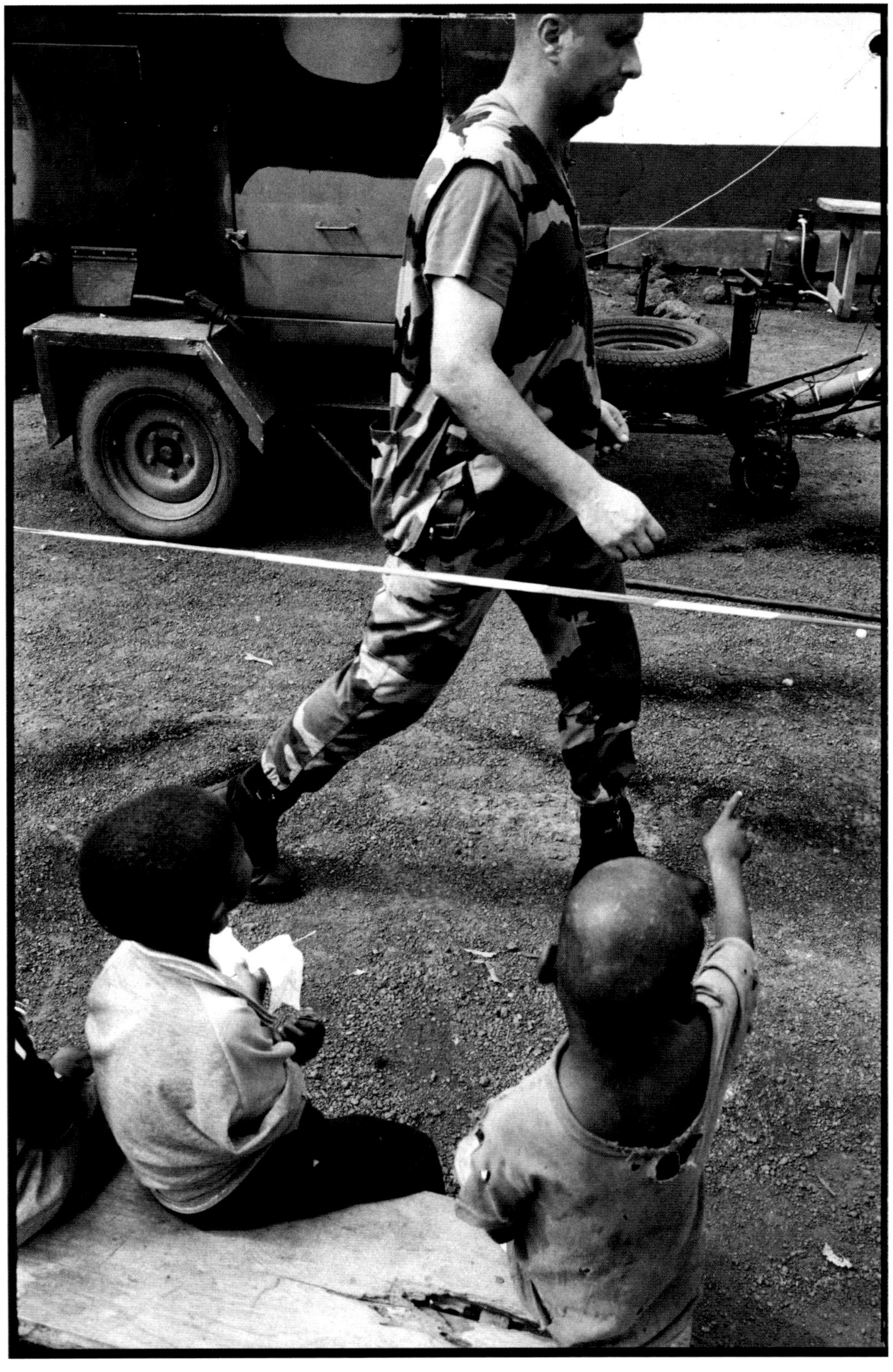

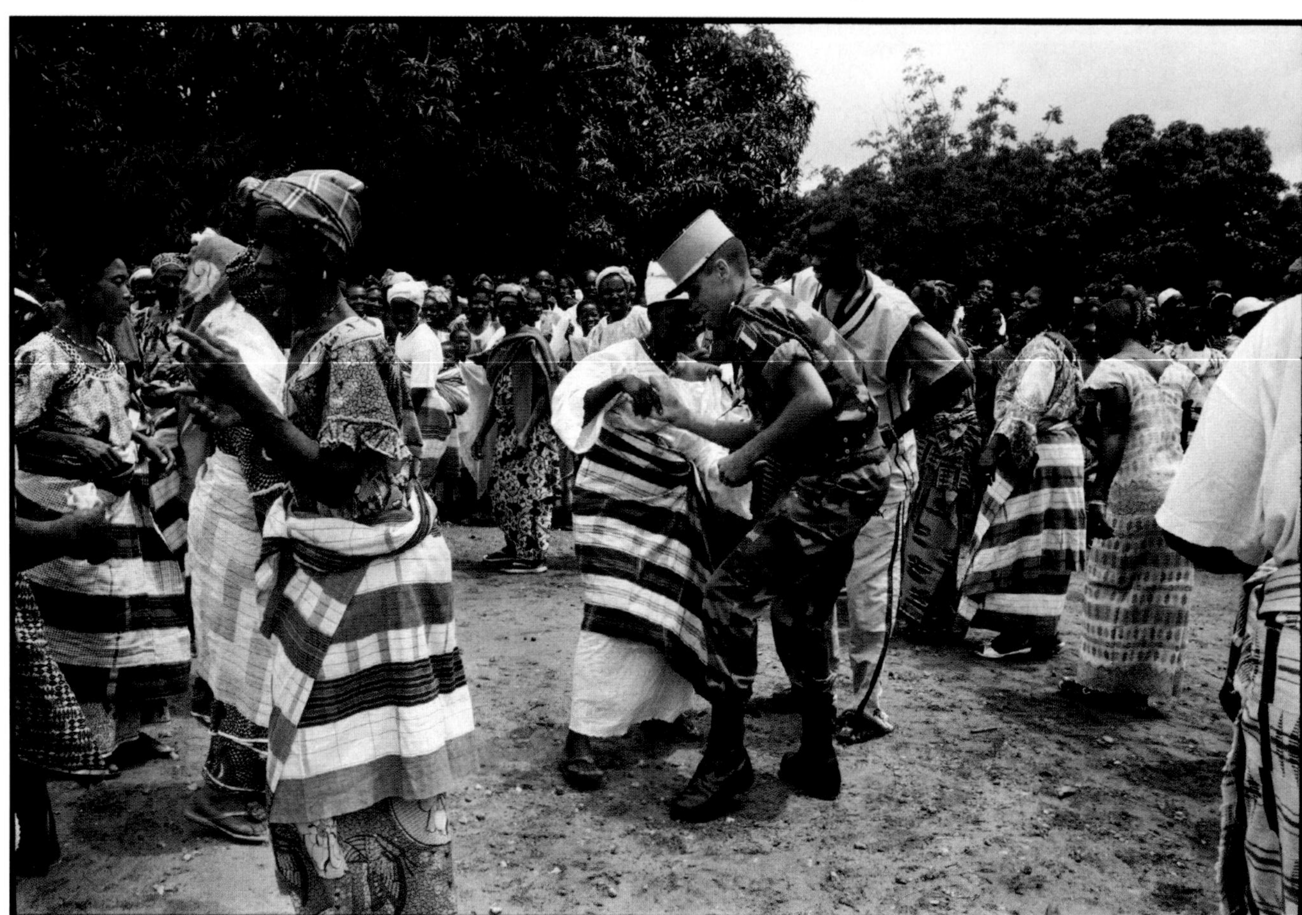

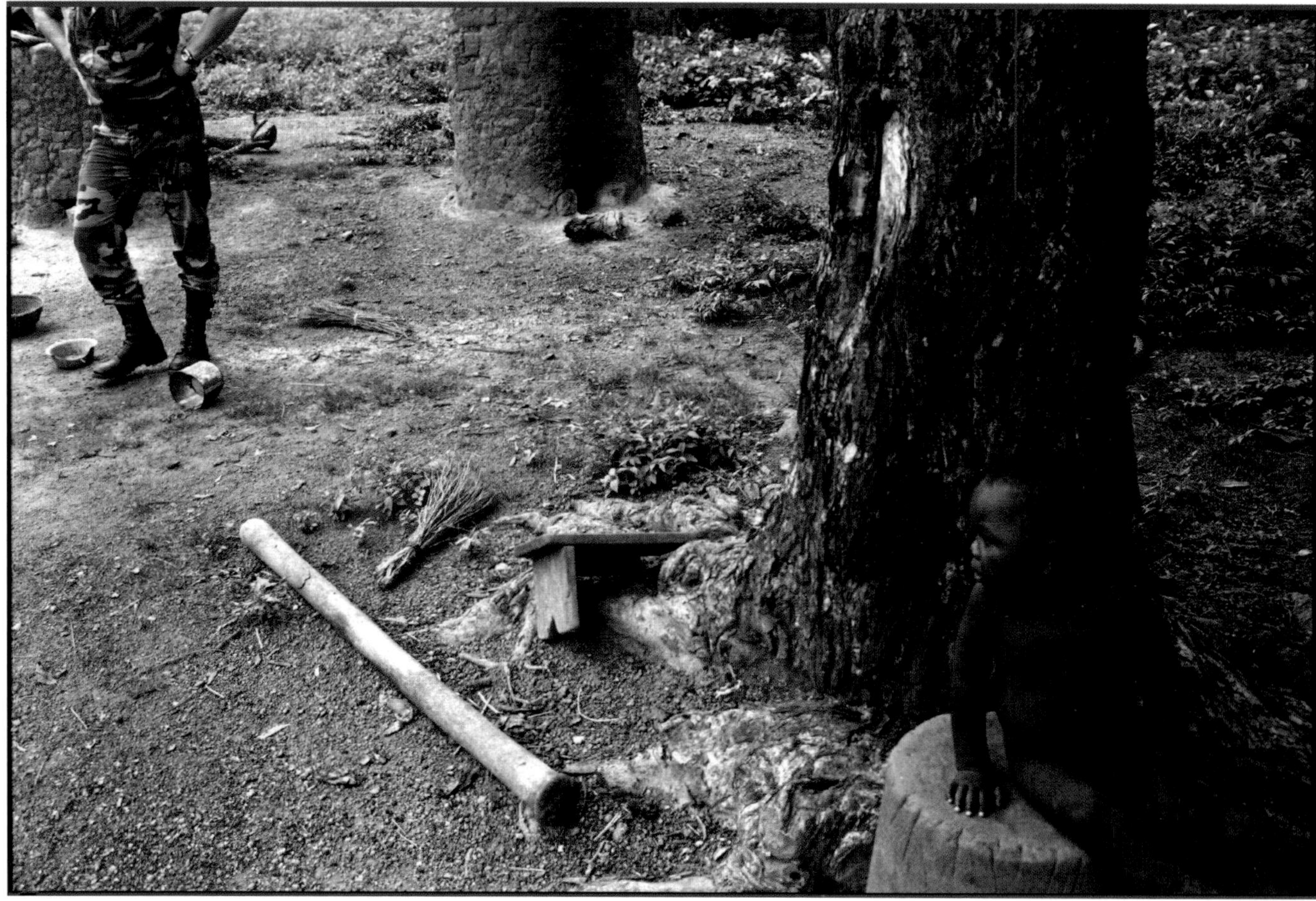

Côte d'Ivoire, zone ex-rebelle from the series *Embedded*, 2008

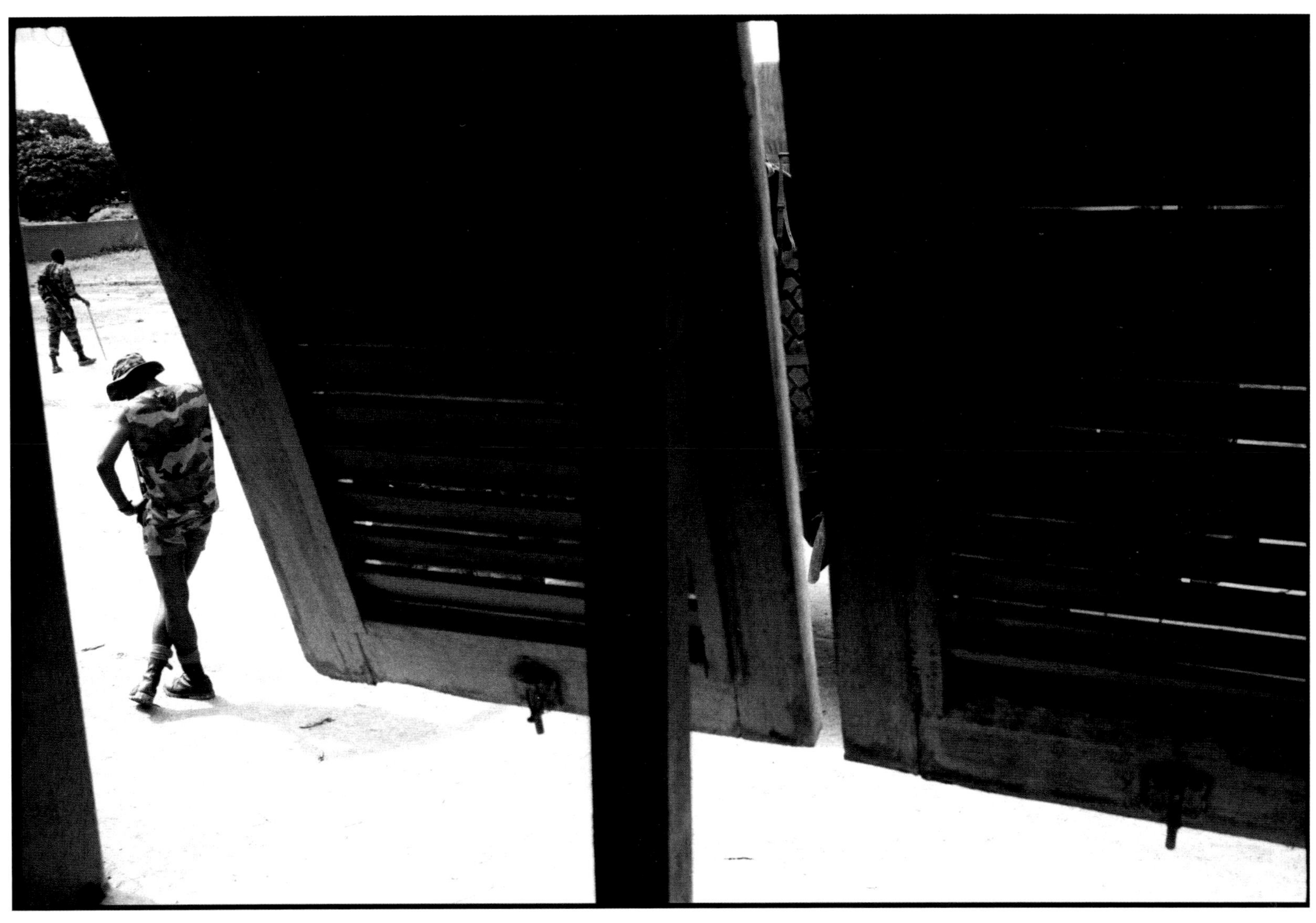

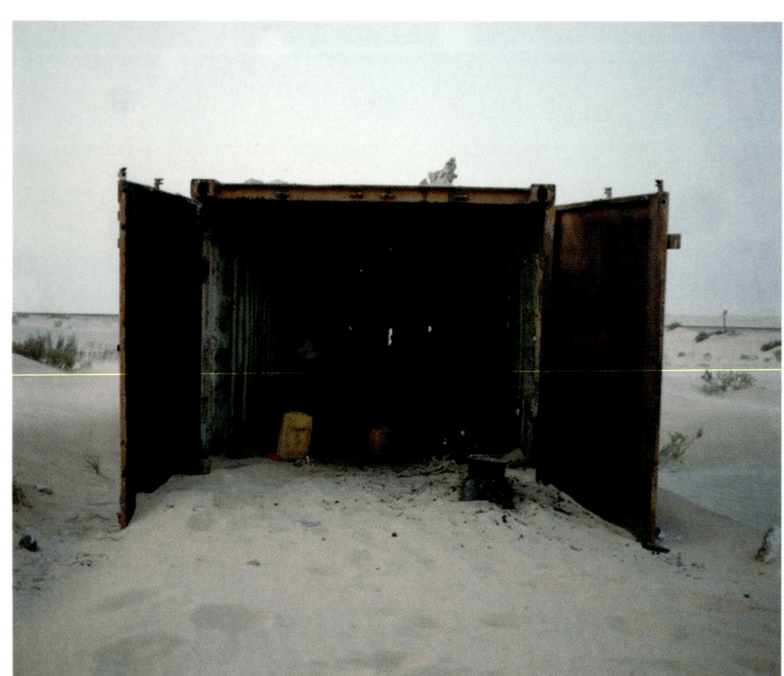

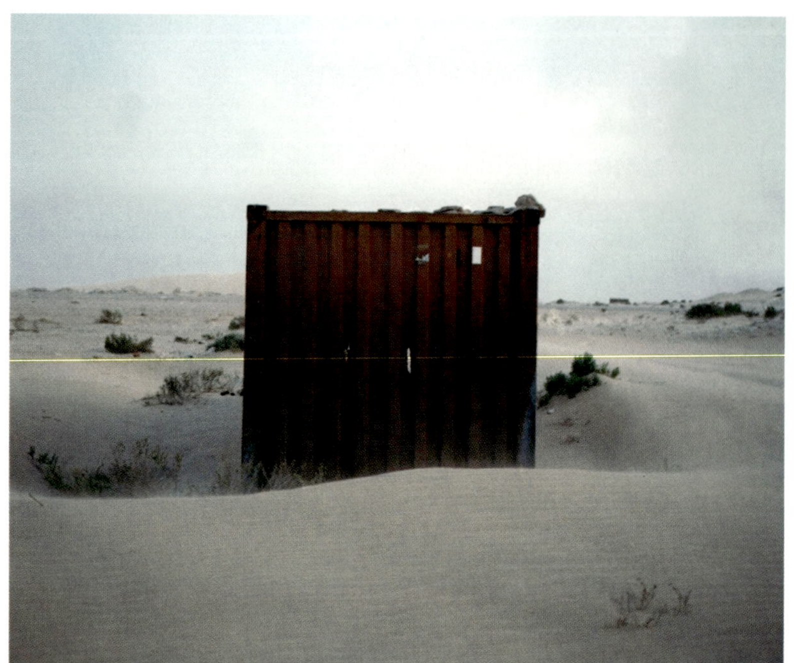

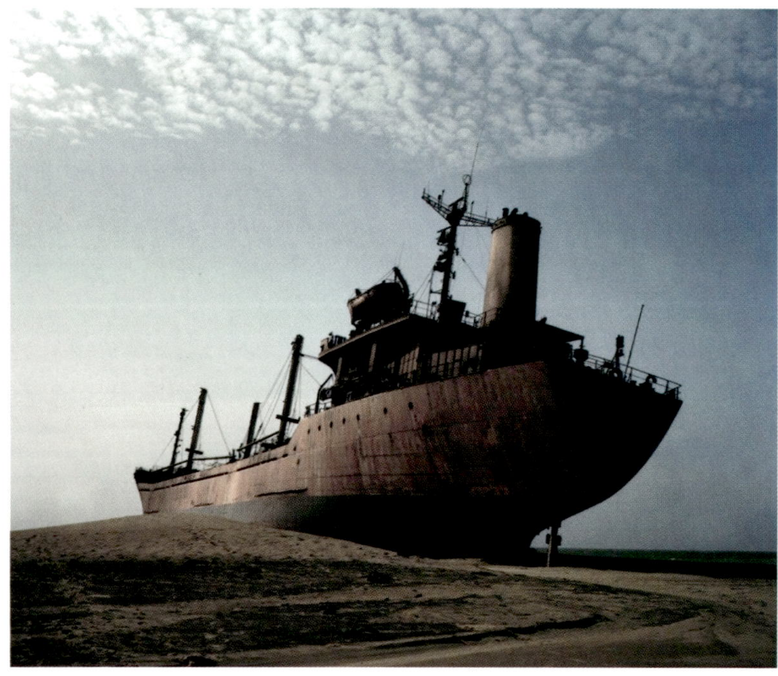

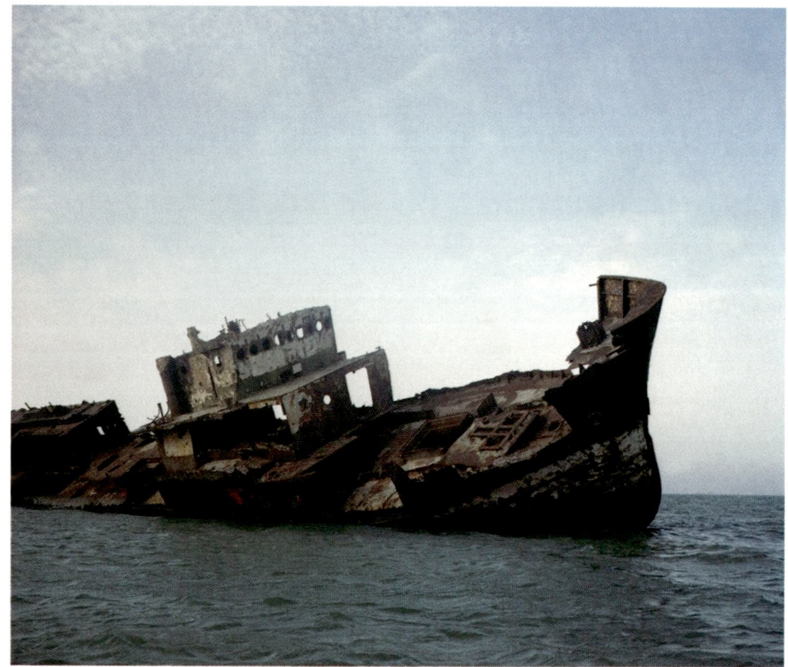

Reusable Spaces, 2008
Shipwreks 5, 2008

Reusable Spaces 2, 2008
Shipwreks 2, 2008

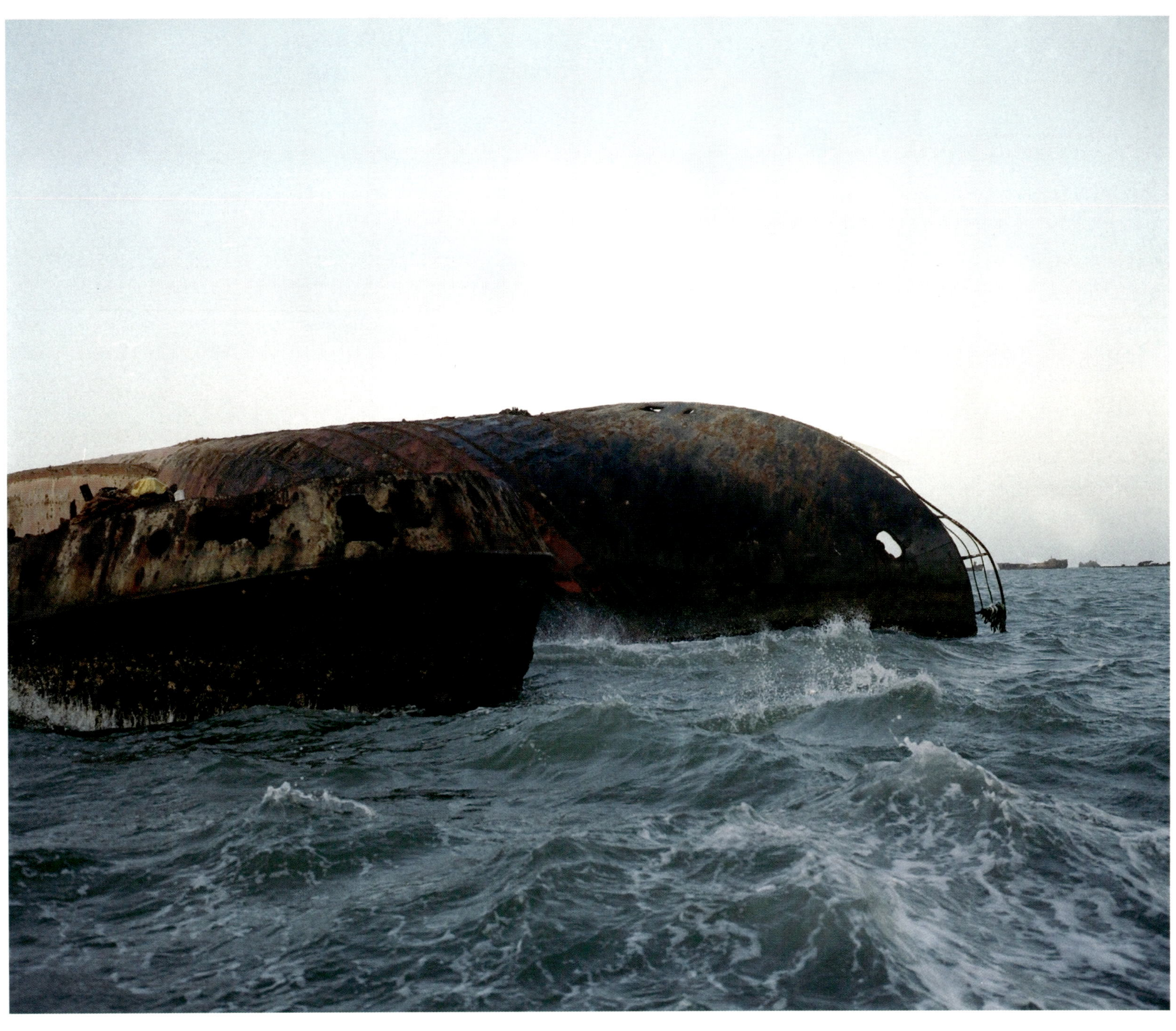

Shipwreks 1, 2008

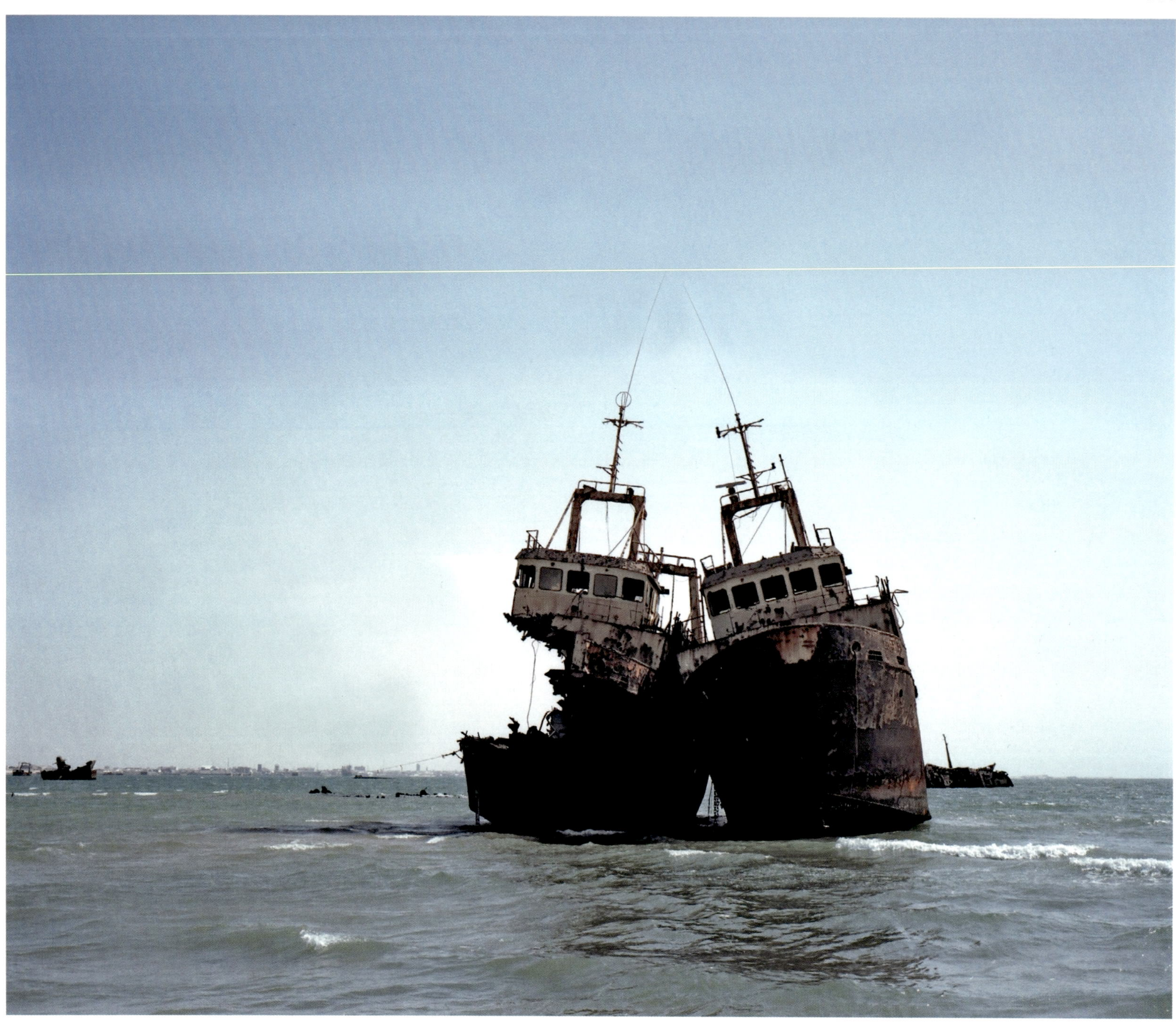

The lovers, 2008

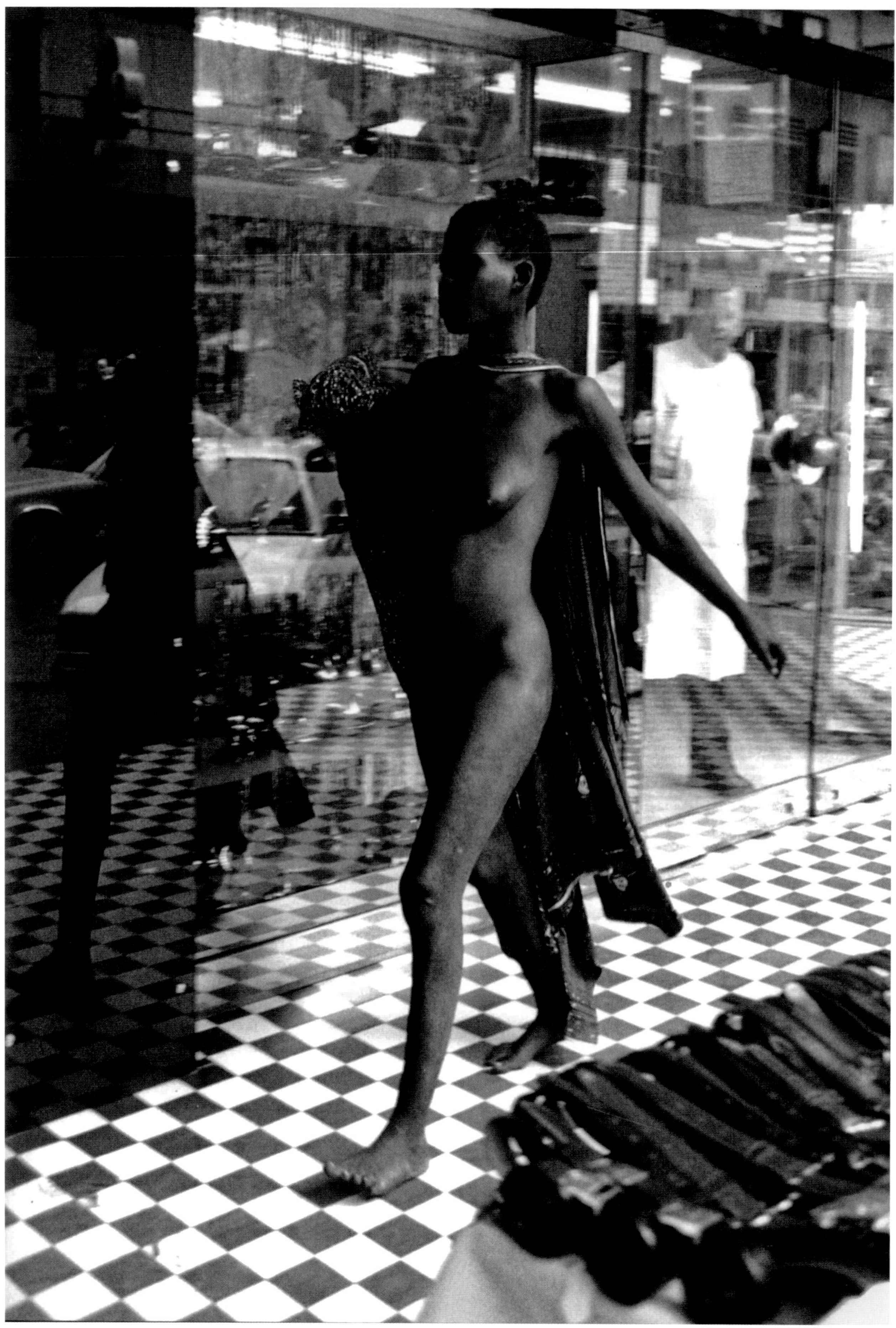

No name
in the street[*]
1990 1999

* James Baldwin

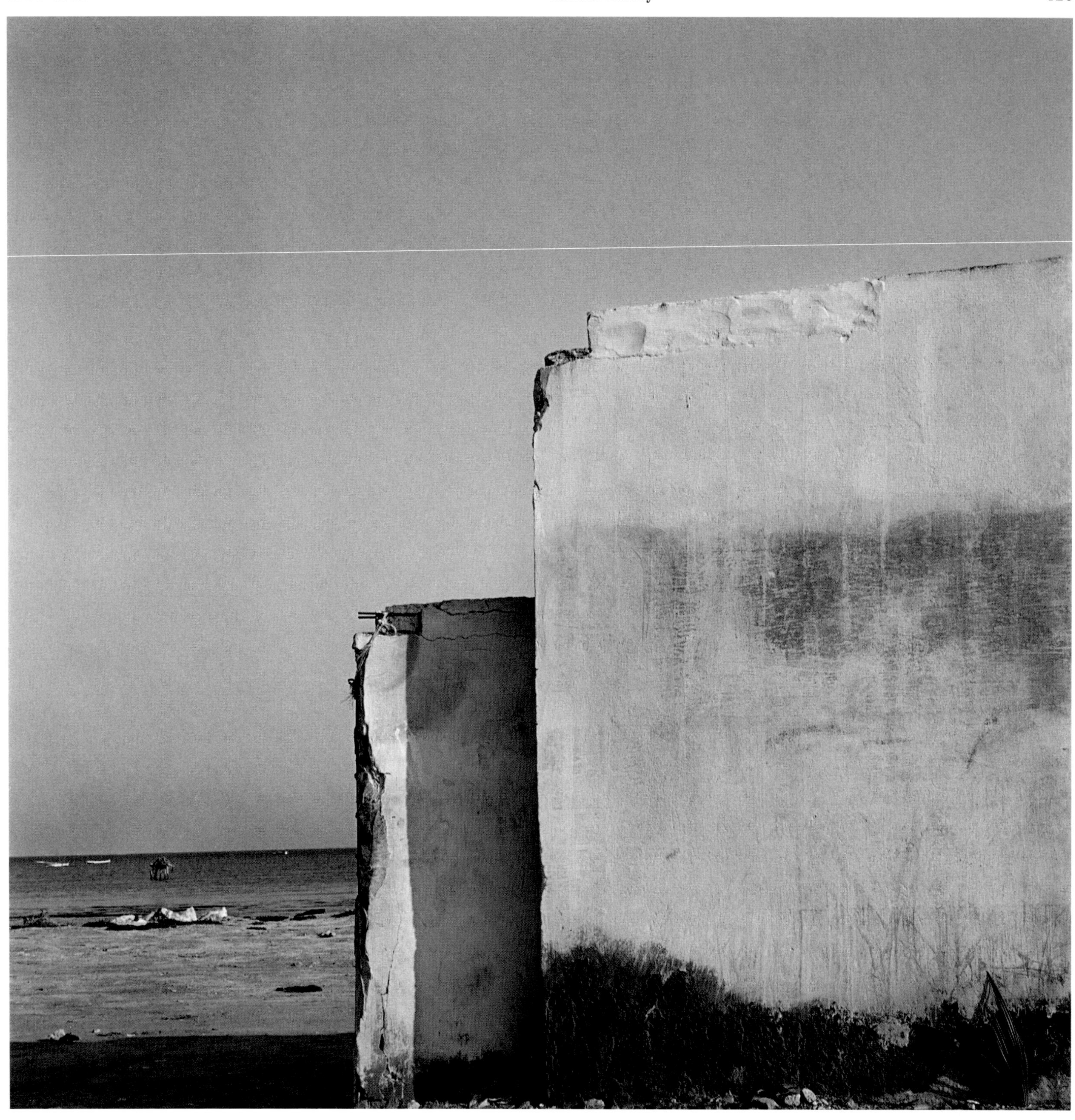

from the series *Murmurer*, 2007

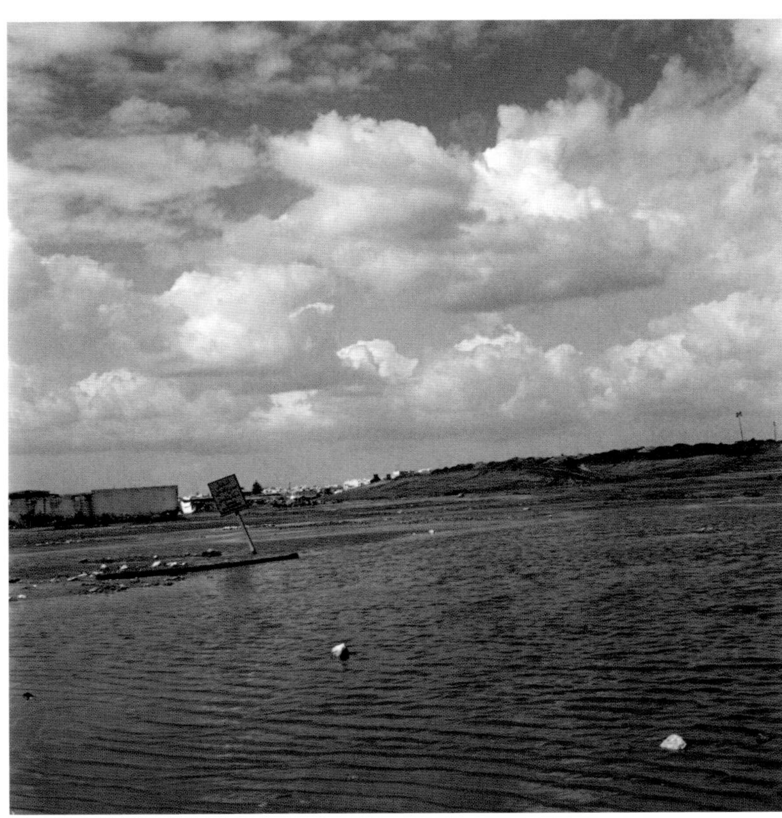

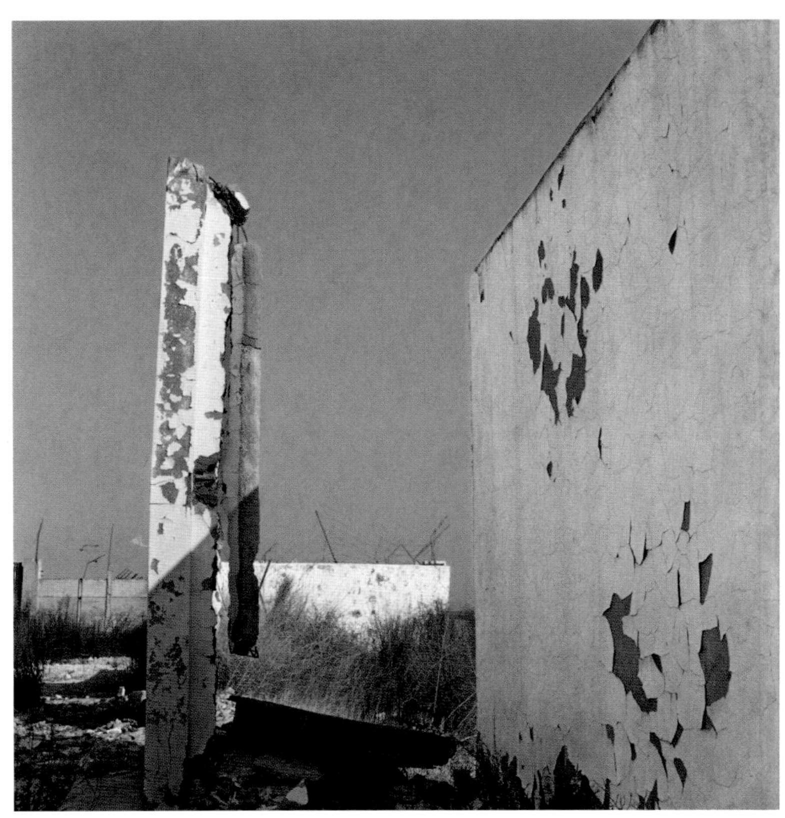

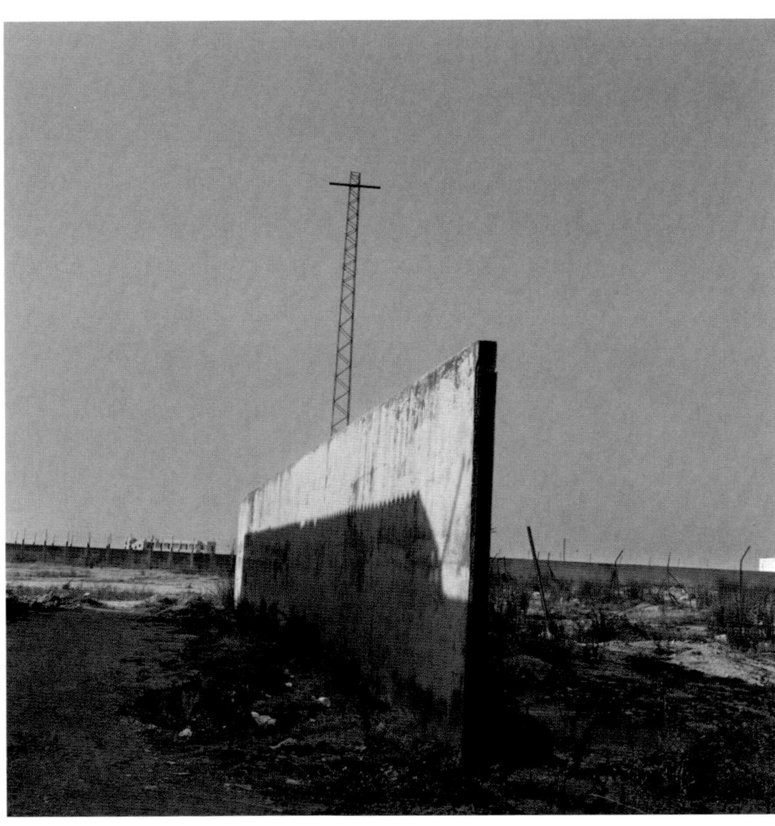

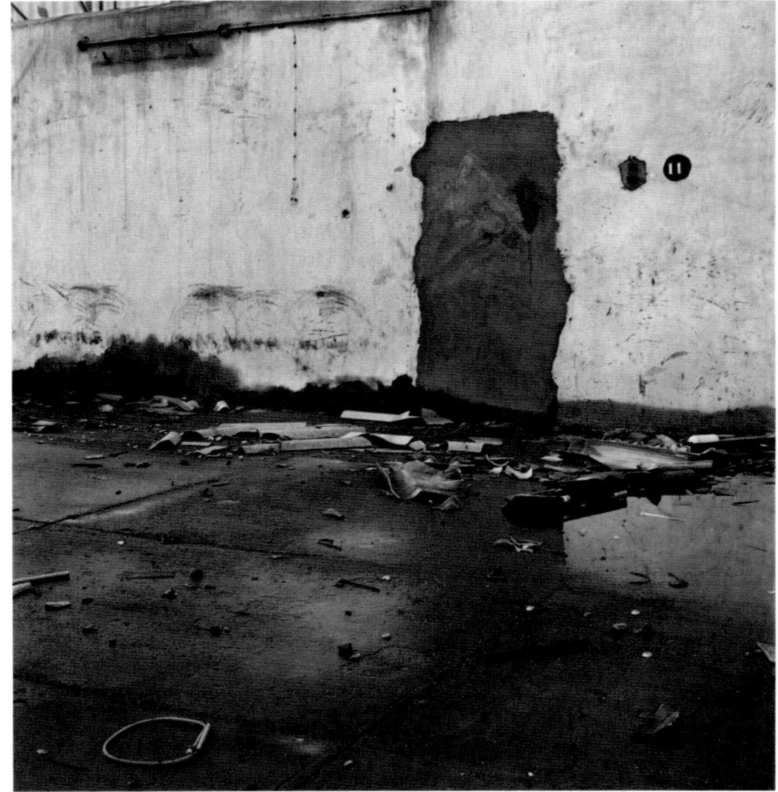

from the series *Murmurer*, 2007

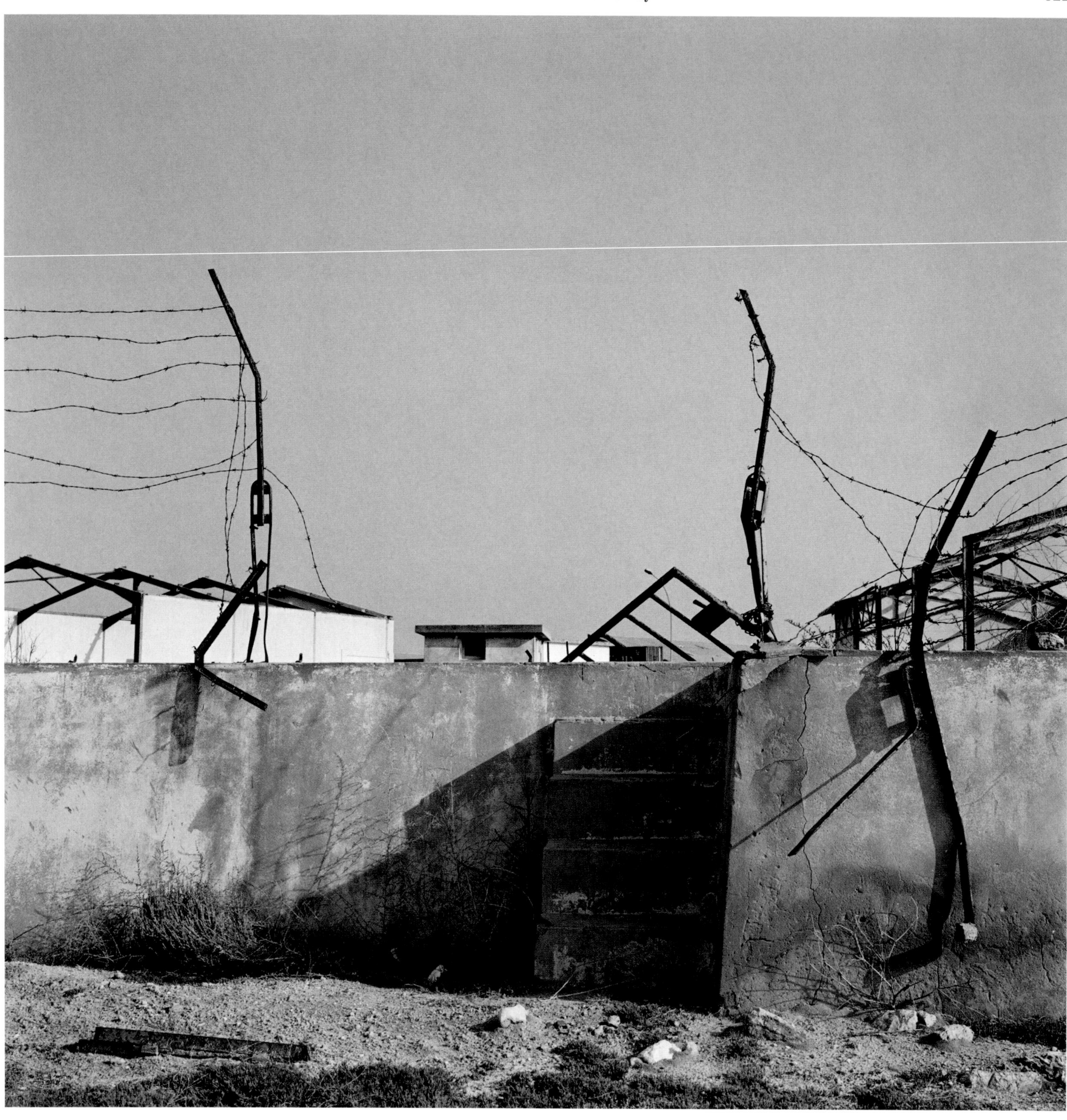

from the series *Murmurer*, 2007

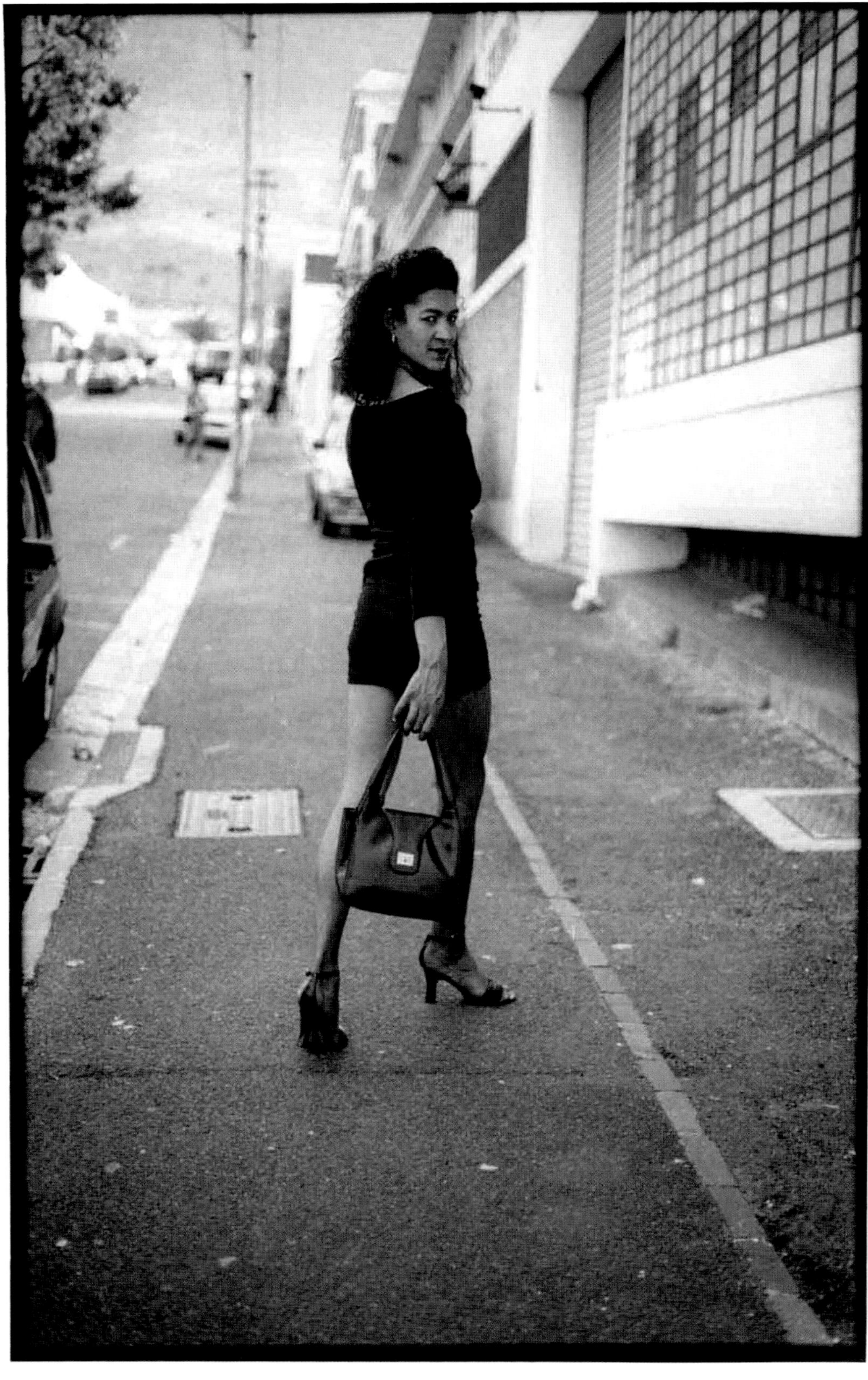

Basha in Woodstock from the series *Basic Necessity*, 1997

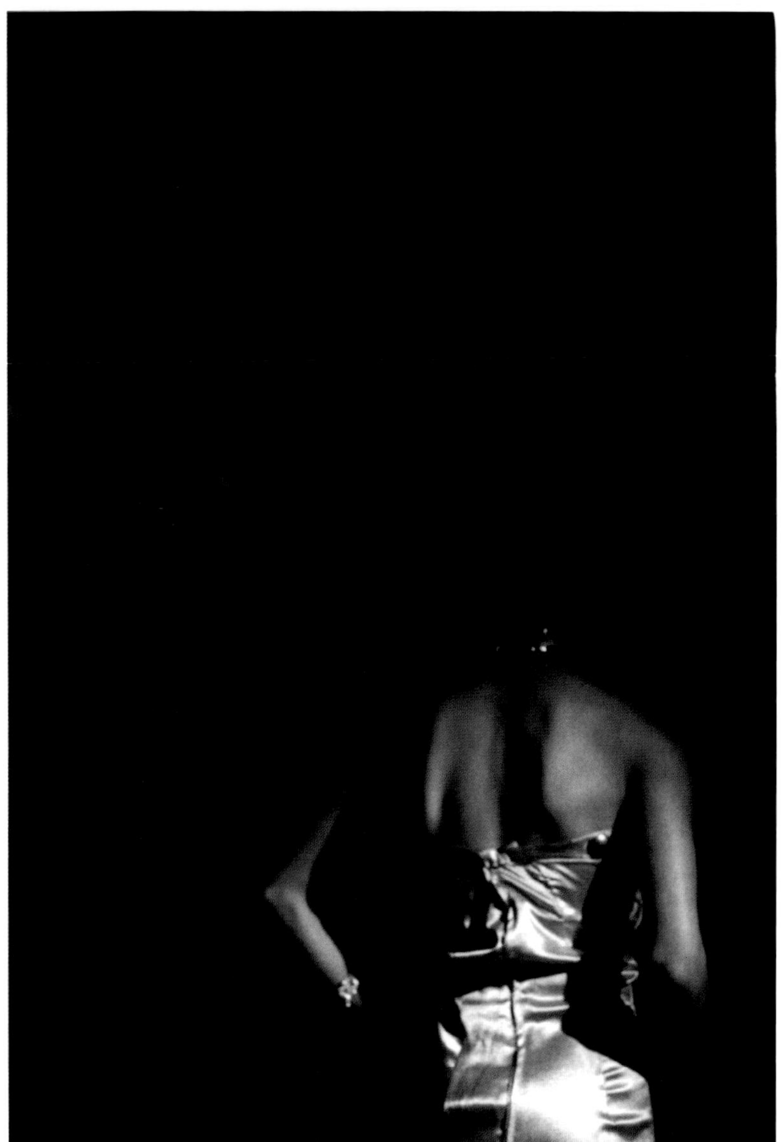

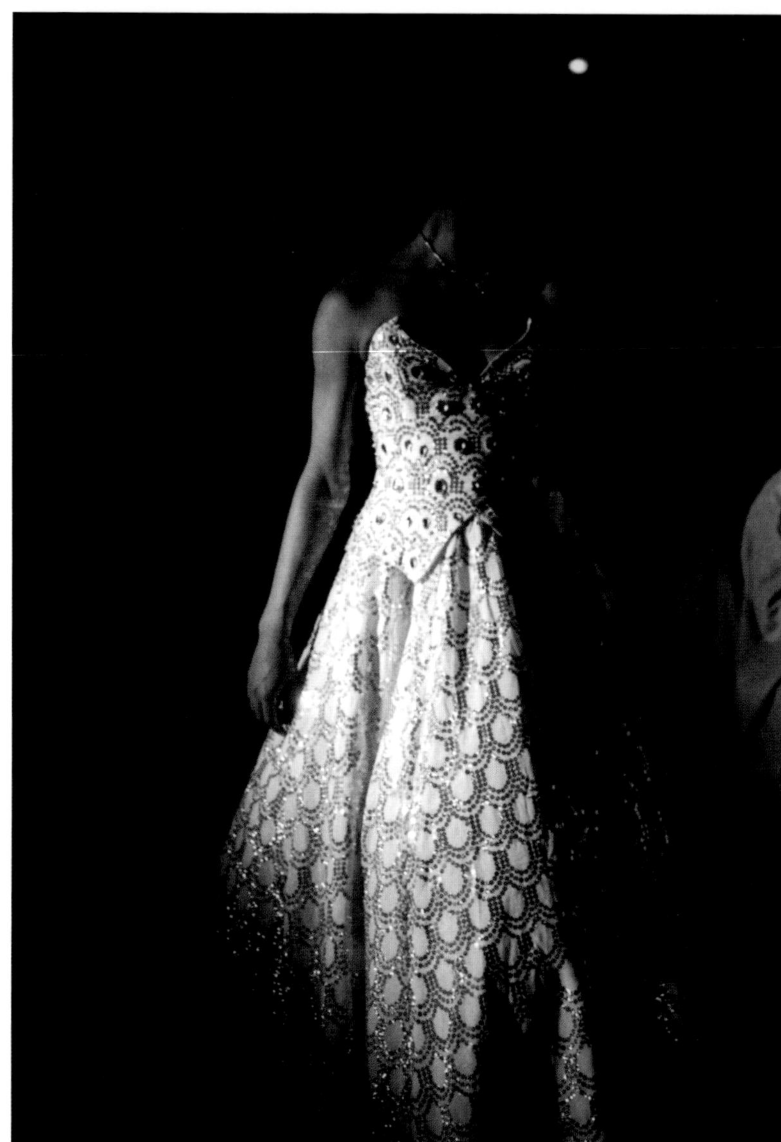

Miss Gay Hollywood Look a-like Competition from the series
Basic Necessity, 1997

Miss Gay Hollywood Look a-like Competition 2 from the series
Basic Necessity, 1997

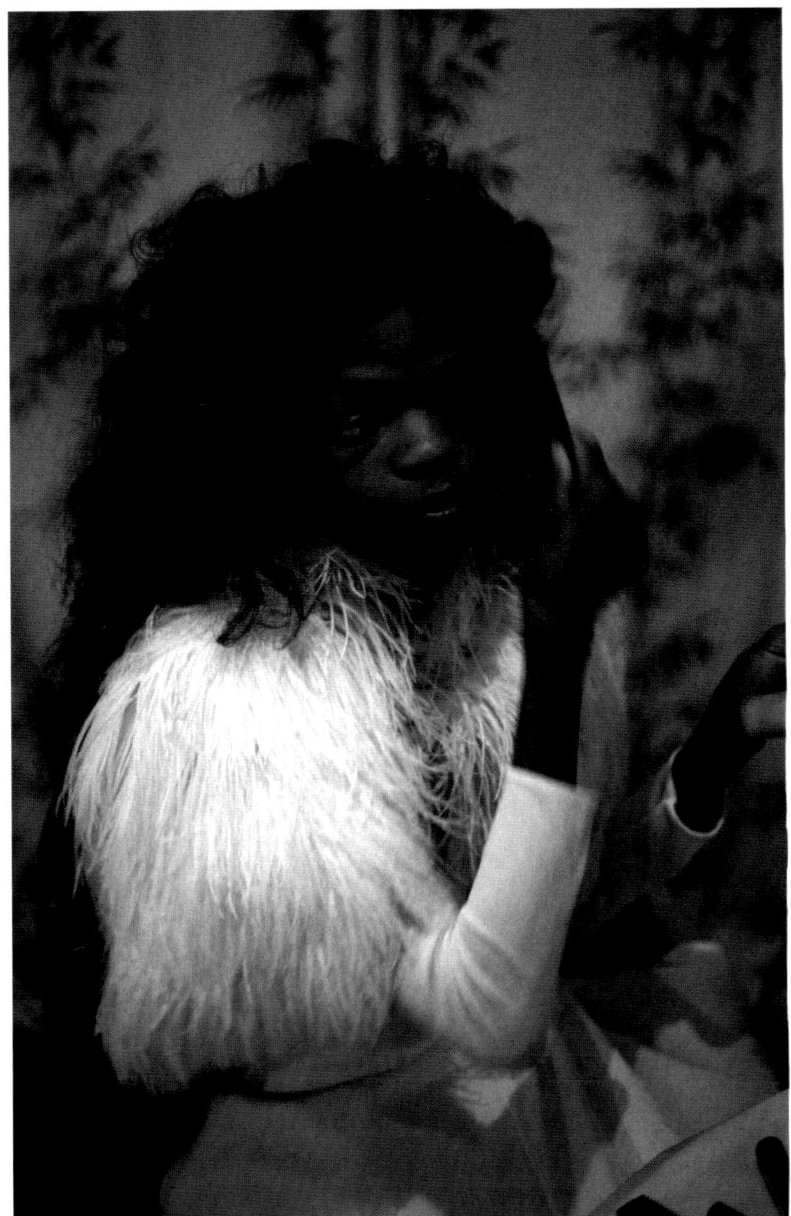

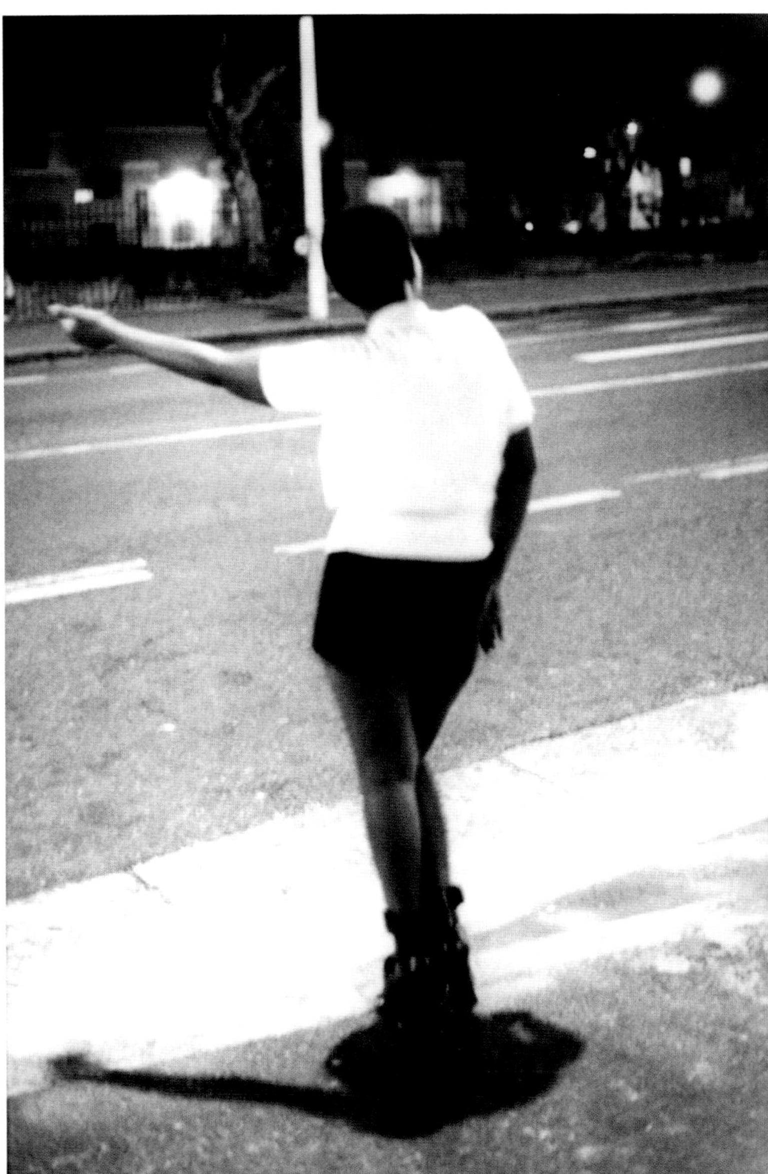

Peter preparing for Wjore's ball from the series *Basic Necessity*, 1998   *Rachel, Salt River Main Road* from the series *Basic Necessity*, 1998

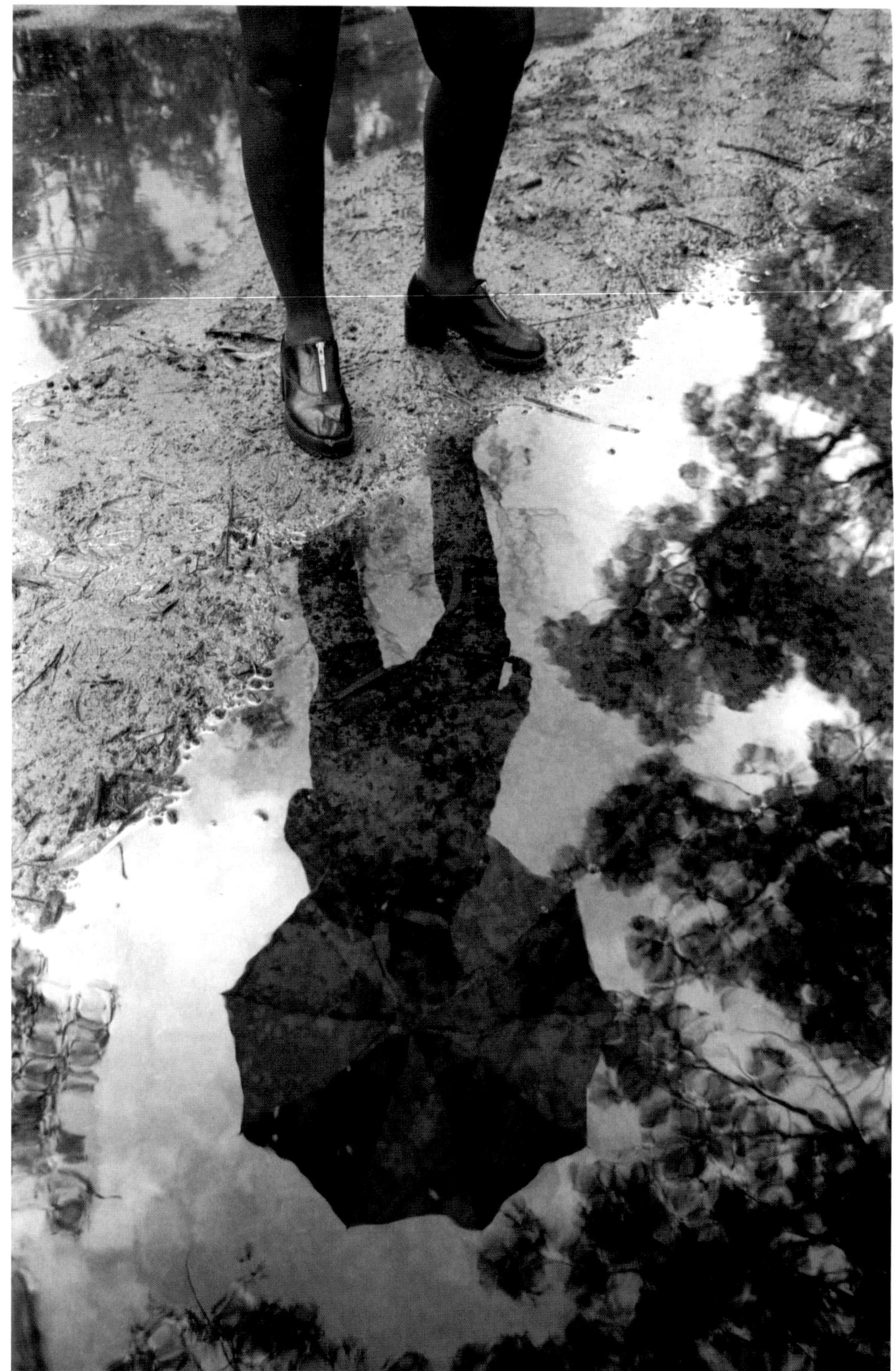

Van Schoorsdrift, N7 highway from the series *Basic Necessity*, 1998

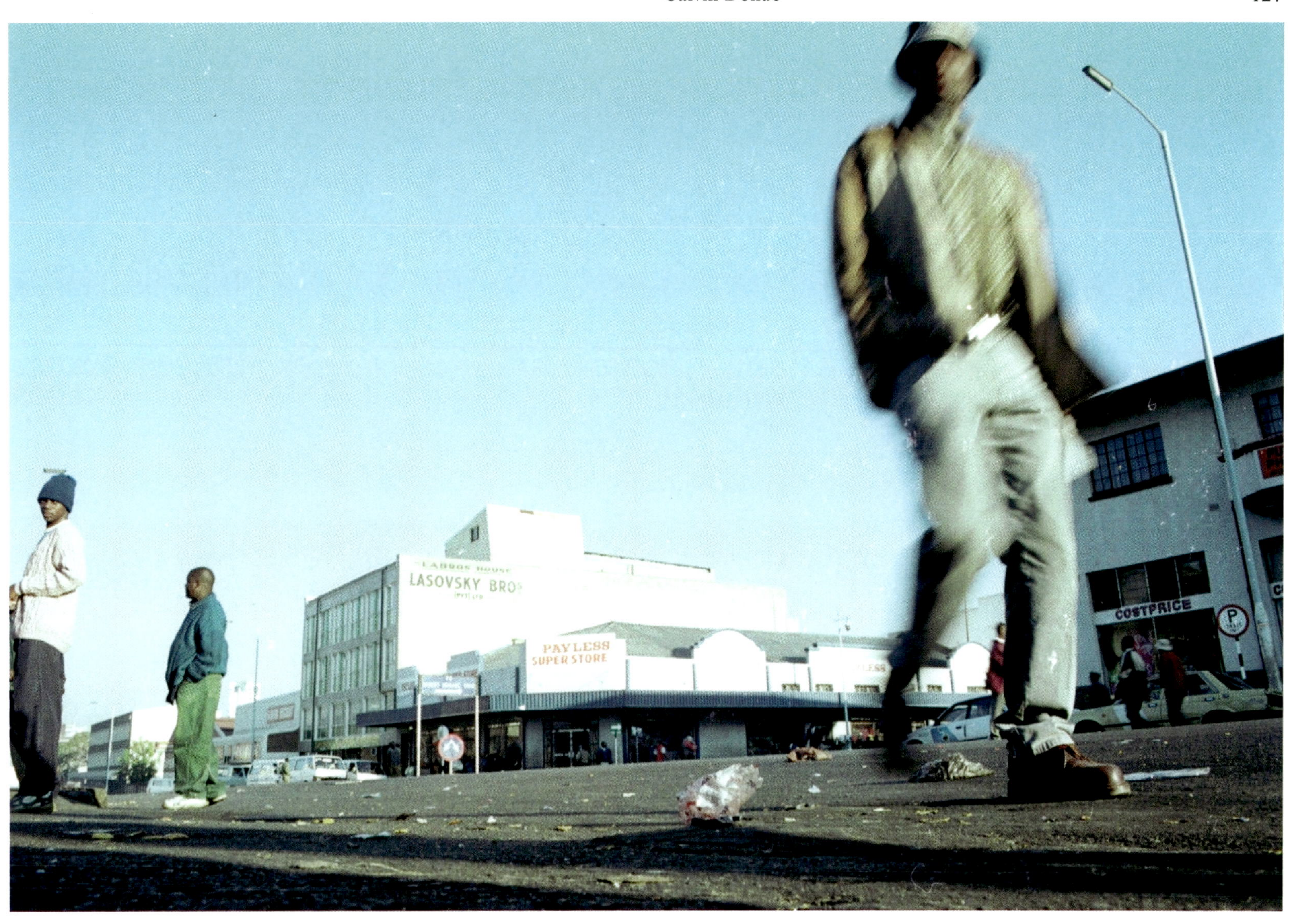

from the series *Harare street*, 2000

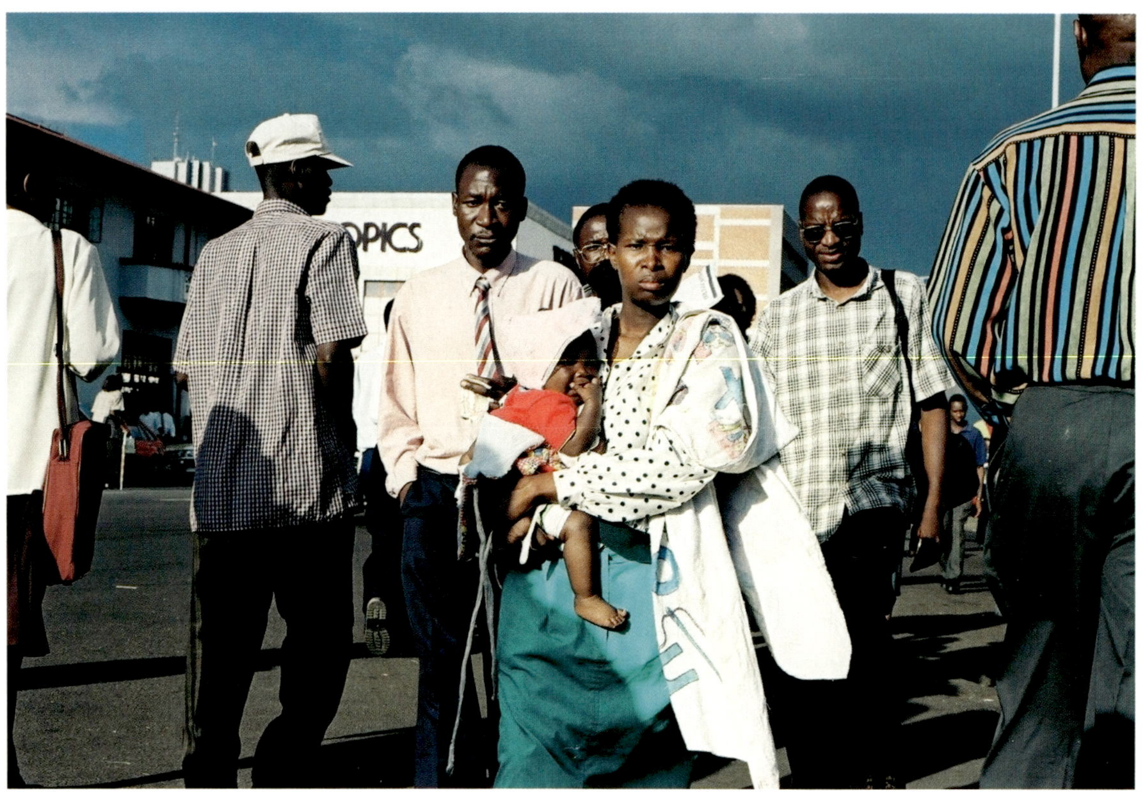

from the series *Harare street*, 2000

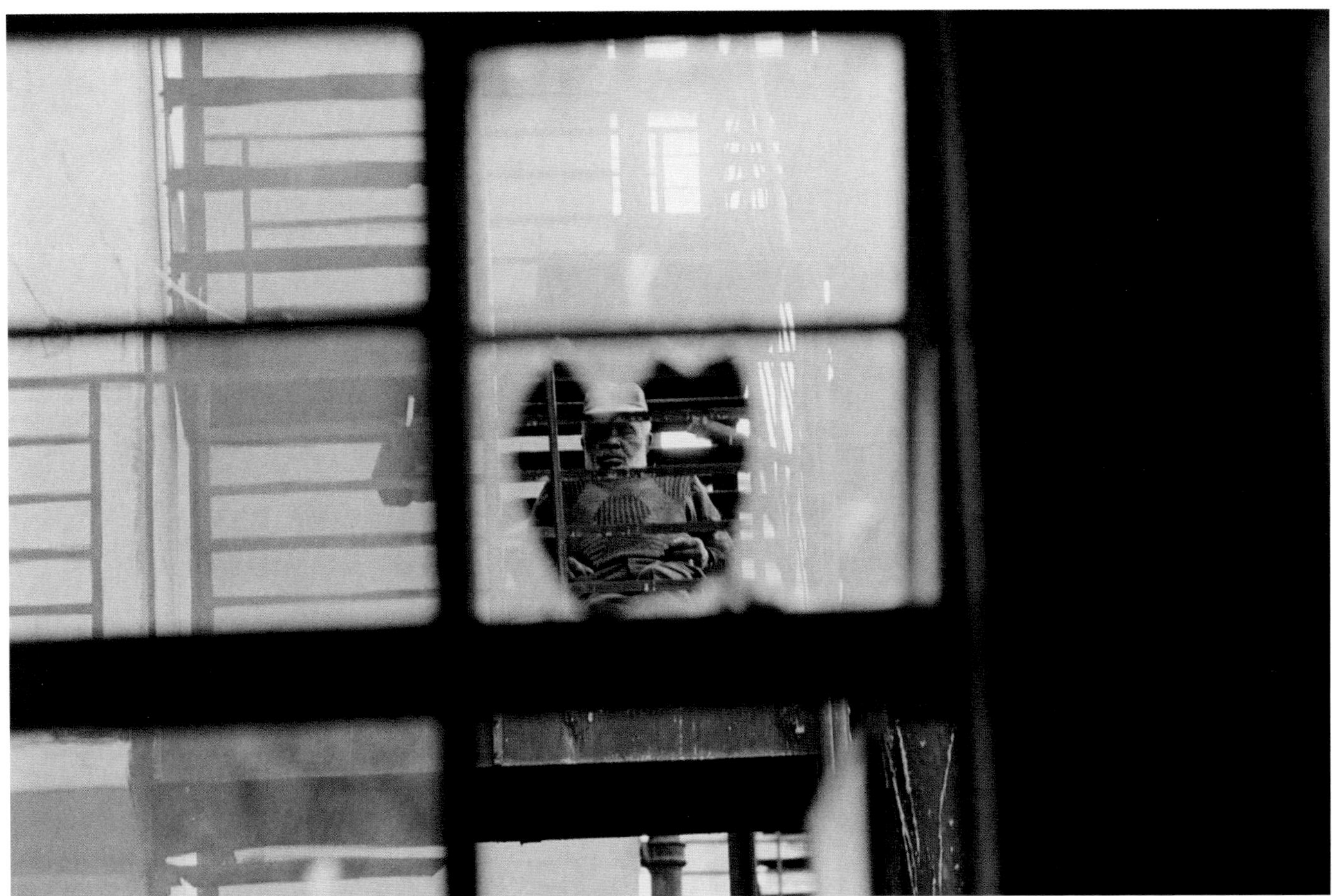

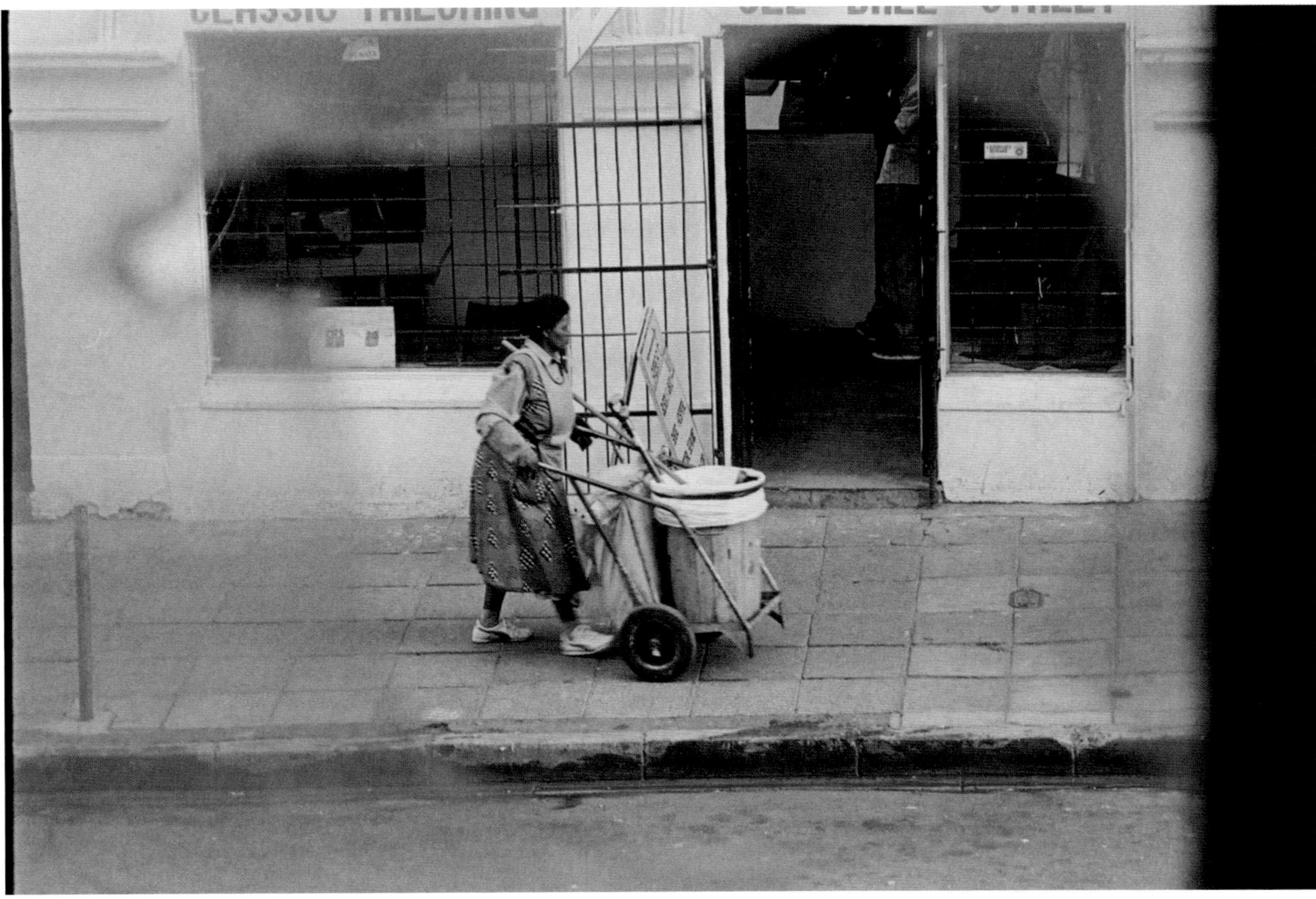

Broken Flat Window Old Man, 2004   *Classic Tailoring*, 2004

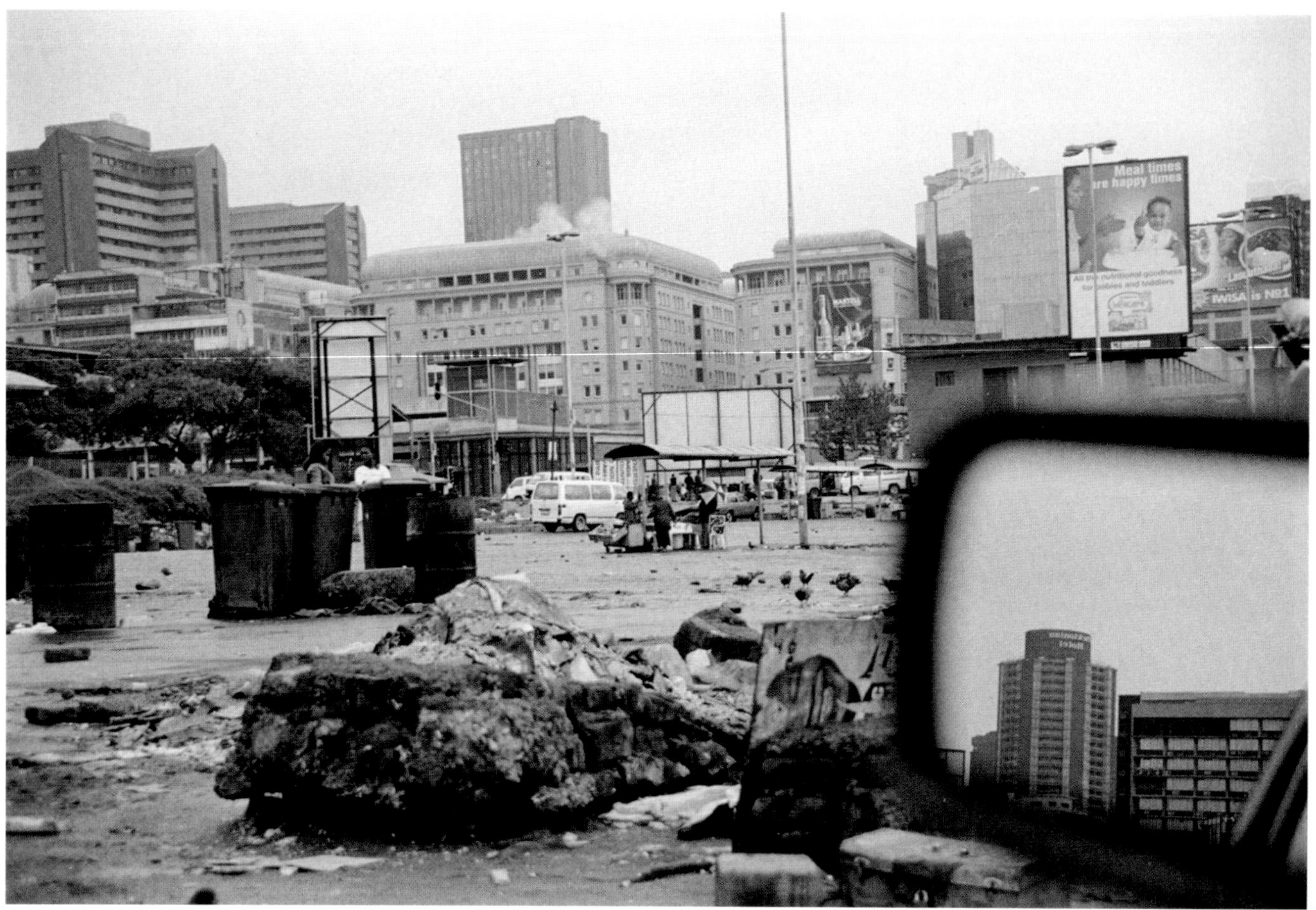

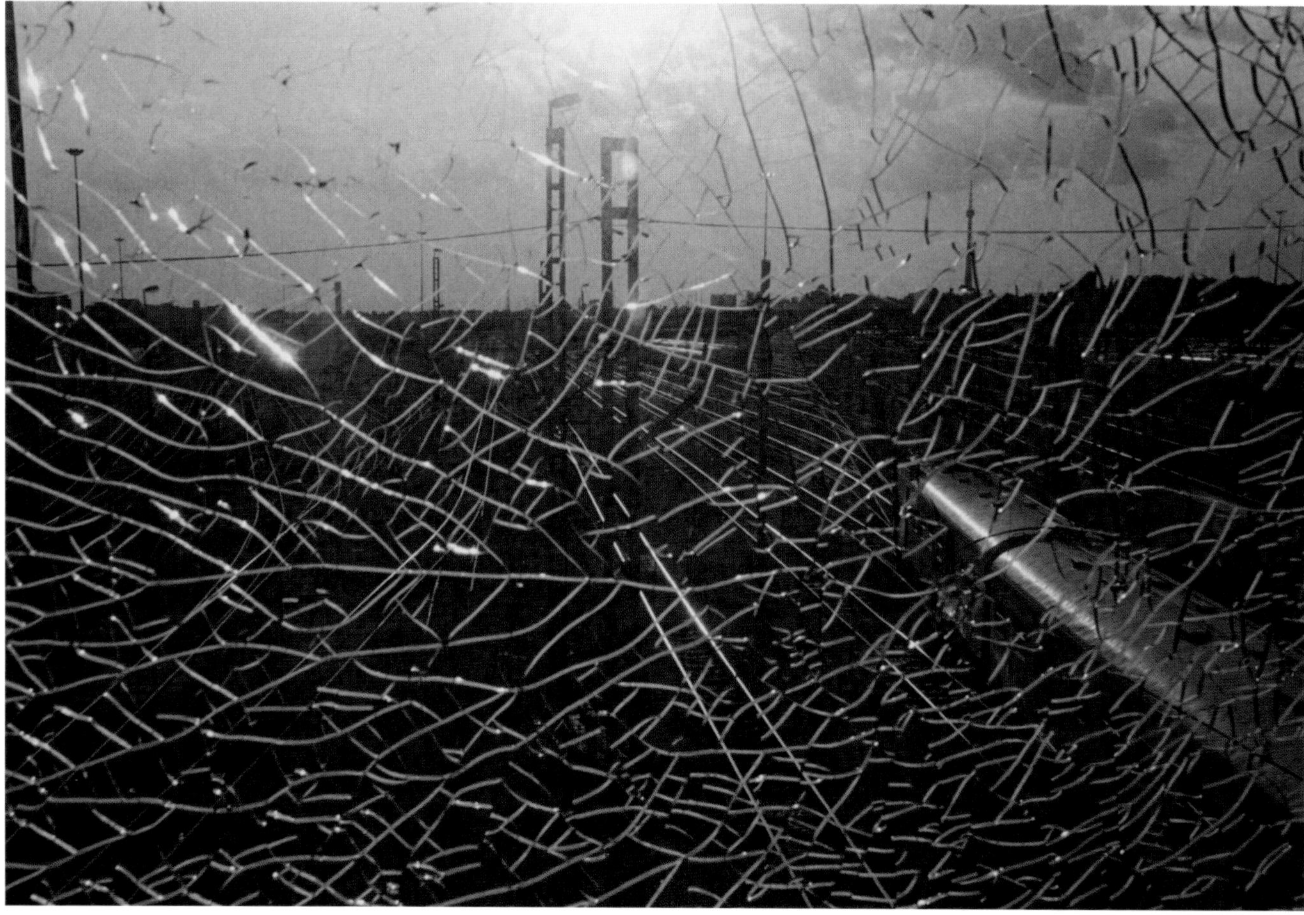

City Informal Trading Place, 2004   *Broken Window and railway lines*, Mandela Bridge

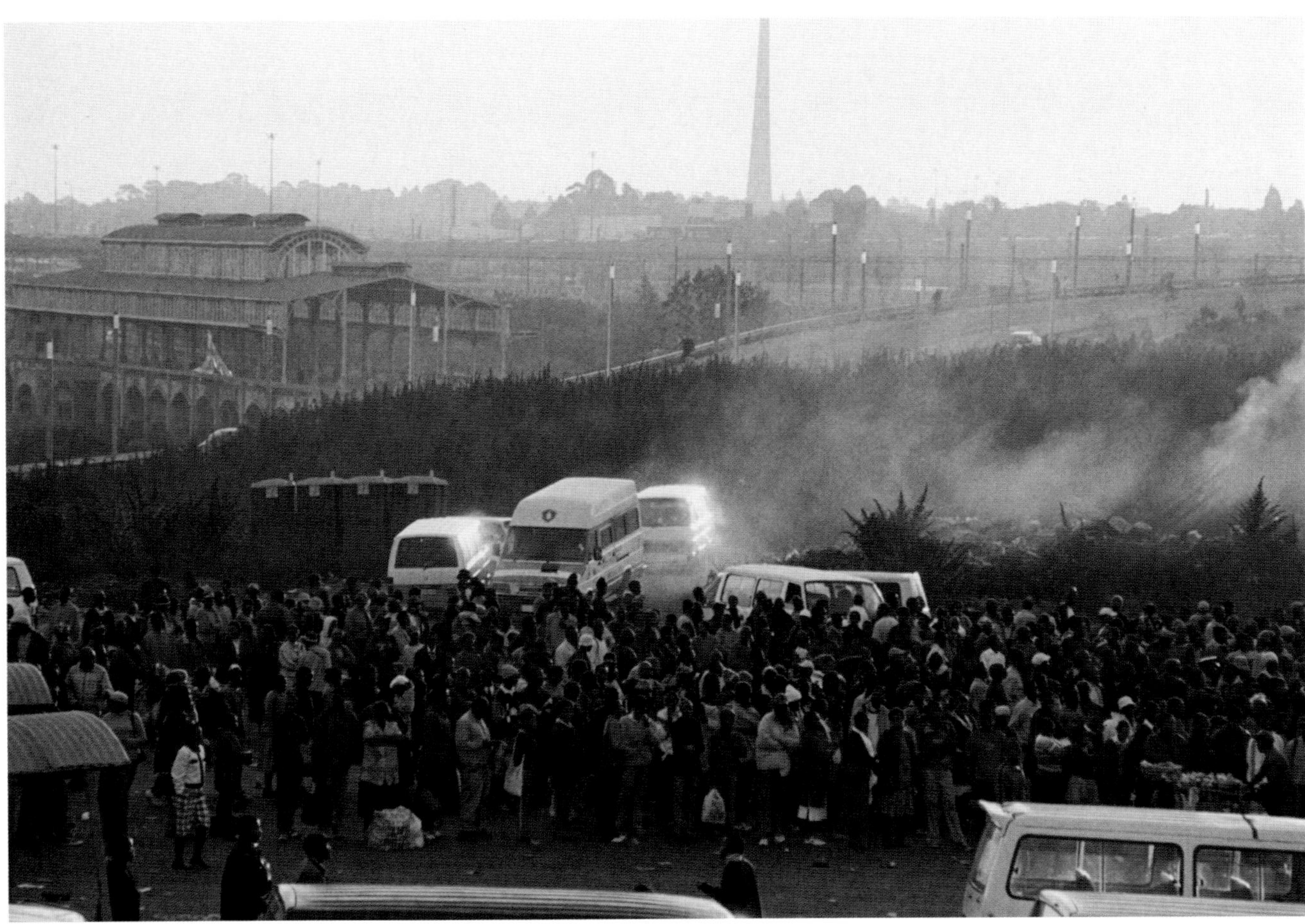

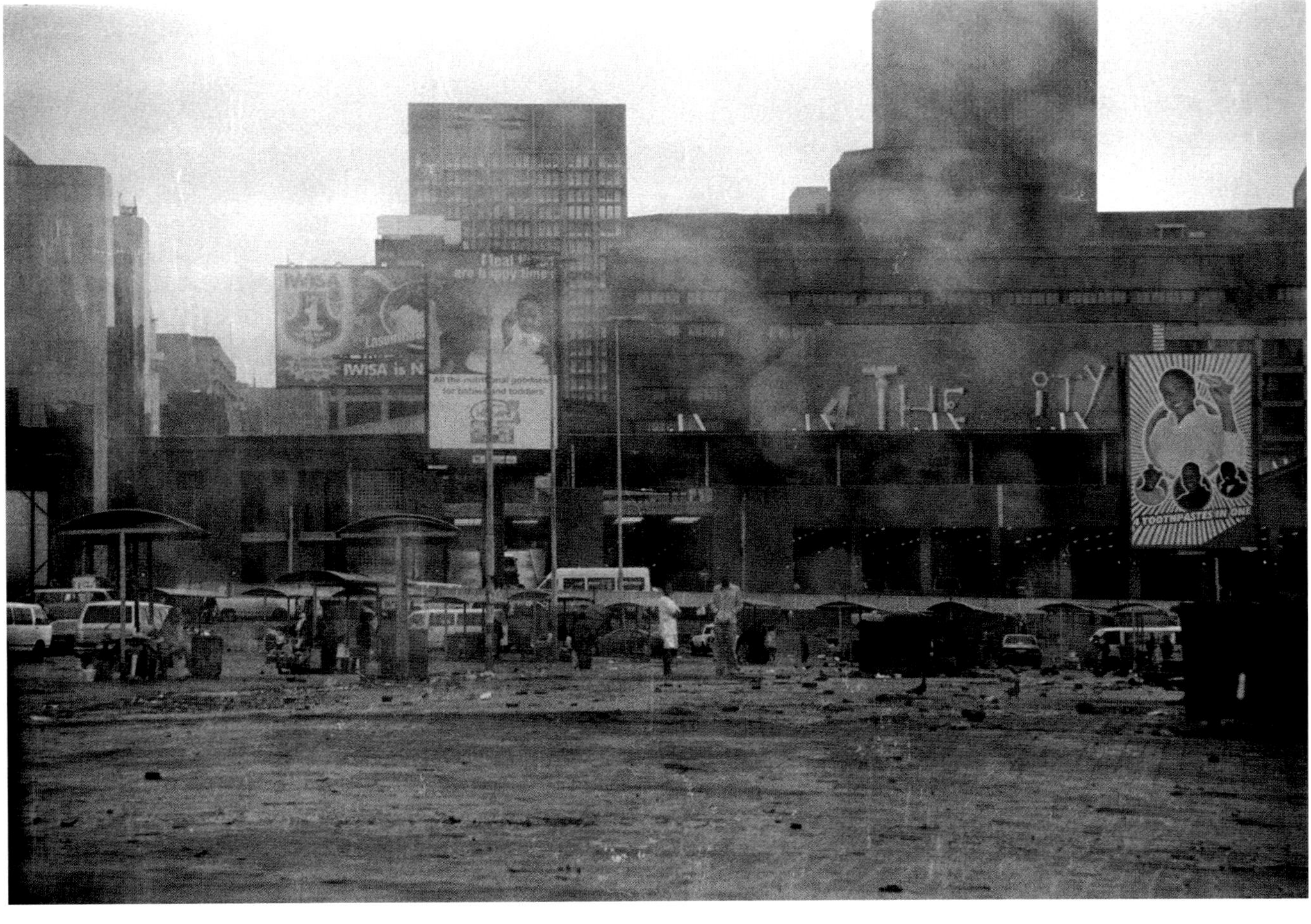

Taxis near Mandela Bridge, 2004

The City Near Bree Street Taxi Rank, 2004

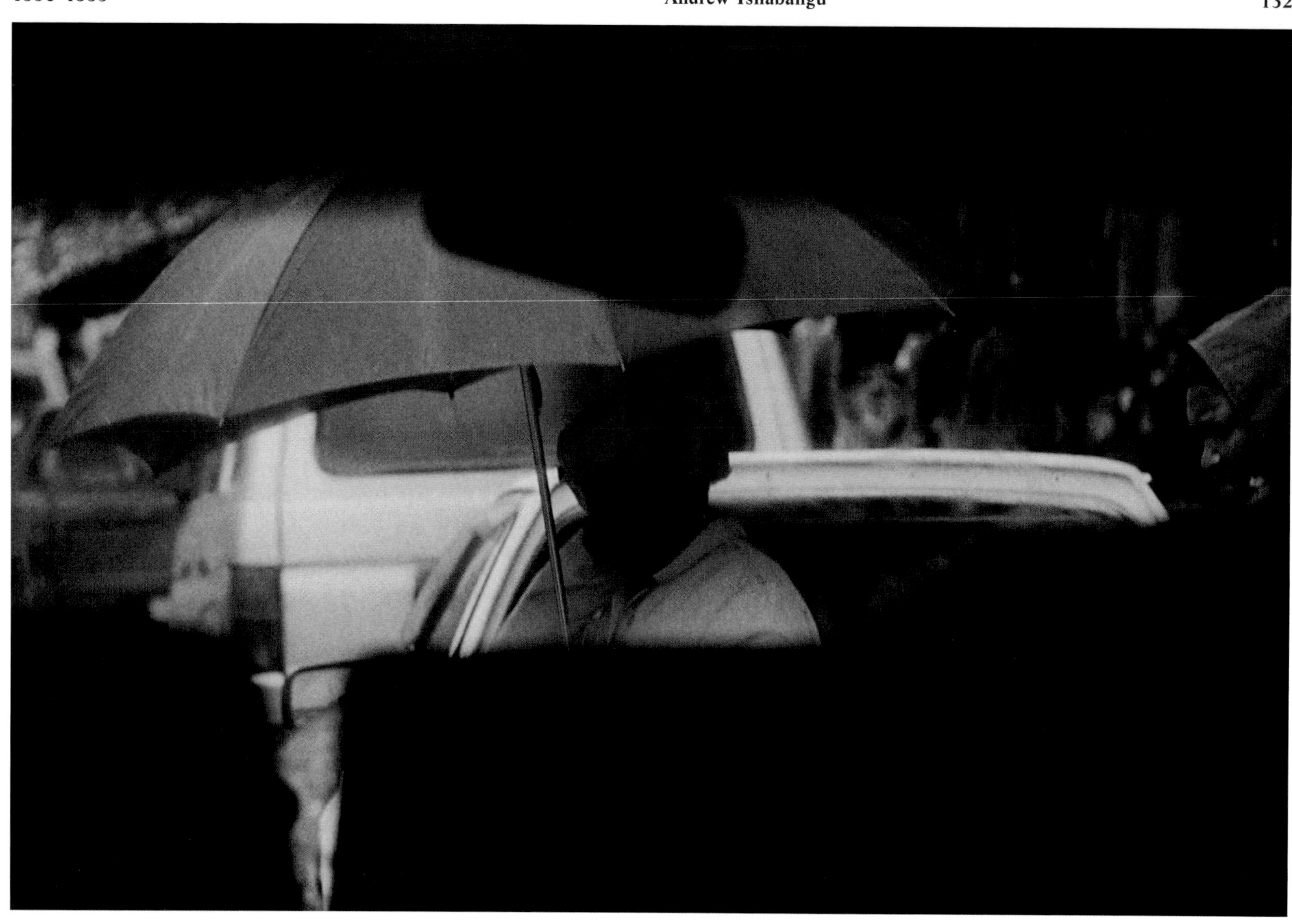

Umbrella Lady, 2004

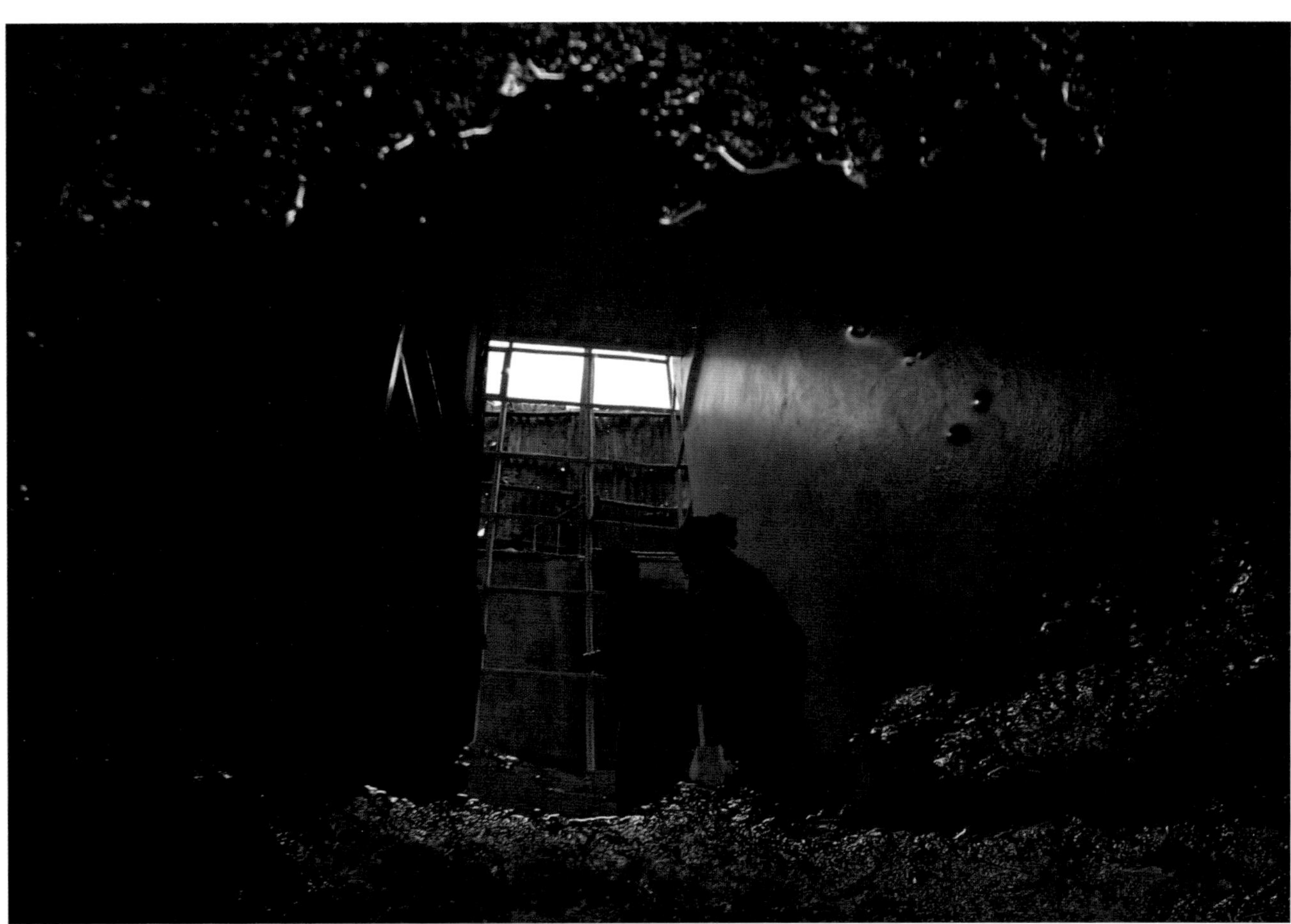

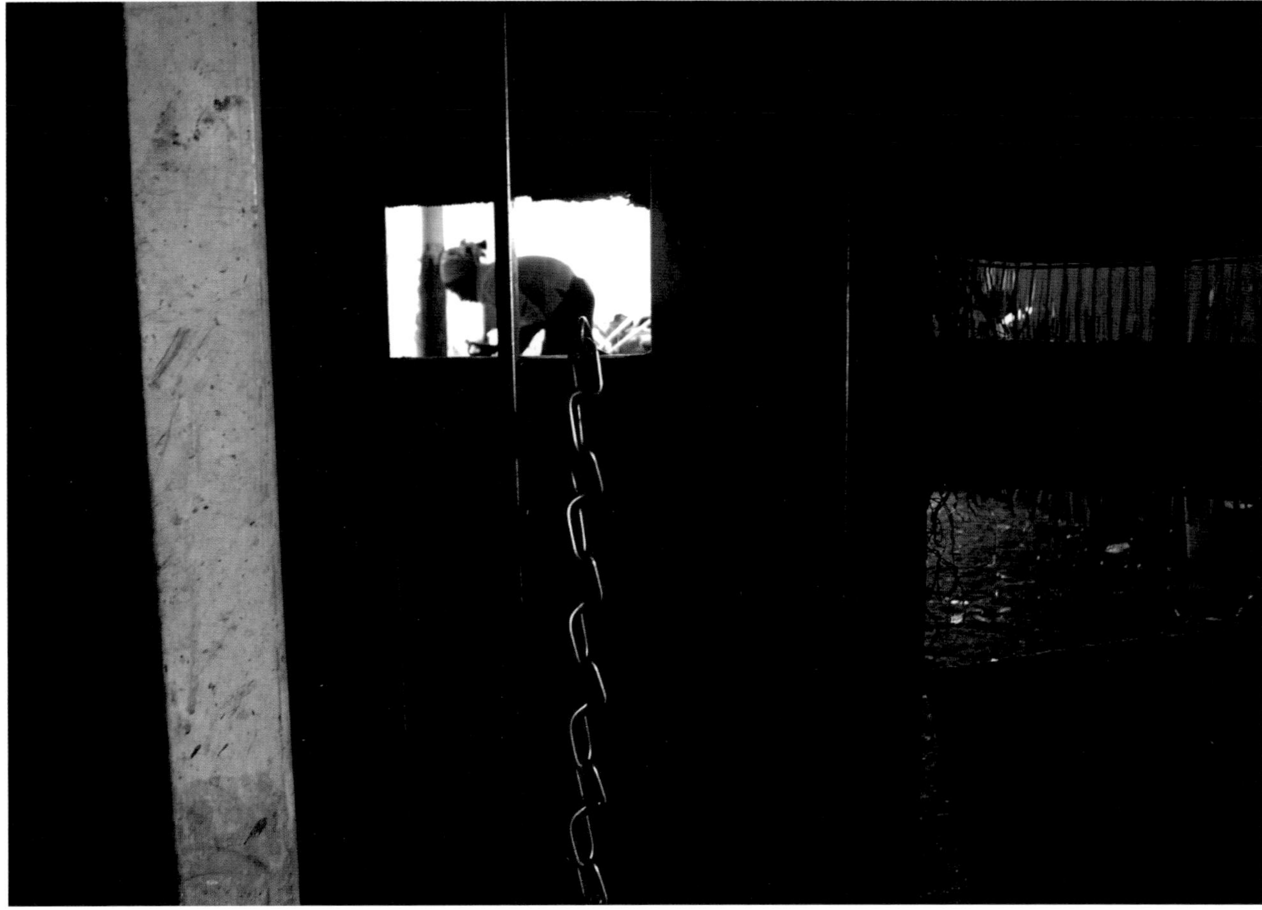

Stairway Reflection in a Puddle, Dese, Welo, Ethiopia, 2002-2008   *A Woman making Juice*, Dese, Welo, Ethiopia, 2002-2008

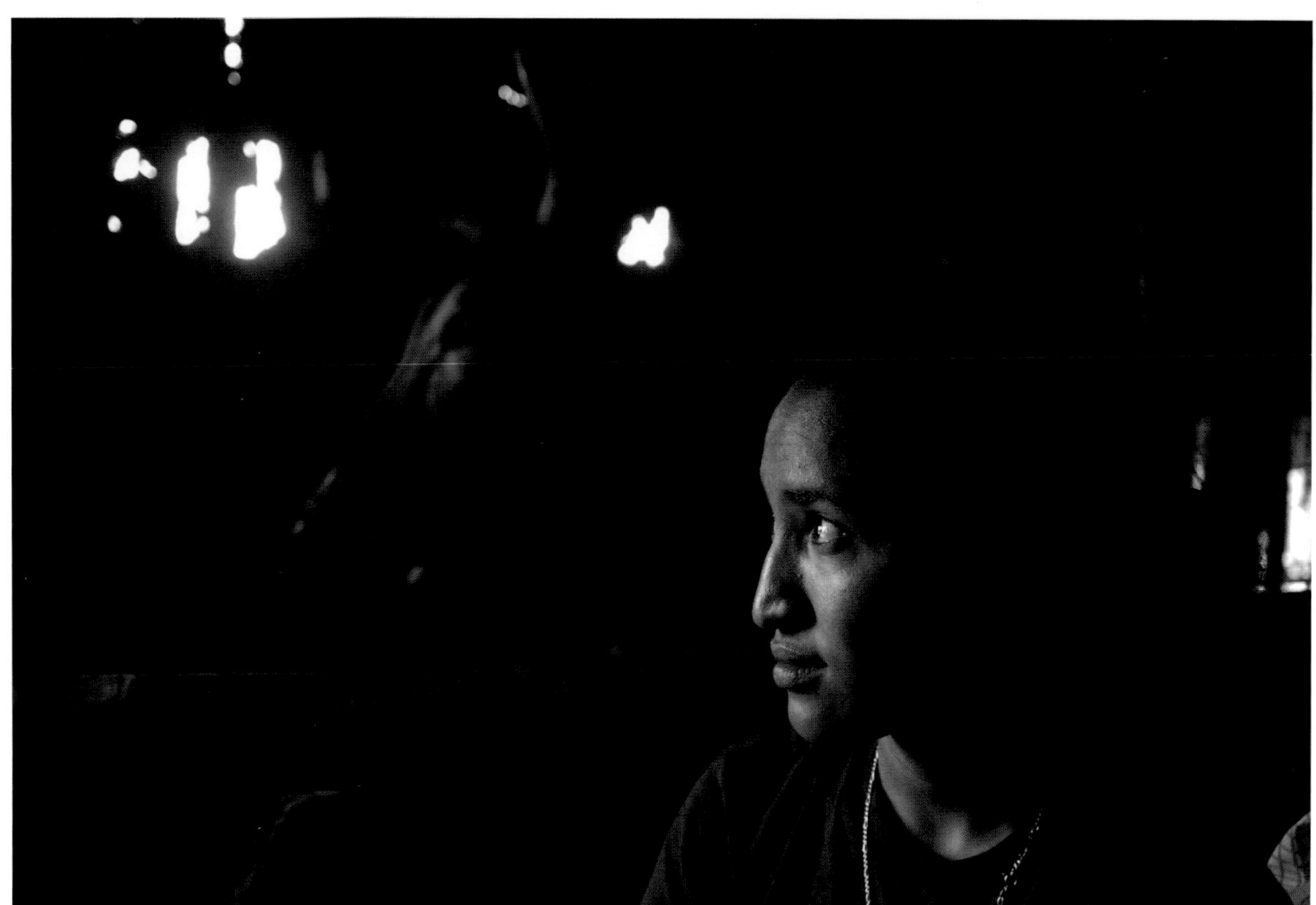

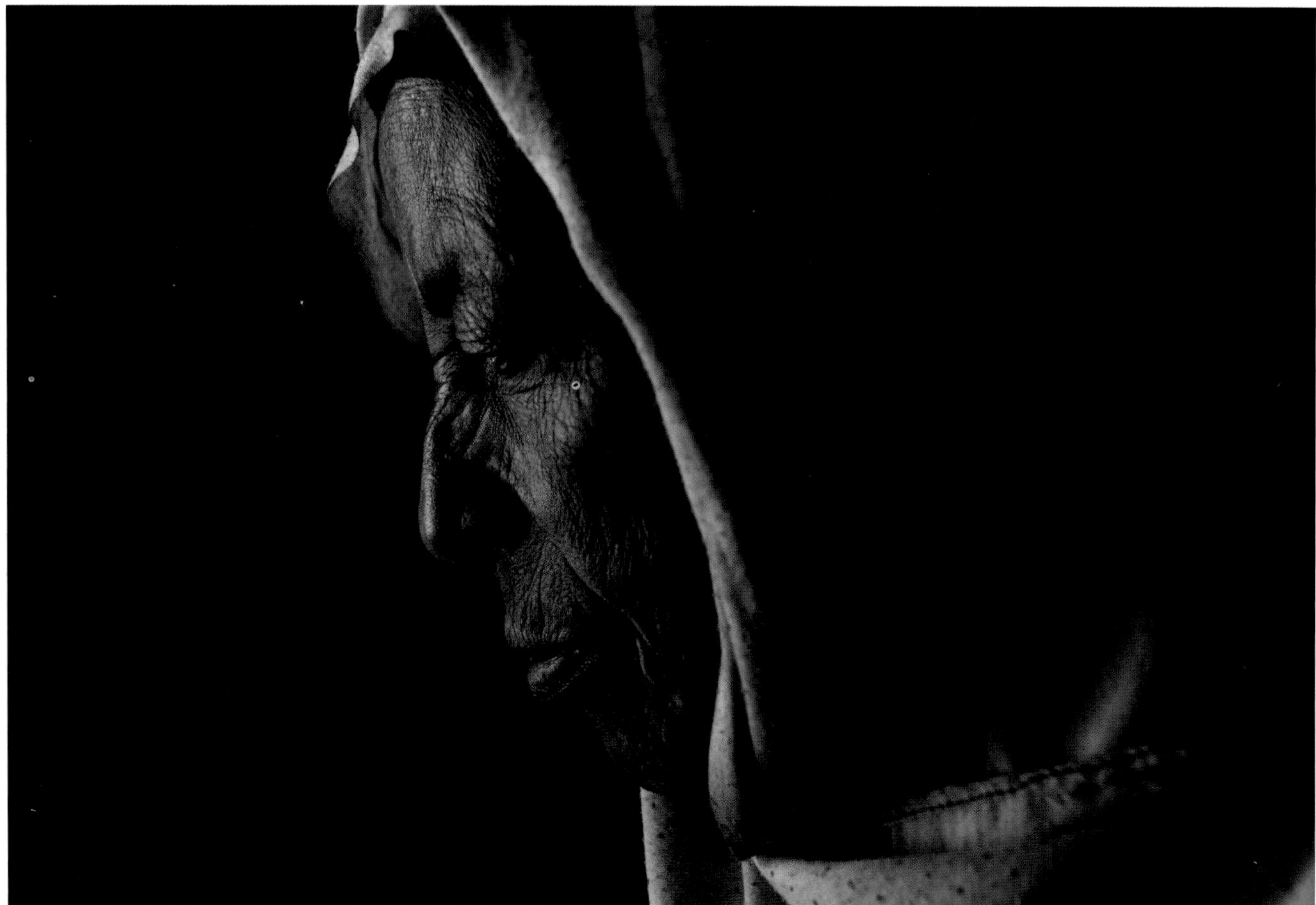

Interiors, Segorah Aba Abo, Welo, Ethiopia, 2002-2008   *Woman in doorway,* Dese, Welo, Ethiopia, 2002-2008

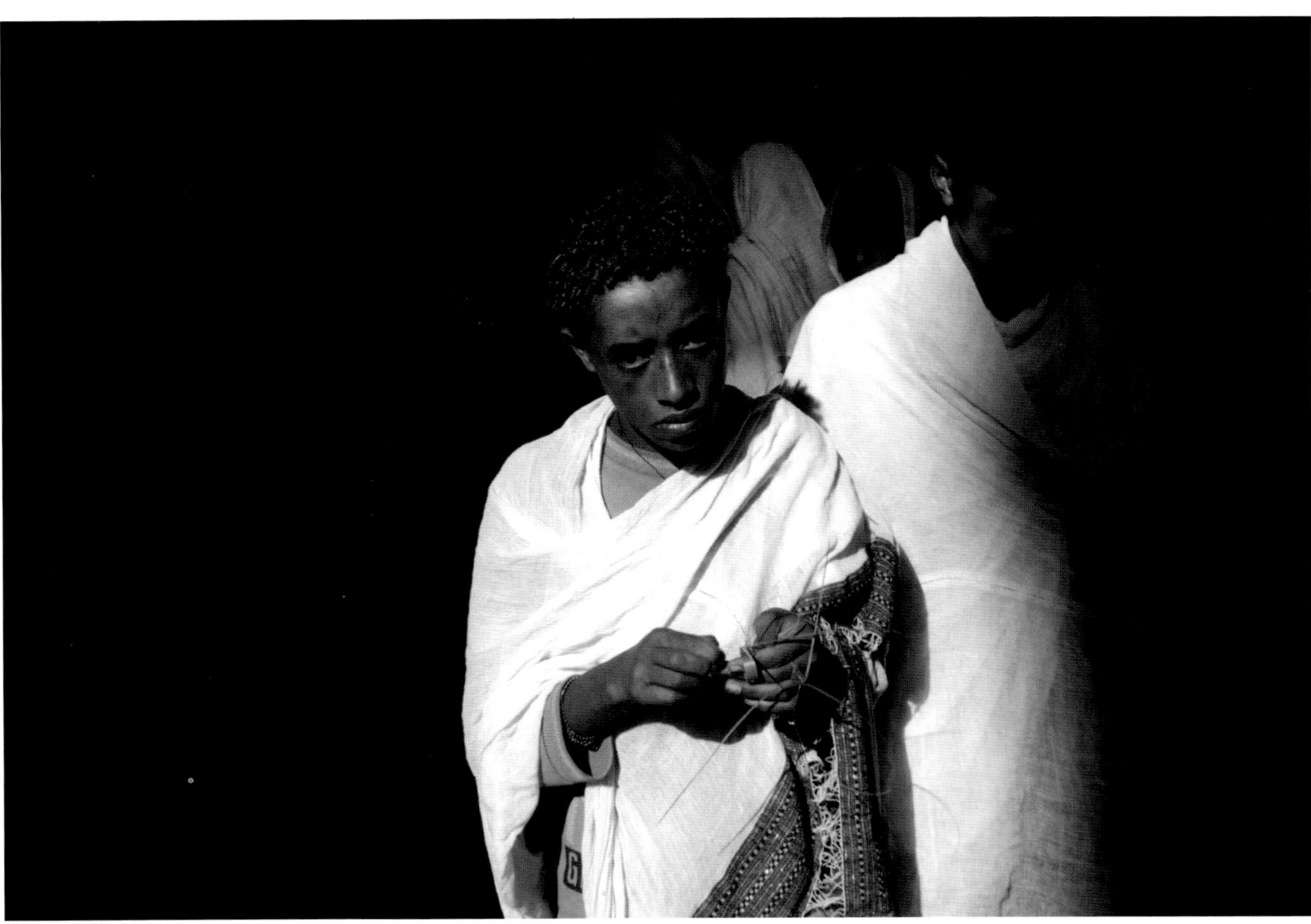

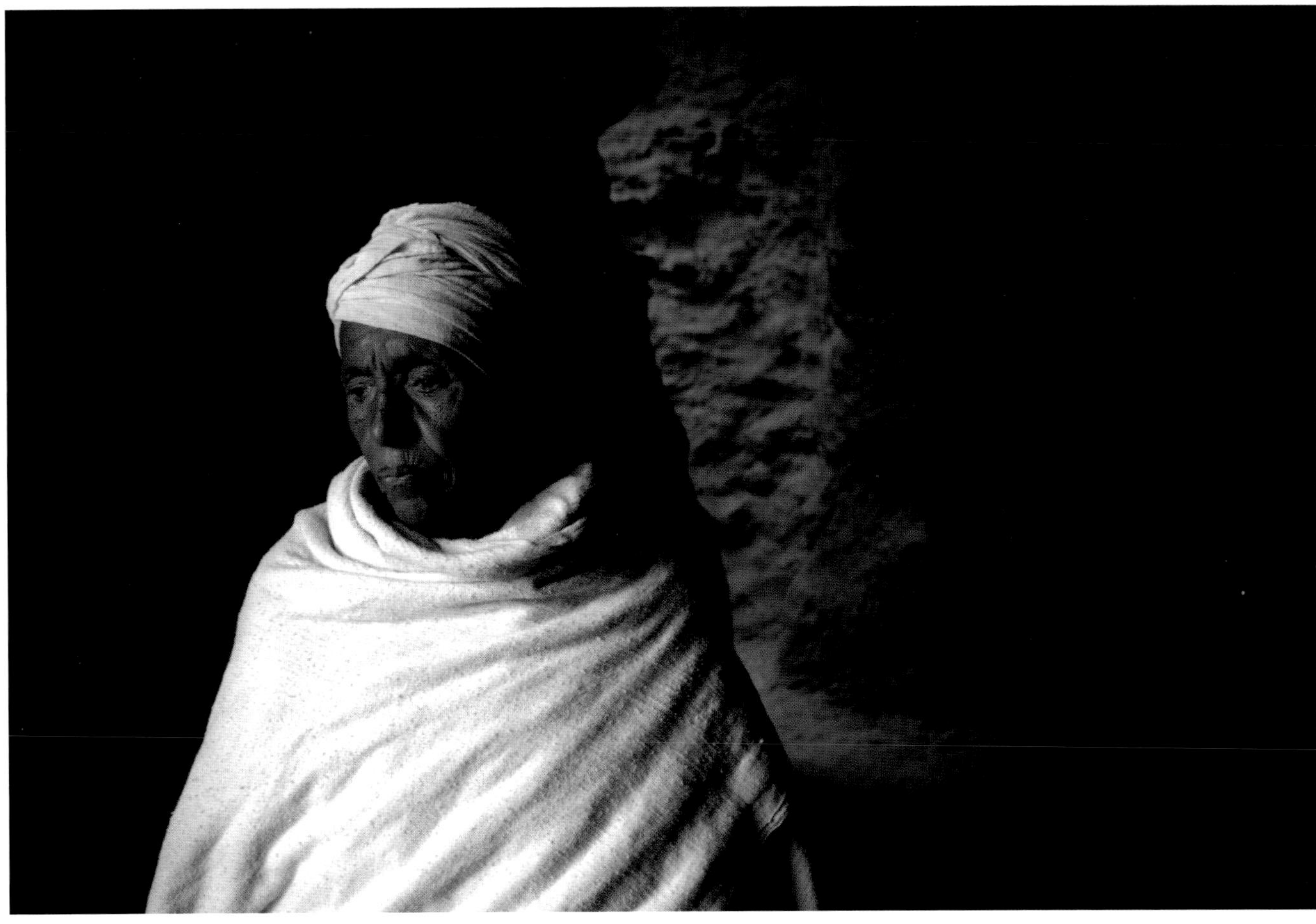

Boy Coming out of Church, Lalibela, Welo, Ethiopia, 2002-2008

Woman in Church Passageway, Lalibela, Welo, Ethiopia, 2002-2008

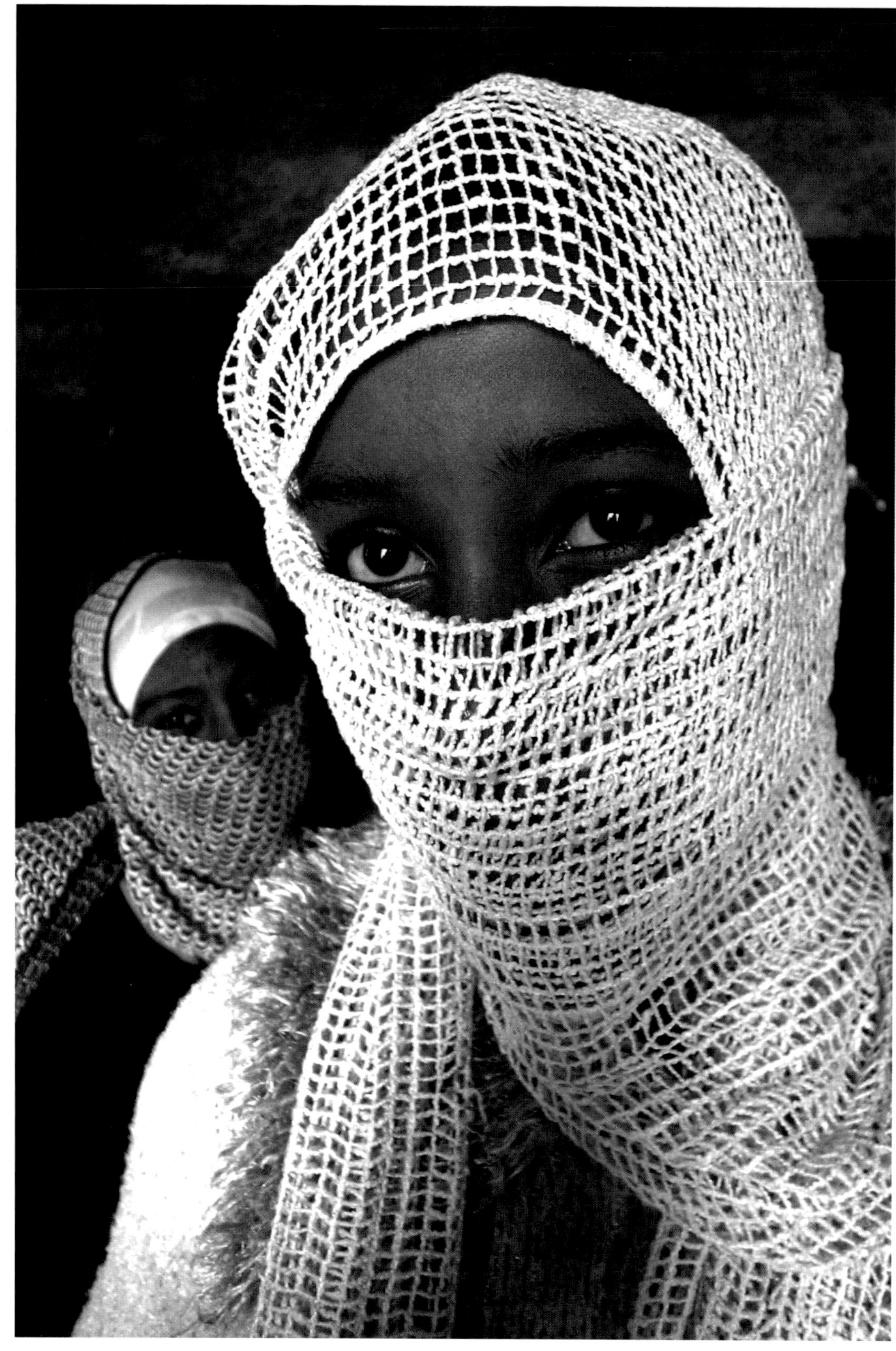

Shy Girls in Quran School from the *Islam in Ethiopia* series.
Dese, Welo, Ethiopia, 2002-2008

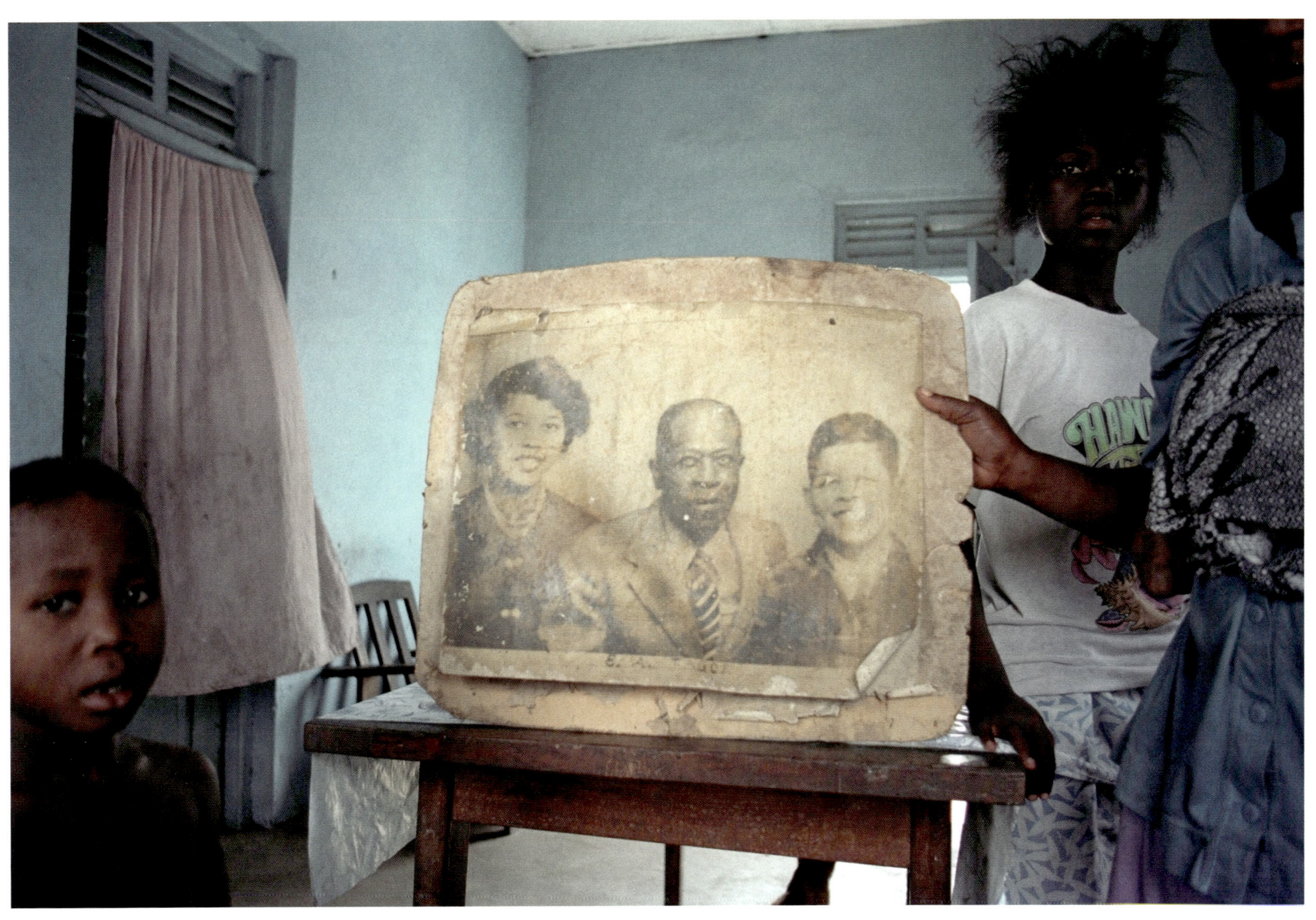

Untitled, 1996

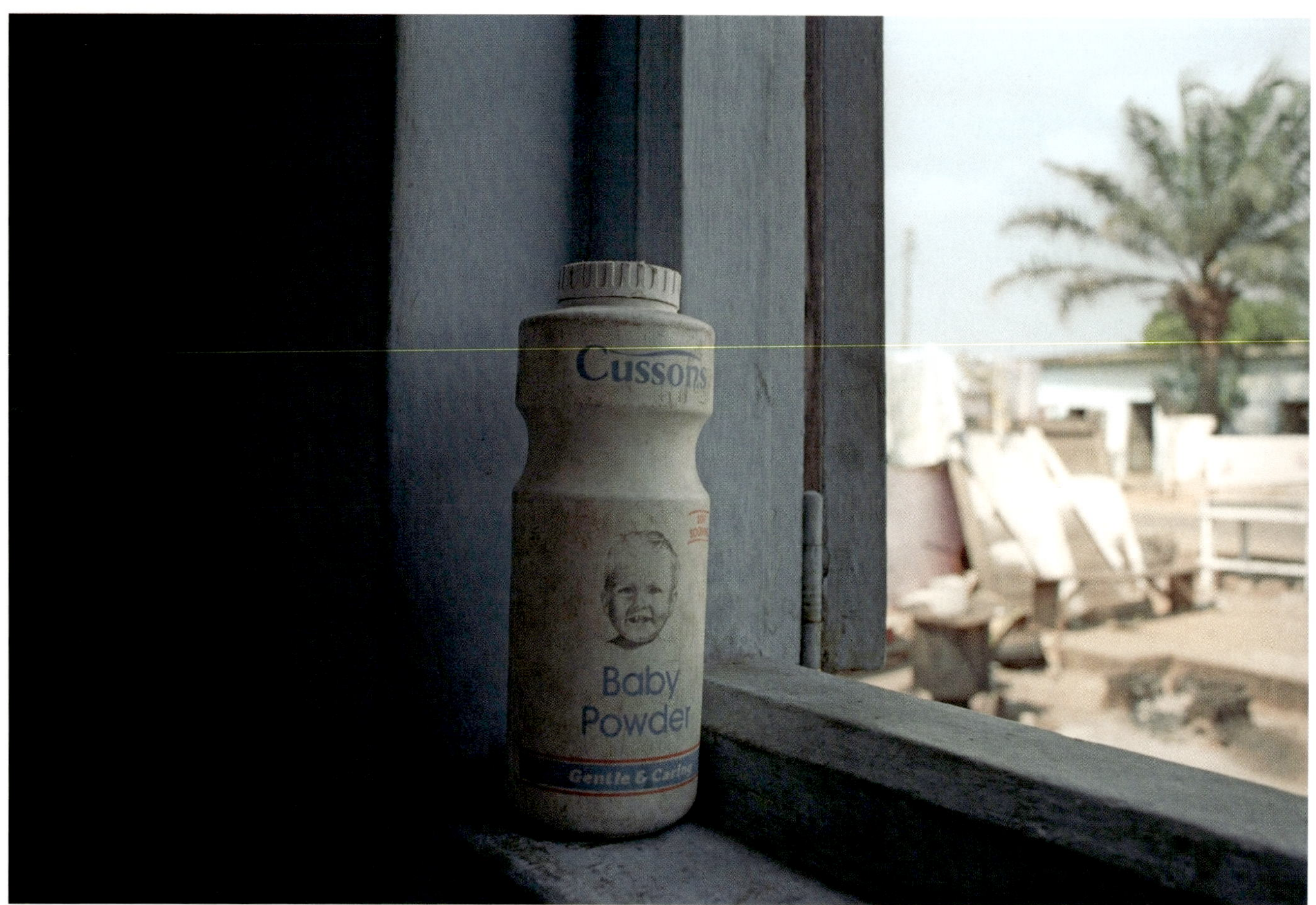

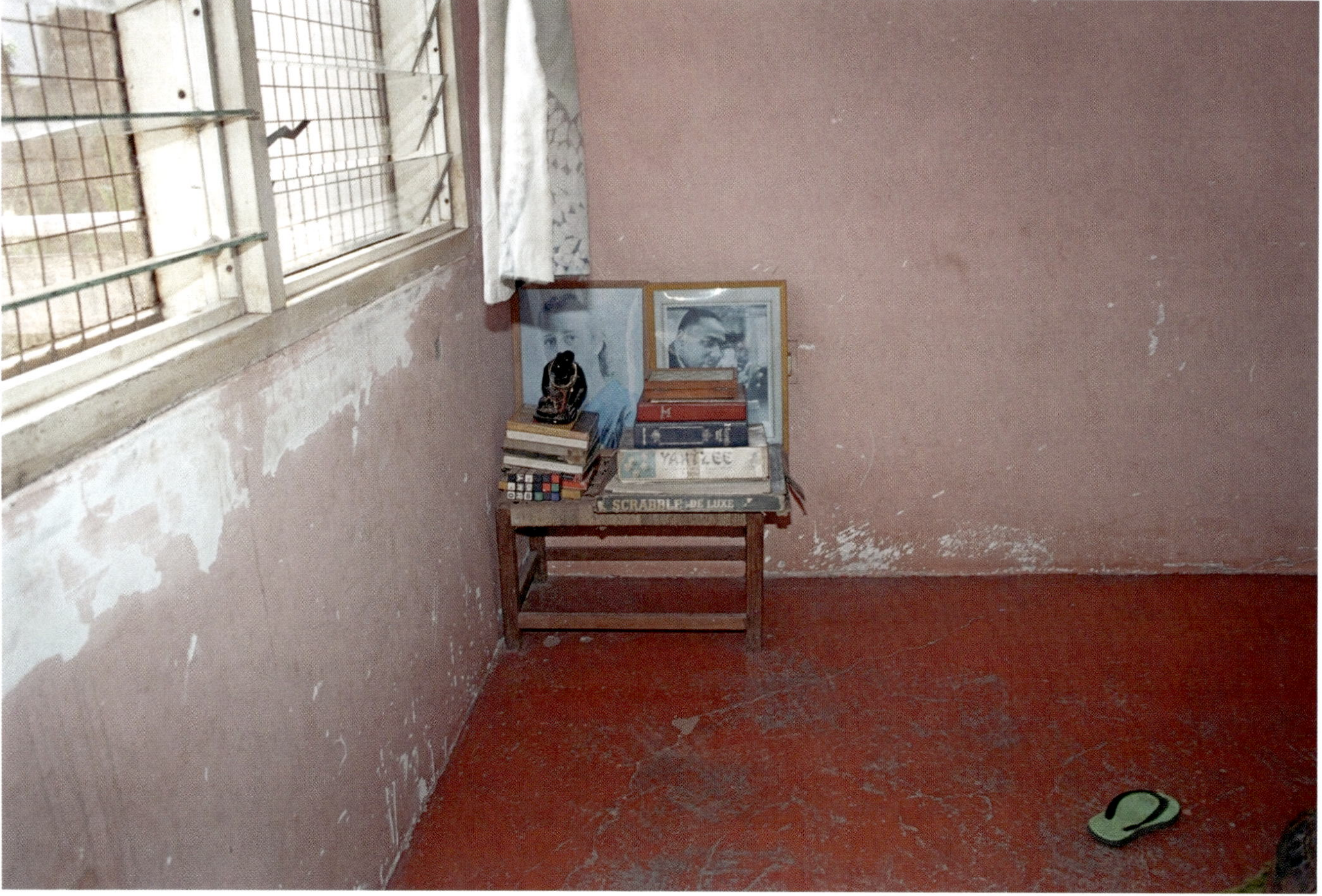

Untitled, 1996

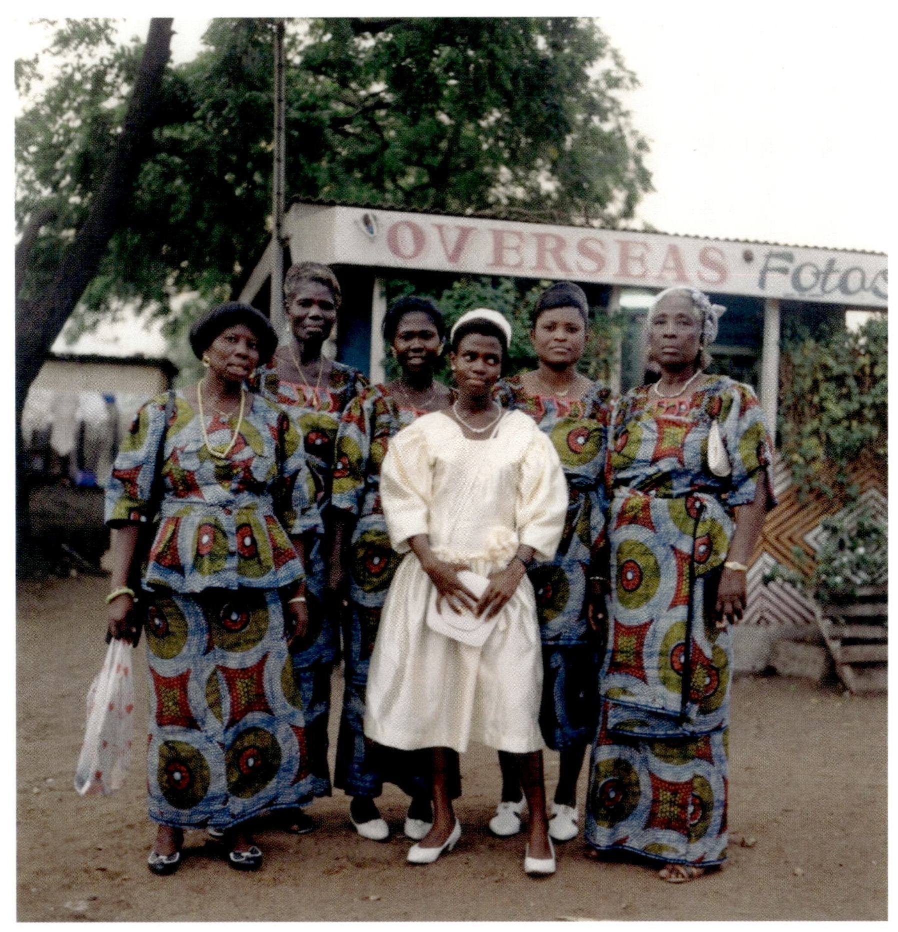
OVERSEAS Fotos

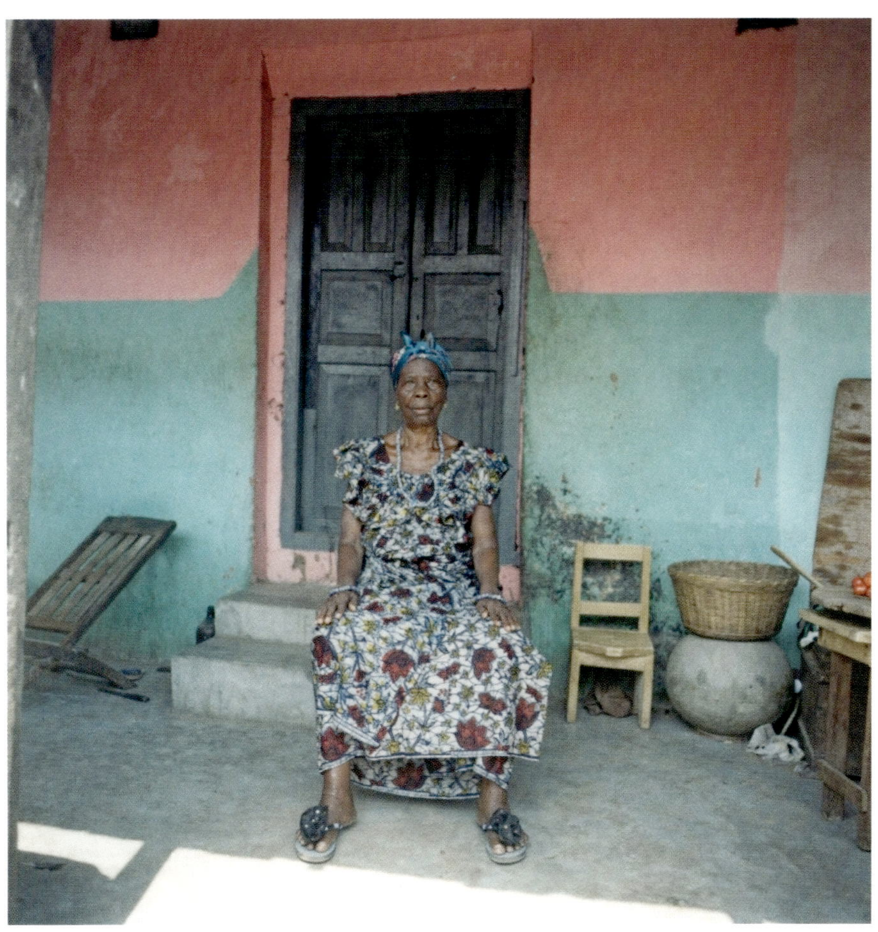

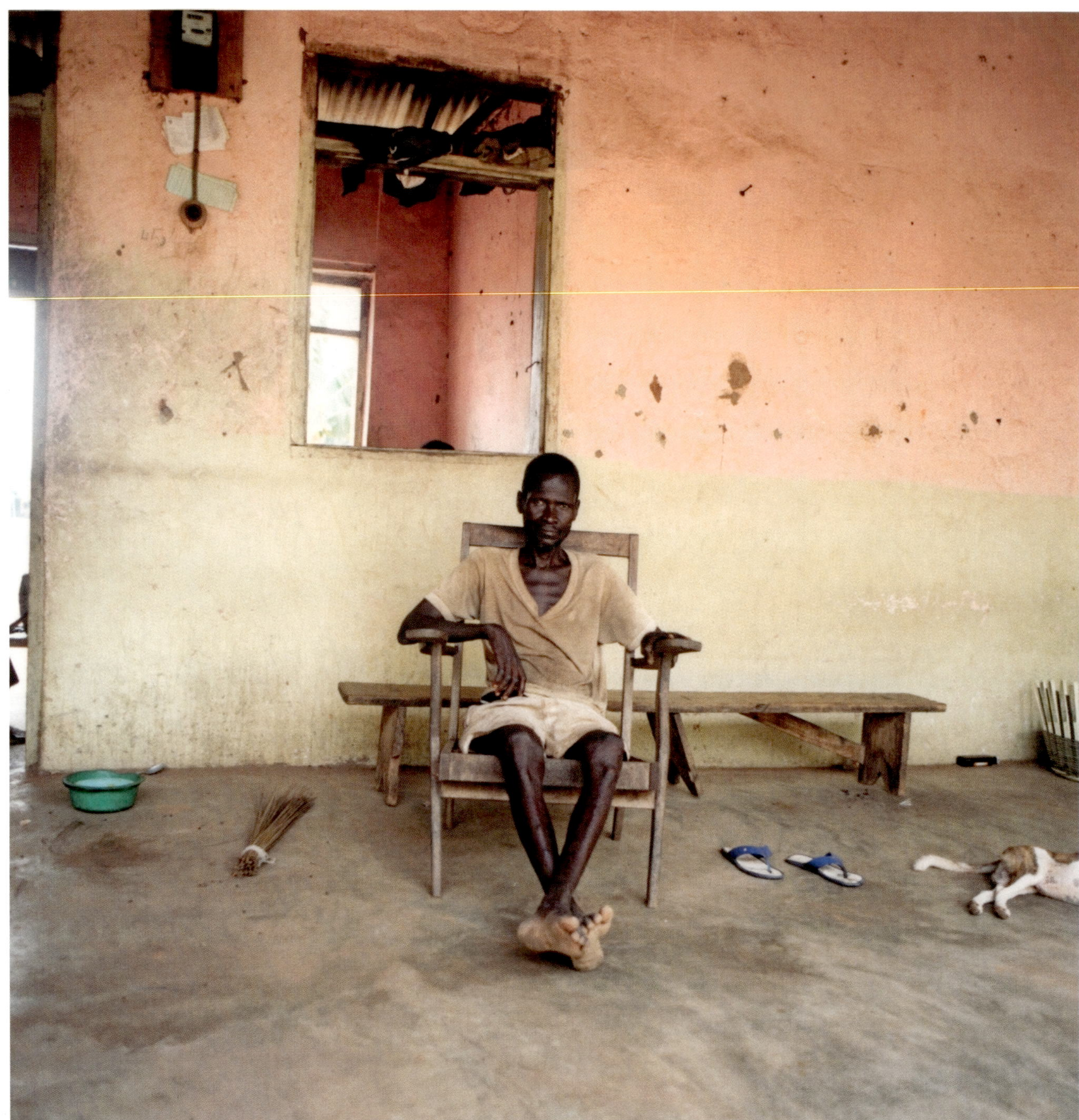

Untitled, 1996

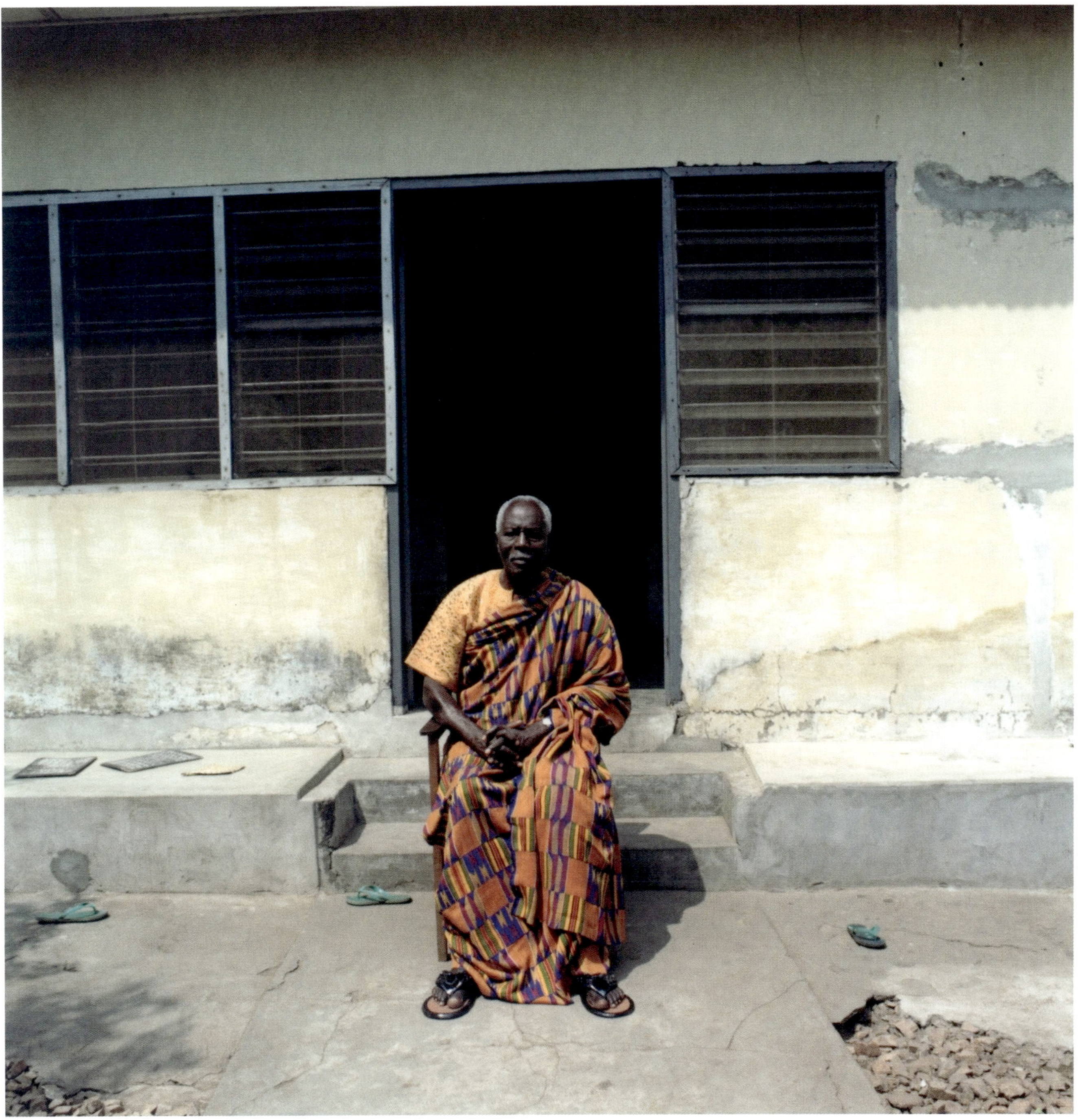

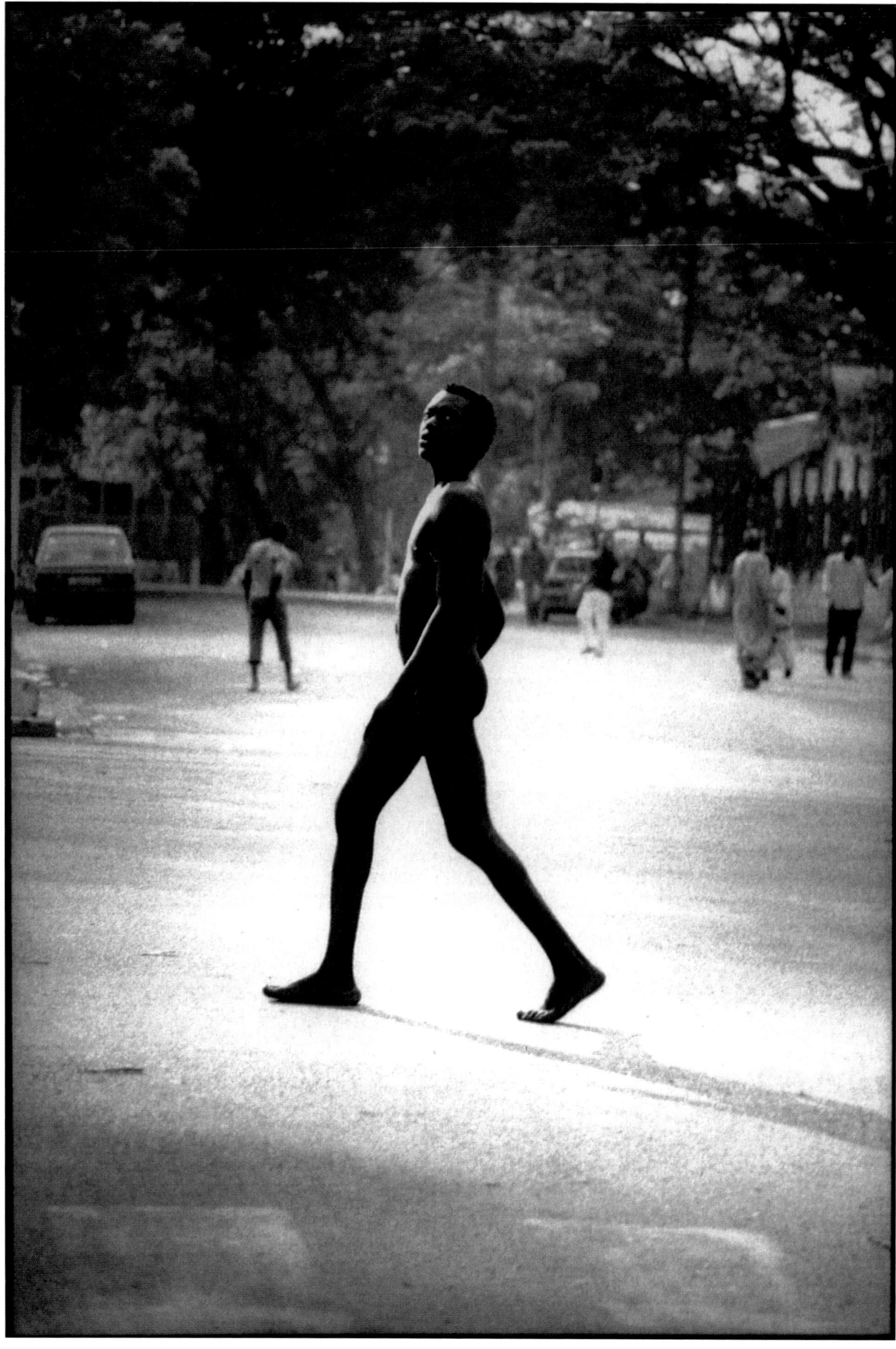

Un fou nu dans la rue, Abidjan, ca 1990-1992

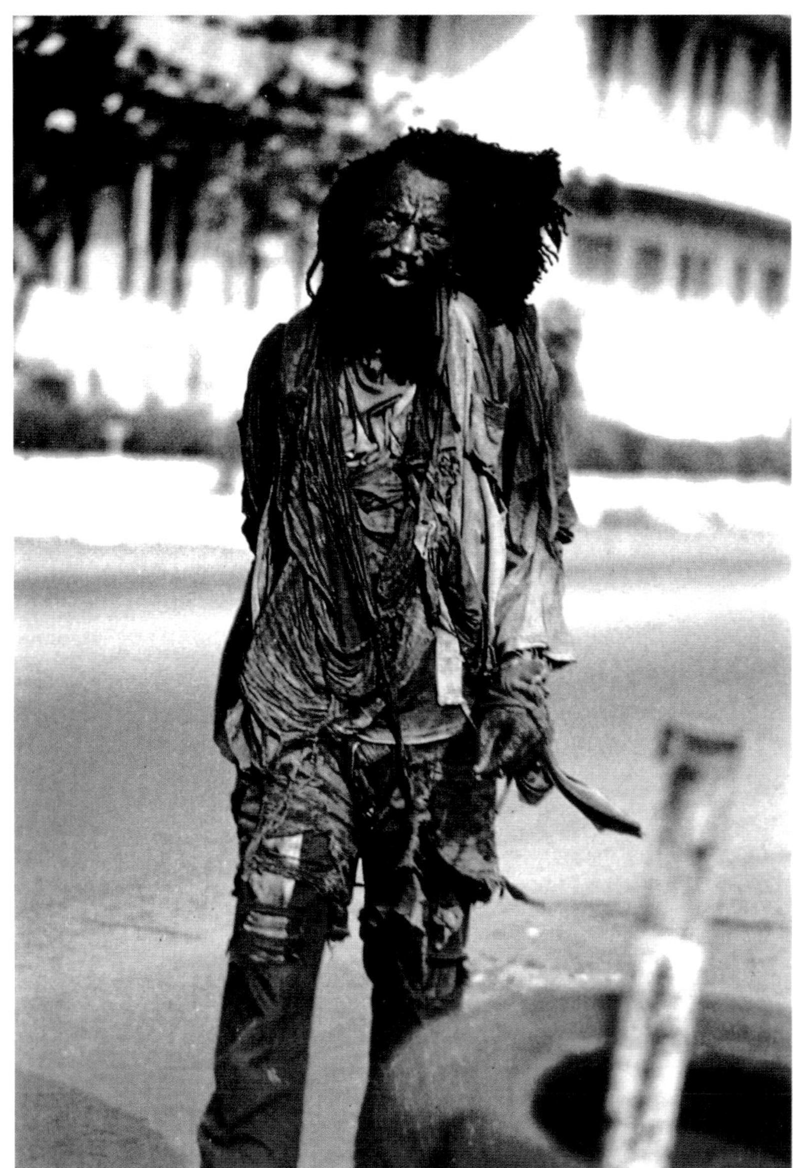

Errer dans les rues, Abidjan, ca 1990-1992

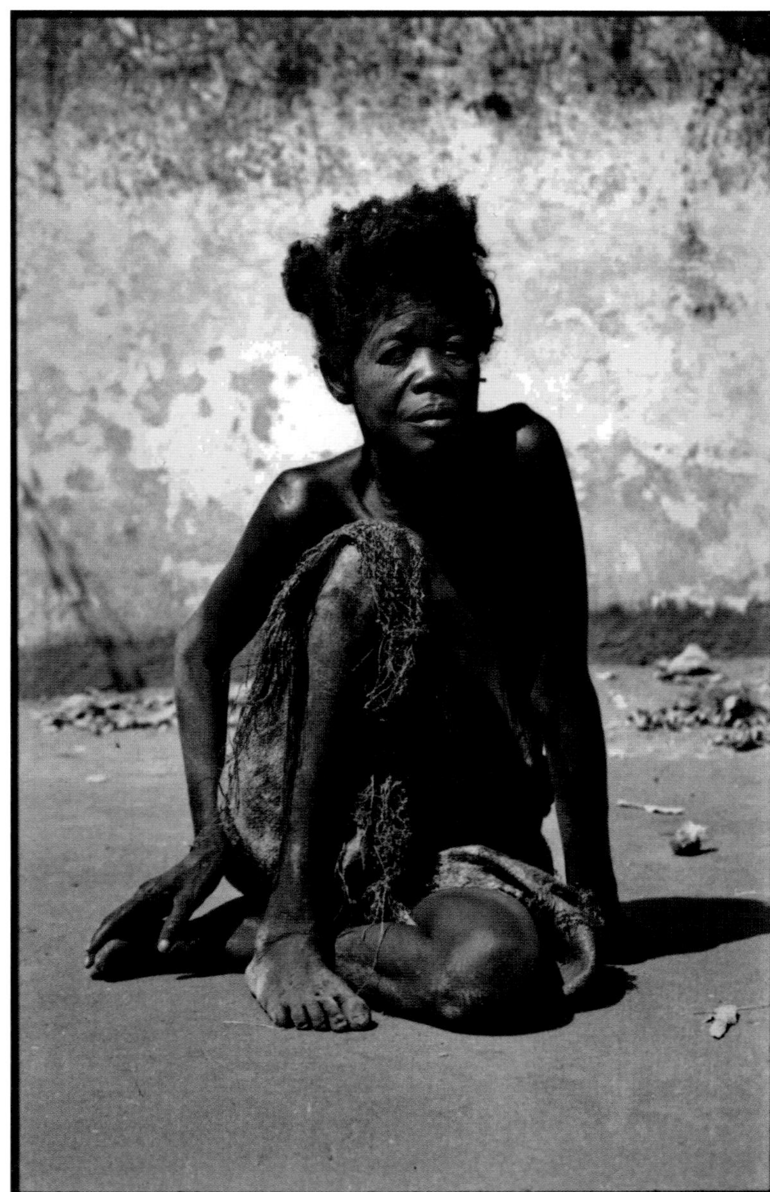

Seule dans la rue, Abidjan, ca 1990-1992

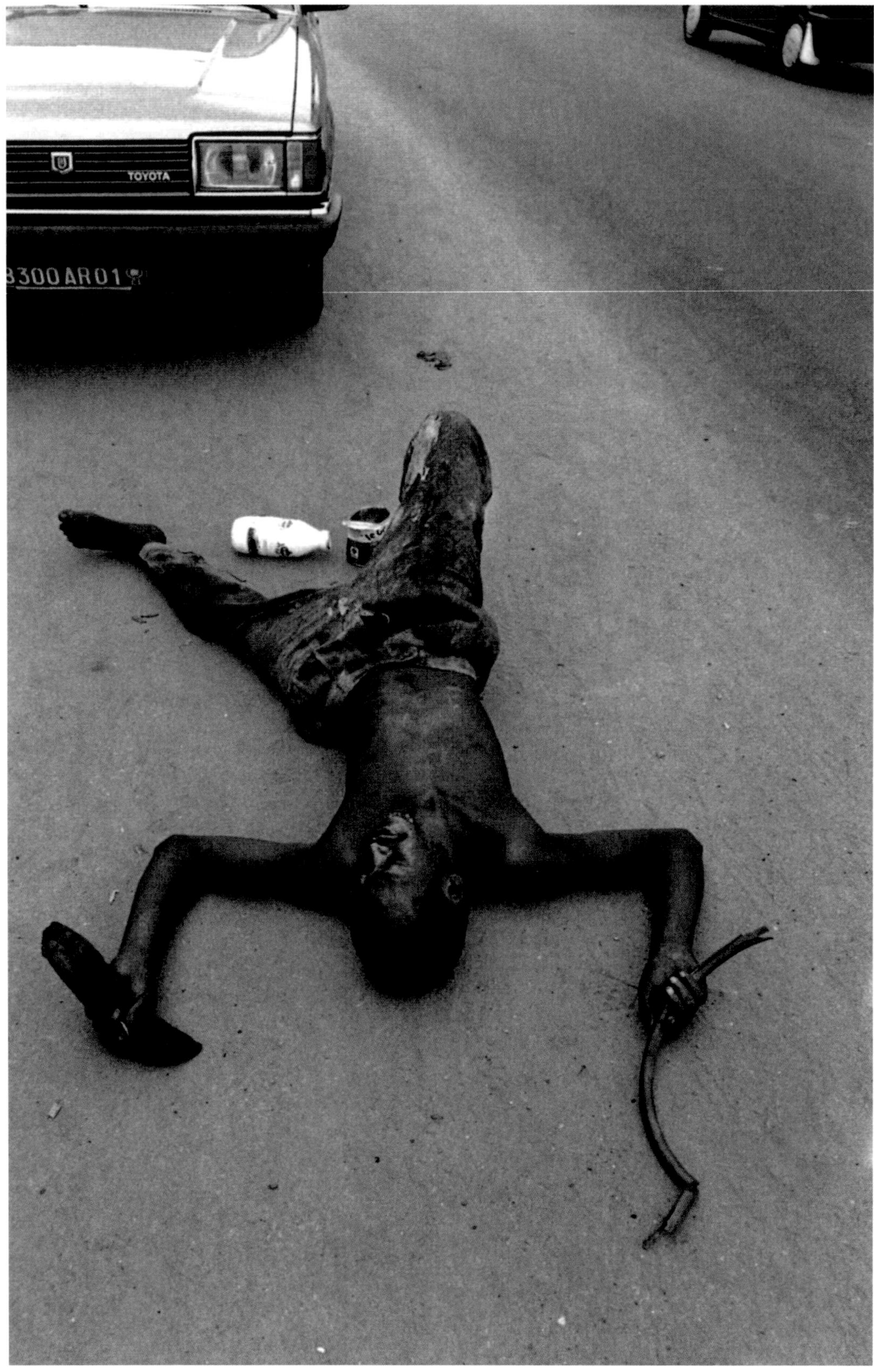

En transe, Abidjan, ca 1990-1992

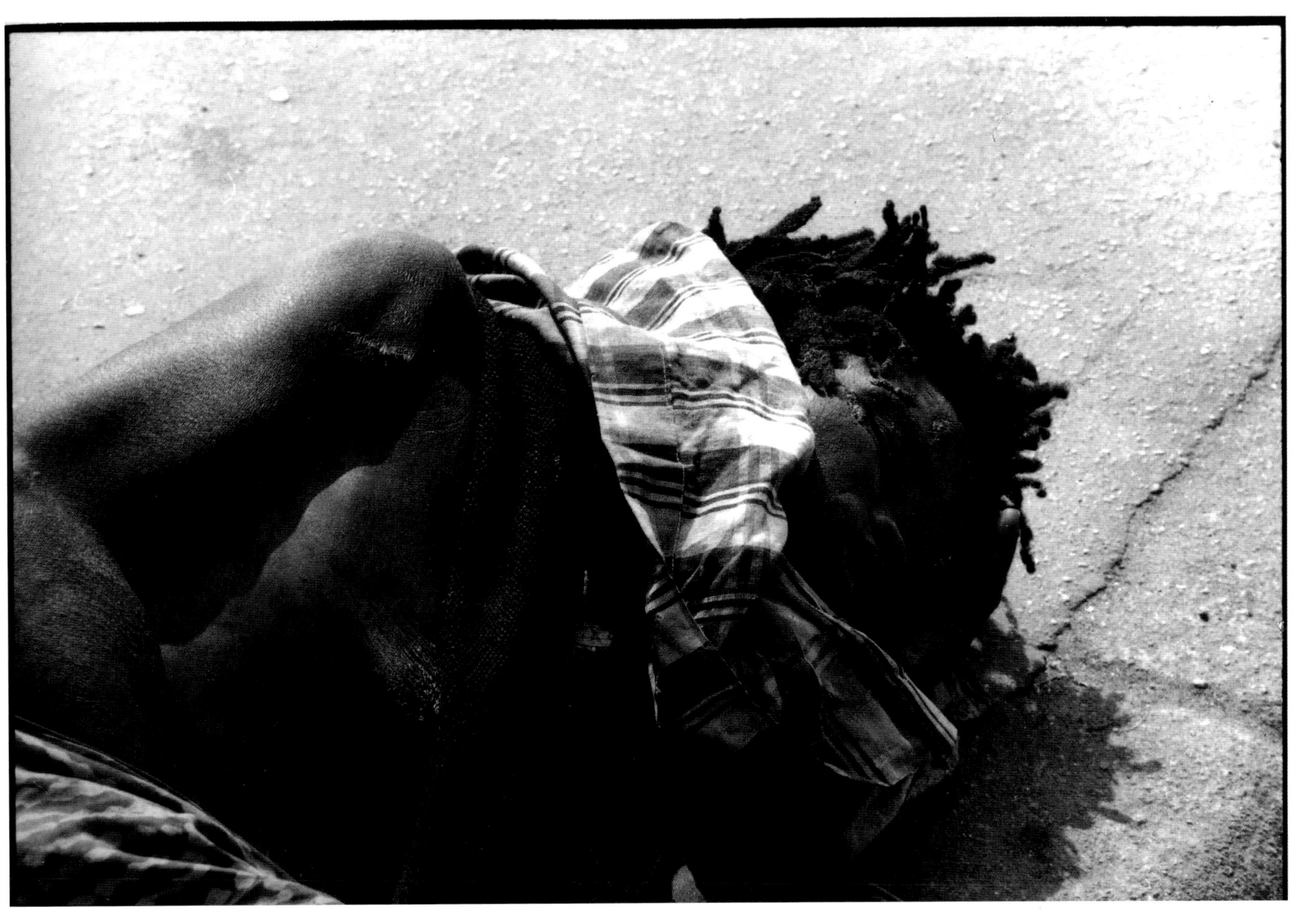

Dormir, Abidjan, 1990-1992

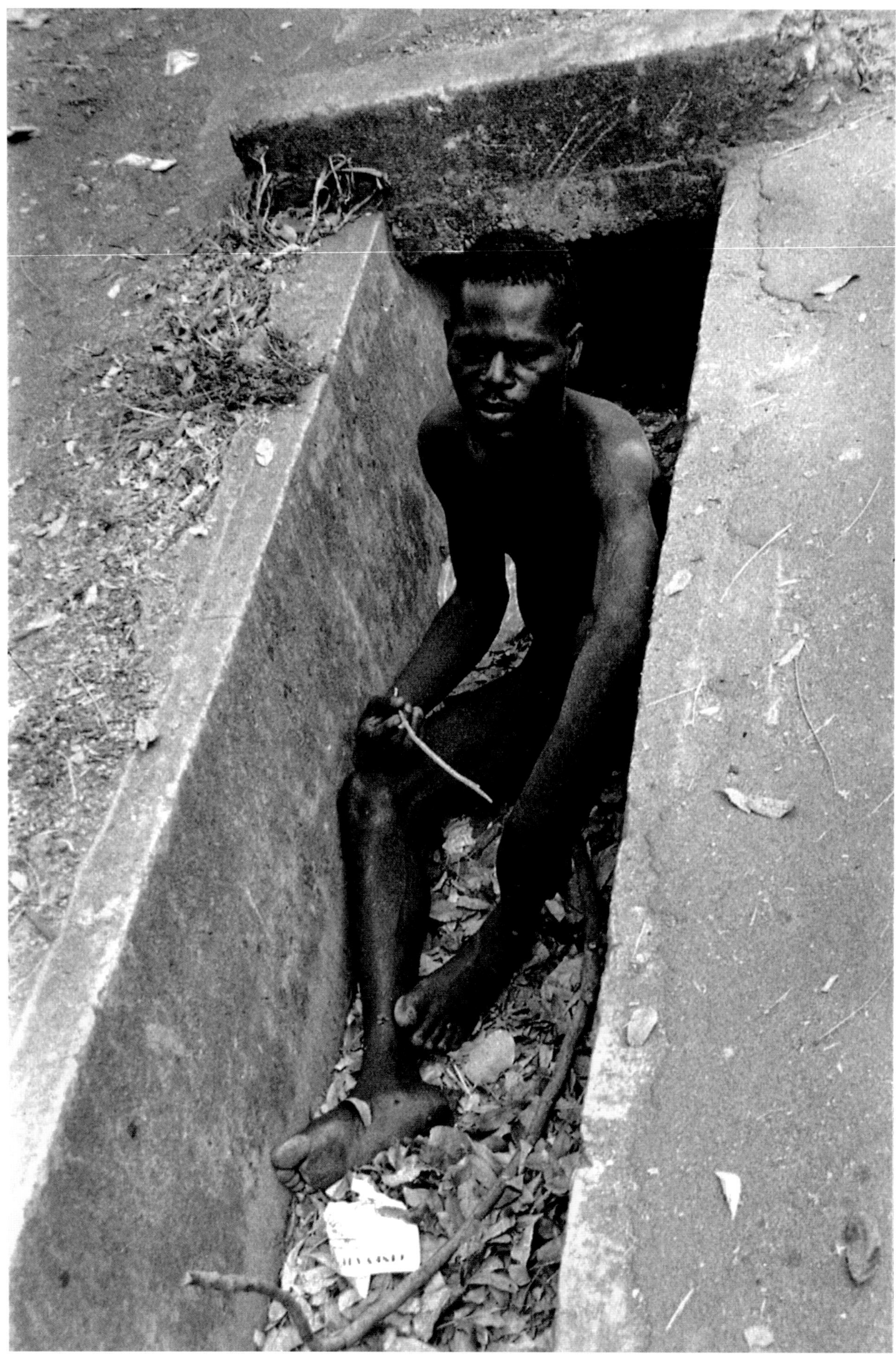

S'isoler, Abidjan, ca 1990-1992

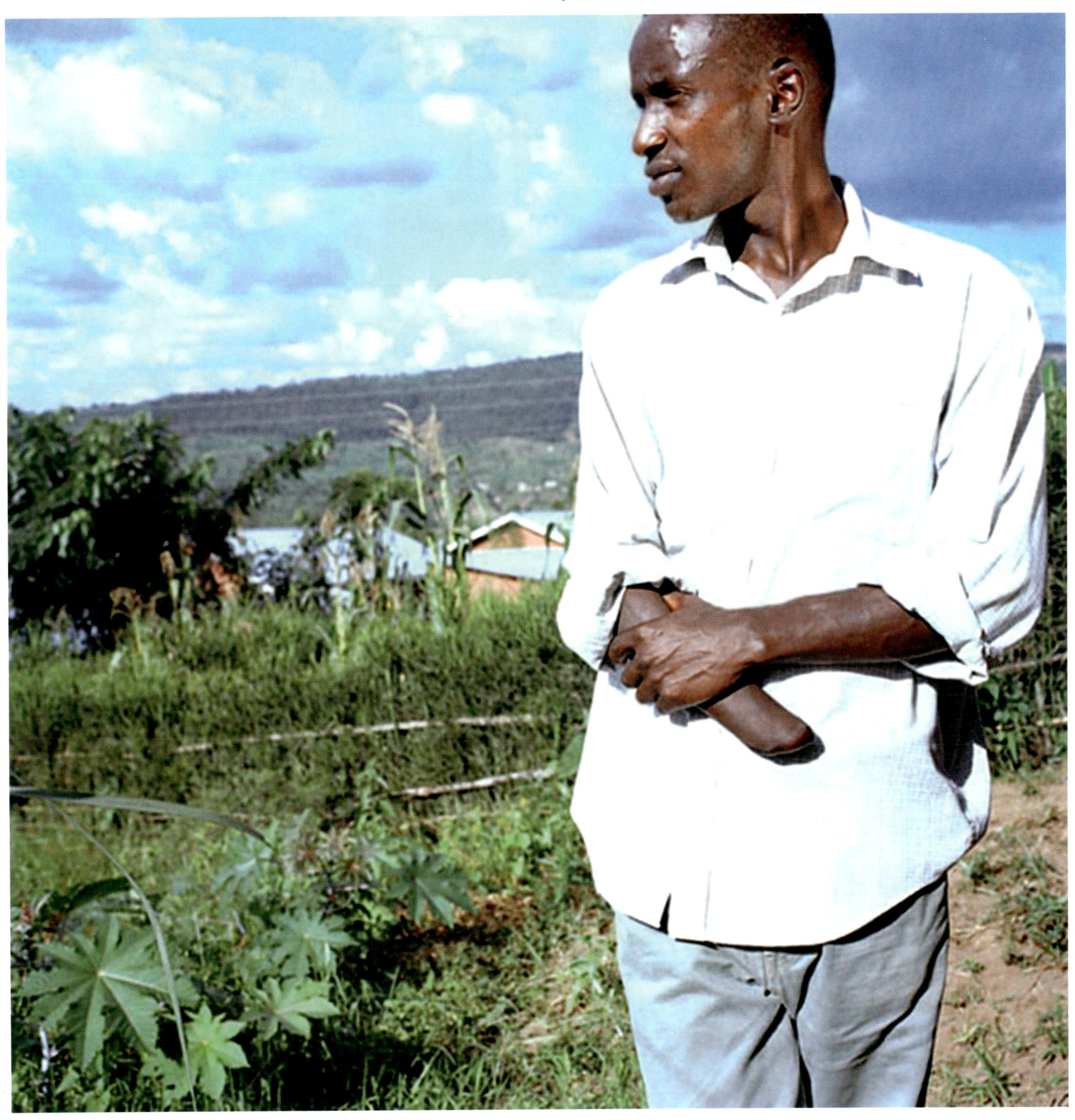

*'I have been encircled by armed men. I was so afraid that I fainted.
When I woke up, my hand was lying next to my body'. Fred Murisa* from
the series *Portrait of a Genocide*, 2007

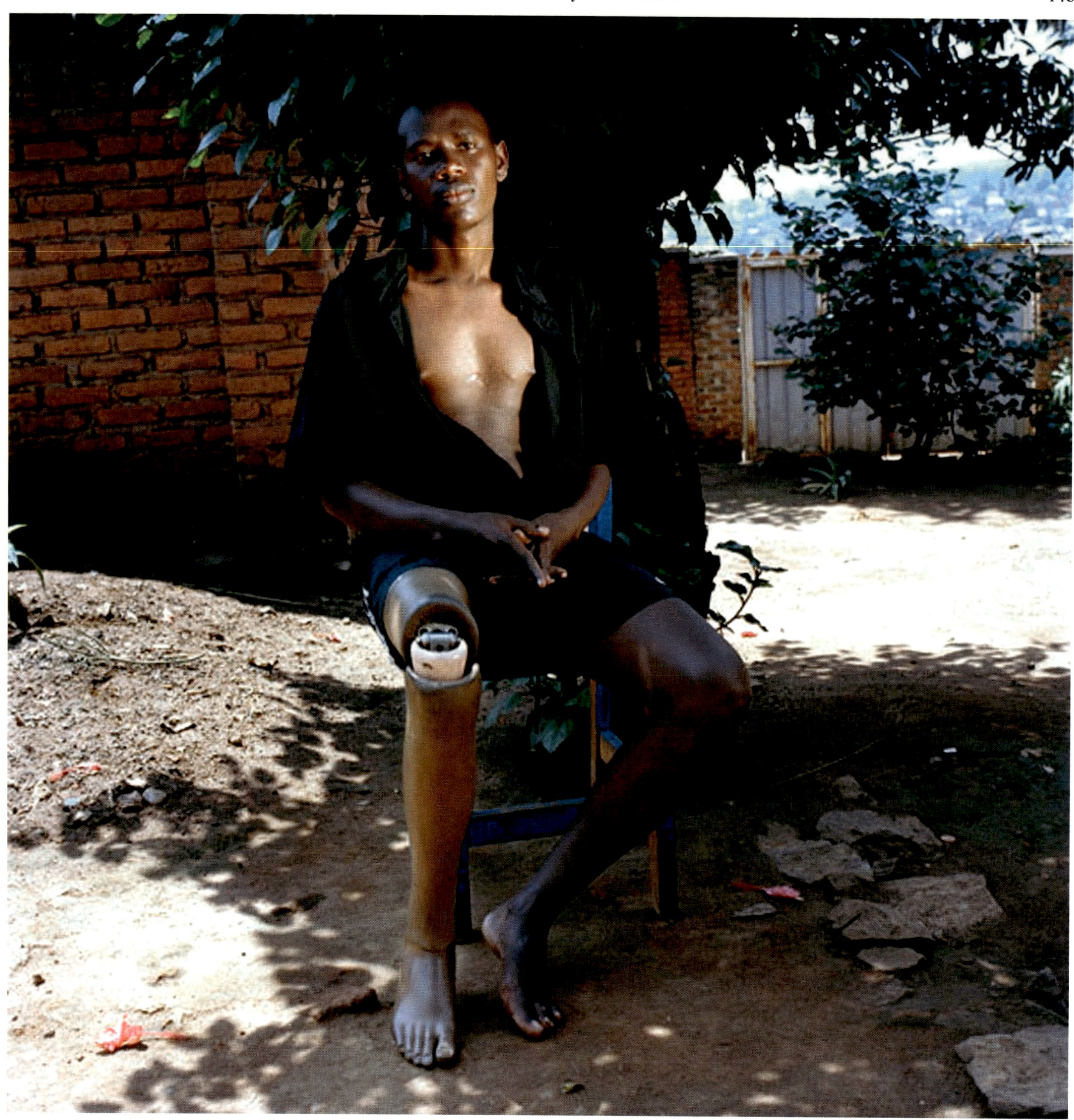

*'After I lost my leg and my entire family, I lived 4 years all by myself
in an abandoned house I had found. I was 13'. Jean Pierre Sibomana*
from the series *Portrait of a Genocide*, 2007

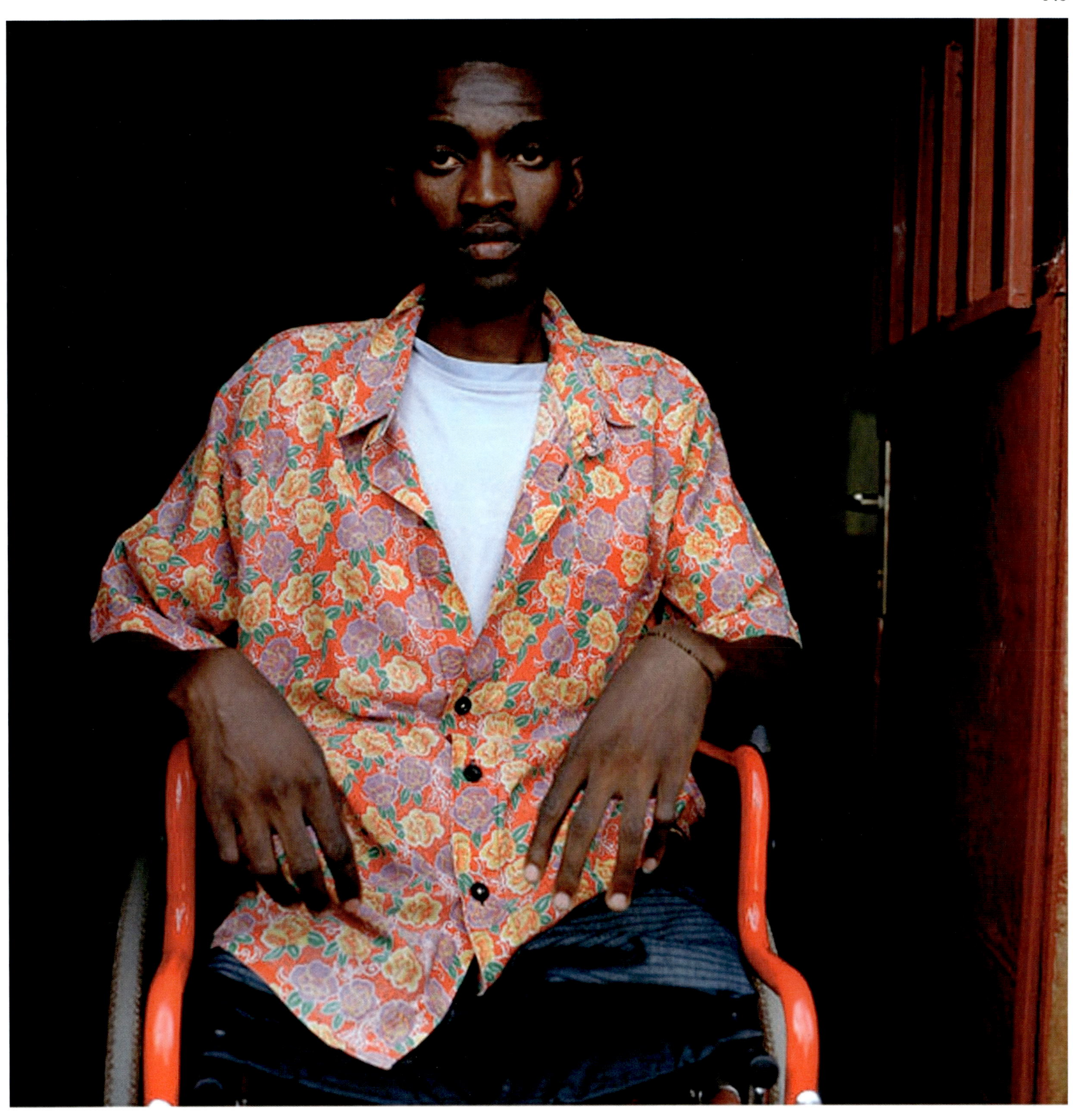

'I have nothing to say. I have too much pain, and there would be too much to say anyway'. Theoneste Muvunyambo from the series Portrait of a Genocide, 2007

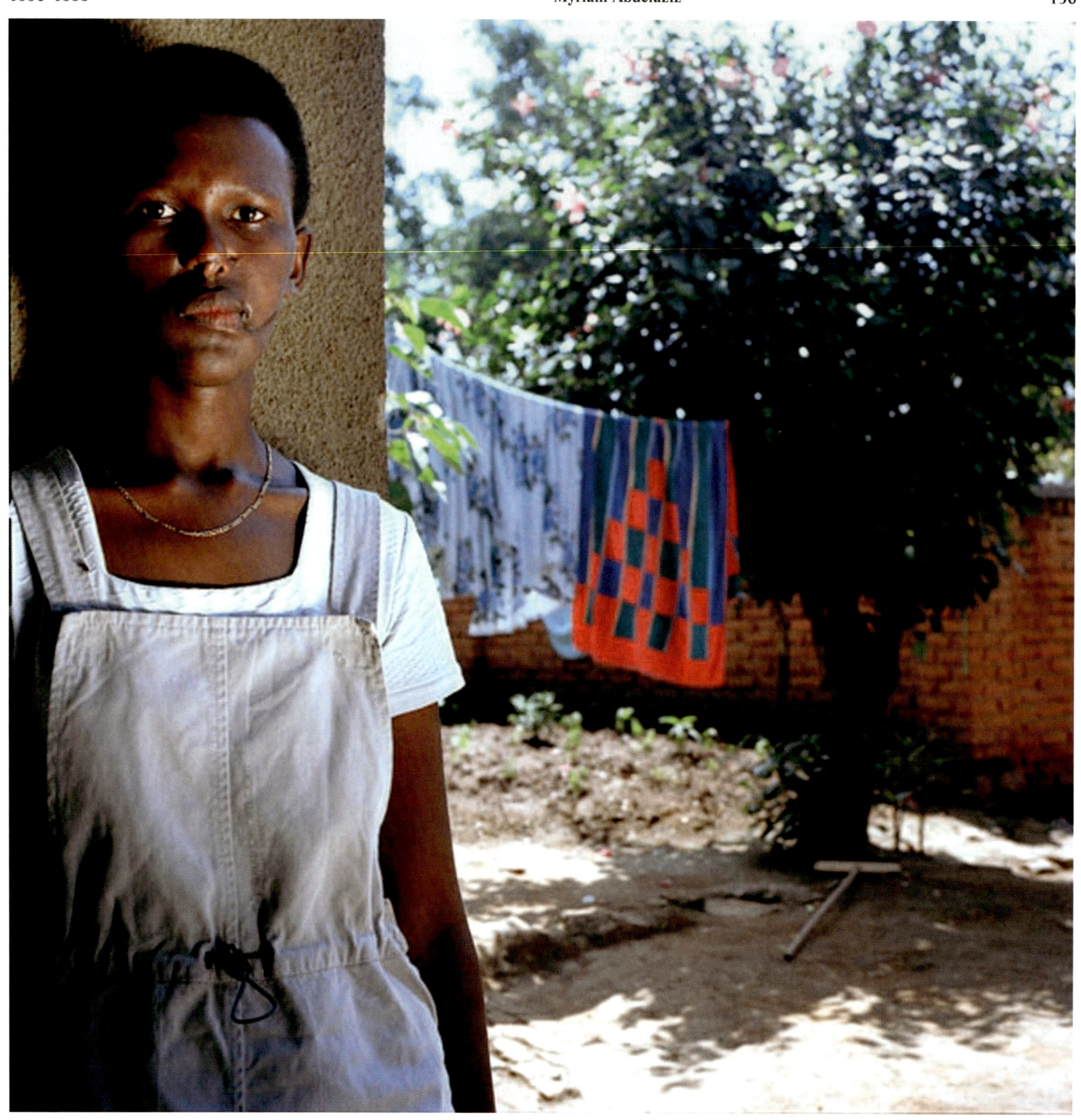

*'One of the genocide perpetuator had pity on me and was able to con-
vince the others to leave me alive. It was a miracle. I was 8'. Godiose
Mukakahisa* from the series *Portrait of a Genocide*, 2007

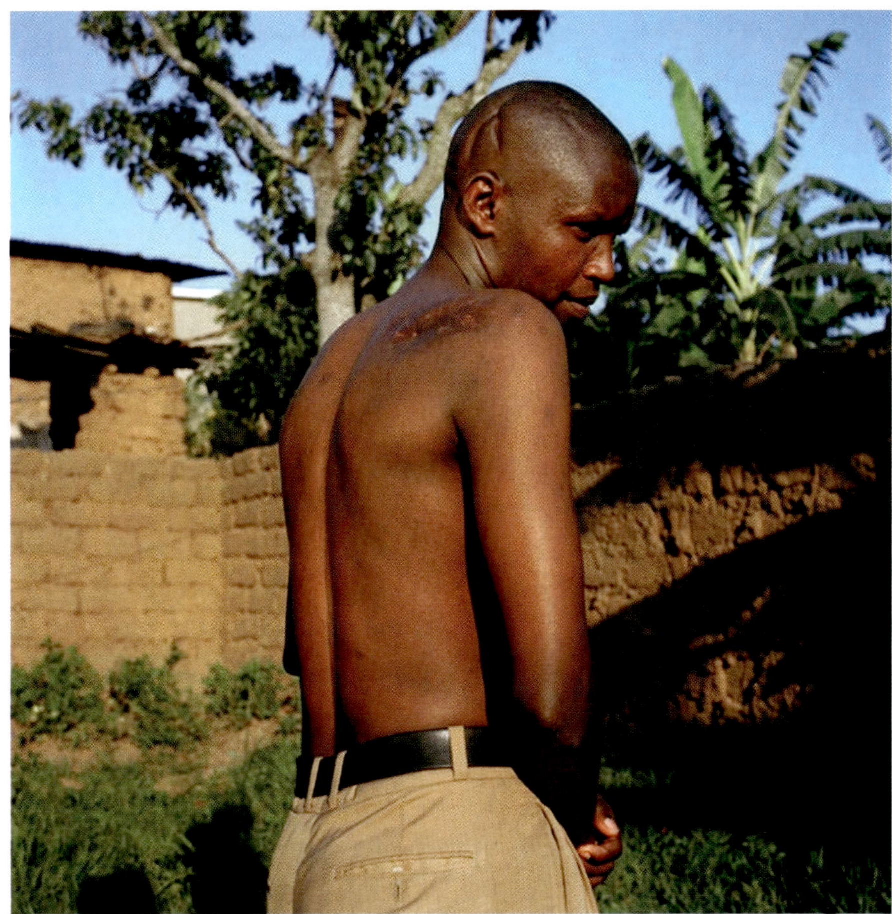

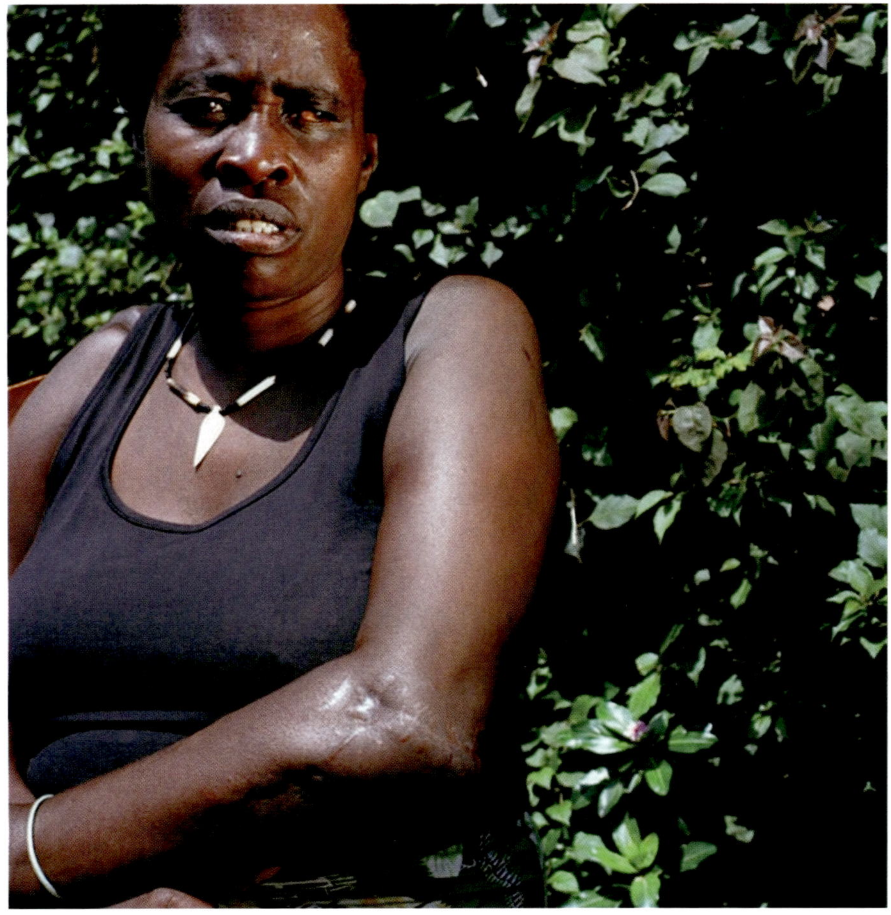

'I still receive intimidation letters and death threats. I know it is my neighbors who send them'. *Samuel Nduwayo* from the series *Portrait of a Genocide*, 2007

'I can't move my arms anymore. I have no husband or any family anymore. How was I supposed to take care of my children?' *Beatrice Bazayirwe* from the series *Portrait of a Genocide*, 2007

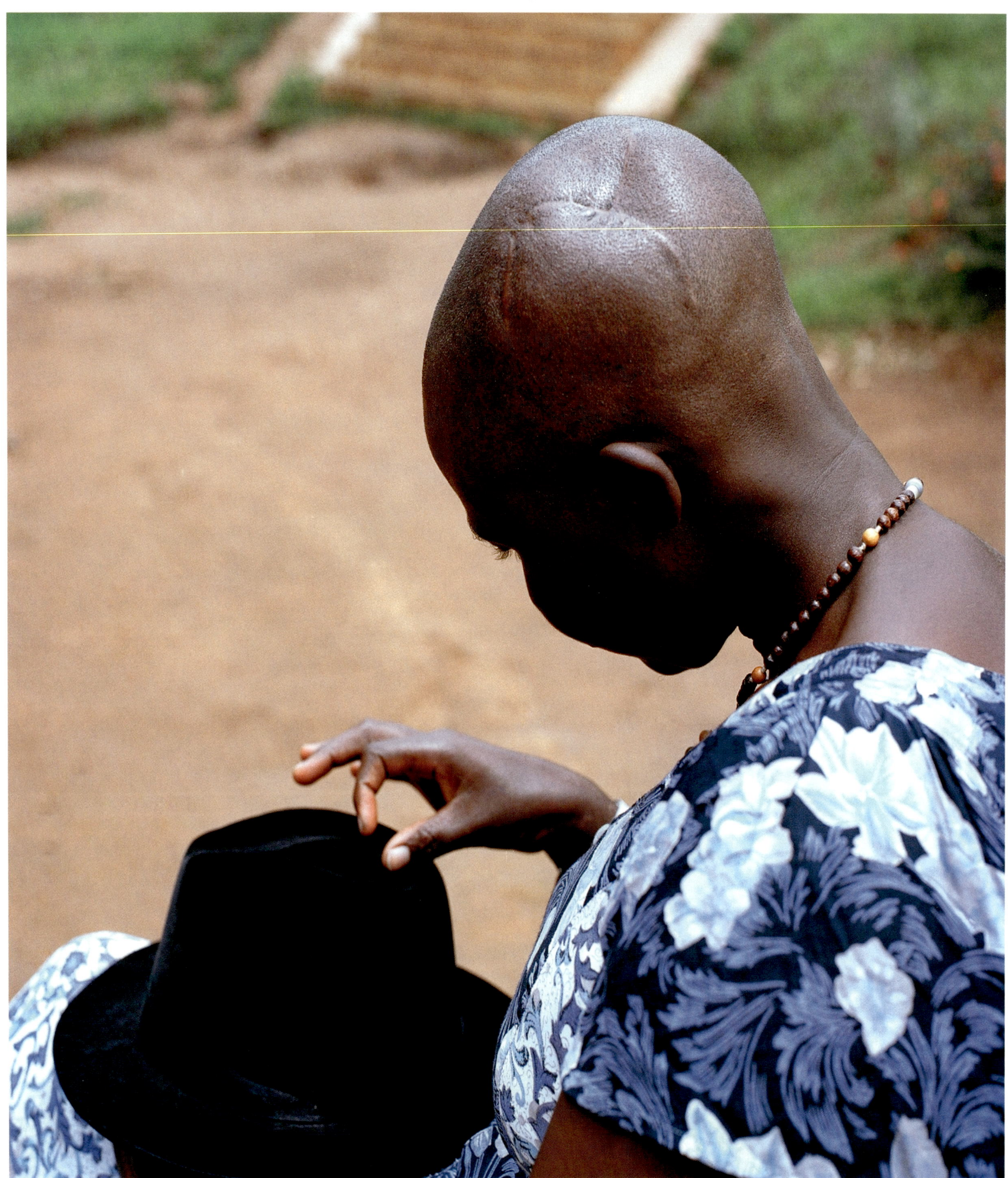

'My head still hurts. I hear noises, like very strong wind blowing in my skull, like a storm in my head'. Winny Murekatete from the series *Portrait of a Genocide*, 2007

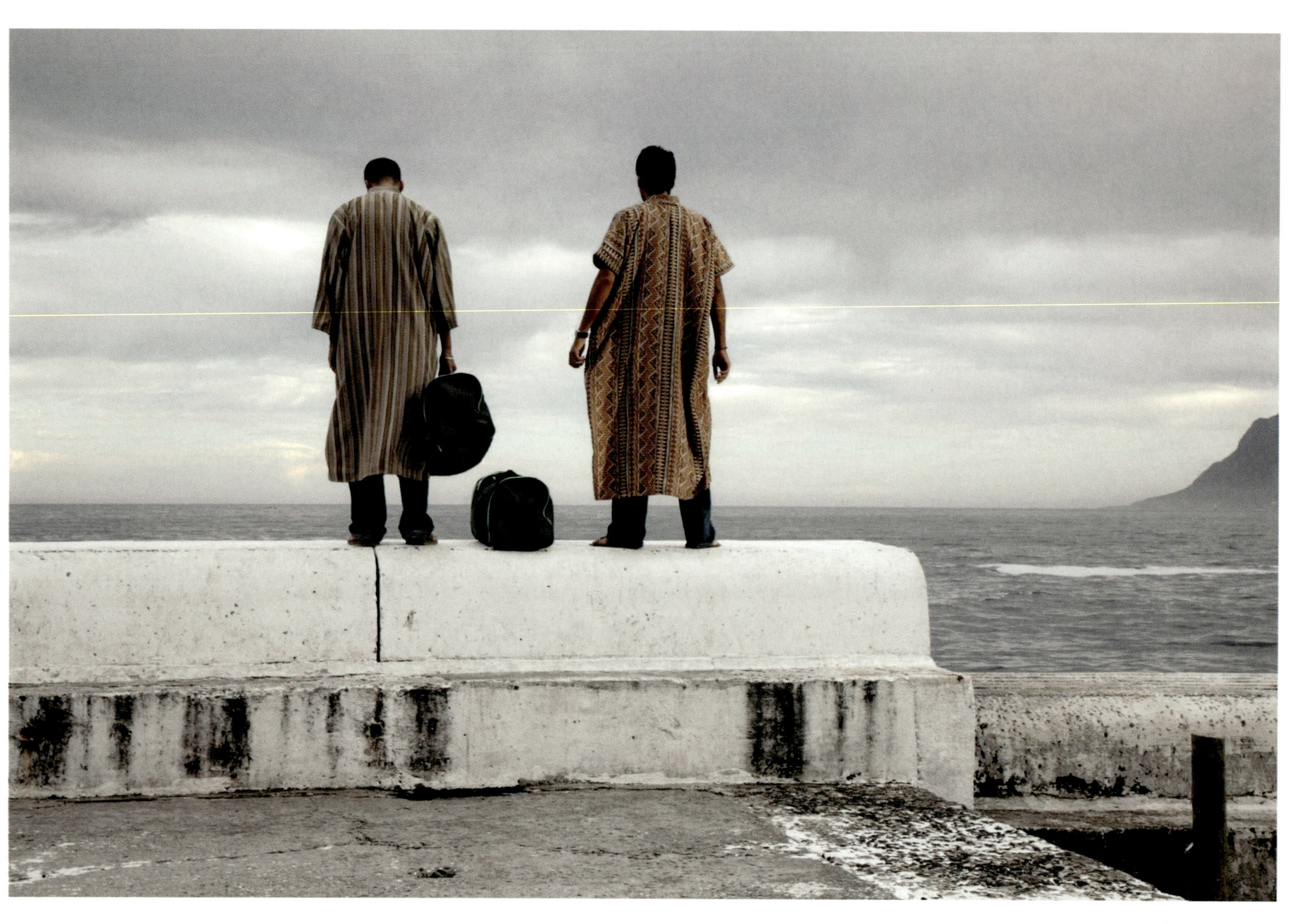

Another country* 2000 2010

* James Baldwin

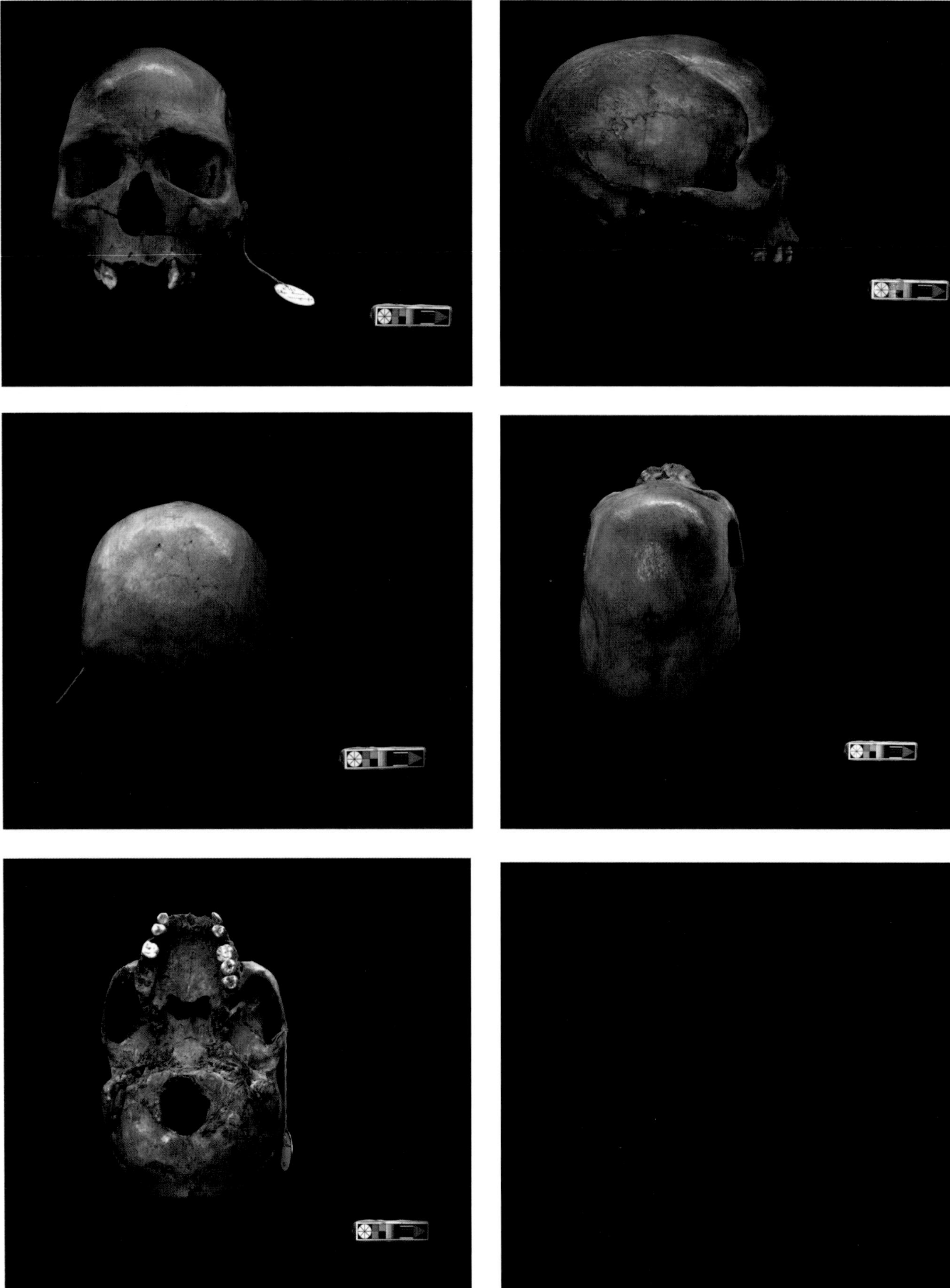

Aller et retour, 2009

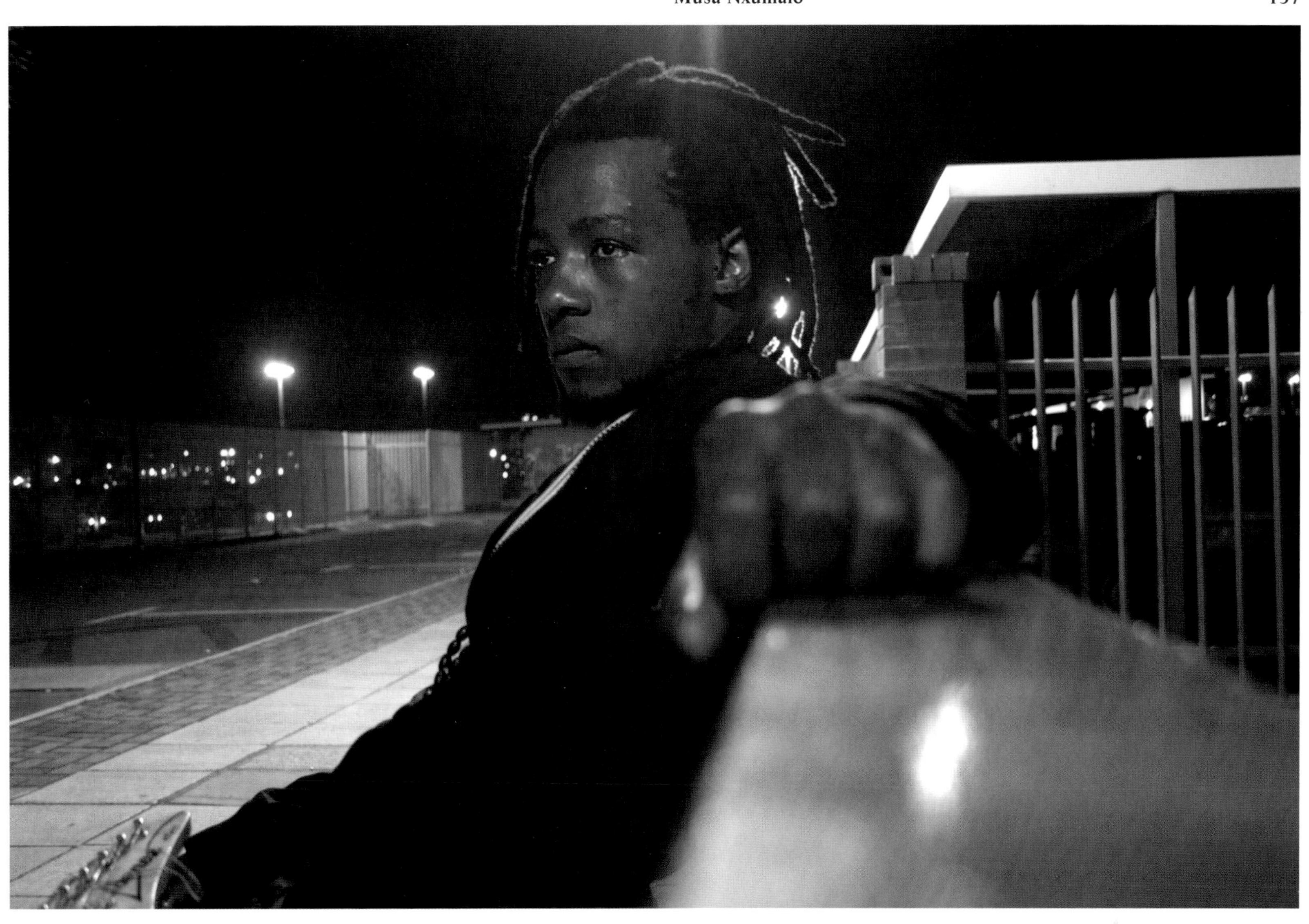

Bongani Msiza, Bat centre (Durban), 2009

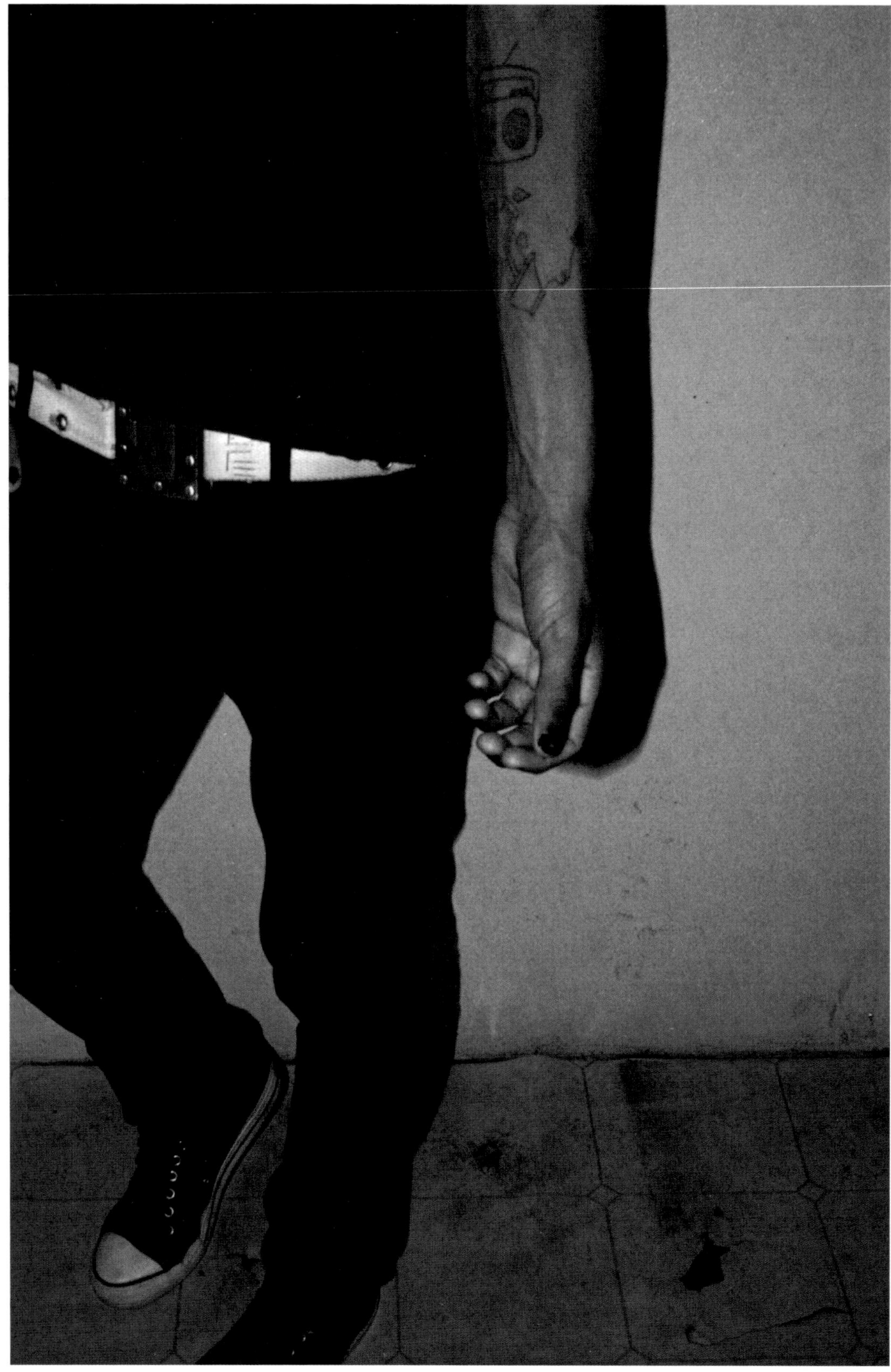

Alternative-kidz. Self-portrait, Naledi, 2008

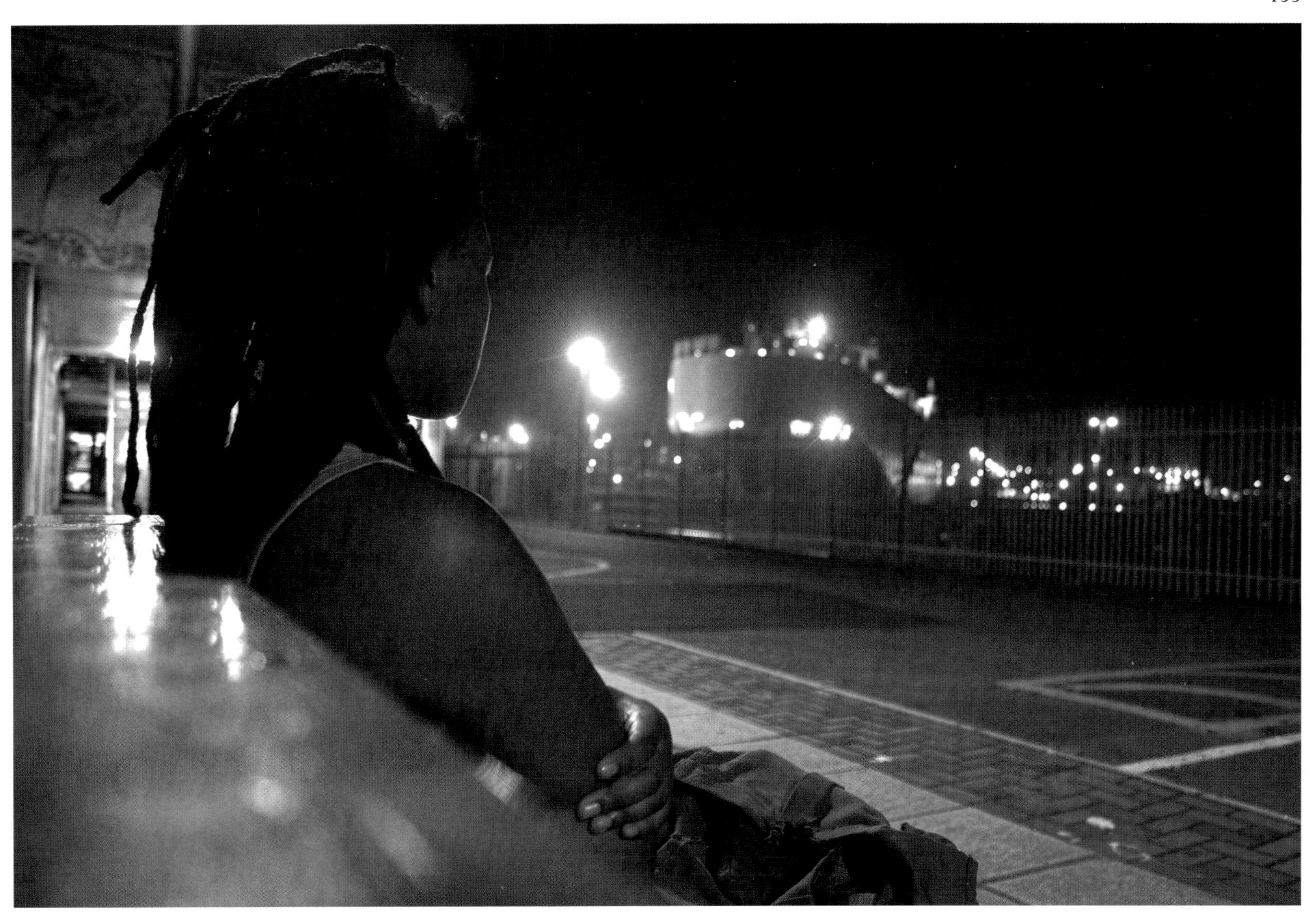

Mamaki Rakotsoana, Bat centre (Durban), 2009

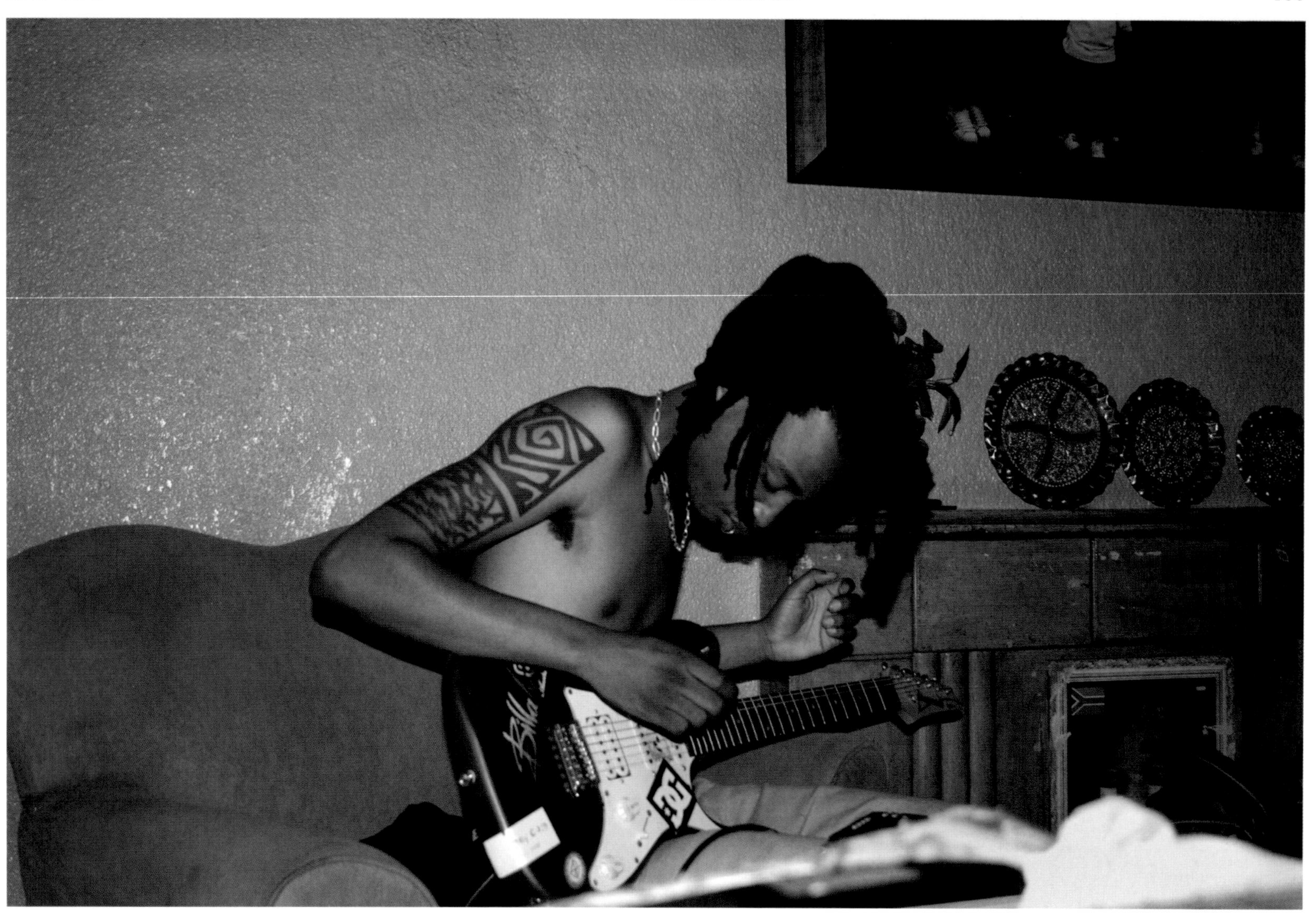

Alternative-kidz. Bongani Msiza, Durban, 2008

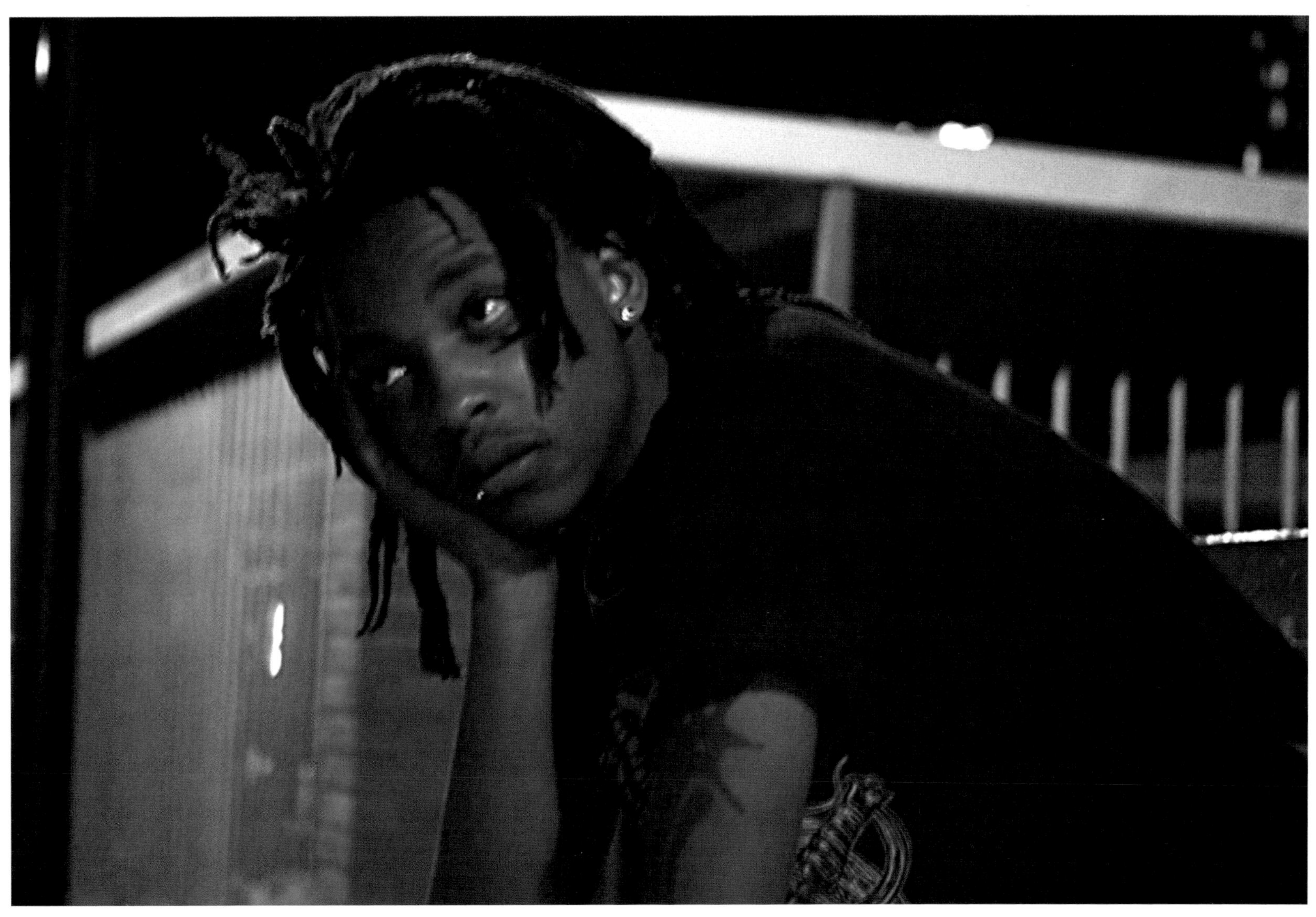

Thato Khumalo, Bat centre (Durban), 2009

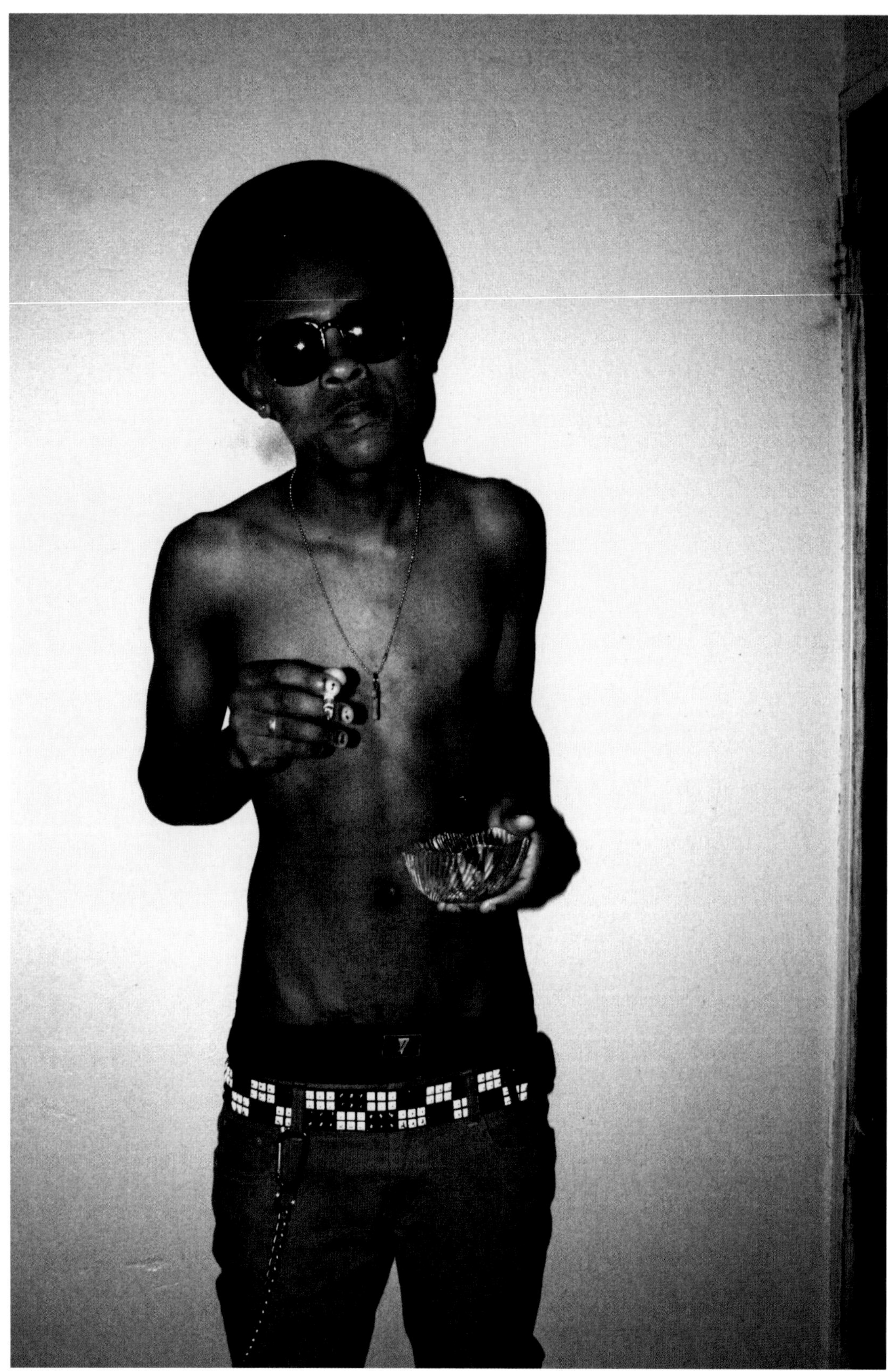

Alternative-kidz. Self-portrait, Naledi, 2008

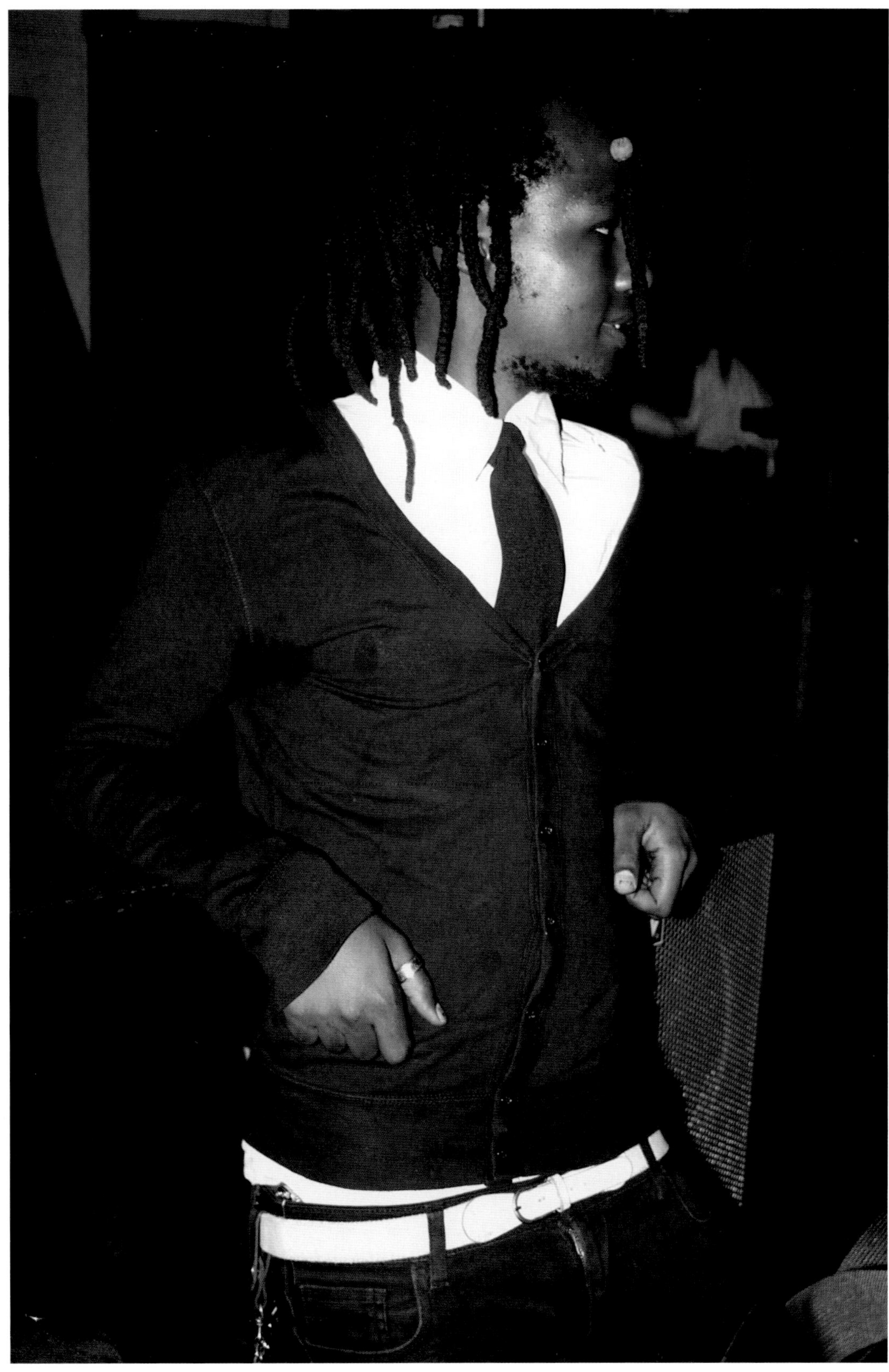

Alternative-kidz. Thato Khumalo, Vaal, 2008

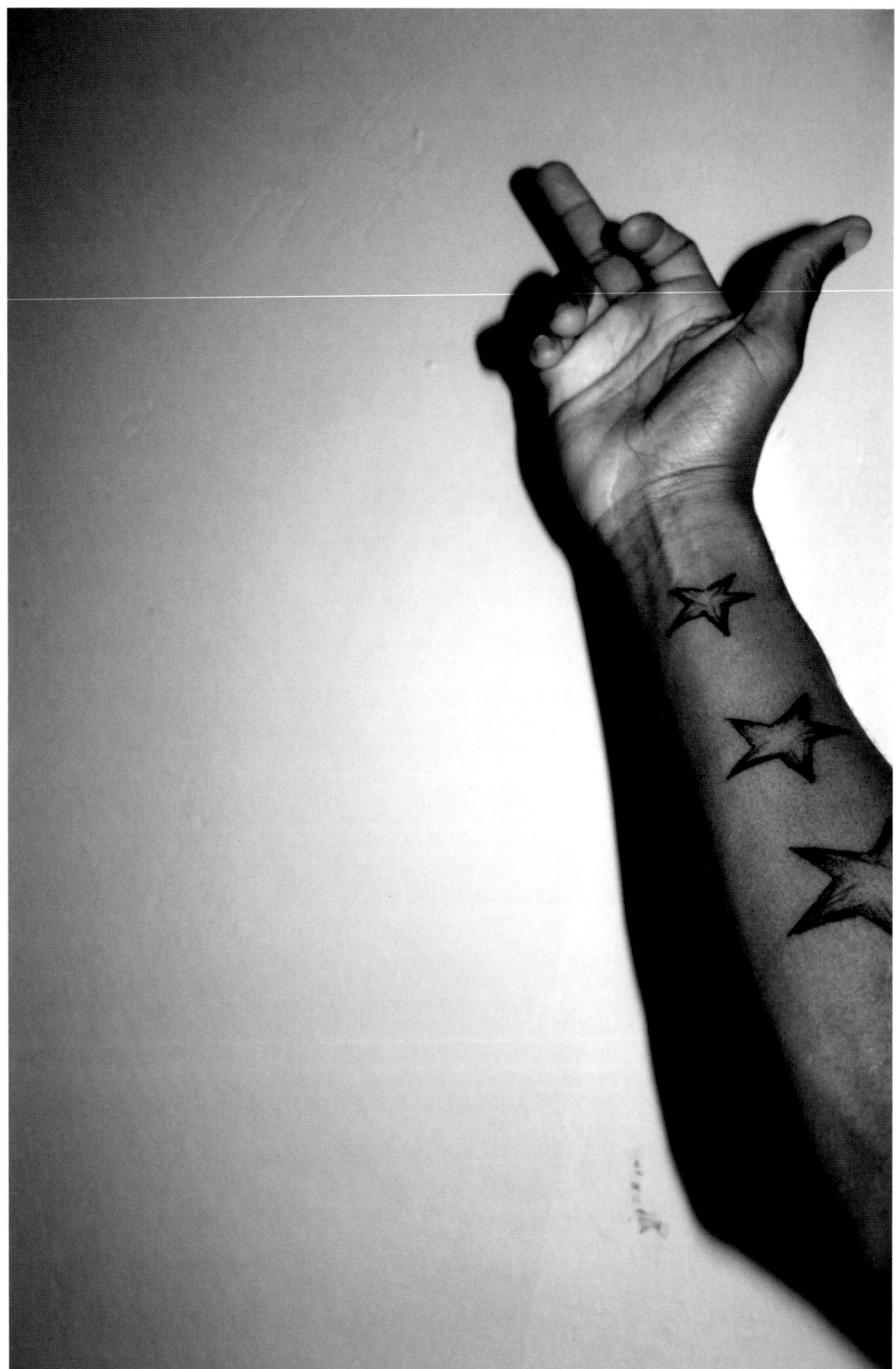

Alternative-kidz. Self-portrait, Naledi, 2008

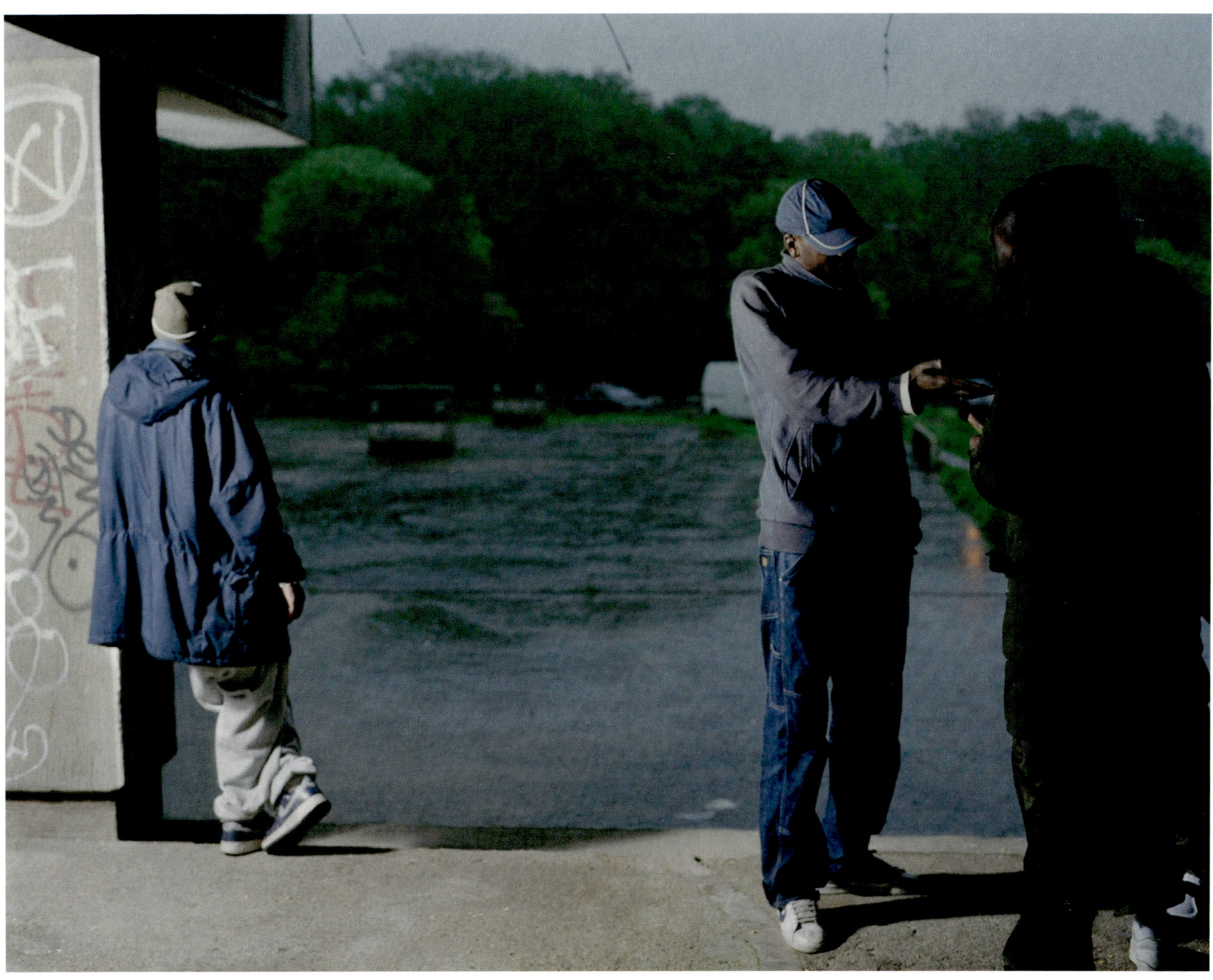

Le hall, 2007

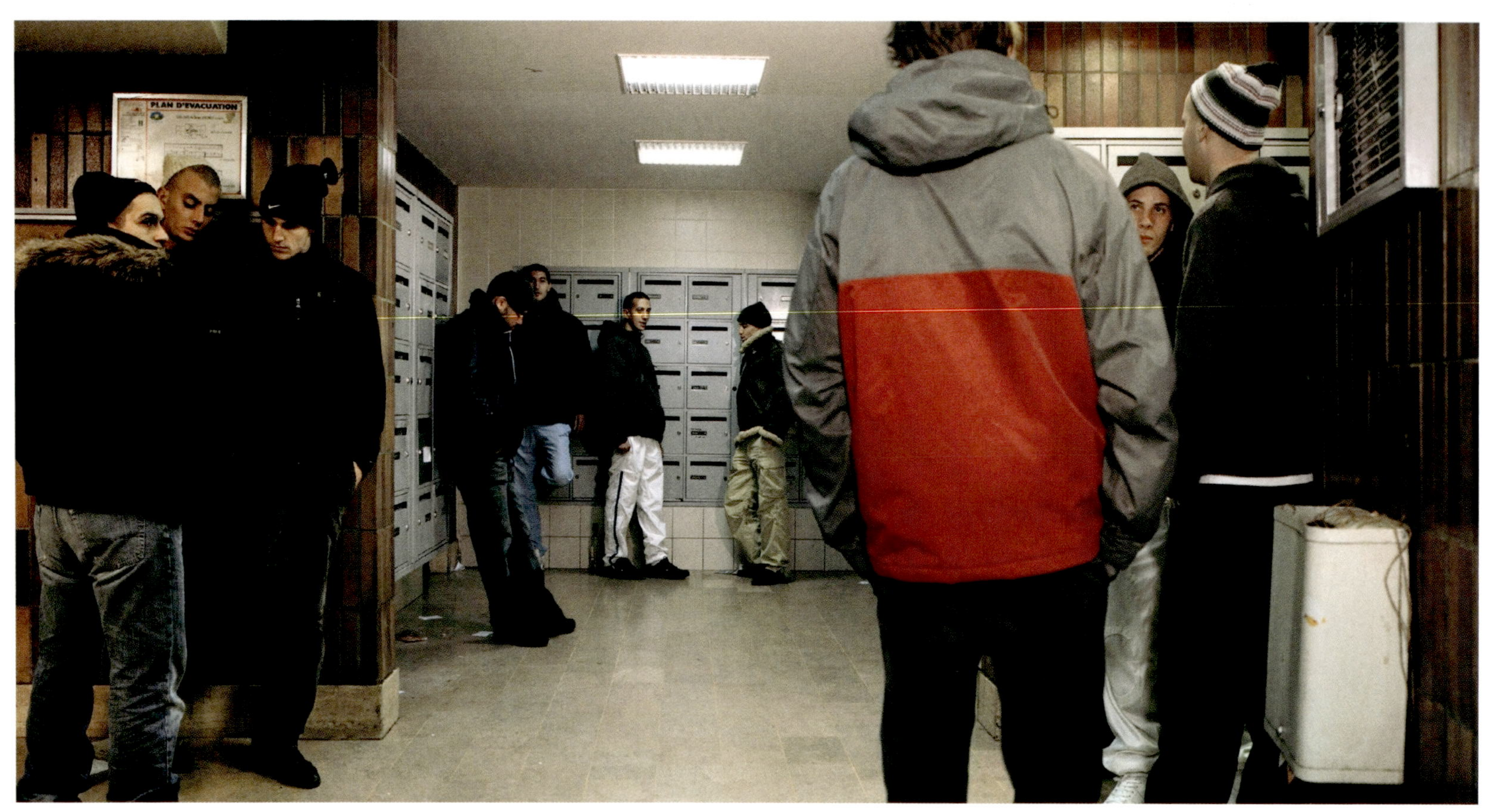

Carré rouge, 2005

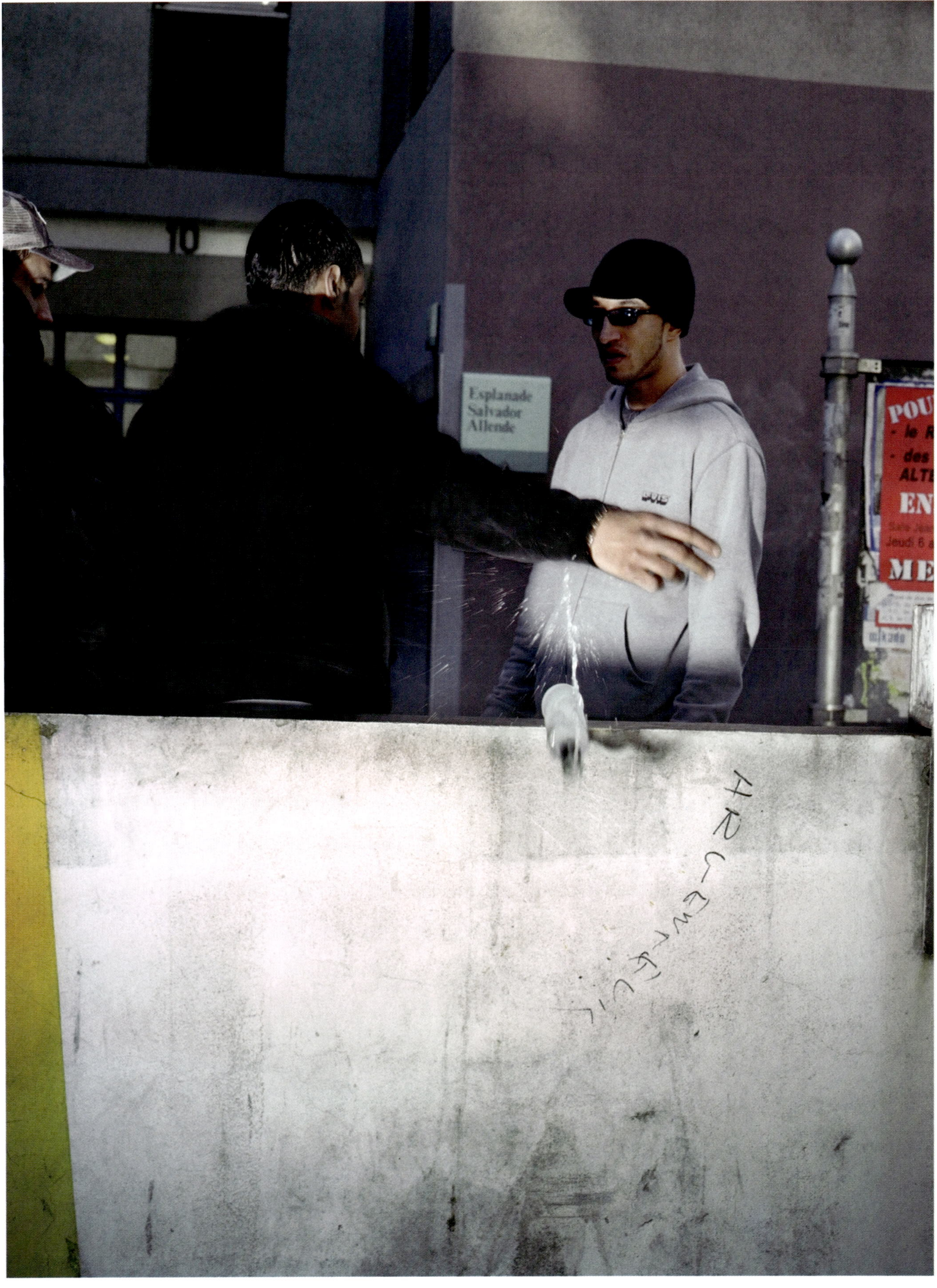

Bascule, 2006

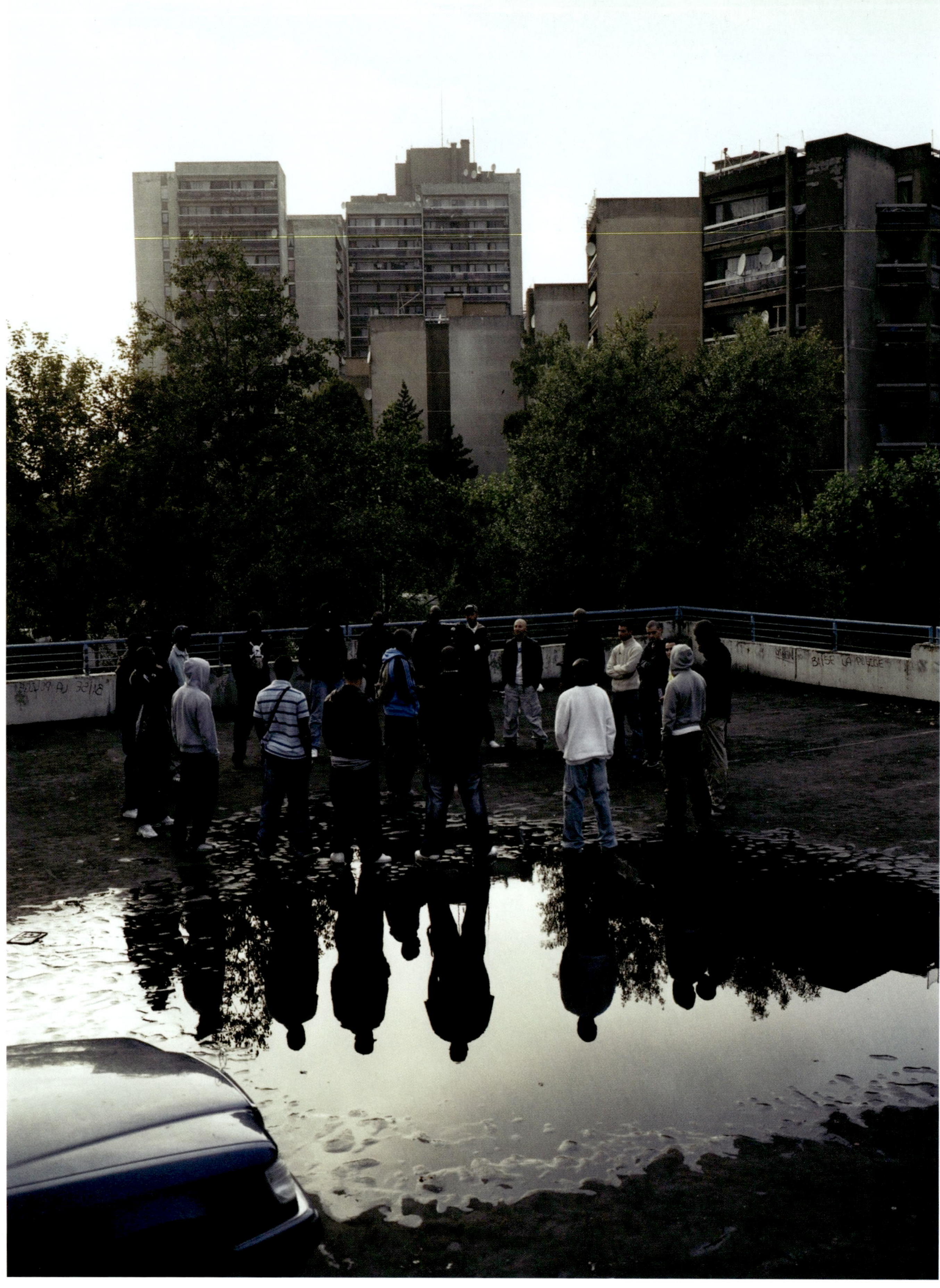

Le miroir, 2006

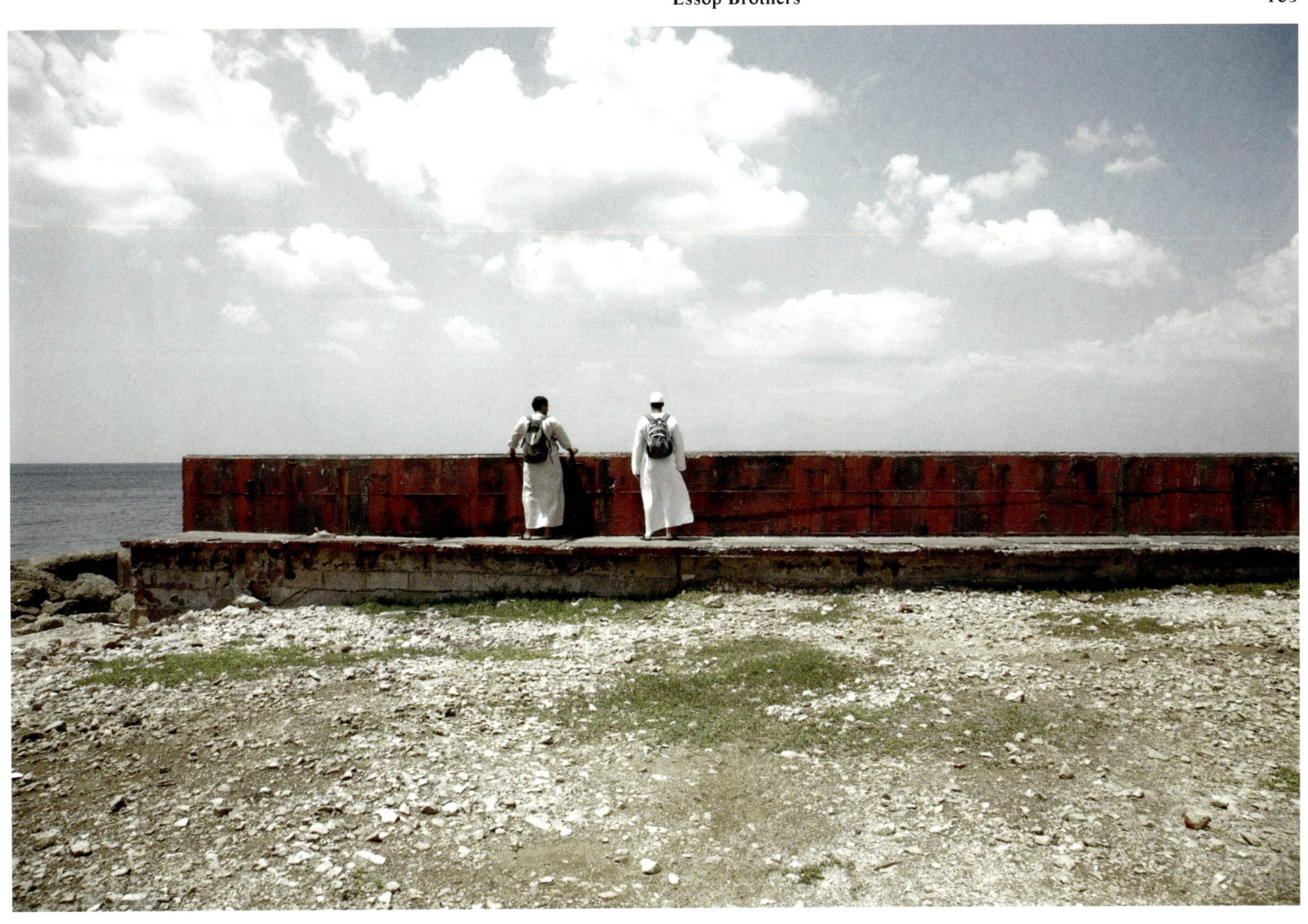

Havana, 2009

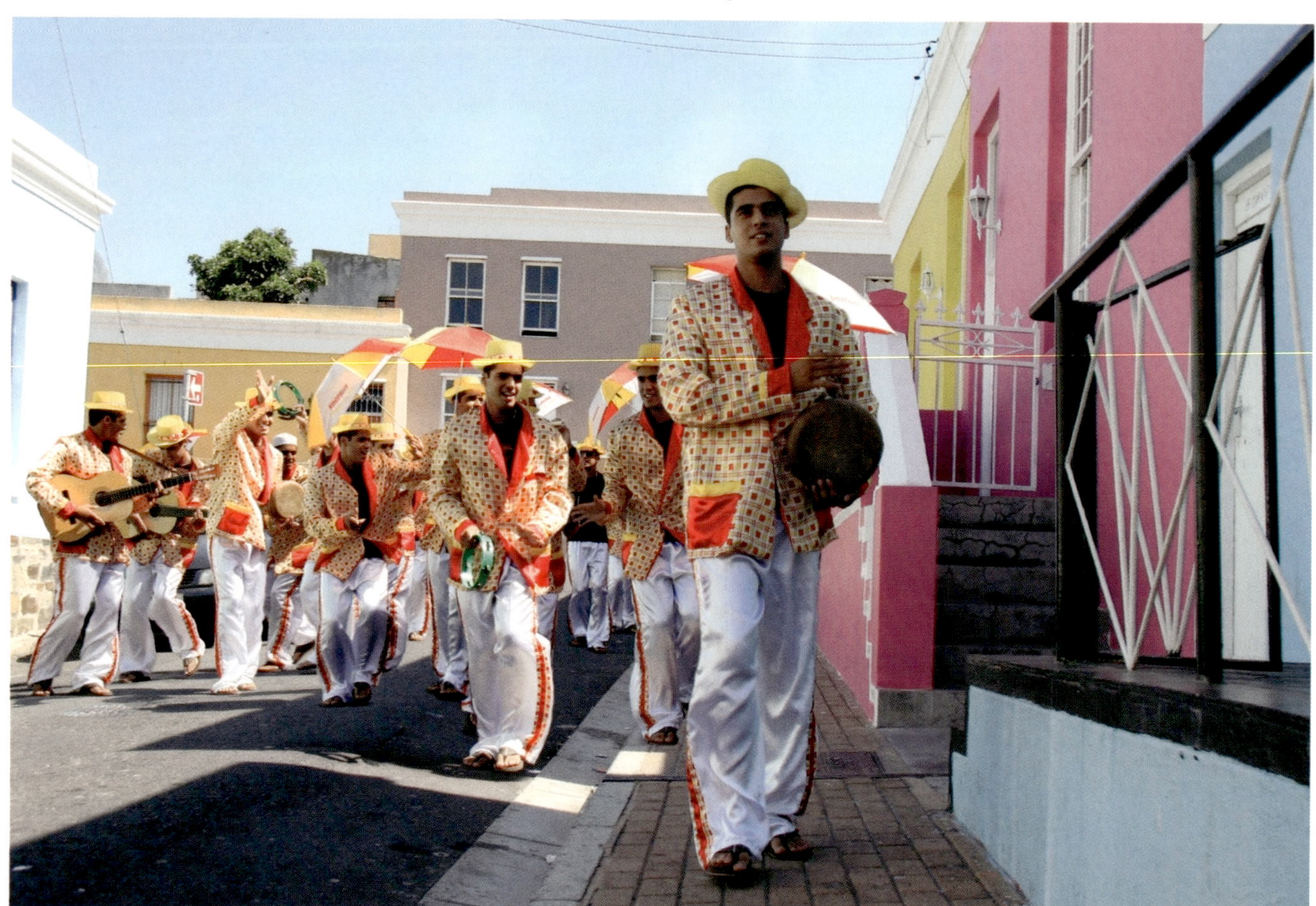

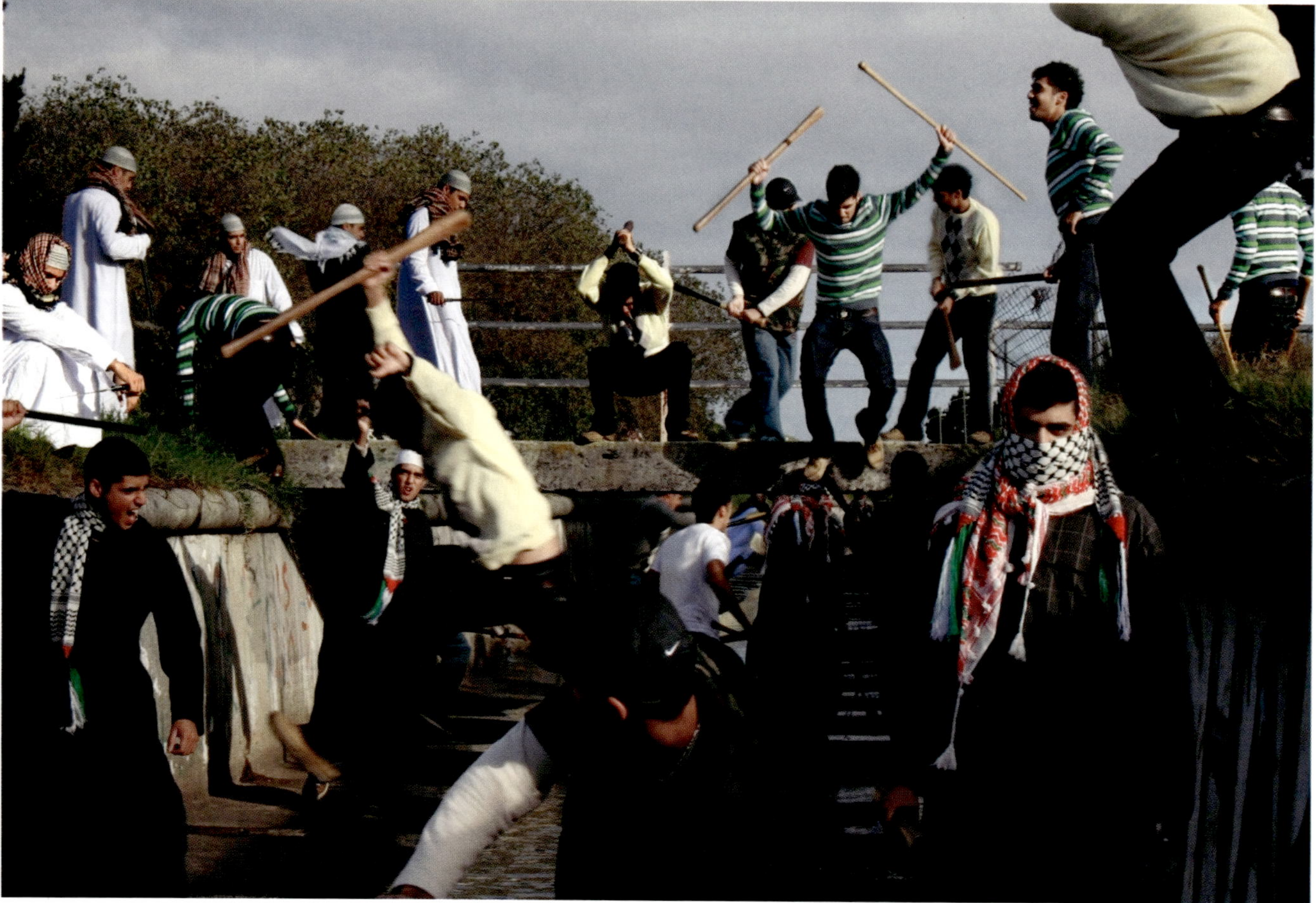

Pensylvanians, 2009   *Black River*, 2007

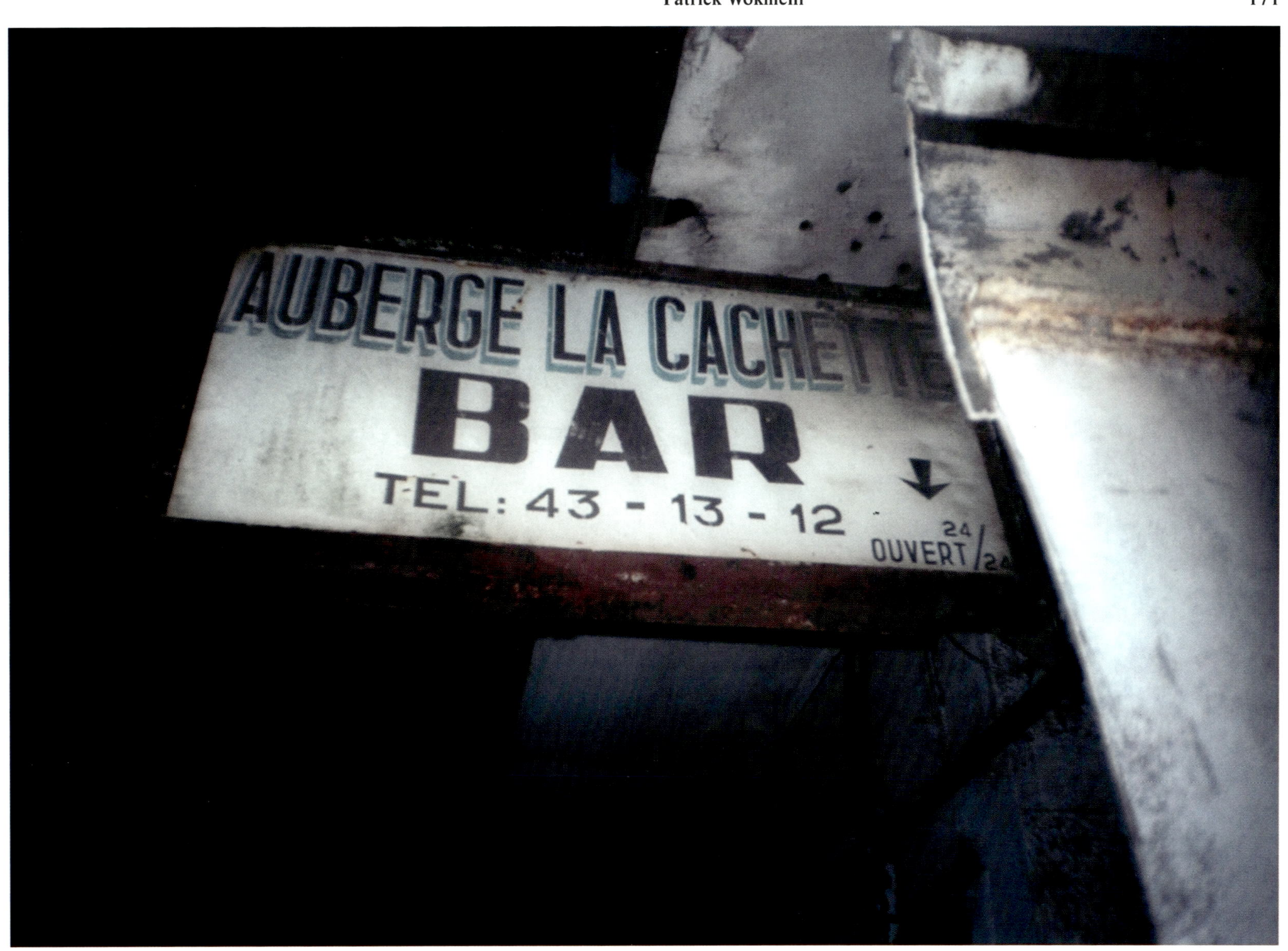

from the series *Les Belles de New Bell*, 2008

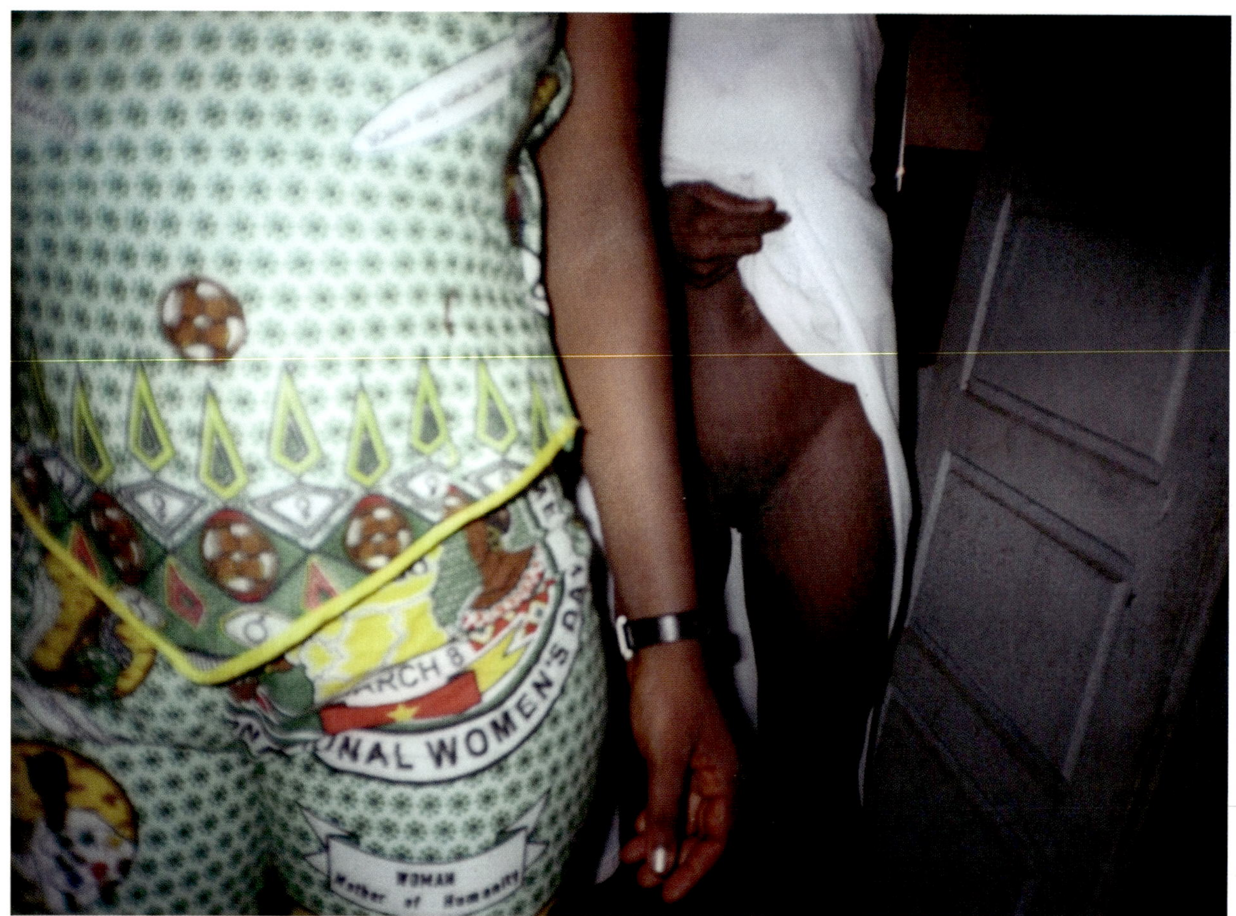

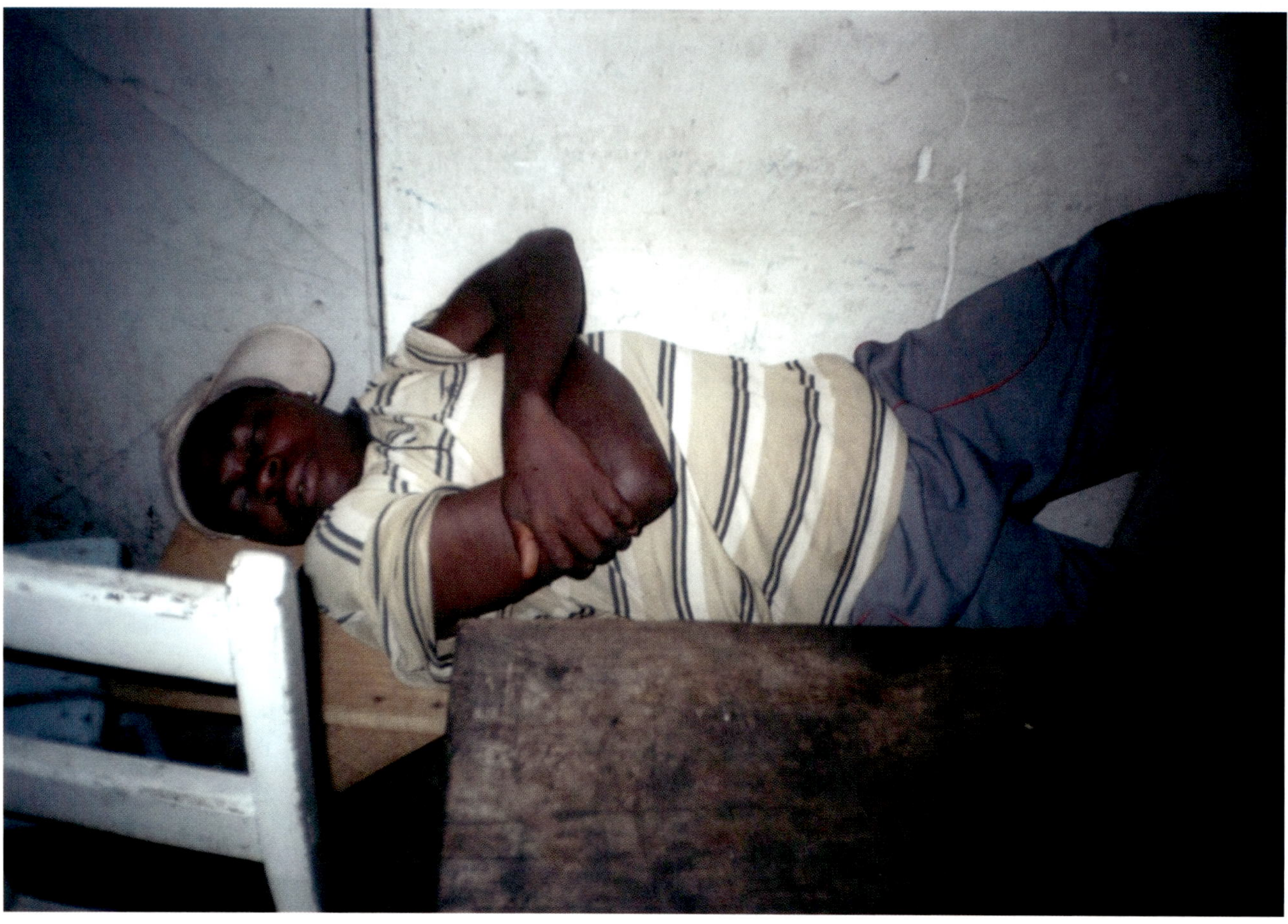

from the series *Les Belles de New Bell*, 2008

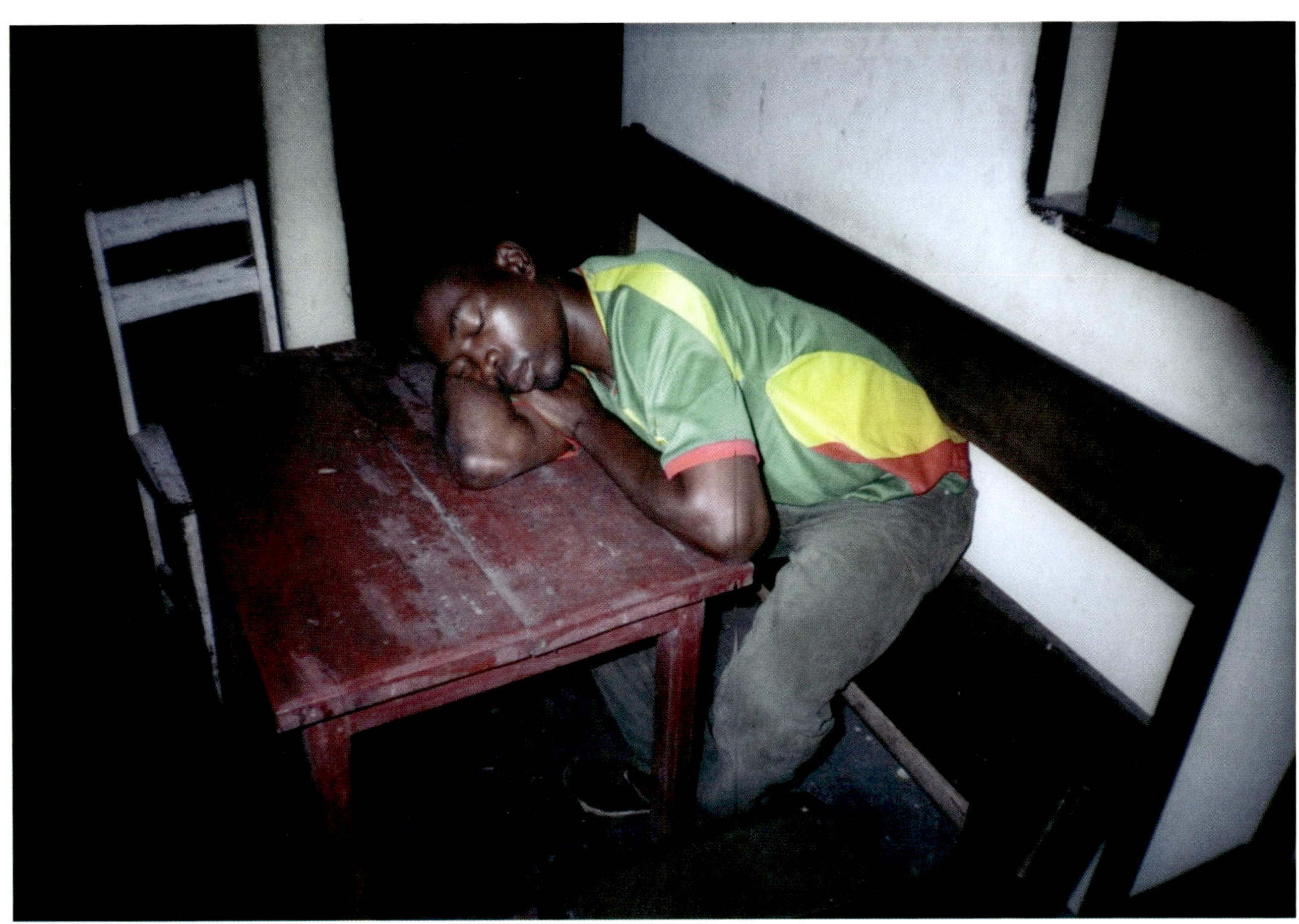

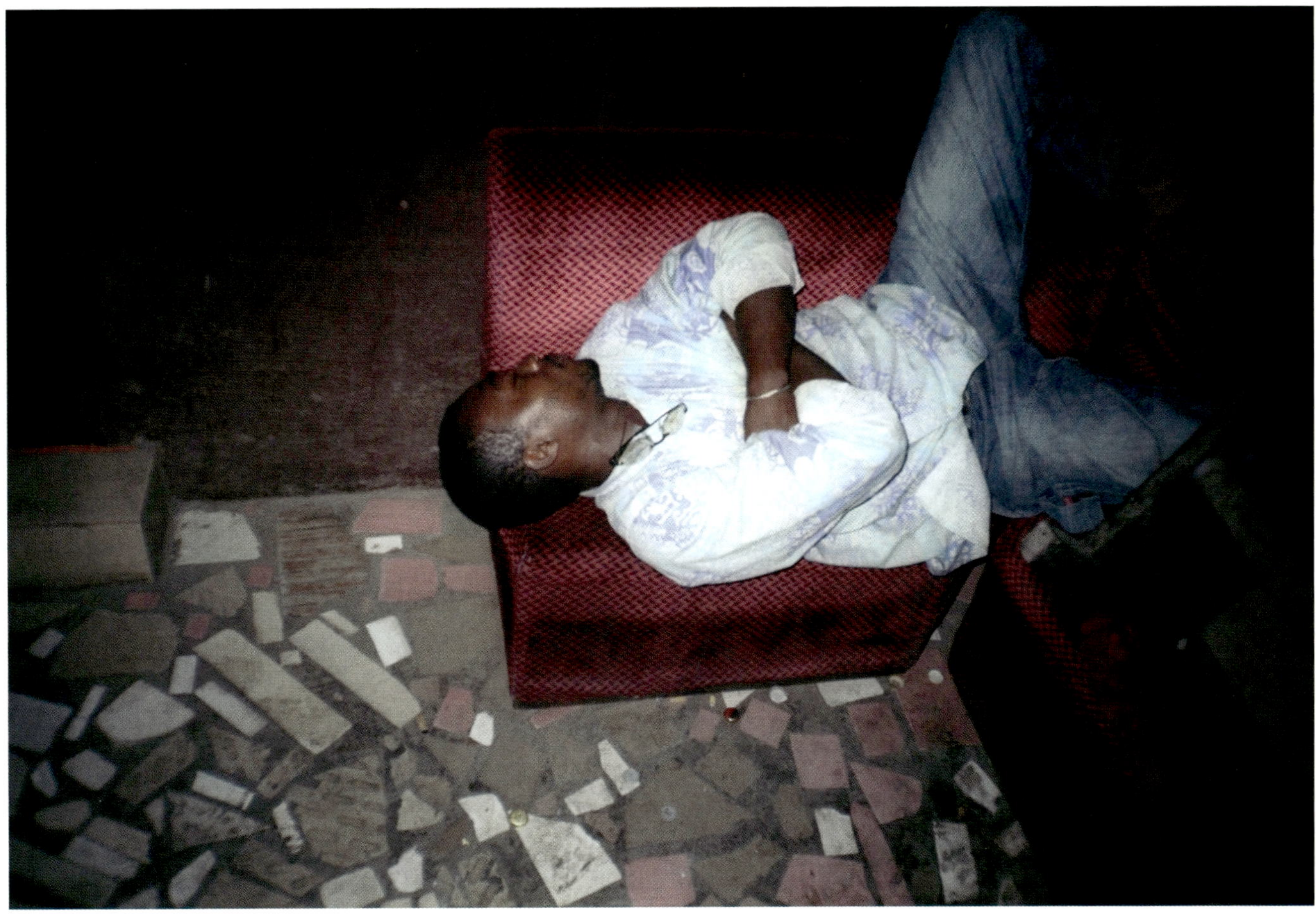

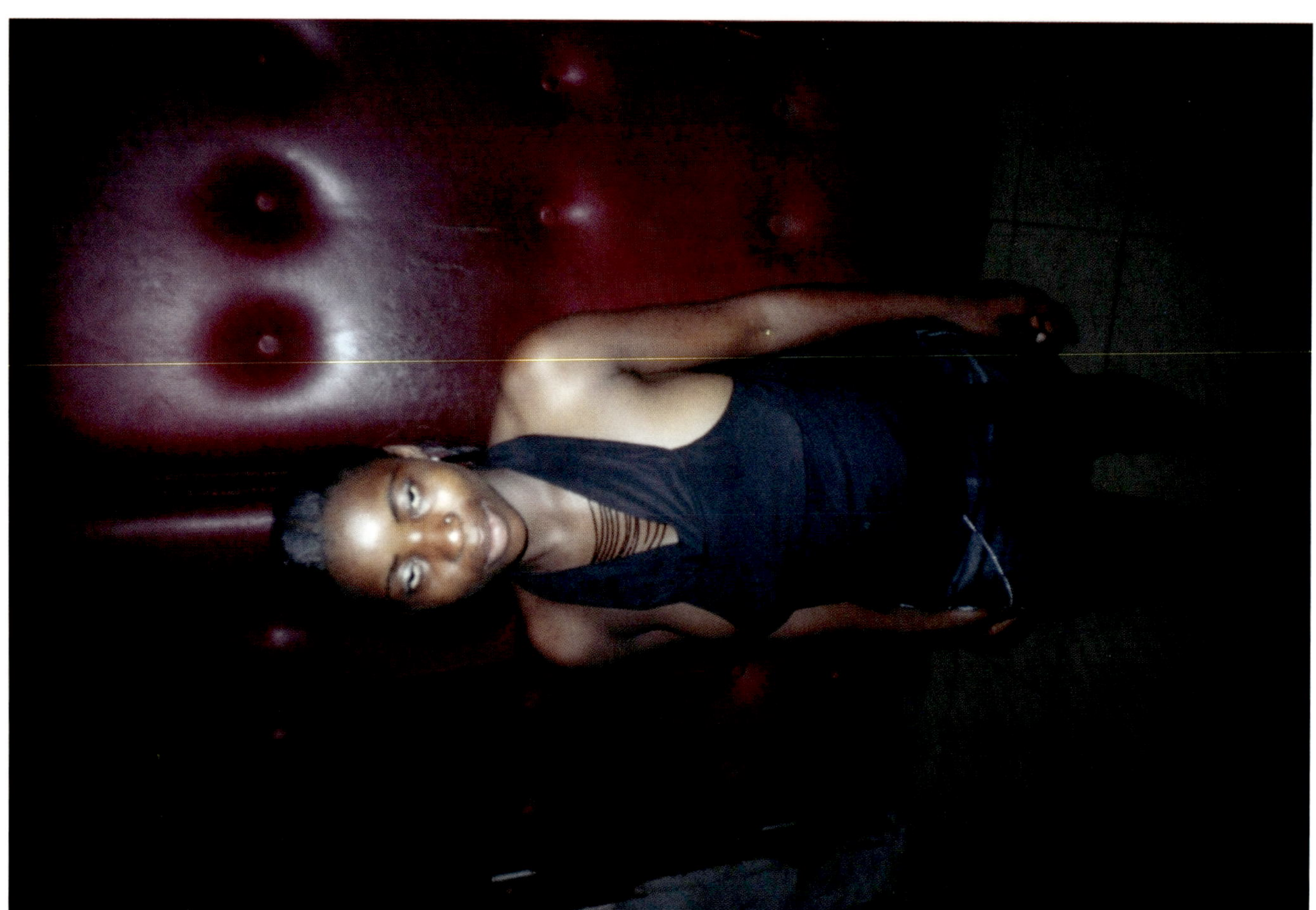

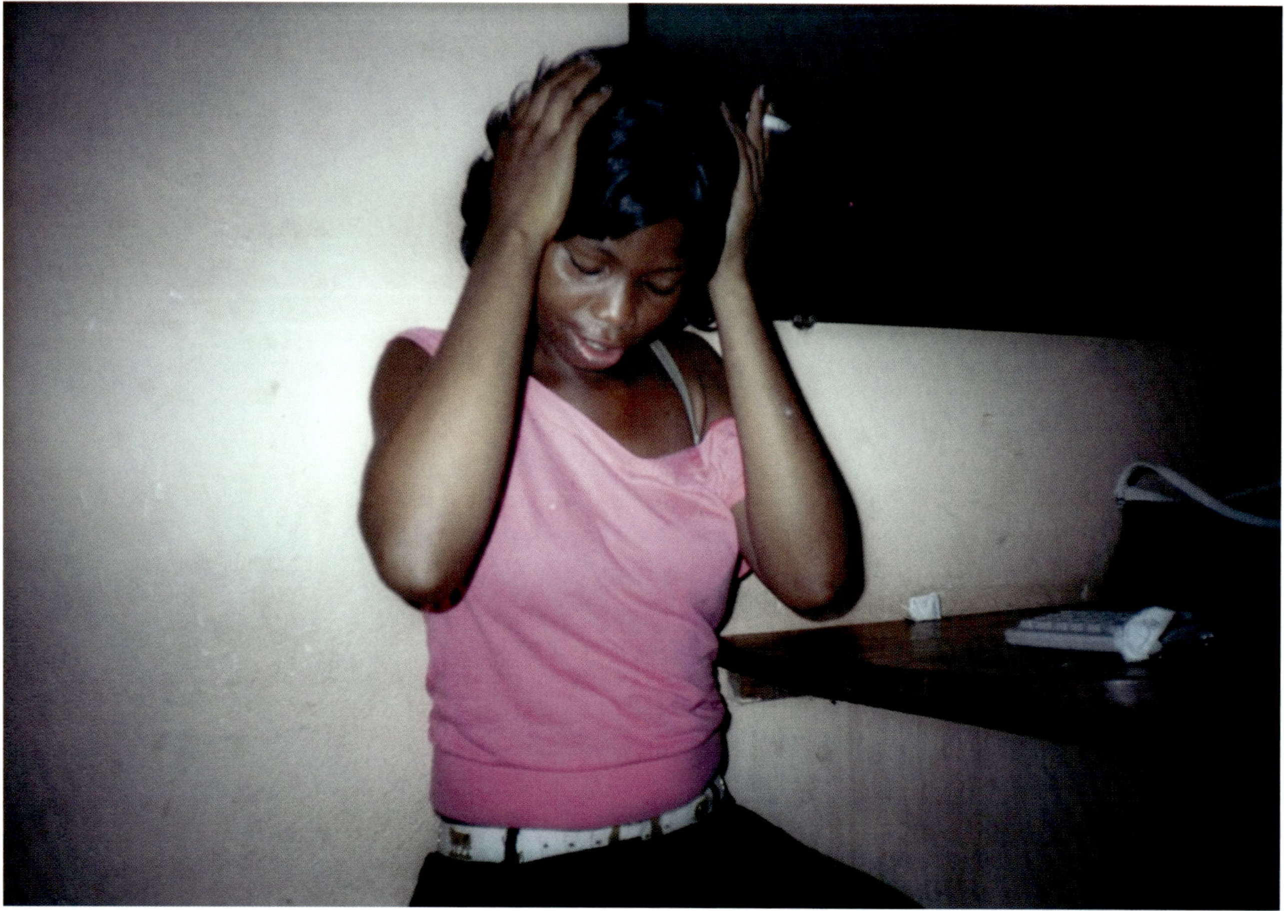

from the series *Les Belles de New Bell*, 2008

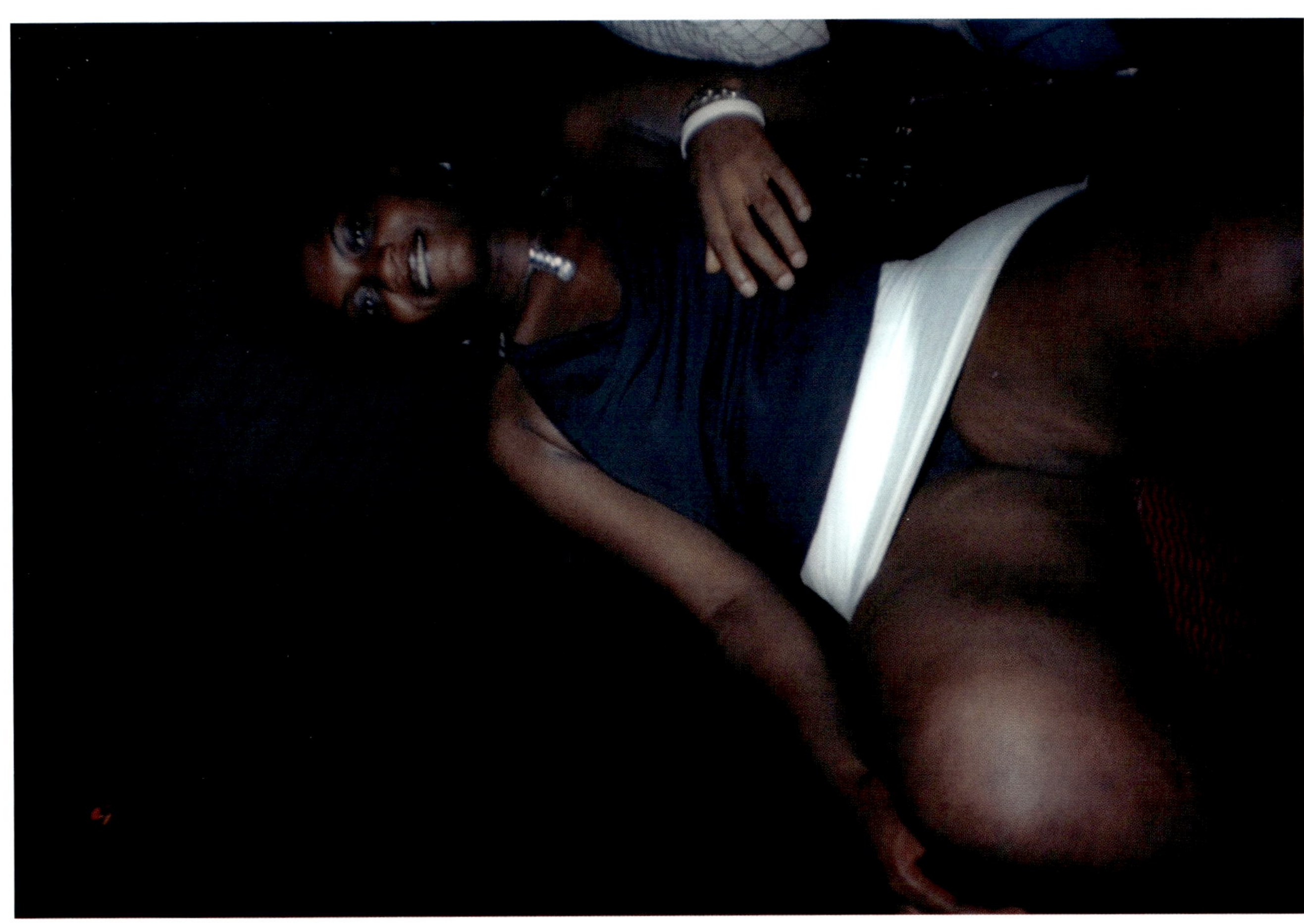

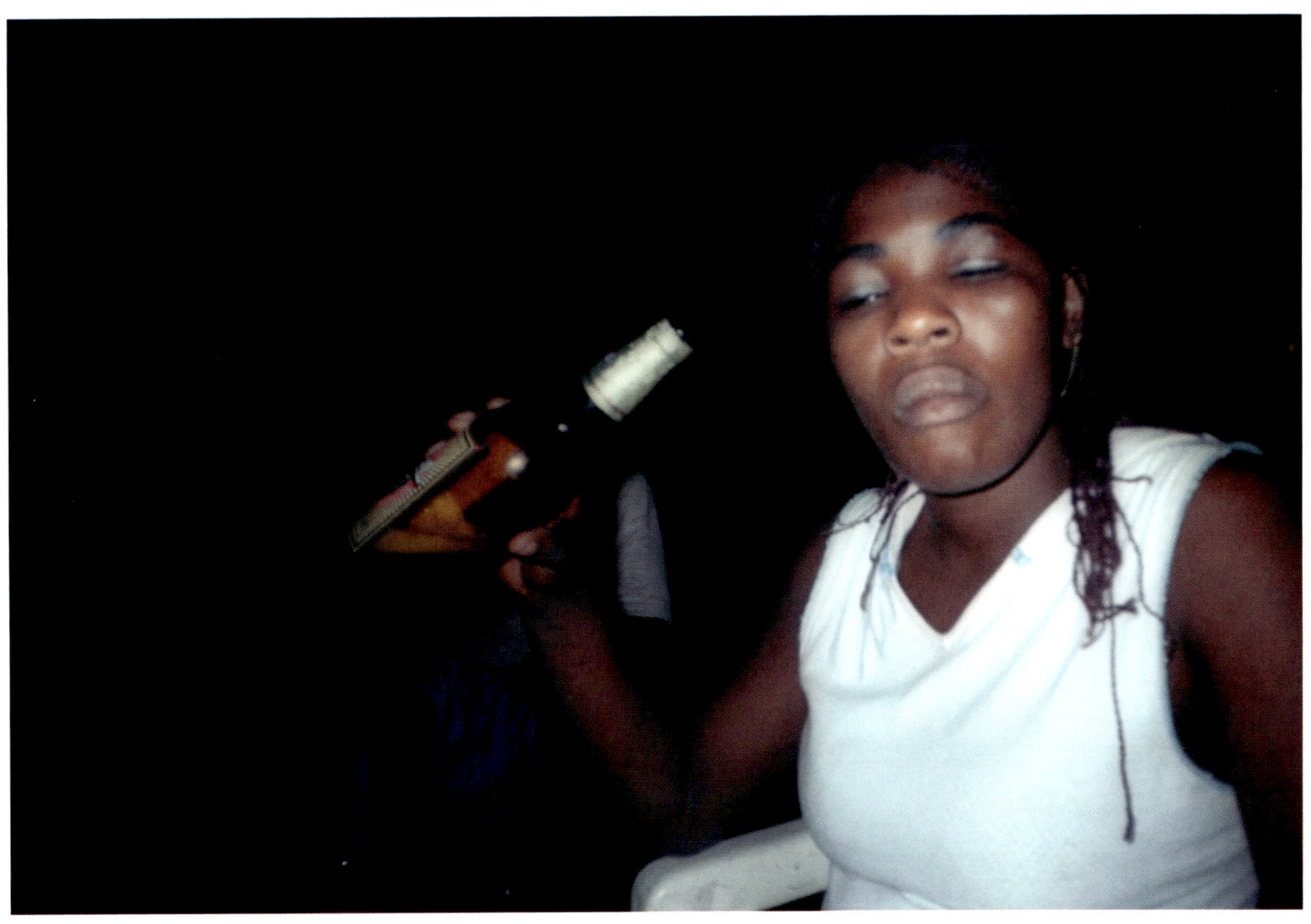

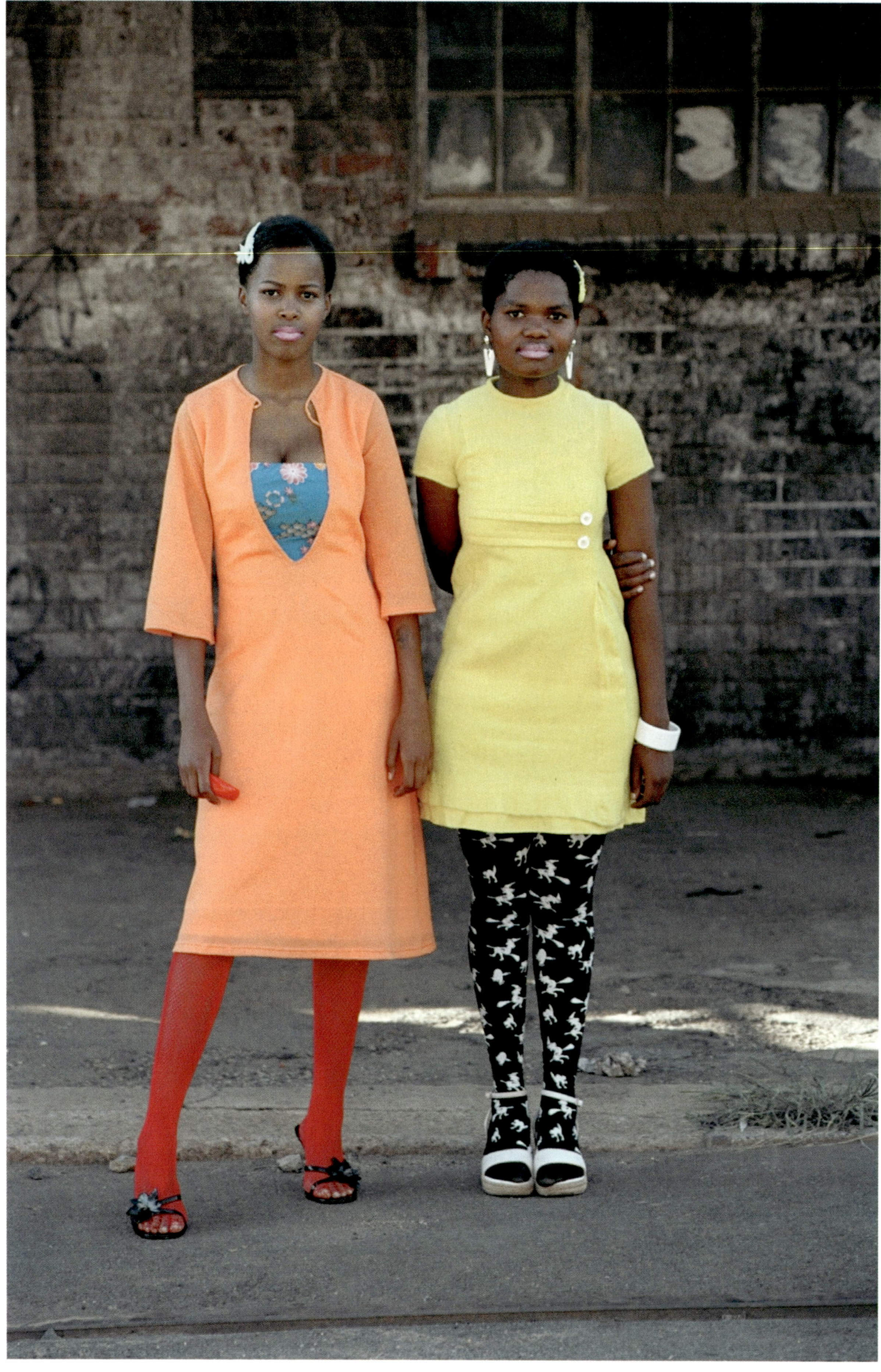

Cindy and Nkuli, 2003

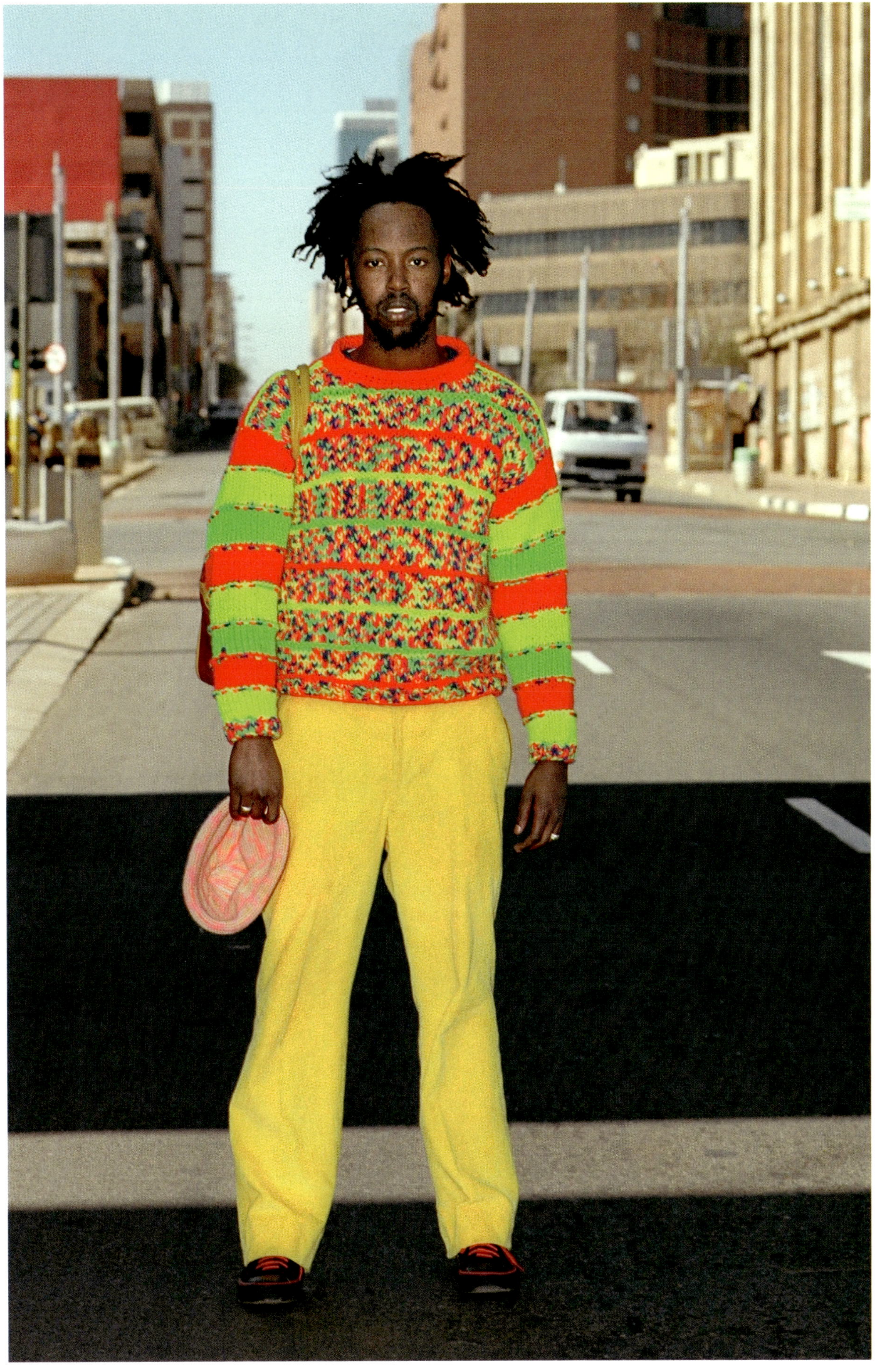

Hloni, 2004

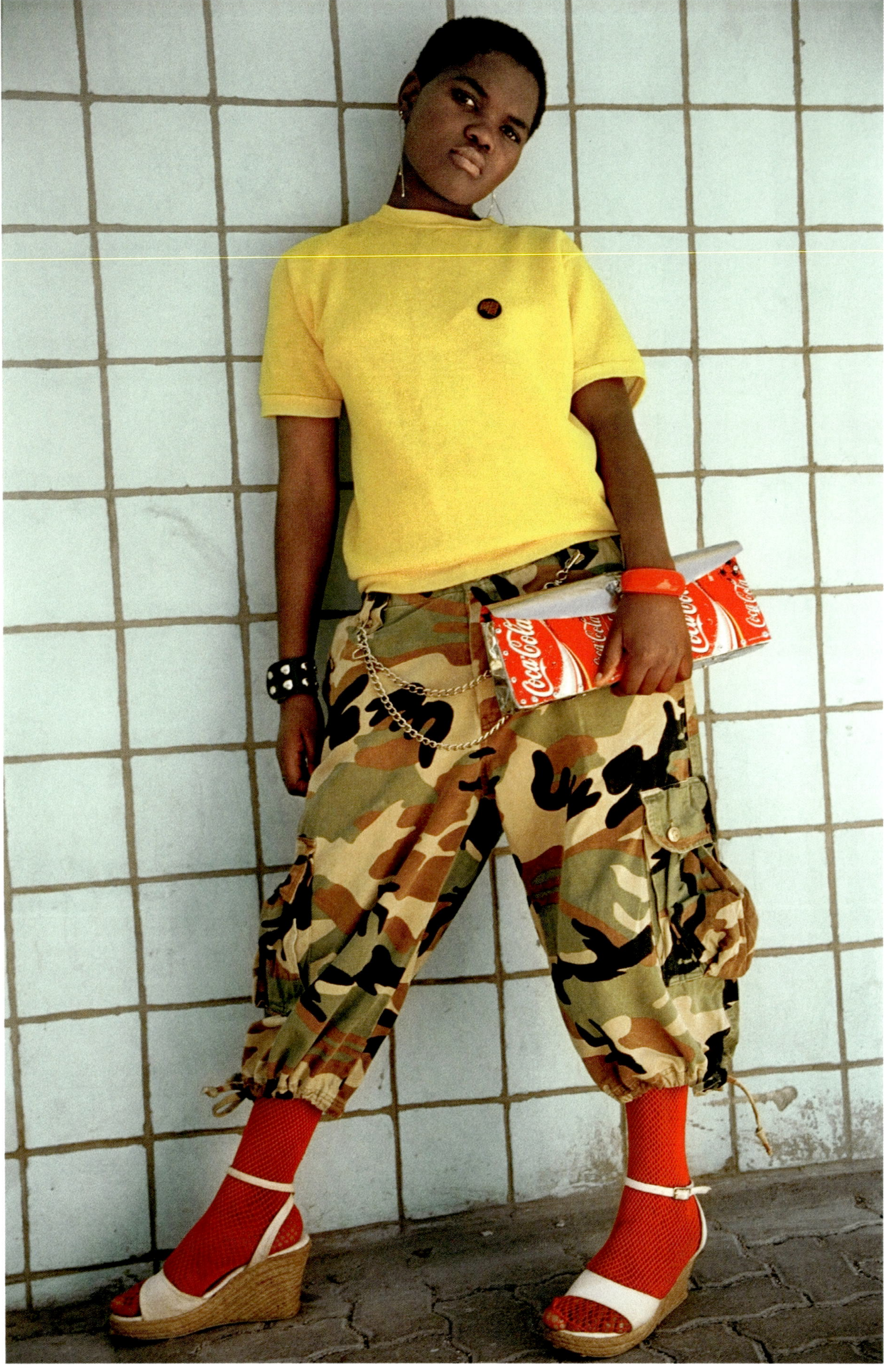

Nonkululeko, 2003

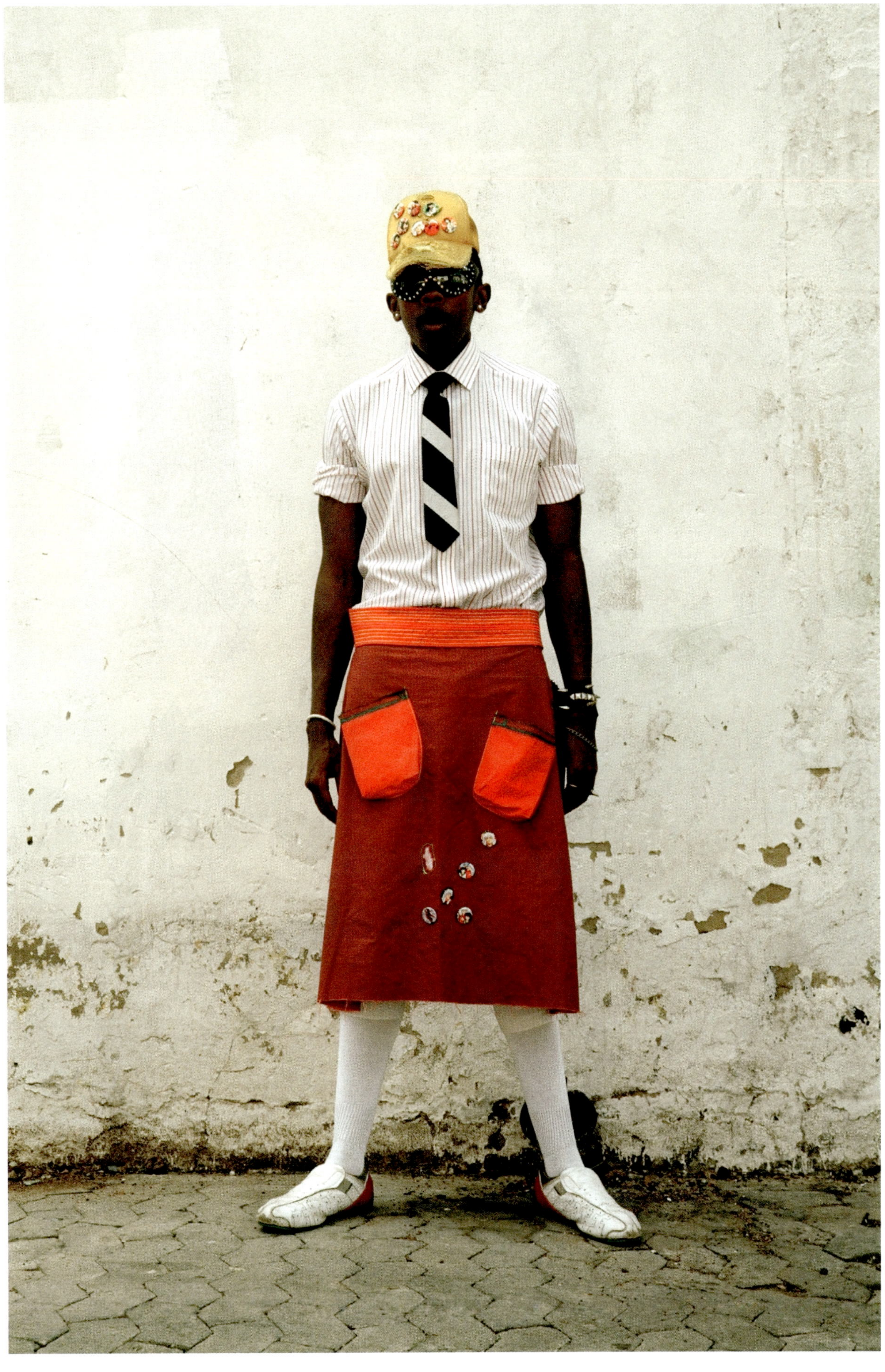

Sibu i, 2006

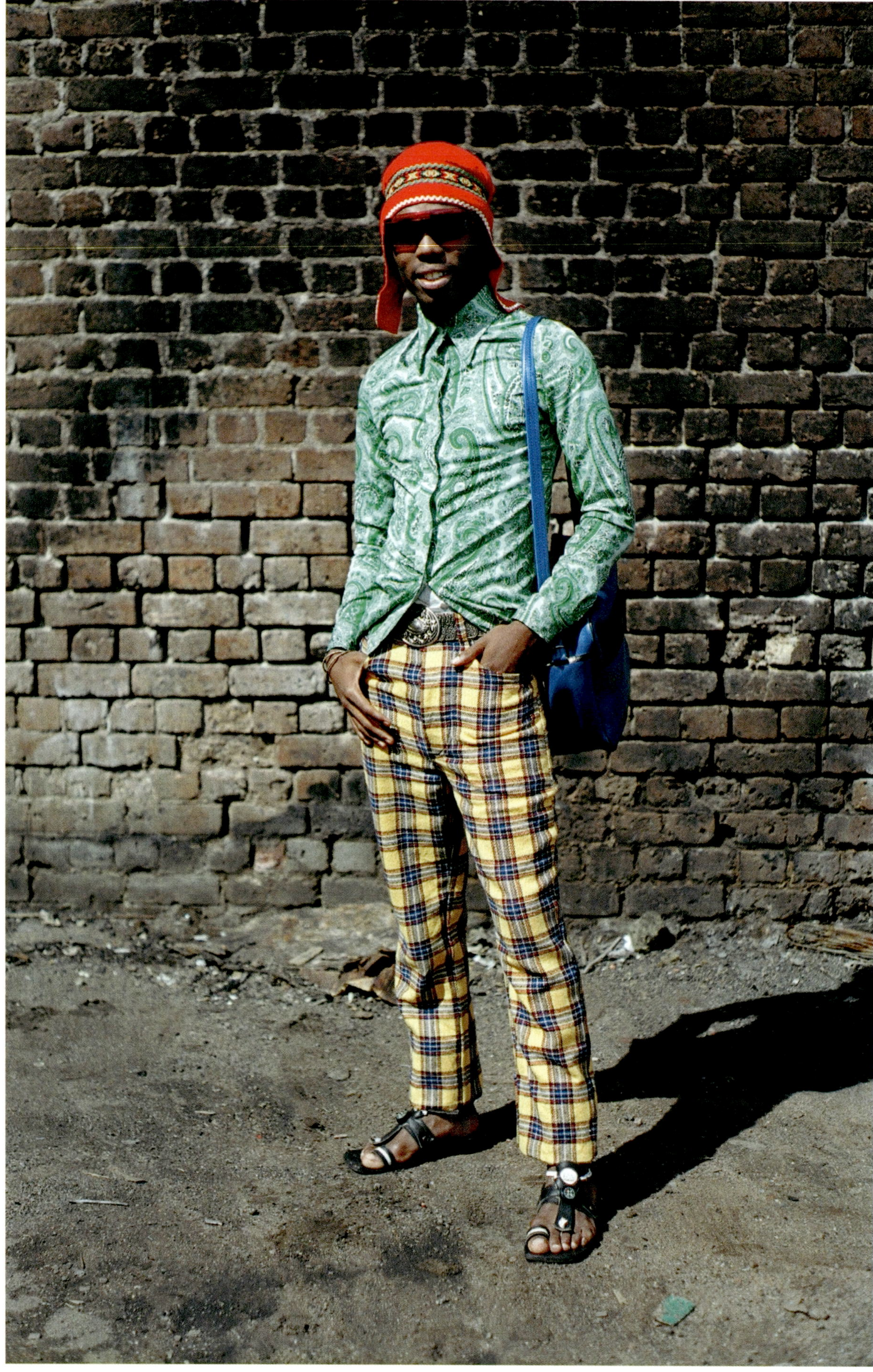

Thulani, 2003

BIOGRAPHIES

Abdelaziz, Myriam
Cairo (Egypt), 1976

After spending her childhood in Switzerland and her adolescence in Egypt, Abdelaziz settled in Paris in 1996. She discovered the world of photography in 1992. Her studies in political science, journalism and marketing led her to work in various international companies, and this provided her with the opportunity to travel and develop her eye. She began to exhibit her work in Paris in 2004, just before moving to New York, in 2005, to take courses in photojournalism at the ICP (International Center of Photography). She currently splits her time between New York and Cairo.
No name in the street, p. 147

Akinbiyi, Akinbode
Oxford (United Kingdom), 1946
of Nigerian parents.

After finishing his studies in literature in Nigeria and England, Akinbiyi took up photography—he is self-taught—in 1972. He has lived in Berlin, where he works as a free-lance photographer, since 1977. He photographs the megalopolises of Europe and, especially, of Africa: Cairo, Lagos, Kinshasa, and Johannesburg. He sees himself more as a writer whose task would be to document human condition as it is, with no romanticism or despair. In 1997, thanks to financial backing from the German magazine Stern, he travelled to Lagos, Kano and Dakar. He is the co-founder of the cultural centre Umzamsi, in the township of Durban, South Africa. Akinbiyi is a writer and curator. He has exhibited at the Bamako Biennale and in Germany.
Crossroads, p. 105

Amin, Mohamed Mo
Nairobi (Kenya) 1943; died 1996.

At the age of fifteen Mo Amin sold his first photograph. In 1963, five years later, he founded the company Camerapix. He covered major events on the African continent and the Middle East, bringing meticulously prepared, exclusive images back from his assignments. His images are often shocking testimony of violent conflicts and dictators. Nicknamed 'Lucky Mo', he survived being beaten, tortured, shot at, and several car accidents. Because of his incredible ability to communicate, he was able to get close to despots and reveal their injustices. In 1991, during Ethiopia's civil war, he lost his left arm in an explosion in Addis Abeba, but took up work again using an artificial arm. His frenetic life was tragically terminated when an Ethiopian Airlines plane was hijacked and plunged into the Indian Ocean. He died while trying to negotiate with the hijackers.
Lost illusions, p. 73

Azaglo, Cornélius Yao Augustt
Lomé (Togo), 1924; died in 2000
in Côte d'Ivoire.

Azaglo started working in administration while he trained as a photographer in labs and studios. In 1955 he became a traveling photographer, using a 'box camera' to take pictures of people in the markets, instantly developing them in his mobile lab. With Independence in 1962, he travelled across the country to photograph people for a census of the rural population, creating an impromptu studio with a simple curtain for the backdrop. With the arrival of color photography, his studio work slowed down. There are more than one hundred thousand, well conserved negatives stored and arranged in boxes and indexed in notebooks. In 1994, his entire collection was exhibited for the first time at the French Cultural Centre in Abidjan then, in 1996, with *Revue Noire*'s exhibition *L'Afrique par elle même*, at the Maison Européene de la Photographie, at the Pinacoteca de São Paulo, at the Bamako Biennale, among others.
A useful dream, p. 42

Baloji, Sammy
Lubumbashi (Democratic Republic of the Congo), 1978

With a degree in the Humanities, Boloji began his career as a comic strip artist before turning to photography and video. His first work captures the vestiges of colonialism in the Upper Kantanga region. He produced photomontages by superimposing archival black and white prints of slave-like workers on contemporary, color images of mining sites that show devastated landscapes. Presented in 2007 at the time of the 7th Rencontres Africaines de la Photographie, he was awarded the prize for most promising young talent. He has been commissioned by museums like the Quai Branly, the Royal Museum for Central Africa, and the Museum for African Art in New York.
Another country, p. 156

Bieber, Jodi
South Africa, 1966

After taking classes in photography at the Market Photo Workshop in Johannesburg, Bieber began a ten-year project with South Africa's marginalised youth culture. *Between Dogs and Wolves*, much like the project that followed, is an essay on Afrikaners and gangs from the black districts that she made while working for newspapers such as *The New York Times*, *Geo*, and *The Sunday Times*, and for NGOs like Doctors without Borders. She has written on AIDS and drugs in Spain, and her work has received awards from the World Press, the Fondation Blachère, and the Rencontres de la Photographie de Bamako. In 2008, she began her project *Real Beauty*, an ongoing series of portraits of contemporary women in South Africa. In 2010 she published a book on Soweto's youth.
Crossroads, p. 84

Bourouissa, Mohamed
Blida (Algeria), 1978

Having earned his degree from the École Nationale Supérieure des Arts Décoratifs in 2006, Bourouissa undertook a project to photograph staged scenes using the suburbs of Paris as his set. The project, *Périphéries*, immediately convinced him of the value of photography and brought him recognition from his peers and professionals in the field. Since then, he has exhibited widely France (at Galérie du Château d'Eau in Toulouse, at the Cité de l'Histoire de l'Immigration in Paris, at the Le Fresnoy: Studio National des Arts Contemporains in Tourcoing), and the world (Finland, Brazil, United States, and Mali). His practice also includes video and sculpture. In 2010 he participated in numerous artistic events: Manifesta Murcia, Biennale Berlin, Biennale Brighton, and his first solo exhibit was held in New York at Yossi Milo Gallery.

Another country, p. 165

Boutros, Nabil
Cairo (Egypt), 1954; lives in Paris.

Boutros studied in Paris, first at the École Nationale Supérieure des Arts Décoratifs and then at the École Nationale Supérieure des Beaux-Arts. In 1986, after having worked as a painter and designer, Boutros dedicated himself to photography. After ten years of absence, he returned to Egypt, where he focused on his country of origin and began *Alexandrie revisitée*, a project inspired by the texts of Edouard Al Kharrat and populated by black-and-white portraits of anonymous nocturnal figures. It documents 'inhabited' places, as well as traditional and Egyptian folk musicians. His recent work, in color, explores 'modernity' in Egypt and Jordan. He has exhibited and published in France and abroad, in places like New York's Aperture Gallery, Sevilla's Centro de Arte Contemporáneo, and the 2003 Bamako Biennale.

Crossroads, p. 96

Depara, Jean
Kboklolo (Angola), 1928; lived in Kinshasa (Zaire, now DRC). He died in 1997.

Depara settled in Kinshasa (formerly Leopoldville) and began taking photographs while doing working as a camera repairman, a bicycle mechanic, and a cobbler. He opened a studio, Le Jean Whisky Depara, where he photographed the West African community in a series of portraits called *Sénégalais*. His love of Westerns led him to photograph the hip, urban youth as modern-day cowboys. Later on, he became the official photographer of Franco, the famous national rumba singer. He photographed the trendy nightclubs he liked to frequent, unwittingly capturing with his photographs the first winds of freedom. Depara left his studio in 1966. He converted to Islam and made a series of self-portraits. In 1975 he became a photo lab assistant for Parliament. He retired 1989.

A useful dream, p. 47

Derrick, Tracey
Cape Town (South Africa), 1961

Derrick's social documentary photographs, mainly in black and white, show the contradictions of a system scarred by the effects of apartheid. Her images, taken without flash or special effects, concern the daily and individual conditions of homeless children, women in prison and displaced persons. Her 1997 photo-essay *Basic Necessity* is based on the sex workers of Cape Town. From her first images, her eye has been attracted to the wretched of the earth, whose humanity and grace she captures with disarming sympathy, and projects as a denunciation of the conditions under which society forces them to live. Tracey Derrick covered the UN peace process in Mozambique, and traveled extensively the world, especially Brazil.

No name in the street, p. 123

Dib, Mohamed
Tlemcen (Algeria), 1920; died in La Celle-Saint Cloud (France) in 2003.

Dib was a teacher, accountant, translator and journalist for the *Alger Républicain* and *Liberté*; both papers were connected to the Algerian Communist Party. With his trilogy, *Algérie: La grande maison* (1952), *L'incendie* (1954), and *Le métier à tisser* (1957), he came to be considered the founder of Francophone Algerian literature. In 1959, the colonial authorities expelled him from Algeria because of his activism and support for independence and he only returned in 1983, to bury his mother. Settling in France, he worked on a collection that included fiction, poetry, and plays; he would publish more than thirty books. He was the first writer from the Maghreb to receive the Grand Prix de la Francophonie in 1994. He claimed that his memories, his imagination and his writing were prompted by a set of photographs of his hometown taken in 1946, and that these images were the only evidences of what he attempted to express. These photographs were published under the title *Tlemcen ou les lieux de l'écriture* by *Revue Noire*. He died in 2003 at the age of eighty-three.

A useful dream, p. 34

Dondo, Calvin
Harare (Zimbabwe), 1963

Dondo studied photography at the Bulawayo Polytechnic College in Harare from 1985 to 1988. Since then, he has been a freelance photographer, a teacher, and the curator of Gwanza, the Month of Photography in Harare, which he created. He works regularly for the *Associated Press*, *Agence France Presse* and *Black Star USA*. Trained as a photojournalist, Dondo is interested in recording people in their daily life, in capturing apparently banal gestures, thus exploring with his lens what Henri Cartier-Bresson once called *the decisive moment*. He was awarded the Grand Prix at the 2007 Bamako Biennale.

No name in the street, p. 127

DRUM Magazine, see page 24

El Rassoul Younis Khalil, Mohammed Abd
Kaas (Sudan), 1922

El Rassoul began to photograph when he joined the Army Special Forces (Sudanese-Anglo-Egyptian). In 1954, as independence loomed over the country, he became the official state photographer. He worked for the Ministry of Foreign Affairs, answering directly to the minister himself, Ahmed Delwa, whom he accompanied as the latter toured Africa and the West in 1958. He then went with General Eguero Yaten to Kampala (Uganda), as a reporter and photographer. El Rassoul is an example of a policy and practice that was common among many newly independent African states, many of which employed photographers whose task it was to praise the state's deeds and generally to be griots of power. El Rassoul was of fixture of the Sudanese government; from the time of its independence to his retirement in 1982, he served every incoming government, whether democratically elected or militarily installed.

A useful dream, p. 54

Essop Brothers
Cape Town (South Africa), 1958

Twin brothers Hasan and Husain graduated from the School of Fine Art Michaelis in Cape Town in 2006. Since graduating, the Essop Brothers have been working collaboratively, producing digitally composited photographs, picturing a profusion of twin clones, engaging in various pursuits and altercations. Dressed in designer gear, traditional garb and army camouflage, the twins' doubles, triples and multiples act out contradictory stereotypical identities. Through their photographs, the two brothers question the people of their generation, their social background, their community and their beliefs. They write: 'Our work questions global and local hegemonies. We explore the influence of Western popular culture and the distorting effects it has on existing religions and cultures. Internal conflicts are expressed through performance'.

Another country, p. 169

Fosso, Samuel
Douala (Cameroon), 1962; lives in the Republic of Central Africa.

Samuel Fosso grew up in Nigeria but had to flee during the Biafran War, in 1972. Taking refuge in Bangui, RCA, he worked as an assistant photographer and eventually went on to open his own studio. In the evenings, after photographing his clients, he would take pictures of himself and send these to his grandmother, to show her he was still alive. His interest in self-portraiture grew and he began to explore the use of costumes and settings, portraying himself in a growing assortment of genres and probing into questions of self-identity. Samuel Fosso is one of Africa's most eminent photographers. His photographs are shown all over Europe and America, from the Guggenheim in New York to galleries in Barcelona, Paris and Amsterdam.

Lost illusions, p. 64

Gosani, Bob
Johannesburg (South Africa), 1934; died in 1972.

In 1952, at the age of sixteen, Gosani started working as a courier for *Drum* Magazine. He soon became an assistant in the photo department's darkroom, and it was not long before he found himself out working the streets with a camera in his hands, shooting some of the magazine's most stunning, and exclusive, images, such as that of a young Nelson Mandela sparring with a famous boxer. He was to become one of the magazine's best photographers, and his iconic images bear witness to the society of oppression he came from. He spent his entire professional life at *Drum*; he died in 1972, at thirty-eight, without knowing the end of apartheid.

Before dawn, p. 26

Kasco, Dorris Haron
Abidjan (Côte d'Ivoire), 1966; lives in Montpellier (France).

Kasco began his photographic practice in the world of fashion and then chose to explore the social demons that haunt African cities. He spent three years documenting the mentally ill people of Abidjan, people we find in many African cities, walking naked or talking to themselves, or both. This series was shown for the first time in 1993, and the book *Les Fous d'Abidjan* was published a couple of years by *Revue Noire*. Kasco undertook the first extensive research project into the history of photography in Cote d'Ivoire. This resulted in the discovery, among many others, of Cornélius Augustt, about whom he made a movie for the the 2001 Bamako Biennale.

No name in the street, p. 142

Karray, Mouna
Sfax (Tunisia), 1970; lives in Paris (France).

In 1989, Karray entered the Institut Supérieur d'Animation Culturelle in Tunisia, where she was introduced to cinema, video and photography. She had her first solo exhibition, *Alchimère*, in Tunisia in 1995. She then received a scholarship to go to Japan and, in 1997, she enrolled at Nihon University and then at the Tokyo Institute of Polytechnics and Arts, earning a Masters of Media Image in 2002. She returned to Tunisia, where she taught photography at the School of Arts and Crafts of Gabes, and then at the École des Beaux-Arts de Sousse. In 2005 Karray was awarded an artist residency at the Cité Internationale des Arts in Paris and settled there. She developed her series *Murmurer*, photographs of abandoned and unexplained walls in Sfax.

No name in the street, p. 120

Koudjina, Philippe
Lomé (Togo) 1940; lives in Niamey (The Republic of Niger).
Koudjina left Lomé for Niamey in 1959 and, once there, he eked out a living with a variety of jobs. At night, though, he would roam clubs and bars, taking photographs of the regulars that he would then sell to them. In 1962 he became the official photographer of the French Military. During those twelve years, he photographed all the official demonstrations of the decade. Although his work is an important part of Niger's heritage, the arrival of color photography forced him to close his workshop and sell his equipment.

Lost illusions, p. 68

Leki Dago, Ananias
Côte d'Ivoire, 1970; lives in Paris (France).

After his studies in Abidjan, he traveled extensively through the Caribbean, the Middle East, Europe and Africa. He initiated the Rencontres du Sud, the month of photography in Abidjan, in 2000, and was its coordinator that year as well as in 2002. Dago collaborates with publications such as *Africultures*, *Photonews*, and *Regards*, and his first book, *Le Goff*, was published by Les Éditions de l'Oeil. He has participated in numerous exhibitions, among them *Africa Remix*, and his work has been featured at the Bamako Biennale. Dago's black-and-white photographs, now part of several permanent collections in Europe, Africa and the US, show contrasting and sometimes brutal images in which fragments of male and female bodies are cut up by the play of shadow and light.

Crossroads, p. 109

Men, Pierrot
Midongy-du-Sud (Madagascar), 1954; lives in Fianarantsoa.

Men developed a love of photography early on his life, and his first experiments with photos date back to his teenage years. His career took off in 1994, when he was awarded Leica's Mother Jones Prize. Since then, he has been invited to show his work at different parts of the world, and he was awarded the Gold Medal at the 3rd Francophone Games in 1997, and the UNEP/Canon Prize in 2000. His photographic depictions of the people of Madagascar, specially the inhabitants of Fianarantsoa, are suffused with a poetry suggestive of the intimate bond between natural and human realms. The photos, with their proclivity for landscapes haunted by silhouettes, are captivating for how they show Men struggling to find the meeting point of the images' component elements.

Crossroads, p. 91

Mofokeng, Santu
Johannesburg (South Africa), 1956; lives in Johannesburg.

Mofokeng began his career as a street photographer in Soweto. In the early 1980s his practice centred around documentary photography, with Mofokeng risking his life time and again to cover anti-apartheid rallies and demonstrations. He became a freelance photographer and member of the collective Afrapix in 1985. Mofokeng continued to explore the identity of the black middle class through topics like religious ceremonies. His landscapes are spaces invested with public memory and spirituality, and he investigates them in relation to ownership, ecological impact and power. The series *Chasing Shadows* documents religious ceremonies in caves, public parks and urban wastelands. It includes photographs taken at the Motouleng Caves in the Free State, some of which feature his brother Ishmael shortly before his death from HIV. In 1992, he received the prestigious Mother Jones Award for Africa and, in 2009, the Prins Claus Award.

Lost illusions, p. 76

Muluneh, Aïda
Addis Abeba (Ethiopia), 1974; lives in Addis Abeba and New York (USA).

Muluneh discovered photography while studying cinema, radio and television in the USA. After a long period of living abroad, she returned to Ethiopia, where she was brutally confronted with the social and culture situation of her country. Her reaction was to use photography to show what the country's official media kept from the foreign press. It was at that time that she began to organise, in parallel to her work as a photographer, workshops with young students, and this led to the creation of Africa DESTA (Developing and Educating Societies Through the Arts), a nongovernmental organisation designed to promote cultural development through the use of photography. In 2008, she directed a documentary in Cuba entitled *The Wound Unhealing*, which chronicles the journey of Ethiopian orphans of war sent to study in Havana. Her book *Ethiopia: Past / Forward* was published in 2009 by Africalia.

No name in the street, p. 133

Mtethwa, Zwelethu
Durban (South Africa), 1960; lives in Cape Town (South Africa).

Mtethwa is a graduate of the Michaelis School of Fine Arts, University of Cape Town, where he was one of the few black students admitted to art school under the apartheid regime. He started out as a painter, and subsequently took up photography. In his work he favours large-format, color photography, and his images question the economic and political realities of South Africa. They recount the lives of people forced to leave countryside, following their journeys to the megalopolises of the country, where they invariably become marginalized. His work is now part of permanent collections of cultural institutions around the world. His first personal book was published in 2010 by Aperture.

Crossroads, p. 101

Nxumalo, Musa
Soweto (South Africa), 1986

Nxumalo lives and works in and around Johannesburg. He studied photography at the Market Photo Workshop between 2006 and 2008. He was the recipient of the Edward Ruiz Mentorship Award (2008) and took second prize at the MTN CIT: Y Festival (2009). He seeks to explore the constant flux of urban youth culture in contemporary South Africa, particularly in black communities, and hopes to document the 'first' generation of democratic South Africa.

Another country, p. 157

Perrier, Eileen
London (United Kingdom), 1964 of Ghanaian parents; lives in London (UK).

Perrier studied at the Surrey Institute of Art and Design and graduated from the Royal College of Art. She has always been fascinated by classic British portraiture and her photographs are an attempt to convey their atmosphere through photography. Since 1999, she has exhibited at places like the The Photographers Gallery, Tate Britain, Whitechapel Gallery, and in shows like *Africa Remix*. She has received Space Studio's Cultural Diversity Award, and the National Magazine Award, and she has also contributed to the journals *Revue Noire* and *Creative Camera*. In the wake of her first visit to Ghana, in 1995, Perrier's work starts to reflect her engagement with the long tradition of the studio portrait in Africa. In response to her own upbringing, her work addresses questions about cultural identity, diversity and individual awareness.

No name in the street, p. 137

Rangel, Ricardo
Maputo, formerly Lourenço Marques (Mozambique), 1924; he died in 2009.

Rangel began his career in the 1940s, working as a developer for Studio Focus. In 1952, he became the first non-white photographer employed by a Mozambican paper, the daily *Notícias da Tarde*. Over the next two decades he worked on several papers in Lourenço Marques and Beira and, in 1970, he was among the progressive journalists who set up an opposition publication, the weekly magazine *Tempo*, the first color magazine in Mozambique. He photographed history through the actions and daily activities of the people. He was jailed several times and subjected to censorship. Among his famous series we find *Pão Nosso de Cada Noite*, in which he depicts the prostitutes of Rua Araújo, in the capital's port district. In the wake of independence, in 1975, Rangel played an important role in training a new generation of young Mozambican photographers, all of whom passed through the Centro de Formacao Fotografica (CFF), which founded in 1983, and which directed until his death in 2009.

A useful dream, p. 37

Sedira, Zineb
France, 1963 of Algerian parents; lives in London (UK).

Born in the *banlieux* of Paris, Sedira settled in London in 1986. Between 1998 and 2003 she studied at St Martin's School of Art and the Slade School of Art, followed by a research fellowship at the Royal College of Art. Already in her student days, Sedira's work shows a preoccupation with the veil and a propensity for challenging the simplistic imagery ascribed to it. The introspective nature of her work is never restrictive; one the contrary, her look inwards opens up into a world of multiple selves and homes—notably Algeria, France, and the United Kingdom. In this journey she is sometimes accompanied by friends, family, and by her professional, artistic or literary mentors. She uses video, photography, writing, installation, and computer technology to examine themes of sexuality, representation, family ties, language, and memory. Sedira prefers to live in England, 'where the media represents little to nothing of Algeria, in stark contrast to France'; this, she says, gives her clearer perspective onto her history, and provides a horizon against which she can articulate her penchant for self-erasure.

Crossroads, p. 114

Sidibé, Malick
Sodaba (Mali), 1936

In 1952, Sidebé joined the École des Artisans Soudanais in Bamako, where he graduated as a artisan, a jeweler. A French photographer introduced him to photography and delegated some reporting work to him. He opened his own studio in Bamako, Studio Malick, in 1958, and this has been his professional work space since. His interest in Bamako's youth culture resulted in a series of photos of them as they discovered Western music, the twist, the cha-cha, and as they danced to recordings of rock and roll, pop and soul music, sometimes in clubs, sometimes on the banks of the River Niger. He was discovered in 1994, at the first Bamako Biennale, where his international career took off. His work has been exhibited at the Fondation Cartier in Paris, the Guggenheim Museum in New York, and at the National Portrait Gallery in London. At the age of sixty-seven, he became the first African photographer to receive, in 2003, the International Prize awarded by the Hasselblad Foundation; he was also awarded the Golden Lion at the 2007 Venice Biennale, for his lifetime achievement.

A useful dream, p. 46

Studio 3Z: Ambroise Ngaimoko
1949, Angola

In 1961, Ngaimoko moved with his family to Kinshasa. There he worked as a mechanic, then as a technician for an open-air cinema, before he became an assistant to his uncle Marques Ndodão in 1968, who ran two photo studios, and who gave him a Yashica 6x6 camera. It was in Kitambo in 1971 that he opened the Studio 3Z, a named picked to symbolise three Zaïres: the country, the currency, and the river. Young people who came to the studio remember it because of the constantly changing backdrops. He gained recognition in the course of the 1970s due to an unprecedented technique, in which he developed two portraits on the same sheet, using the same negative twice. This cult of cloning is reminiscent of the rites performed for a lost twin. In the full swing of *Zaïrization* there was a shortage of 6x6 black-and-white film and, with the eventual arrival of color film, Ngaimoko lost his clientele. He resigned himself to using the format 24x36 to make his identity-based work. In 1997, he renamed his studio 3C (for the three Congos).

Lost illusions, p. 60

Tshabangu, Andrew
Soweto (South Africa), 1966

Tshabangu studied at the Alexandra Community Art Centre in Johannesburg. He taught photography at the Children's Photography Workshop in 1995 and 1998 and, in 1999, he taught at post-matric photography courses at the Market Photo Workshop. His first exhibit was organised at the 2006 Bamako Biennale. Shortly thereafter he took part in the African artists exhibit at MoMo Gallery in Johannesburg. He works on several projects at once. For example, his portrait of a family in a village of the northern province, his project on spirituality in the black Diaspora of Johannesburg, London and New York, and the one on the township Alexandra were carried out simultaneously. For years he has also photographed the rituals of religious ceremonies in the black communities. While his practice is strong on social documentation, his photographs are distinguished by a smoky atmosphere that creates a mystical element and a dramatic intensity.

No name in the street, p. 129

Veleko, Nontsikelelo (Lolo)
South Africa, 1977; lives in Johannesburg (South Africa)

Veleko studied graphic design in 1995 in Cape Town and photography at the Market Photo Workshop in Johannesburg from 1999 to 2004. Her photographs have been exhibited in prestigious places and she has received numerous awards and been invited to residencies in Switzerland and the United Kingdom. Her preferred subject is the urban youth of South Africa–young adults blurring the lines of social class and ethnicity by using clothes and fashion as forms of crossbreeding. Somewhere between fashion photography and documentary photography, Lolo Veleko's 'flashy' portraits look at how identity is perceived, and often assumed, and how her subjects use their clothes to construct their own guises of identity. She celebrates the vibrant and creative culture of South Africa's youth.

Another country, p. 176

Wokmeni, Patrick
Douala (Cameroon), 1985

Wokmeni photographed the area of New Bell in Douala during the 2008 February riots. These photos were published in *L'Ivresse du Papillon*, by Lionel Manga (SARL Edimontagne, France, 2008). The photos show children returning from their schools, closed down as a result of the riots, a city gripped by chaos, more than 150 people dead and, also, the idleness and prostitution that continued to be a part of New Bell. Wokmeni is self-taught. He comes from a deprived and disenchanted youth and practices photography as a form of therapy. His photos started to attract the attention of peers and professionals during a workshop he attended in Ghana in March of 2009.

Another country, p. 171

This book was published on the occasion
of the exhibition
A useful dream
Centre for Fine Arts, Brussels,
26 June 2010 — 26 September 2010
in the framework of the platform
Visionary Africa and the *Summer of
Photography 2010*

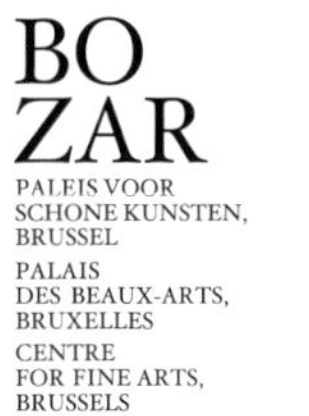

BOZAR
PALEIS VOOR
SCHONE KUNSTEN,
BRUSSEL
PALAIS
DES BEAUX-ARTS,
BRUXELLES
CENTRE
FOR FINE ARTS,
BRUSSELS
WWW.BOZAR.BE | + 32 (0)2 507 82 00

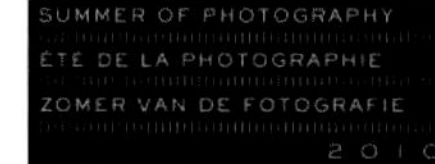

BOOK

Publisher
BOZAR EXPO and Silvana Editoriale

Editor
Simon Njami

Assistant to the editor
Mikaela Zyss

Editor Biographies
Mikaela Zyss & Emiliano Battista

Publication coordinator
Emiliano Battista

Translators
Popahna Brandes
Gail de Courcy-Ireland

Proofreaders
Viviana Vai

Graphic design and layout
Studio Luc Derycke, Gent

Printer
Arti Grafiche Amilcare Pizzi S.p.A.

Cover Image
One, two, three and… The Ennerdale Academy of Dance, south of Johannesburg, 1997
© Jodi Bieber, courtesy Goodman gallery

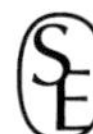

Silvana Editoriale

Direction
Dario Cimorelli
Art Director
Giacomo Merli
Copy Editor
Ondina Granato
Production Coordinator
Michela Bramati
Editorial Assistant
Elena Piaggesi
Iconographic office
Deborah D'Ippolito, Alessandra Olivari
Press office
Lidia Masolini, press@silvanaeditoriale.it

EAN 97890-7481636-6
97888-3661659-6

Mohamed Mo Amin
© Mohamed Amin, Camerapix, A24 Media

Cornélius Yao Augustt Azaglo
© Dokolo, Revue Noire

Sammy Baloji
© Sammi Baloji. With the support of
Musée du Quai Branly, Paris

Jodi Bieber
© Jodi Bieber, courtesy Goodman gallery

Mohamed Bourouissa
© M Bourouissa, courtesy Galerie Filles
du Calvaire

Jean Depara
© Dokolo, Revue Noire

Mohamed Dib
© Dokolo, Revue Noire

DRUM Magazine
© BAHA, courtesy Bailey Seippel Gallery

Mohammed Abd El Rassoul
© M Abd El Rassoul, Elnour

Essop Brothers
© Essop Brothers, courtesy Goodman
gallery

Samuel Fosso
© Samuel Fosso, courtesy Jean Marc
Patras, Paris

Bob Gosani
© BAHA, courtesy Bailey Seippel Gallery

Dorris Haron Kasco
© Dokolo, Revue Noire

Philippe Koudjina
© Dokolo, Revue Noire

Pierrot Men
© Pierrot Men

Zwelethu Mtethwa
© Zwelethu Mtethwa, courtesy Jack
Shainman gallery
& galerie Anne de Villepoix

Ricardo Rangel
© Ricardo Rangel, courtesy Afronova

Zineb Sedira
© Zineb Sedira, courtesy galerie Kamel
Mennour

Malick Sidibé
© Malick Sidibé, courtesy André Magnin

Studio 3z
© Dokolo, Revue Noire

Lolo Veleko
© Lolo Veleko, courtesy Goodman gallery

This publication was made possible thanks
to the initiative of Paul Dujardin and the
support of the Belgian Ministry of Foreign
Affairs

Acknowledgements *A useful dream*

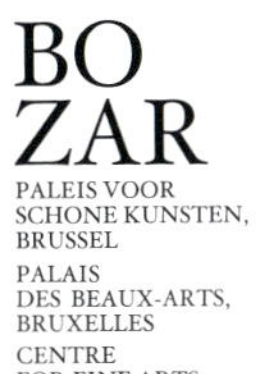

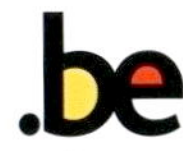
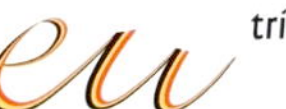
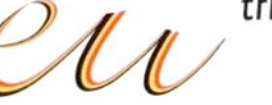
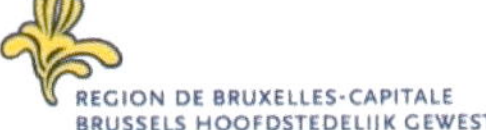

PALEIS VOOR
SCHONE KUNSTEN,
BRUSSEL
PALAIS
DES BEAUX-ARTS,
BRUXELLES
CENTRE
FOR FINE ARTS,
BRUSSELS
WWW.BOZAR.BE | + 32 (0)2 507 82 00

This exhibition was made possible
thanks to the support of:
Chancellery of the Prime Minister
Foreign Affairs Federal Public Service
Région de Bruxelles-Capitale
Brussels Hoofdstedelijk Gewest

In the context of the Belgian Presidency
of the European Union

EXHIBITION

Curator
Simon Njami
Assistant to the curator
Mikaela Zyss
Exhibition Coordinator
Frank Vanhaecke
Technical Coordinator
Joris Erven
Art Handling and Installation
Aorta

The Centre for Fine Arts and Simon Njami
are grateful to the following institutions
and people:

All the photographers, Revue Noire, Pascal
Martin Saint Léon, Goodman Gallery, Liza
Esser, Nikki Berriman, Emma Laurence
Storm, Janse Van Rensburg, Lunetta Bartz
Jane B. (for her wonderful birthday),
Afronova, Henri Vergon, Madame Béa-
trice Rangel, Madame P. (the spy from
Odessa), Marie Lelièvre, Berry Bickle,
Dunja Herzog, Galerie Anne de Villepoix,
Antoine Laurent, Shainman Gallery New
York, Galerie filles du Calvaire, Marie
Doyon, Galerie Sieppel Köln/Johannes-
burg, Ralf Seippel, Tobias Lehr, Delia
and Lily McLeish, Galerie Kamel Men-
nour, André Magnin, Olivier Souchard,
Salim Amin, Camera Pix, David Mutua,
Elnour, Claude Iverne, Jean Marc Patras,
Gallery Momo, Karen Brusch, Marta C.
(for her commitment), Gabriel & Lucas
N., Paolo Regini, Sindika Dokolo Foun-
dation, Luanda Triennial

BOZAR

Centre for Fine Arts
Chief Executive Officer—
Artistic Director
Paul Dujardin
Deputy Artistic Director
Pablo Fernandez Alonso

BOZAR EXPO

Deputy Exhibitions Director
France de Kinder
Collaborators
Axelle Ancion
Ann Arend
Emiliano Battista
Eva Bialek
Helena Bussers
Ann Flas
Vera Kotaji
Sophie Lauwers
Laurence Leunen
Alberta Sessa
Maïté Smeyers
Christel Tsilibaris
Elizabeth Vandeweghe
Frank Vanhaecke
Bozar Architecture
Iwan Strauven
Scientific Adviser
Jan Van Alphen
Project Managers
Anne Judong
Nicola Setari
Artistic Consultants
Kurt Deboodt
Hélène Vandenberghe

BOZAR TECHNICS

Director Technics, IT, Investments,
Safety & Security
Stéphane Vanreppelen
Collaborators
Rudi Anneessens
Nicolas Bernus
Joris Erven
Jo Heyvaert
David Roels
Roger Vander Meulen
Ward Vansteenwegen

BOZAR GUEST SERVICES

Manager Guest Services
Erwin Verbist
Collaborators Planning
Anne Geeraerts
Sanne Fetlaar
David Mommens
Cédric Orban
Frédéric Vandervelde
Field Coordinator

Jeroen Hallaert
Field Supervisors
Fatima Absisan
Mira Dejonge
Corinne Meijers
Olivier Smaers
Isabelle Speybrouck
Matthieu Vanderdonckt

BOZAR FUNDING

Head of Funding
Elke Kristoffersen
Membership
Catherine Carniaux
Corporate development
Miek Declercq
Annik Halmes
Vanessa Lakhanisky
Lydia Vandam
Katrien Desrumeaux

BOZAR STUDIOS

Coordinator
Tine Van Goethem
Collaborators
Vera Claessens
Sarah Deloenen
Laurence Ejzyn
Lieve Raeymaekers

BOZAR COM

Director Marketing,
Communication & Sales
Sabine Jonckheere
Audience Development Expo
Geraldine Jonville
Catherine Mussely
Bettina Saerens
Press Bozar Expo
Leen Daems
Annelien Mallems
Hélène Tenreira
Eve-Marie Vaes
Webmaster
Wendy Schuppen
Content Assistant
Danielle D'haese

BOZAR FINANCES

Director
Benoît Provost
Financial Controller
Florence Absalon

GENERAL ADMINISTRATION

Director
Didier Verboomen
Legal Affairs
Els Brokken

VISIONARY AFRICA

From 30 May to 26 September, the festival Visionary Africa is mounting four exhibitions at the Centre for Fine Arts, and five at the Royal Museum for Central Africa. Additionally, over twenty concerts and performances will be offered as part of *48 hours in Brussels* and *CONGO@BOZAR*.

April

27.04 — 09.01.2011 (@RMCA)	*Fleuve Congo. 4700km de nature et culture en effervescence*	**Exhibition**

May

30.05.2010	*MO*Debate Congolese Diaspora in Belgium*	**Debate**
	Heritage, collective project initiated by Pitcho Womba Konga	**Music**

June

01.06 — 11.07.2010 (@RMCA)	*South Africa 2010: World Cup*	**Screening**
09.06 — 26.09.2010	*GEO-graphics: a map of art practices in Africa, past and present*	**Exhibition**
09.06.2010	Lecture architecture David Adjaye	**Archi**
11.06.2010	Opening match, World Cup 2010	**Screening**
11.06 — 09.01.2011 (@RMCA)	*Indépendance! Souvenirs congolais à travers 50 ans d'indépendance*	**Exhibition**
11.06 — 30.09.2010 (@RMCA)	'Bonjour Congo' en Belgique	**Exhibition**
14-15.06.2010	Walter Verdin & Matchume Zango & Venancio Mbande: *Timbila Tracks*	**Music & Cinema**
17.06.2010	*Soul Boy* – Hawa Essuman	**Cinema**
17—18.06.2010 (@Kaaitheater)	Savion Glover: *Bare Soundz*	**Dance**
24.06.2010	*Kinshasa Symphony* – Claus Wischmann & Martin Baer	**Cinema**
24 — 26.06.2010 (@Kaaistudio's)	Walter Verdin & Panaibra Gabriel: *GUESTS*	**Dance**
26.06 — 26.09.2010	*A useful dream*	**Exhibition**
26.06 — 26.09.2010	*Roger Ballen*	**Exhibition**
26.06 — 26.09.2010	*Pôze III / Africa Town*	**Exhibition**

July

09.07.2010	*Rokia Traoré*	**Music**
	Acoustic rumba concert	**Music**
10.07.2010	*African Gospel Day*	**Music**
	Acoustic rumba concert	**Music**
11.07.2010	World Cup final	**Screening**
	Acoustic rumba concert	**Music**
16.07.2010	50 Years of Congolese music	**Music**
17.07.2010	Acoustic rumba concert	**Music**
18.07.2010	Acoustic rumba concert	**Music**
22.07.2010	Angélique Kidjo	**Music**

September

11.09.2010	*Moloch Tropical* – Raoul Peck	**Cinema**
21.09.2010 (@Halles)	Sophiatou Kossoko & Latifa Laâbissi: *Lore Dream Song*	**Dance**
22.09.2010	Germaine Acogny: *Songook Yaakaar*	**Dance**
25.09.2010	*African Renaissances* Literary closing events & Awadi: *Présidents d'Afrique*	**Literature & Music**

At the Horta Hall, the heart of the Centre for Fine Arts, a special tribune was designed by David Adjaye and SUM for visitors to enjoy the broadcast matches of the World Cup in South Africa. This space will also be used to host several events of the *Visionary Africa* platform.

The exhibitions *GEO-graphics* and *A useful dream* will be adapted for a travelling exhibition in several African capitals starting with Tripoli, where the Africa-EU summit will take place in November 2010. The project is launched by the European Commission.

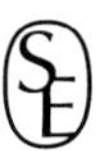

Silvana Editoriale Spa

via Margherita De Vizzi, 86
20092 Cinisello Balsamo, Milano
tel. 02 61 83 63 37
fax 02 61 72 464
www.silvanaeditoriale.it

Reproductions, printing and binding by
Arti Grafiche Amilcare Pizzi Spa
Cinisello Balsamo, Milan

Printed
June 2010